The Worth of Goods

The Worth of Goods

Valuation and Pricing in the Economy

Edited by
Jens Beckert and
Patrik Aspers

Great Clarendon Street, Oxford OX2 6DP

Oxford University Press is a department of the University of Oxford.
It furthers the University's objective of excellence in research, scholarship,
and education by publishing worldwide in

Oxford New York

Auckland   Cape Town Dar es Salaam Hong Kong   Karachi
Kuala Lumpur Madrid Melbourne Mexico City   Nairobi
New Delhi Shanghai Taipei Toronto

With offices in

Argentina Austria Brazil Chile Czech Republic France Greece
Guatemala Hungary Italy Japan South Korea Poland Portugal
Singapore Switzerland Thailand Turkey Ukraine Vietnam

Oxford is a registered trade mark of Oxford University Press
in the UK and in certain other countries

Published in the United States
by Oxford University Press Inc., New York

© Oxford University Press 2011

The moral rights of the author have been asserted

Database right Oxford University Press (maker)

Reprinted 2011

All rights reserved. No part of this publication may be reproduced,
stored in a retrieval system, or transmitted, in any form or by any means,
without the prior permission in writing of Oxford University Press,
or as expressly permitted by law, or under terms agreed with the appropriate
reprographics rights organization. Enquiries concerning reproduction
outside the scope of the above should be sent to the Rights Department,
Oxford University Press, at the address above

You must not circulate this book in any other binding or cover
And you must impose this same condition on any acquirer

ISBN 978-0-19-959465-8

Printed in the United Kingdom by
the MPG Books Group Ltd

ACKNOWLEDGMENTS

This volume is part of a larger research project on markets at the Max Planck Institute for the Study of Societies in Cologne. Issues of valuation and pricing on markets are important aspects of this project: understanding how value is constructed in markets and how prices for goods emerge is key to understanding the operation of the economy. In recent years, valuation and pricing have generated great interest among economic sociologists and now comprise a significant research area in the discipline.

This book assembles research articles from some of the core contributors to the debate on value and pricing in economic sociology. The chapters were presented at two conferences on the topic of valuation and pricing that we organized in the summer of 2009. The first conference, "Valuation and Price Formation on Markets," took place in June 2009 at the German–Italian conference center of Villa Vigoni in Menaggio. A second miniconference on "Price and Value in Markets and Firms" took place in July 2009 in Paris as part of the annual meeting of the Society for the Advancement of Socio-Economics (SASE). We would like to thank all participants, including those who commented on the papers presented, for their contributions. We are grateful to the director of Villa Vigoni, Gregor Vogt-Spira, for his hospitality, and to his staff for their generosity at this truly remarkable place. We thank the president of the SASE, Kathleen Thelen, for supporting the miniconference during the Paris meeting. Thanks also to Martha Zuber and her staff, Annelies Fryberger and Miranda Richmond-Mouillot, for their outstanding organizational support.

The path from the conferences to the publication of this book is by no means the result of our efforts alone. We would not have been able to succeed without the help of many people, above all Astrid Dünkelmann and Cynthia Lehmann from the Editorial and Public Relations Unit at the Max Planck Institute. Casey Butterfield carefully edited all contributions and coordinated much of the communication of the project between authors, editors, and the publisher. Scott Kushner translated the chapters by Marie-France Garcia and Lucien Karpik from the French. Emma Lambert of Oxford University Press organized the production of the volume at the publisher. To all of them, our warmest thanks for their very thorough work. Finally, we would like to thank David Musson of Oxford University Press for his support of the project. Patrik Aspers gratefully acknowledges the support of Research Grant No. M2007-0244:1-PK from the Riksbankens Jubileumsfond and Research Grant No. 2009-1958 from the Swedish Research Council.

Jens Beckert
Patrik Aspers

Cologne and Stockholm, October 2010

CONTENTS

LIST OF FIGURES ix
LIST OF TABLES x
NOTES ON CONTRIBUTORS xi

INTRODUCTION

1 Value in Markets 3
  Patrik Aspers and Jens Beckert

PART I WHAT IS VALUABLE?

2 Price and Prejudice: On Economics and the Enchantment
  (and Disenchantment) of Nature 41
  Marion Fourcade

3 What Is the Price of a Scientific Paper? 63
  Lucien Karpik

4 The Value of Ethics: Monitoring Normative Compliance
  in Ethical Consumption Markets 86
  Peter Gourevitch

5 The Transcending Power of Goods: Imaginative Value in
  the Economy 106
  Jens Beckert

PART II AESTHETIC MARKETS

6 Symbolic Value and the Establishment of Prices: Globalization
  of the Wine Market 131
  Marie-France Garcia-Parpet

7 Pricing Looks: Circuits of Value in Fashion Modeling Markets 155
  Ashley Mears

8 Damien's Dangerous Idea: Valuing Contemporary Art at Auction 178
  Olav Velthuis

9 Infinite Surprises: On the Stabilization of Value
  in the Creative Industries 201
  Michael Hutter

PART III FINANCIAL MARKETS

10 Forecasting as Valuation: The Role of Ratings and
   Predictions in the Subprime Mortgage Crisis in the United States   223
   Akos Rona-Tas and Stefanie Hiss

11 Selling Value in Kenya's Nairobi Stock Exchange   247
   Christopher Yenkey

12 Coping with Contingencies in Equity Option Markets:
   The "Rationality" of Pricing
   Charles W. Smith   272

PART IV ORGANIZATIONS

13 Valuing Products as Cultural Symbols: A Conceptual
   Framework and Empirical Illustration   297
   Davide Ravasi, Violina Rindova, and Ileana Stigliani

POSTSCRIPT

14 What's Valuable?   319
   David Stark

INDEX   339

LIST OF FIGURES

2.1	The two roles of economics	47
5.1	Typology of value	111
6.1	Wine investment: Capital gains in a bottle	139
7.1	Editorial and commercial worlds in the fashion field	161
11.1	Creating familiarity with the industry in awareness phase advertisements	259
11.2	Establishing firm performance in awareness phase advertisements	260
11.3	Countdown phase advertisement	263
11.4	IPO advertising relative to regional population	265
11.5	IPO advertising relative to regional wealth	266

LIST OF TABLES

7.1	Range and averages of models' earnings per job	164
8.1	Summary of conditions determining the use of price mechanisms	182
11.1	Descriptive statistics of each initial public offer	254
11.2	Correlations between number of new NSE accounts opened and firm, offer and market-level attributes	254
11.3	"Psychographic types" of consumers, as defined by advertising agency	257
11.4	Four-stage advertising strategy used in Kenyan privatizations	258

NOTES ON THE CONTRIBUTORS

Patrik Aspers is Associate Professor of Sociology at Stockholm University. Aspers' topics of research include economic sociology and sociological theory. His research in the field of economics has concentrated on markets, with particular emphasis on the question of market constitution. He has conducted empirical work on the garment industry. His recent books include *Markets* (Polity Press, 2011) and *Orderly Fashion: A Sociology of Fashion* (Princeton University Press, 2010).

Jens Beckert is Professor of Sociology and Director of the Max Planck Institute for the Study of Societies in Cologne. His general research interests include economic sociology, organizational sociology, sociology of inheritance, and sociological theory. Beckert's current work focuses on the sociology of markets. He is the author of *Beyond the Market: The Social Foundation of Economic Sociology* (2002) and *Inherited Wealth* (2008), both published by Princeton University Press.

Marion Fourcade is Associate Professor of Sociology at the University of California, Berkeley. A comparative sociologist, she is interested primarily in cross-national differences in political and economic cultures. She has worked comparatively on the formation of knowledge, disciplines, and professions; the making of economic policies; the forms of political organization; and international processes and dynamics. Her first book, *Economists and Societies* (Princeton University Press, 2009), explores the institutions and cultural forces that have shaped the professional identities, practical activities, and disciplinary projects of economists in the United States, Britain, and France in the twentieth century.

Marie-France Garcia-Parpet is a French anthropologist who presently works for the French National Institute for Agricultural Research (INRA) and is a member of the Centre de sociologie européenne (Ecole des hautes études en sciences sociales). Her research focuses on the social construction of markets. She has recently published a book on the globalization of the wine market and its repercussions for the field of wine-production in France.

Peter Gourevitch is Founding Dean of the School of International Relations and Pacific Studies and Distinguished Professor of Political Science at the University of California, San Diego. His research interests include corporate governance regulation, the role of NGOs in a global economy, and political responses to economic crises, on which he has published books and articles. He is the former coeditor of *International Organization*.

Stefanie Hiss is an Assistant Professor of Economic Sociology and the Sociology of Financial Markets at the University of Jena in Germany and a Schumpeter Fellow funded by the Volkswagen Foundation. Her research interests include economic sociology and new institutionalism in sociology; financial markets and socially responsible investment; rating and scoring; and corporate social responsibility. Her recent publications include articles on the role of rating and scoring in the subprime crisis and the institutional change of corporate responsibility in Germany.

Michael Hutter is Director of the "Cultural Sources of Newness" research unit at the Social Science Center Berlin and a Research Professor at the Technische Universität Berlin. His current research interests include processes of interdependence between economy and art, cultural conditions of innovation, markets for cultural goods, and social systems theory. His recent publications deal with media economics, price differentials in art markets, and notions of value in culture, economics, and the arts.

Lucien Karpik is a French Senior Sociologist at l'Ecole des Mines and the Centre d'études sociologiques et politiques Raymond Aron (Ecole des hautes études en sciences sociales) in Paris. The focus of his research is on economic sociology and the sociology of justice. His most recent publications in English are *Valuing the Unique: The Economics of Singularities* (Princeton University Press, 2010) and *Fighting for Political Freedom: Comparative Studies of the Legal Complex and Political Liberalism* with editors T. Halliday and M. Feeley (Hart Publishing, 2007).

Ashley Mears is Assistant Professor of Sociology at Boston University. Her research focuses on the intersections of culture, markets, gender, and inequality. Her recent publications include articles on precarious labor and bodily capital, color-blind racism in aesthetic markets, and the mitigation of uncertainty in the cultural economy. Her first book, *Pricing Beauty*, traces the production of the fashionable "look" in the fashion modeling markets of New York and London.

Davide Ravasi is Associate Professor of Management at Bocconi University in Milan. His research interests include the interrelations between organizational identity, strategy, and culture; organizational symbols and artifacts; the management of design and design firms; and the creation of symbolic value. His works have appeared in the *Academy of Management Journal*, *Organization Science*, the *Journal of Management Studies*, *Journal of Business Venturing*, and *Industrial and Corporate Change*, among others.

Violina Rindova is Ralph B. Thomas Regents Professor in Business, an Ambassador Clark Centennial Fellow, and a Fellow of the IC2 Institute at the University of Texas at Austin. Her research focuses on perception, interpretation, and meaning-making in markets and their role in the social construction of markets, value, and advantage. Her work has been published in the *Academy of Management Journal*, *Academy of Management Review*, *Journal of International Business Studies*, *Organization Science*, *Strategic Management Journal*, and *Strategic Organization*.

Akos Rona-Tas is Associate Professor of Sociology at the University of California, San Diego, and a Research Associate at Met@risk, INRA, Paris. He is currently working on the problem of rationality and uncertainty in two research contexts: in economic sociology, credit and credit assessment; in sociology of science, the effect of scientific uncertainty on policy decisions in food safety. His publications include "Uncertainty, Risk and Trust: Russian and American Credit Card Markets Compared" (with Alya Guseva; in: *American Sociological Review*, 2001) and "Consumer Credit and Society in Transition Countries" (in: Victor Perez Diaz, ed., *Markets and Civil Society*, Berghan Books, 2009).

Charles W. Smith is Professor Emeritus of Sociology at Queens College and the Graduate Schools of CUNY. His primary research interests are auction markets, including financial markets. From his early work, "The Mind of the Market," to his more recent "Markets as Definitional Practices" (*Canadian Journal of Sociology* 32[1]), his focus has been on how these markets cope with ambiguity and contingencies. He is also the editor of the *Journal for the Theory of Social Behaviour*.

David Stark is Arthur Lehman Professor of Sociology and International Affairs at Columbia University, where he is Chair of the Department of Sociology and also directs the Center on Organizational Innovation. Stark studies how organizations and their members search for what is valuable. His most recent book, *The Sense of Dissonance: Accounts of Worth in Economic Life*, was published by Princeton University Press in 2009.

Ileana Stigliani is a Research Associate with Design London and the Innovation and Entrepreneurship Group of Imperial College Business School. She holds a PhD in Business Administration and Management from Bocconi University, Milan. Her dissertation focused on the role of artifacts and aesthetics in product design and was based on a ten-month ethnographic study of a leading design consulting firm located in Boston, Massachusetts. Her research interests include the emergence of service design as a design discipline, the role of artifacts in designers' creative processes, designers' aesthetic knowledge and learning, and the collaborations between business firms and design consulting firms.

Olav Velthuis is Assistant Professor in the Department of Sociology and Anthropology of the University of Amsterdam. His research interests include economic and cultural sociology. Velthuis is the author of *Imaginary Economics* (NAi Publishers, 2005) and *Talking Prices: Symbolic Meanings of Prices on the Market for Contemporary Art* (Princeton University Press, 2005), which received the Viviana Zelizer Distinguished Book Award of the American Sociological Association.

Christopher Yenkey is a PhD candidate at Cornell University in Ithaca, New York. His research applies economic sociology, organization theory, and behavioral finance to the study of emerging financial markets. In addition to his work on the legitimation of shareholding throughout Kenyan society, Yenkey is studying the social structure of speculative trading and the effects of fraud on ongoing participation in the Nairobi Stock Exchange.

Introduction

1 Value in Markets*

Patrik Aspers and Jens Beckert

The question "How much is it?" is often posed. We hear it when we buy something in the supermarket, but the businessman who wants to know the cost of having his bank help him to close a deal might pose the same question. "How much is it" often comes in the context of another question: "How much is it worth?" These are different questions, but they have been connected to each other since Aristotle. The centrality of these questions and the difficulties in understanding the underlying problems have not diminished since (Spates 1983).

This book focuses on value and prices in markets. Several recent events have brought the importance of this issue to the forefront. First came the collapse of Enron in 2001, where the fraudulent misrepresentation of profits and the value of the company's assets misled financial investors and finally culminated in the bankruptcy not only of Enron but also of Arthur Andersen, the accounting company approving Enron's financial statements. Then, in the financial crisis of 2008, the erroneous assessment by rating agencies of the value of financial products like asset-backed securities and collaterized debt obligations triggered a bubble and the subsequent collapse of financial markets. Questions of value, however, are also important much more generally. For products to be sold in markets, customers must value them and assess their value in relation to other products. Firms must produce products and position them in the market where customers will consider them valuable. Financial investors must assess the value of assets through judgments of the opportunities and risks involved.

The problem of value is not restricted to contemporary capitalism. Assessments of value must be also made by exchange partners in the barter system that dominates exchange in traditional societies. The absence of money does not mean the absence of valuation. Questions of pricing and valuation appear in socialist economies as well, even when prices are not generated in and communicated through markets but are politically determined. The issue of value and valuation in production, consumption, and distribution appears whether we have a traditional or a modern economy, a socialist or a capitalistic system. However, the more the market has become the dominating mechanism steering the production and distribution of goods—substituting for

---

* For helpful comments on earlier versions of this introduction, we would like to thank Susanna Alexius, David Dequech, Pierre François, Kristina Tamm Hallström, Jörg Rössel, and the members of the research group on the sociology of markets at the Max Planck Institute for the Study of Societies.

householding and redistribution as the dominant coordination mechanisms of traditional and state-run economies—the more significant the questions of valuation and pricing in markets have become.

The contributions to this volume focus on the value and prices of goods and on processes of valuation and pricing. By goods, we refer to consumption goods and capital goods as well as to financial assets.[1] Despite the spotlight on markets, the scope of the chapters goes beyond markets because valuation and pricing cannot be understood as the outcome of markets viewed in isolation. Value is created by organizations and through networks; economic value is connected to social values and can be established independently from any intention to exchange a good on the market.

In this introduction, our aim is to contribute to the analysis of value and price. Economic sociologists have analyzed questions of value and price primarily in empirical case studies. Our ambition is to strengthen the tools for this kind of analysis by highlighting the multifaceted aspects involved in processes of valuation and locating the relevant features in relation to each other. We will start with markets, since discussing markets will lead us to identify the problems of uncertainty and order as the core problems underlying issues of valuation and pricing in markets. We will then discuss the notion of value in its economic and noneconomic dimensions and conceptualize how these facets interrelate. This is followed by a brief overview of the different perspectives on economic value that have developed in economics and sociology. In the subsequent section, we distinguish several dimensions of economic value and discuss the valorization of goods as part of the market process. We then discuss how market actors evaluate goods: the classification and categorization of goods that allows market actors to distinguish their value in relation to one another is one of the principal issues of the sociological treatment of economic value. Supported by concepts developed in economic sociology in recent years, we highlight the social devices allowing for the classification and categorization of goods. This analysis is followed by three sections which deal with additional topics crucial for a sociology of economic value: the relationship between organizations and valuation, the dynamics of economic value, and the link between value and price.

Markets

Markets are arenas of social interaction in which rights for goods and services are exchanged for money under conditions of competition (Aspers and

---

[1] Throughout this text, the term "good" is used interchangeably with the term product and comprises services as well. Goods can be consumption goods or capital goods. Except where otherwise indicated, we subsume financial assets under the notion of goods, though economists usually distinguish between goods markets and financial markets.

Beckert 2008; Fligstein 2001). Ideally, this exchange is voluntary and peaceful (Weber 1968: 17, 1922: 383), which follows from the assumption of respect for property rights.²

Markets are one form of coordination in the economy; others are hierarchies and networks. What distinguishes markets from these other forms of coordination is the role of competition.³ A market exists only if there is competition on at least one side of the market—demand or supply. Competition is a social relationship between two or more actors aiming for an end that cannot be shared (cf. François 2008). Market interaction is a form of indirect conflict (Simmel 1978). Suppliers or purchasers compete with each other based on offers that are mutually observed, evaluated, and eventually countered by new offers. For competition to emerge, actors must not only desire the goods offered and have the necessary purchasing power but they must be able to assess their qualities relative to each other and compare them in terms of their value. What makes a good valuable? How are they evaluated in markets and how are they priced?

These topics speak to the issue of uncertainty and order in markets. Order is the key question from which to understand the operation and the dynamics of markets (Aspers 2009, 2011; Beckert 2009b; Fligstein 2001). Order in a market presupposes that uncertainty in the market has been reduced (Beckert 1996; Jagd 2007). With regard to the issue of value and price, this uncertainty stems from the contingency of the value of products and from the difficulties in judging the qualities of the products offered in the market. The first issue refers to the valorization of products; the second issue to the assessment of the evaluation of goods in relation to one another (see Vatin 2009). Only if these issues can be resolved can the production and distribution of economic goods be coordinated through markets. Imagine yourself in a wine store or a gallery, or as a financial investor, and not knowing anything about wine, art, or equity. How could you make a sensible choice between the different offers? Would not the prices attached to the bottles, artworks, and stocks appear completely random?

[margin note: ORDER = Risk reduction]

[margin note: Appadurai: valuing occurs according to scales — hence differing valuations.]

Value

What makes a product valuable? Value has several interrelated dimensions. In social life, different forms of value are present simultaneously, such as moral

---

² The return of something else (usually money) for the property rights surrendered sets market exchange apart from gifts; the voluntary character of the exchange sets market exchange apart from robbery.

³ A correlate is the market's price-setting function. A hierarchy may well have internal transfer prices, for example a purchase or sale between different departments, but these prices are not set under competition; to have competition, outside actors must be involved for comparison as well.

value, aesthetic value, and economic value. Each form of value has a scale used for evaluating the things that value covers. An activity may be judged as more or less ethical, and an object may be more or less beautiful, more or less appropriate, or more or less expensive. These different scales of value exist concurrently, leading to different ways of evaluating social events, people, organizations, or objects. In this sense, Arjun Appadurai talks of different "regimes of value" (Appudarai 1986; cf. Moeran and Pedersen 2011). Being judged as a commodity is only one sort of "life" that a thing can have. Valuing something means measuring and comparing it according to a scale. Worth is a covering concept, encompassing all the different scales through which the value of an object or event can be assessed (Stark 2009).

Moral values such as solidarity, regard for human rights, or preservation of the environment are used to express something that is seen by a group or a society at large as right and good (cf. Graeber 2001: 1). Moral values can motivate action and form the basis for the assessment of goods. Moral values may also stand in opposition to one another (Boltanski and Thévenot 2006; Weber 1946), which is to say that they may be incommensurable.

Such clashes in the evaluation of an action, a person, an organization, or an object can also have their source in the use of the different scales applied for judging them. Objects can be assessed using aesthetic criteria, referring to their beauty, or using economic criteria, referring to the (monetary) equivalent an actor is willing to surrender in order to obtain property rights in the object. An action can be of high moral value but of little economic value, as when someone is caring for an animal that is ill. These valuations according to different scales may lead to conflicts over the assessment of the value of a good or an activity. To translate value from one scale to the other seems to be a categorical mistake, since there is no "exchange rate." This lack of a common scale is also why it is wrong to subsume the different forms of value constituting the worth of an actor, a product, or an organization under the notion of capital, as Bourdieu did, or to reduce these different forms of value to utility, as economists do.

Nevertheless, these kinds of translations do take place. Observing how actors perform them and what kind of frictions emerge in the process is one of the main questions in sociological studies of valuation. In this volume, Marion Fourcade (Chapter 2) presents a highly informative case on the challenging relationship between economic evaluation and moral values. Fourcade studies the civil lawsuits that followed the devastating oil spills in Alaska. The question in these lawsuits was how to assess the destroyed value in animal and plant life: "goods" that were never intended to be evaluated economically or to be traded in a market. She shows that given the cultural framework of the United States, it was legitimate to translate the environmental damages into a measure of economic value. This translation was done by judging the economic value of the natural environment at Prince William Sound—the location of the oil spill. She thereby shows how economic theory is part of the technology used to evaluate the worth of the natural environment.

Some of the most important work on the interface between economic value and moral valuation has been conducted in numerous studies by Viviana Zelizer. An example is her analysis of the early stages of the life insurance industry in the United States (Zelizer 1979), which shows that the emergence of this industry was initially blocked by religious beliefs that held life insurance to be morally offensive because the beneficiary would profit from the death of a loved one. Thus, moral values prohibited the economic value of the good from being considered.

Zelizer's historical analysis alludes to a much larger phenomenon: To be valuable in the market, goods must not only fulfill a need but must also find legitimation as being tradable in market terms. This means that valorization and normative evaluation are closely entangled. Which products find legitimacy is historically contingent. Following the taxonomy of Michael Walzer (Walzer 1983), it seems that at least in modern societies, the market exchange of objects related to the human body and to human life itself is considered particularly morally offensive, as is the market exchange of (political) decisions. This holds true for organ trafficking as well as for human trafficking, enslavement, and the purchasing of votes (Healy 2006; Steiner 2010). If potential customers consider the market exchange of a certain good as illegitimate and do not demand the product, no market will emerge. This happened with life insurance policies when they were first introduced in the United States. If the moral offensiveness of the exchange leads markets for this product to be prohibited, but demand exists for it nonetheless, then illegal markets will emerge. Examples of this are the alcohol market in the United States during prohibition (Welskopp 2010), as well as the illegal markets for drugs, counterfeit consumer products, and human organs (Scheper-Hughes 2004). Another response to a situation in which economic evaluation seems illegitimate is to obscure the economic dimension of the exchange (Bourdieu 1996). The art market provides an example of this case (Velthuis 2005).

That economic criteria must be judged as a *legitimate* basis of evaluation of the product to be exchanged shows *one* important connection between markets and morality. Moral values can block markets. Moral values, however, can also contribute to the value of products.[4] Goods produced organically or with a social conscience are in high demand in many consumer markets today. "Fair trade" is a small but rapidly growing market segment (Zick-Varul 2009). The rise in demand holds true for groceries, sport shoes, flowers, wood furniture, or other products produced under morally defined criteria. Consequently, demand must be understood in relation to values of good health, care for workers, animals, and the environment at large (see also the chapter by

---

[4] Emile Durkheim alluded early on to the close connection between the values held in a community and the value of the objects exchanged on the market. His most important example of this connection was the value of labor. Durkheim lamented the low wages paid to workers, seeing them as a pathological deviation from the rule that the wage a worker obtains should reflect the value society sees in his labor (Durkheim 1984).

Peter Gourevitch in this volume). In financial markets, we find small but rapidly growing segments of Islamic investment and ethical investment, both of which combine moral values with economic value in assessing the worth of an asset. In other cases, the connection of a product to moral values constitutes the very thing that makes it possible for a market to develop, for example the emergence of a tourist market for whale watching (Lawrence and Phillips 2004). The "product" in this market consists of a boat ride off the coast that provides tourists the opportunity to observe whales swimming in the ocean. This product only became valuable once whales had become symbolically associated with values of freedom and unspoiled nature. Hence, what is valued in markets correlates with what is valued outside of markets. Moral values are distinct from economic values; they are, however, *economically relevant* (Weber 1978).

Economic Value in Social Science

Economic value in markets refers to the assessment of goods or services in terms of how much money an actor is willing to surrender to obtain property rights to the good in question. Money is used as the common denominator to assess the value of goods: it makes qualitatively different objects commensurate on a common scale of prices. Money is the means of account for economic value, but it is also a means of storing economic value.[5] The discussion of money in sociology (Carruthers and Ariovich 2010; Dodd 1994; Ingham 2004; Simmel 1978) shows how money affects social relations. Money thus cannot be seen as a neutral measuring rod if we want to understand how economic values emerge.

The question of where the economic value of products derives from has a long history in economic thought that is closely related to fundamental transformations of the economic order. Aristotelian ideas of use value and exchange value formed an important foundation for thinking about the matter of value in relation to markets. The physiocrats, writing before the industrial revolution and at a time when political power was rooted in landed property, held the idea that only agriculture could yield a surplus—a *produit net*. According to the physiocrats, the manufacturing process used the same amount of value as input as what it produced as output, and hence created no added value. Classical political economy, most notably in the works of Adam Smith and David Ricardo, prospering in the early stages of the industrial and the bourgeois revolutions, challenged this position. Its labor theory of

---

[5] Money can be any means of exchange that is valued in local communities, such as within the Kula ring (Malinowski 1922). But money of this kind has no clear exchange rate with other currencies and stands separate from other circuits of commerce (Zelizer 2004). Today, most monies are currencies (Dodd 2005). A currency like the euro is legal tender and has exchange rates with other currencies.

value—which has a forerunner in Aristotle—saw the value of goods as stemming from the transformation of natural assets through labor. The value of a product could be measured as the work hours needed to produce it. Karl Marx followed the assumption of classical political economy that value is produced by the laborers in the labor process.

In Marx's theory, the market has at best an indirect role in the determination of value, because value is created in production.[6] This theory misses the essential point that economic value expresses a relationship between the qualities of products offered in the market and the wants of customers *and* sellers. The intuition that goods have no intrinsic value has paved the way for modern economics. Most notable is the idea of marginal utility, developed at about the same time by William Jevons, Carl Menger, and Léon Walras, who saw value as utility, or more specifically the utility of the last added item. Instead of continuing to differentiate between market price and value, marginal utility theory took the sweeping step of giving up on any objective measure for assessing economic value—be it land, labor, or anything else—and anchoring value exclusively in the sphere of market exchange. This also means that *valorization* and *evaluation* (Vatin 2009) cannot be clearly distinguished anymore.[7]

Neoclassical economics advocated a radical subjectivation of value through the introduction of the notion of marginal utility. During the 1930s, Lionel Robbins defined economics as "the science which studies human behavior as a relationship between ends and scarce means which have alternative uses" (Robbins 1935: 16). This formal definition is narrow, and it excludes noneconomic values; these become relevant only as inputs of what people desire.[8] The subjective notion of economic value has also been advocated by sociologists. For Georg Simmel, looking at the demand side of markets, value follows from the distance between an actor and an object he desires: "The object...which is characterized by its separation from the subject, who at the same time establishes it and seeks to overcome it by his desire, is for us a value" (Simmel 1978: 66).

While we agree with marginal utility theory that economic value is an effect of the wants of potential purchasers—however manipulated by the producer side—we also maintain that the theory of exchange offered by marginal utility

---

[6] Marx (1977), however, connects the value of a commodity to the "socially necessary labor time" for its production. This can be interpreted as an influence of market competition on the value of goods.

[7] The focus on subjective utility and on using the desire of actors as the basis for economic value does not imply that the costs of production—some of which are labor costs—are irrelevant. The production costs are relevant to the question of whether a product is produced at all. Only products whose expected price in the market is high enough to generate a profit for the producer will be produced. Hence, production costs influence market supply but the cost of production must not affect how market actors evaluate goods.

[8] More recently, some economists have broadened the utility function to also include noneconomic values. Akerlof and Kranton suggest that economists should account for who the actors are and how they want to live their lives, and have labeled this approach Identity Economics (Akerlof and Kranton 2010), an approach that also draws on sociological research.

theory does not suffice to develop a theory of economic value. This is most obvious in the failure of neoclassical economics to develop a theory of preference formation. Marginal utility theory treats preferences as exogenous and does not take interaction in markets into account as a factor that may form and re-form preferences. The assumption made is that market participants each enter the market with fixed preferences for a bundle of goods and are restricted in their purchases through the respective budgets available to them. Neoclassical theory is interested in the questions of how demand changes against changes of relative prices and how prices change with variations in the demand for products. Hence it offers a theory of market exchange. What remains necessarily opaque in such a theory is the explanation of actors' preferences themselves. "De gustibus non est disputandum" is the famous formula employed by George Stigler and Gary Becker (Stigler and Becker 1977) to bar questions of preference formation from the theory, but this has led to a situation in economics where "no one knows why people want goods" (Douglas and Isherwood 1979: 15).

Exogenizing preferences is possible only to the extent that neoclassical theory limits itself to explaining how market equilibria emerge based on *existing* preferences. However, such a theory remains incomplete because it remains silent on the origins of preferences. To start from a situation in which "all actors have a perfectly defined utility function is to suppose that the 'market question' is already partially solved" (Jagd 2007: 84). And to the extent that market equilibria are affected by endogenously changing preferences, a theory that exogenizes preferences cannot reach its goal of explaining the observable equilibria. It is this systematic point at which sociological approaches to the question of valuation in the economy set in.

To be sure, the limitations of neoclassical economics do not apply to all economists. Some strands of economics have taken up issues of endogenous changes in preferences and of explaining the origins of preferences. The bandwagon and snob effects refer to changes in demand due to the consumption patterns of others (Leibenstein 1950), violating the assumption that preferences are independent from the preferences of others. For some products, demand increases with price, meaning that price is itself valued as a cultural signal in markets and influences demand (the Veblen effect). While recent branches of economics are beginning to open the black box of preferences to scientific exploration,[9] they do so primarily on psychological grounds.

---

[9] Endogenous changes of preferences (Lichtenstein and Slovic 2006) have been observed in situations where actors adapt their preferences to the situation—for instance, when actors declare that goals are no longer desired once they seem unreachable (Elster 1983). One challenge is to integrate such adaptive preferences into welfare theory (von Weizsäcker 2005). Another challenge is to explain the constitution of preferences. Some economists have suggested answers to this question based on psychological theories. Witt, for instance, has recommended a behaviorist theory of wants that distinguishes between innate wants and acquired wants, the latter of which can change over time (Witt 2001). Both types of wants can be expanded chiefly through new product designs and the instruments of marketing. Other economic approaches dealing with the constitution of preferences

The scope of psychological assessments is limited if desires for objects are seen as natural rather than cultural and social. It is the conviction expressed throughout this volume that investigations of the valuation of goods and changes of these valuations need to focus on the *meanings* that goods obtain for actors and on the social and institutional structure of markets.

Dimensions of Economic Value

[handwritten annotation: 1. use/investment 2. individualistic/relational 3. functional/symbolic]

A theory of economic value must explain both how economic value is socially constituted and how economic value is the result of markets. To examine value assessments in markets, it is helpful to distinguish analytically between the questions of *what* it means to say that a good provides value for an actor and the question of *how* actors determine the value of a good. The first question refers to the dimensions in which a product or an asset can be valuable, the second to their evaluation.

Value is not intrinsic to the materiality of an object but rather is inseparably connected to the concept of meaning (Richins 1994: 504). Even products whose value consists of the satisfaction of innate needs must be "understood" by the user as fulfilling this need and legitimated as a means for the satisfaction of the need. Despite this general dependence on meaning, it is possible to distinguish different forms in which goods can become economically valuable to the purchaser. Three such distinctions are especially illuminating to understand the sources of value:

1. *The distinction between use value and investment value.* Use value refers to what is gained from the *qualities of a good* through its use. Buying a soft drink at the soccer game, an axe to cut wood for heating, or a car for transportation are all purchasing decisions in which the value of the objects is based on the satisfaction stemming from their use. Investment value of a good, in contrast, derives from the expectation of a monetary gain to be realized. Investments in financial markets are an example of this. Financial assets may gain in value but also provide a stream of revenue through interests or dividends. In addition, liquid financial assets, including money, may provide implicit revenue in the form of what Keynes called the liquidity premium. Purchases of capital goods and the contracting of workers are based on the expectation of deriving a profit. To buy a car and use it as a taxi to make a profit is based on its investment value; to buy the car for leisurely trips on the weekend is based on its use value.

---

may take into account the desire for social integrity (acting cooperatively and fairly), for example, or the beliefs and evaluations of actors as they are expressed in attitudes toward goods (Binder and Niederle 2007).

The distinction between use value and investment value is analytical, because in many cases both dimensions overlap. Buying a house is based on its use value in providing shelter, but it is also an investment if the buyer speculates that the house will go up in value. Purchases of artwork are characterized by a similar mixture of use value and investment value. Conversely, objects that seem to have their primary value in their investment dimension are also not entirely separated from use value. Setting up a production site can provide an intrinsic satisfaction and confer social status on the owner. Investment value and use value may also be connected through a prolonged means-ends chain. The profits from the investment might—though not necessarily (Deutschmann 1999)—be intended for consumption purposes. A person who buys stocks may do it because he wants to use the expected profit to buy a sports car. The distinction between use and investment hence has nothing to do with the inherent qualities of the items; it is purely a matter of the economic flow of meaning in which it is embedded.

2. *The distinction between individualistic value and relational value.* Individualistic value refers to the satisfaction of a buyer's desire regardless of any social interaction effects associated with the purchase. A person who buys a cake for an afternoon snack or a bouquet of flowers for their home may do so independently of any orientation to third parties. "Individualistic value" does not mean that the desire for cake or for a bouquet of flowers would not be socially shaped. The purchase, however, can be made regardless of the reactions of third parties to it. Conversely, buying the same cake for a social gathering or giving the bouquet of flowers as a gift are examples of the relational sources of value. Relational value is based on what other people think, or are perceived to think, about the purchaser of the good based on what has been bought. The teenage boy who buys a pair of expensive sneakers to avoid being bullied by his peers is as relational as the father who replaces his car so as not to fall behind in status among his colleagues.

Again, this is an analytical distinction because the very same good can have individualistic and relational value at the same time, depending on the flow of meaning in the exchange process. In this volume, Michael Hutter (Chapter 9) testifies to the importance of individualistic value in his analysis of how the "amazement" and "surprises" experienced by the spectators in a theatre, opera, or any other cultural event create value. Conversely, Pierre Bourdieu (Bourdieu 1984) has investigated the relational dimension of goods by showing how different consumption patterns express differences in cultural capital and how people employ this cultural capital to position themselves in the social field. Different tastes in music or different styles of home furniture are tools that actors use to distinguish their lifestyles and to signal their place in the social space.

3. *The distinction between functional and symbolic value.* A good that is bought because of its function allows its owner to use it to alter a state of the world based on the physical effect of the good. Symbolic value, by contrast, refers to the meaning a good has for its owner and in the owner's social environment that extends beyond the good's physical effects. Symbolic value is also only *analytically* independent from functional value, because often both come together in the same object. The house not only provides shelter (its physical effect) but is also a home. It can be a status symbol, signaling the social position of the owner to his social surroundings. In general terms, the ownership of products is part of the construction of the identity of the consumer (McCracken 1988) or the firm (Podolny 1993; Uzzi and Lancaster 2004) and therefore always has symbolic dimensions.

Symbolic value has been central in sociological research. It is based on intersubjectively shared meanings. What an object symbolically stands for is established in the community and emerges in social practices.[10] Jens Beckert (Chapter 5) discusses in this volume a specific form of symbolic value he refers to as "imaginative value." Some goods not only position their owners in the social space through their symbolic signification but are also symbolic representations of espoused ideals and values that can be imaginatively appropriated through the purchase of goods. Goods can serve as bridges to the transcendental. There are examples of this potential for transcendence in consumer goods as well as in financial investments and entrepreneurial activity.

Seen on the aggregated level, the symbolic meaning of goods is an important element of the reproduction of class structures. Thorstein Veblen's classic description of conspicuous consumption (Veblen 1953) still provides the most graphic representation of how goods are utilized to symbolically demarcate social positions. Subsequent research has demonstrated with much broader scope how purchasing decisions in general are used to communicate identification with specific social identities (Warde 1994).

Though value based on symbolic meanings of goods is as old as the production of wealth beyond mere physical survival, it plays an especially important role for economic growth in affluent contemporary societies in which basic needs have already been satisfied (see also the chapter by Hutter in this volume). Now that land and labor have been identified as dominant sources of value in earlier times, the question arises: Are symbolic meanings to be understood as the leading sources of value today?

---

[10] Symbolic and relational value overlap if the possession of goods contributes to the social identity of the owner. Value is symbolic, but not relational, if the satisfaction does not derive from recognition by third parties, as in the case of the amazement experienced in a theatre performance. Value is relational, but not symbolic, if the relational part refers to the use value of the good. A father buying a pair of shoes for his daughter's hiking trip would be an example.

Value through Evaluation

Identifying the different dimensions in which goods and services become valuable to the buyer does not yet address the question of *how* market participants arrive at their judgment of the value (desirability) of the good offered in the market. This question refers to the evaluation of goods. How do financial actors make choices between different assets, given the uncertainty they confront? How do consumers choose between hundreds of models offered in the car market? These questions might seem trivial at the outset, because experience tells us that, at least in consumer markets, we have seemingly spontaneous ways to assess the goods we confront in most situations. And indeed, many purchasing decisions are made routinely.

A more detailed look at the question of how value is determined, however, reveals a highly complex world of social mechanisms standing behind the seemingly unproblematic task of producers and consumers to make value judgments in the market. This issue is directly connected to the problem of uncertainty in markets and forms one of the core issues in the sociological investigation of economic value. Only if buyers are capable of "forming clear subjective values for goods in the market" (Koçak 2003: 8), meaning that they are in a position to distinguish between the values of goods, and if sellers can reliably demonstrate the value of their goods, will uncertainty be reduced and a disposition to buy arise (Koçak 2003: 5–6). Market coordination presupposes a shared understanding of the qualities of goods (Eymard-Duvernay 2002: 268). This connection of the problem of the order of markets with the issue of valuation manifests itself among purchasers as well as among producers. On the demand side, customers need to compare goods offered in the market and make judgments on the desirability of these goods in relation to other offers. On the supply side, producers must demonstrate the value of their offers in relation to other products offered in the market.

The symbolic qualities of products that constitute their economic value must be constructed. This is done through practices of qualification of products. In the financial markets, for instance, the existence of a representation of the future is not given a priori but is the result of market exchange itself (Beunza and Garud 2005; Jagd 2007). In consumer markets, signification systems are produced and reproduced through the practices of consumers, producers, and market intermediaries, and the interactions between them (Callon et al. 2002). The process-driven character of the valuation of goods in social practices counters the idea of exogeneity of preferences. An empirical investigation of such practices is provided in this volume by Christopher Yenkey (Chapter 11), who analyzes the birth of the stock market in Kenya. Until recently, shareholding was unknown to private investors in Kenya. With the privatization of formerly state-owned firms and a nascent field of initial public offerings, a new market became possible. Potential buyers of shares, however, had to be "attached" to this form of investment by becoming convinced of the worth of shareholding before the market could develop. Yenkey shows how advertising campaigns led by state agencies were actually creating the value of the shares offered.

The role of producers is crucial in these processes. Product differentiation as a form of value creation among producers is mentioned by Alfred Marshall (1920: 300–2), but today it is especially associated with the work of Edward Chamberlin (1948). Product differentiation is also the starting point in Harrison White's theory of producer markets (White 1981, 2008). White argues that firms competing in producer markets establish market niches that correspond with their identities. On the one hand, producers share the identity of being producers in the same market; on the other hand, they have different identities because they produce heterogeneous products. Product differentiation and the perceived value of the products is the outcome of the reciprocal orientation of producers toward each other.

Producers and market intermediaries are actively pursuing the creation of the value of goods. According to Alfred Marshall, value emerges from wants, which in turn result from activities. Wants make up the demand side and activities represent the supply side (1961). To understand the evaluation of products by customers, one needs to look at how producers and market intermediaries judge products in markets. There is a plethora of strategies and techniques that producers and sellers may employ to create, establish, and attribute value to their products. One field in which such strategies can be observed especially well is the fashion industry (Aspers 2010), which perhaps more than any other industry is characterized by symbolic rather than functional value production. By creating identities for firms and products through the means of narratives, visual communication, and connections between customers, and by using advertising, producers create niches and rank orders among themselves, as a result of interaction in the market.

This weight of the producer side in the valorization of products can also be observed in business-to-business markets, for example in the purchasing decisions of companies and in financial investments. Brian Uzzi and Ryon Lancaster provide an example of this in their findings that price differences between corporate law firms are based on the different symbolic value they offer to their clients (Uzzi and Lancaster 2004). Customers derive "the 'emotional part' of a purchase" from their perception of a law firm as having high status (Uzzi and Lancaster 2004: 328). The influence of status on the price charged by the law firm is based on two mechanisms: the desire of the client firm to improve its own image by associating itself with a high-status law firm, and a logic of appropriateness: Hiring a high-status law firm protects the internal counsel responsible for the decision "from potential criticism and raises their worth in the eyes of others" (Uzzi and Lancaster 2004: 328). This symbolic value allows higher prices to be charged for the legal service.

What does the situation look like when we turn to the consumers? Not only are market actors confronted with a large heterogeneity of different types of goods among which they must allocate their budget, but these actors often have a myriad of products to choose from within each category. The main issue in the evaluation of goods is their classification—an issue whose investigation has a long history in sociology (Durkheim and Mauss 1963; Espeland and Stevens 1998; Lounsbury and Rao 2004; Schneiberg and Berk 2010; Zuckerman 1999). To classify objects means to put them into categories that establish distinctions and at the same time make the objects commensurable. The classification of commodities leads not only to differentiation between different markets but also to recognized distinctions between the objects traded in one market, thereby reducing complexity (Musselin and Paradeise 2002: 257). For instance, four-wheeled motor vehicles form a market category that is distinct from motorcycles. Within that market, trucks are distinguished from passenger vehicles. Within the market for passenger vehicles, family cars are distinguished from sports cars and from SUVs. Within the category of family cars, there are models from Toyota, Volkswagen, Renault, and other producers.

Producers may try to impose categories, but consumers may accept or reject these attempts. The classifications of products according to perceived differences contribute to the ordering of the complex and almost infinite world of commodities. However, the classification of products as such does not yet resolve the problem of valuation. Viewed from the demand side, making a decision in favor of an SUV depends on a value judgment: given the purpose for which the car is intended, the SUV is a *better* or *more appropriate* choice than a sports car. Similar choices must be made when deciding on a Volkswagen instead of a Toyota. How do potential purchasers of commodities arrive at such value judgments? How do they decide on a lawyer without having full information on what that lawyer's services are worth (Karpik 2010)? How do financial analysts assess the value of a stock or a bond despite the uncertainty involved (Beunza and Garud 2006; Zuckerman 1999)? How do consumers arrive at a choice between products that are interchangeable but not identical? These questions can only be answered based on judgment of the goods' qualities, that is, the qualification of a good—a process that requires the good's "individualization" (Callon 2002: 267).

Note that the problem of judging qualities is not limited to the "market for lemons problem" described by information economics (Akerlof 1970). The problem is not one of asymmetrically distributed information but of establishing what qualifies as quality. Much research in economic sociology has focused on the processes of qualification of goods as an indispensable part of the constitution of market value. Concepts like framing (Beunza and Garud 2005; Biggart and Beamish 2003; Fiss and Kennedy 2009), status (Aspers 2009; Podolny 2005), networks (Granovetter 1995; Uzzi and Lancaster 2004; White 1981), qualification (Callon 1998; Callon et al. 2002), market devices (Callon et al. 2007), judgment devices (Karpik 2010), and circuits of commerce (Zelizer 2004) have been applied to investigate how market actors arrive at judgments on the qualities of products offered in the market.

In addition to approaches in economic sociology, the economics of conventions (Eymard-Duvernay 1989; Favereau and Lazega 2002; Orléan 2004; Salais and Thévenot 1986) has addressed this question from within (heterodox) economics. The economics of conventions starts out from the problem of uncertainty, posing the question of how actors coordinate their activities on markets. One of the uncertainties actors confront in markets stems from the contingency in the qualification of goods. Qualification refers to the development of shared cognitive and normative understandings of the qualities of the products exchanged. The approach stipulates that shared understandings of product qualities emerge through processes of interaction in the market field, processes which lead to the formation of conventions. Conventions allow that actors base their expectations and actions on joint knowledge. These emerging frames, however, are not homogeneous. On the contrary, conflicting "orders of worth" (Boltanski and Thévenot 2006) can be institutionalized simultaneously in a field, making it necessary for the actors to negotiate between them. This is an important source of the dynamics of valuation processes (Stark 2009). The theoretical framework of the economics of convention has been applied to evaluation processes in markets as distinct as the labor market (Eymard-Duvernay and Marchal 1997; Marchal and Rieucau 2010; Salais 1989), the wine market (Diaz-Bone 2005), and financial markets (Orléan 1999). Considered in systematic terms, the concept of conventions—like status, standards, judgment devices, circuits of commerce, or frame—is a response to the failure of neoclassical theory to explain preferences.

STANDARD AND STATUS MARKETS

One of the most insightful vantage points when disentangling processes of product qualification is to observe *what* is actually being judged in the market. Intuitively, it seems to be obvious that it is the qualities of the product that are evaluated in relation to the qualities of other products in the market. However, this holds true for only one kind of market, which can be called the standard market (Aspers 2009). Standard markets are defined by the existence of a scale of evaluation for what is offered in the market that exists independently from the buyers and sellers. Buyers and sellers orient to this scale when evaluating goods. Gold markets as well as stock exchange markets are examples of standard markets.

The standard may be constructed by the market actors themselves, for example by an industry organization (Ahrne and Brunsson 2008) or by market intermediaries, or imported from outside, for instance when the state sets the standard. The applied measuring techniques are not simply "objective," but are deeply culturally (and politically) entrenched. The chapter in this volume by Marion Fourcade on the techniques used for the economic assessment of environmental damages shows an example of such entrenchment, as does the chapter by Akos Rona-Tas and Stefanie Hiss on credit rating agencies.[11]

---

[11] What is not yet clear is how the object is economically rated, meaning how it gains an economic value in the form of price. The standard is independent of the price setting of what is traded in the

A *status market*, by contrast, lacks a scale of value that is independent of its actors. Instead, offers are evaluated with reference to the actors who offer or purchase the product or service. Buyers and sellers stand in rank order of interrelated status positions. The value of what is traded in this kind of market is a function of the participating actors. Stated in generalized terms, in status markets value is established as a consequence of activities that are oriented to the social status of the market actors. Actors shift "their orientation from what is exchanged to the social structural positions of their potential exchange partners" (Podolny 1994: 459). The social structure of the market is relatively more entrenched for the assessment of value than any scale measuring product qualities. Here, one can also see how evaluation and valorization are inseparably linked.

Though the role of status can be relevant in all markets, it becomes especially visible for products where value reflects aesthetic judgments. Garments and modern art, and also cars, furniture, and wine provide examples of markets in which objective differences in quality can be established only partially or not at all. The fashion industry provides especially illuminating examples (Aspers 2010). The quality of a sweater is not assessed on the basis of a ranking of the material qualities of different sweaters; the categorization derives rather from the assessment of the status of the brand that is selling it. That we value a sweater from Armani so much more highly than one from H&M is based on the known status order of brands in this industry. The value, however, can also derive from the status of the users, from who buys a certain product or label. Is the label "in" or "out" among purchasers who have high social status in the market?

The role of status for the value of products is investigated in Ashley Mears' chapter (Chapter 7) on the pricing of fashion models. Her starting point is the apparent arbitrariness of aesthetic evaluation that actors in this industry face. This leads to uncertainty regarding the value of the "look" to be sold, in the same way that the art market must confront the uncertainty of what establishes quality in art. The status of models in the market emerges, Mears argues, from a reputation that is gained by working for prestigious magazines and photographers, even though these jobs typically pay very badly or not at all.[12]

The relevance of status orders in markets is not limited to consumer markets. Joel Podolny, for example, investigated the prices that investment banks charge their clients when underwriting corporate securities and has

---

market. Regardless of the price of one kilo of silver, the determination and rating of silver as silver is unaffected. We will come back to this when discussing the relationship of value and price.

[12] This demonstrates an interesting paradox of separation of reputation from (immediate) financial rewards. One can assume a mechanism operating here that is also found in the art world (Becker 1982; Bourdieu 1996): artistic value and monetary value stand in a hostile relationship to each other; the obscuring of the monetary dimension aims to protect the "sacred" character of the product that is in danger of being contaminated by money. As Viviana Zelizer has argued, we may speak of circuits of commerce, each of which has its own logic, media of exchange, and clear boundaries against the others (2004). The actors in such a circuit share meanings. In some circuits, money will hence be seen as hostile or immoral, or as damaging to the dignity of the activity or person (O'Neill 2009).

shown the correlation of price and status in this market (1994). One implication deriving from the measurement of quality according to status is that value cannot be separated from social practices. What is "high status" and what is "low status" is the result of definitional struggles taking place in the market field. Such struggles involve not just customers and the supplying firms but also many intermediaries such as critics, designers, and traders.

JUDGMENT DEVICES

The valuation of goods takes different routes in standard markets and status markets.[13] Both types of markets, however, converge in that social devices allow for the categorization of different offers in the market and thereby reduce uncertainty. Standards and status assessments can be described as two principles of categorization of goods allowing for the ordering of offers in markets. But how are standards set, and how is status assessed?

In recent years, several studies anchored in the field of the social studies of finance have analyzed the role of mathematical models as devices for the assessment of the value of financial products. An important basis for this was laid by Michel Callon, who introduced the notion of "calculative tools" (Callon 1998). Calculation of equivalence in financial markets takes place through formulas and accounting rules. Such technologies of valuation have been analyzed by Donald MacKenzie and Yuval Millo (2003), for instance, in their now classic article on the Black-Scholes model of derivatives pricing and its role in making possible the expansion of the derivatives market since the 1970s. More recently, Donald MacKenzie has analyzed the evaluation practices of rating agencies when assessing the risks entailed in collateralized debt obligations (CDOs) and asset-backed securities (MacKenzie 2010). MacKenzie discusses the role of the mathematical formula known as the Gaussian copula that has been used to calculate the risks of the CDOs, and relies on a correlation number that expresses the interdependencies of the securities pooled in one CDO. The formula made it possible to calculate the risks. The low levels of correlation assumed in the models, however, made the securitized debt look much less risky, and hence more valuable, than it turned out to be.

While such calculative tools have seized the attention of scholars in the field of social studies of finance, the French sociologist Lucien Karpik developed a conceptual framework of the mechanisms applied to assess quality in markets for "singular goods" (Karpik 2010). Karpik calls these mechanisms *judgment devices*. With this notion Karpik refers to "guideposts for individual and collective action" (Karpik 2010: 44), which dissipate the opacity of the market by reducing the cognitive deficits of market actors engendered by their incomplete knowledge of products and by providing reasons for choices. Judgment devices create order in markets by flagging out differences in the

---

[13] In any market, however, standard and status can be empirically intermingled as a means to order markets.

quality of products and between the status of producers. Karpik's contribution consists of proposing a typology that entails a large spectrum of different devices through which judgments of products offered on the market are shaped. While this might not be an exhaustive typology of the devices to classify goods and producers, much of the research in economic sociology on the classification of goods refers to one or several of these devices.

1. Personal *networks* refer to the social structure of the demand side. Personal networks provide actors with credible and trustworthy information. When selecting professional services from doctors, lawyers, or accountants, people rely on the contacts that make up their personal networks. They act according to information they receive from personal sources they trust. The use of networks of friends or colleagues as guides for quality assessments, which sometimes is called social capital, is common in markets in which actors only infrequently operate and in which the value of the commodity exchanged is not easily measured (Powell 1990).

2. Karpik uses the term *cicerones* to refer to critics and guidebooks that "embody a soft, symbolic form of authority" (Karpik 2010: 46) and thereby influence the evaluation of the qualities of different offers. These can be travel guides, car magazines, or restaurant guides that steer actors who are choosing a restaurant or a new car. Karpik himself has conducted a study on the role of the Guide Michelin in the French restaurant market (Karpik 2000). The Guide Michelin compares, selects, and rates restaurants. The notion of quality is defined by the Guide through Michelin's own judgment criteria. At the same time, the Guide leaves space for the heterogeneity of principles of worth that will be applied by different customers, by informing the reader through various categories.

   Cicerones are also the experts in a market who shape judgments of the goods through their assessments. One example of a market where critics play an extraordinarily important role is the art market (Beckert and Rössel 2004; Velthuis 2005; Yogev 2010). Aesthetic markets (Aspers 2001: 1) generally have no objective standards by which quality could be measured and compared. Instead, quality is constructed from the judgments of the participating actors. As gallery owners, museum curators, art critics, collectors, or professors at art schools, these experts shape the evaluation of art works through their opinions, reviews, purchasing decisions, and exhibition policies. These authorities are carefully watched by the other actors in the field, who deduce the quality of an artist through the judgments of professionals (see also the chapter by Ashley Mears in this volume). In financial markets, analysts are experts who exercise a soft pressure on investment decisions through their assessments of the financial assets traded.[14]

---

[14] In the financial markets as well as in the art market, one can observe that the influence of these experts depends on their status. Financial analysts can become stars in the field if they have made

3. Karpik uses the term *confluences* for the techniques used by firms to channel buyers, "ranging from territorial location, spatial organization and displays to selling skills" (Karpik 2010: 46). The role of *confluences* can be demonstrated with a recent study on the French funeral market. Pascale Trompette investigated how the organizational structures of the market influence the decisions of families in need of the provisions for a funeral (Trompette 2007). The principal judgment devices relevant in this industry are techniques used by firms to channel buyers. Opening up a funerel home right at the hospital—where most people die these days—puts these services in direct proximity to the families of the deceased. Hence, economic value is created through the location of suppliers. Another example would be the organization of the presentation of merchandise on the shelves in supermarkets.

4. *Rankings* include not only bestseller lists like the ones for music and books but also the rankings for academic journals, universities, hospitals, lawyers, or wine, which are often established by magazines. One market where *rankings* are highly influential judgment devices is the wine market. In contrast to the soft authority of *cicerones* that allows more than one principle of worth to be included, ranking is a way of creating order out of what is offered in a market by reducing complexity to one single scale at the ordinal level. Robert Parker introduced a scale that uses values between 50 and 100 to rank wines. This scale mimics an "objective" standard, though it is in essence subjective. Many studies on the wine market have confirmed the influence of the Parker ranking on the prices for wine (Gibbs et al. 2009; Hay 2007).

Wine has become a frequent object of studies on valuation (Benjamin and Podolny 1999; Diaz-Bone 2005; Hay 2010). In this volume, Marie-France Garcia-Parpet (Chapter 6) provides a case study on quality classification in the wine market. She focuses only indirectly on the influence of rankings and centers on the role a social network can play as a substitute for high rankings. Garcia-Parpet analyzes how the winemaker Aimé Guibert was able to establish a reputation as a high-quality vintner in the Languedoc-Roussillon region, a region with traditionally low status in the French wine market. Finding support in the Anglo-American wine press through his networks, Guibert was able to change how his product was perceived in assessments from the wine press, and even contributed to the re-evaluation of the status of the region itself. The chapter by Lucien Karpik in this volume (Chapter 3) deals with the assessment of scholarly success

---

accurate forecasts in the past, giving their judgments much greater weight compared to other analysts. It makes a crucial difference for the artistic and economic value of an artist whether his or her work is exhibited at the Centre Pompidou or at a local gallery, or whether it is a renowned art critic or a local journalist who reviews the work. The bestowal of value cannot be separated from the activities and voices of actors in the field who have status, and who therefore are in the structural position to define "value."

through the ranking of academic journals. By asking "What Is the Price of a Scientific Paper?" Karpik, like Fourcade in her chapter, shows how mechanisms designed for the assessment of value in market exchange are dispersing into other social spheres.

The chapter by Akos Rona-Tas and Stefanie Hiss (Chapter 10) explores ratings in financial markets. Ratings differ from rankings by providing assessments of the probability of certain events but not positioning the good in relation to the performance of a set number of other goods. Rating agencies provide assessments of the quality of debt. The value of a loan is based on interest rates and assumed risks. Rating agencies deal with the second dimension: they evaluate the promises of borrowers to pay back their loans. The grade given to a security issued by a company, bank, or country is the measure that communicates the risks involved. These ratings might or might not deliver accurate predictions but they are the basis by which markets value the debt. The financial crisis, Rona-Tas and Hiss argue, was foremost a colossal failure of valuation. That the ratings themselves influence the value of the object rated shows how judgments do not just measure value but constitute it. Value is a result of interpretation and not an objective measure of an inherent quality.

5. Finally, *appellations* include all kinds of labels like designations of origin, certifications, brands, and professional titles. They are signals of quality scrutinized by independent third parties. Classifications like the *Appellations d'Origine Contrôlée*, which certify that a product is of a certain origin and produced according to certain standards, are ways of categorizing offers at the nominal level. Roquefort cheese and champagne are products that are labeled according to their place of origin. Appellations, however, refer not only to places of origin for products but also to production standards. Lumber that is certified as having been sustainably logged (Maletz and Tysiatchniouk 2009) and fair trade products are examples of appellations that reference production standards. Fair trade products are valued not for a superior functional value but for the compliance with specific ethical standards in the production process. Though these differences in the production process are invisible in the product itself, some consumers are valuing the products more highly and are willing to pay a premium price for them. Peter Gourevitch (Chapter 4) investigates certification in fair trade markets. Gourevitch is especially interested in the issue of monitoring, which is particularly pressing in ethical markets. Since the products are not different materially, how can producers convince their customers of the truthfulness regarding their claims of compliance with the ethical standards, that is, the value of their product?

While brands are established by firms, certificates and designations of origin are standards that are set and controlled by associations or the state. Though appellations per se do not create rank orders between different regions, for example, singling out a region enables product differentiation, branding, and niche creation to occur at the level of markets instead of firms (White 1981). Appellations reduce uncertainty in the market but also lead to collective monopolies.

Research in economic sociology on calculative tools and judgment devices has taken a perspective that is largely rooted in science studies and in cultural sociology. It is crucial to integrate political sociology much more strongly into this perspective, emphasizing the power-laden political struggles leading to the use of specific judgment devices. If value depends on the contingent assessment of product qualities, the classification of goods is part of a market struggle. There is a *politics of classification* led by rent-seeking actors (Buchanan et al. 1980). The classification of goods is not just a matter of coordination but also of distribution (Beckert 2009a).

The Organizational Basis of Value

The formation of criteria used to assess the quality of goods can emerge spontaneously in the market, developing gradually into taken-for-granted conventions that are used to judge products. Often, however, established criteria for product qualities have their origin in organizational action. Markets are populated by firms, either on one side (such as in the labor market or a final consumer market) or on both sides (business-to-business markets). Studies on valuation in markets demonstrate the crucial role organizations play through their identities (White 2008), their positioning of products in the market (Power and Hauge 2008), their creation of standards (Brunsson and Jacobsson 2000), and their introduction of judgment devices. Organizations play a role in valuation processes not only through the design of market devices but also through the positioning of products under the *given* regime of devices prevailing in the market. Firms attempt to attach customers to products even as they struggle to detach customers from the products of their competitors. "In the economy of qualities, this struggle for attachment and detachment is at the heart of competition" (Callon et al. 2002: 207).

Though this does not imply that processes of valuation of products can be read as a story of manipulation through powerful producers, organizations have the advantage over individuals in that they command collective resources. Organizations also play an important role as market intermediaries, as in the case of rating agencies. Not all organizations in markets are firms. Nongovernmental organizations and consumer associations (Micheletti 2003) also play a role in the valuation of objects, for instance when they monitor claims by producers of ethical production practices, as shown in the chapter by Peter Gourevitch. It is therefore important to take into account how organizations act in markets to affect what is valued and how it is valued.

Some of the most interesting work on the relationship between organization and value in markets has been done by David Stark (2009). In a set of meticulously researched ethnographic studies, Stark focuses on the organization of work practices for the creation of worth in production processes. In one of his ethnographies, a study on a trading room in Manhattan's financial district, Stark analyzed the spatial distribution of the work places of traders and analysts in the trading room to show how work organization is designed to increase the chances of traders to discover trading opportunities. Traders following different trading strategies are positioned in the room in ways that allow them to interact easily. This creates a morphology prone to "creative disturbances," and an organizational form which Stark calls heterarchy.

Other studies on the relationship of organization and economic value stress the crucial role of practices as well. Value emerges from practical activities, including discourses within the firm or between the firm and its competitors or customers (Ansari and Munir 2008; Mützel 2009) . In this volume, Davide Ravasi, Violina Rindova, and Ileana Stigliani (Chapter 13) address the relationship of organizations and valuation in an empirical study on corporate museums. Firms whose products are especially valued for the symbolic meanings they carry for customers must themselves maintain a precise "feeling" for these symbolic connotations in order to be able to design and market products that fulfill the expectations of their customers. Corporate museums, Ravasi, Rindova, and Stigliani show, have the function not only to sustain the "myth" of the product as a form of symbolic value in the perception of (potential) customers who visit the museum but also to maintain this myth in the cognitive frame of the employees and thereby in their work practices.

Value through Friction

Much of the debate in economic sociology on processes of valuation deals with social devices as a basis for individual judgments of products *and* for the intersubjective congruence of quality judgments in the market. Such a perspective, however, finds its theoretical limit in the functioning of markets themselves. Though valuation is a socially structured process, a theoretical conceptualization of the valuation of goods must allow for the *diverse* assessment of qualities by different actors and the simultaneous existence of several possibly contradictory devices. If action is seen as simply conforming to market devices, this leads to an overly static assessment of valuation processes that does not do justice to the dynamic changes of the evaluation of goods and assets. Especially in capitalist economies, the rapid change of the evaluation of products—whether financial assets or consumer goods—is not only empirically observable but also a central element of their growth dynamics. How can one incorporate the dynamics of value in a theoretical model?

Several approaches dealing with questions of valuation have attempted to comprehend the dynamics of the value of economic goods. In the analysis of consumer markets, Georg Simmel was the first to recognize what was later referred to as the trickle-down effect (1971). Simmel observed that once clothing designs that are valued by the upper classes for their representation of social status have found their way to the lower social classes, these designs become devalued in the eyes of the upper classes because the clothes no longer signal social distinction. The distinction is reestablished through the change in fashions among the upper classes. This never-ending process feeds a constant cycle of valuation and devaluation in fashion markets.[15]

In Simmel's days branding was not central, which might explain why he gave so little attention to the role of producers in understanding the dynamics of value. This changed through studies such as Michel Callon's (Callon et al. 2002). The dynamic mechanism Callon describes is not the competition between customers struggling for social distinction but the struggle of firms for profits. In contrast to the trickle-down effect, the mechanism of competition locates the source of the dynamics of valuation on the supply side of markets even if customers are involved in the processes.

David Stark (2009) offers a still different perspective. Stark focuses on the deviation from established routines and scripts in valuation and the deviation from the use of established judgment devices that reduce uncertainty. He argues that value does not derive from following conventions. Quite the contrary: for Stark, value emerges from the *deviation* from routines and devices. Very close to the Schumpeterian notion of the entrepreneur as the type of actor in the economy who breaks with routines and establishes new combinations, Stark argues that worth emerges from "the ability to keep multiple evaluative principles in play and to exploit the resulting friction of their interplay" (2009: 15). Firms discover what is valuable through the interplay among different assessments of value that exist simultaneously in one organizational setting and produce "productive frictions." This theoretically important reflection has its background also in the notion of "orders of worth" (Boltanski and Thévenot 2006).

By emphasizing dissonance over interpretative agreement between actors, Stark stands in opposition to large parts of the sociological literature on valuation in the economy that emphasize the need to reduce this uncertainty through market devices. Stark's position might be exaggerated because he takes order in markets too much for granted, without explaining how order is established from organizational friction. New opportunities are always discovered from the background of established routines, scales, status orders, and judgment devices (Beckert 1999). The principal point is nevertheless highly relevant, especially in the context of dynamic capitalist economies (see also Moeran and Pedersen 2011). The relationship between intersubjective agreement on the one hand and differences between actors in the valuation of objects on the other is a vital theoretical issue in the field.

---

[15] See also Djelic and Ainamo, who show in an excellent article how the telephone industry has attempted to imitate the business model of the fashion industry (2005).

In financial markets and investments in capital goods, the interest of actors—as we have described above—is in *future value*. To realize future value, actors must take risks in largely unpredictable environments. Profit—that is, realized future value—does not result from following established routines but from creative recombinations whose potential has not yet been exploited by others. In this volume, it is Charles Smith (Chapter 12) who takes up the idea of deviating from established script as a condition for creating value. In his chapter on the decision-making of traders in financial markets, Smith argues that decisions on assessments of what is valuable emerge from practices of interpreting *conflicting* information. Smith introduces the notion of "acting sensibly" and contrasts this with a decision style he calls "making sense." When traders are managing their positions, meanings, according to Smith, are "emerging from practices rather than guiding these practices" (Smith in this volume).

While Smith remains less specific about the action-theoretic foundations of "acting sensibly," David Stark develops his understanding of the discovery of worth on explicit action-theoretic grounds (2009). Stark proceeds from John Dewey's notion (1998) of inquiry as a specific mode of action in situations where routines break down and actors are confronted with troubled and perplexed situations. Actors in these situations can only respond to them through social practices in which they discover an understanding of the problem, and possible solutions to it, through processes of trial and error. This finding from Stark alludes to a more general point that was covered in the discussion of Michel Callon's work: valuation takes place in action. The social practices characterizing the valuation of goods, however, have no resemblance to the model of rational action even if actors are purely self-interested.

This is in part because in non-routine purchasing decisions, one can take neither actors' identities nor what is traded as a given. Both are co-constructed in the market process itself, and these processes affect the selves of the actors involved as well as the meaning of the goods exchanged. Actors bring values along when they enter the market, but they will also change their values as a result of being in the market. This implies that at least at the outset, actors' meaning is not directed to specific goals, not least because the problems involved in the valuation of products are not even understood at the beginning. This lack of fixed values at the outset stresses the practical activities of actors, their interpretations, and their construction of meaning. Value and preferences can only be understood in relation to the very social processes in which they are already applied.

The fact that value emerges at least in part from interpretation also shows that innovative activities are not limited to process or product innovations but also emerge from cognitive reconfigurations of existing goods (Thompson 1979). In principle, this is an unlimited source of value. At the same time, it points to the fragility of value in the economy. What would happen to the car industry, for instance, if consumers began to see cars as nothing but profane means of transportation, disconnecting the product from the dream worlds symbolically represented in it?

Value and Prices

So far, the discussion has focused mostly on value and processes of valuation in markets. But what about price? Value and price differ, but markets establish economic value in the form of prices, both as a result of people coming together to trade *and* as an outcome of a specific institutional structure. Each market actor may have an idea of how a certain object or service should be valued in monetary terms because of its beauty, purity, might, or high or low moral standing. All of these values are forced into a single scale when they are ordered according to the money that one would be willing to pay. The amount a person is willing to pay for a good or is willing to sell it for is equal to its economic value from the perspective of the individual market participant.

Market price is not the same as economic value. The market price is the outcome of different assessments of the economic value of a product in the market process. The market price can differ from the economic value individual actors assign to the product in terms of what they would be willing to pay. Market prices, however, are at the same time the outcome of the social structure of the market, of the prevailing institutional rules, networks, and conventions (Bourdieu 2005; Fligstein 2001). Prices result from "the established rules of the game that producers tacitly obey" (Velthuis 2005: 10).

While prices are numerical values assigned to a good, it is important to distinguish between different forms of price. There is price setting (price quoting), set price, and market price. Price setting refers to the process by which offering prices are determined; the set price is the price at which the product is offered; and the market price is the monetary value for which the good changes hands. Set prices have a wider role than to tell purchasers the amount of money for which they can purchase the product. Set prices also act as signals that provide orientation in markets, enabling comparisons within a market and across markets (Schnabel and Storchmann 2010; Spence 2002). Prices are information in a communication process (Luhmann 1988: 18).

In a way, it is ironic to reintroduce the distinction between price and value, since the essential shift of marginal utility theory was to abandon the notion of value altogether and focus exclusively on price. A closer look makes it apparent, however, that to understand markets one must introduce a notion of value that stands apart from price. Prices do not inform customers as long as the customer does not have a standard from which to judge them. The price information itself does not tell the actors what to do in the situation (Luhmann 1988: 20). Calling a product "expensive" or "cheap" is only possible based on the assessment of the price in relation to the assessment of the worth of product qualities. [Without some notion of value, independent of price, there would be no way to judge prices.] This important relation between price and value alludes once more to the point that a theory of exchange, as offered by neoclassical theory, does not in itself suffice to explain the operation of markets and must be complemented by a theory of valuation (Vatin 2009: 16). A remnant of this problem can be detected in neoclassical economics in the notions of "consumer surplus" and "producer surplus."

Hence, the thorny question becomes how prices emerge and change. While supply and demand do influence prices, the question remains where this supply and demand stems from. The answer refers to the social contexts of valuation of goods and assets. Demand is patterned by the processes described above, in which actors constitute the worth of goods by assessing the goods' functional and symbolic qualities, applying judgment devices, and noting their position in the market structure. Supply and demand are the result of the social structuring of markets through institutions that regulate competition (Bourdieu 2005), power structures between buyers and sellers (Marx 1977), social networks (Ingram and Roberts 2000; Podolny 2005; Uzzi and Lancaster 2004), and cognitive frames (Velthuis 2005), which shape the demand for goods and the ways in which firms compete with each other (Fligstein 2001). Hence, "prices are not something that mysteriously emerges from 'the market.' They are part of the terms-of-trade and are socially constructed by the actors involved in the exchange" (White and Eccles 1987: 985).[16]

Prices also depend on the price mechanism used. In the auction market, price is the outcome of a process of bidding among buyers (Smith 1989). In most markets, prices are set by the seller and are not subject to market negotiations. Different forms of markets have different ways of generating prices. Interest in economic sociology has been especially devoted to various forms of auction markets (Garcia-Parpet 1986; Smith 1989; Velthuis 2005). Though there is variation between these auction markets, they are all forms of the market type that Léon Walras theorized based on his observation of the Paris stock exchange. How can we theoretically assess the selection of the price mechanism in a market? In this volume, Olav Velthuis (Chapter 8) deals with this question by addressing the issue of which forms of sale in the art market are considered legitimate. While economic theory would expect that auctions are used above all in the primary art market (Smith 1989), because of the high uncertainty associated with the novel products, and that the sale with fixed prices through galleries would prevail in the more established secondary

---

[16] The reference to the social patterning of supply and demand does not say anything about the efficiency of the prevailing arrangements. The social patterning of competition, for instance, can lead to the inhibition of the price mechanism. Mark Granovetter and Richard Swedberg have argued that social network ties can lead to the stickiness of prices because economic relations "are embedded in networks that restrain the pure economic forces" (Granovetter and Swedberg 1992: 9). If market actors operate within a network in which competitive pricing is negatively sanctioned, as is the case for exchange relations regulated by guilds, prices will not fluctuate even if this would have positive welfare effects.

market, the reality is exactly the opposite. Auctions in fact hardly ever occur in the primary market. Velthuis explains this empirical observation based on conventions of how to legitimately sell art. These conventions are an important structural component of the constitution of worth. Velthuis therefore provides an example of the cultural embeddedness of price mechanisms in the economy. The globalization of the art market that is evident from the entry of countries like China into the market, however, might also challenge such entrenched conventional practices.

Most transaction prices are not the outcome of auctions or of negotiation between suppliers and customers, but are set by the supplier, so that prices emerge from firms. This leads once again to the connection between the sociology of markets and organizational sociology. We find an example of price setting by firms in the producer markets discussed by Harrison White (White 1981); firms carve out a niche, a process in which price setting is crucial. To understand set prices in markets, it is important to understand the market positions and the identities of the firms, while also looking closely at what goes on inside the firm. How are prices calculated?

There is very little research in economic sociology on pricing practices. One of the few exceptions is the work by Mark Zbaracki, who investigated price setting strategies in a large industrial firm (2004). Zbaracki shows that set prices are the outcome of negotiations between different groups within the firm, each attributing different meanings to prices and pricing strategies. The uncertainty regarding optimal strategies makes pricing a process of negotiation, wherein the social order in the organization is "constructed in the ongoing interactions" (Zbaracki 2004: 3). The rationale of economic price theory plays a very important role in this process. But rather than determining prices, the theory holds influence because of its use by some actors as a reference point for legitimating their positions: "Price theory may serve as a rational myth" used by actors to make sense of a situation (Zbaracki 2004: 17).

Finally, we must include the interrelations between price and value in the understanding of price. Prices are not only influenced by the contingent valuations of products by customers but are also reconnected to the valuation process. This is the case when the value actors assign to products is dependent on the products' set price (Schnabel and Storchmann 2010). Customers may interpret the set prices as a quality signal from which they may form their value judgment. A special case of this phenomenon is when customers value a product more highly *because* of its high price, a phenomenon that is especially observable in the markets for luxury products. In the luxury case, price becomes itself a judgment device in the market. This also implies that it is wrong to conceptualize the process of bestowing value as unidirectional. Using the example of the art market, one causal link would be that we first have a painting, then a value assessment, and finally a price for the painting. Theoretically, assuming that the object has no inherent value, our reasoning could also start with a high price and an expert's assertion of the object's value, which would lead to "art" with high value. In other words, it is essential to see the interconnectedness of price, value, and the object in the market process. This does not deny that the costs associated with the production of goods influence their price. It shows, however, that the object in the market becomes what it is as a result of the value bestowed by market actors, of which price can be one source.

Valuation and Pricing on Markets: Lines of Research

Understanding the valuation and pricing of goods is one of the main tasks for economic sociology. The coordination of economic exchange through markets can only be understood if it is made apparent how market actors value goods and assets. Markets fail if the problem of valuation cannot be resolved. Over the last 30 years, a number of instructive studies have been published on these topics from different perspectives. Some of the most interesting work on the issue has been done by French sociologists and economists, but in many cases neither this work nor its authors have found the recognition they deserve outside of France.[17] The field would gain immensely if it were better at overcoming national and language barriers.

Studies on valuation and pricing have provided often fascinating ethnographies of the empirical cases investigated. The empirical scope has chiefly concentrated on three types of markets: first, financial markets (MacKenzie and Millo 2003; Stark 2009; Rona-Tas and Smith, both in this volume); second, markets for aesthetic goods, such as fashion (Aspers 2010), wine (Benjamin and Podolny 1999; Diaz-Bone 2005), art (Beckert and Rössel 2004; Velthuis 2005; Yogev 2010), and food (Dubuisson-Quellier 2003); third, markets in which ethical issues figure prominently, such as the markets for life insurance (Zelizer 1979), whale watching (Lawrence and Phillips 2004), and fair trade products (Zick-Varul 2009). These three types of markets hold a special attraction for sociologists because value seems detached from the materiality of the commodity and in very obvious ways socially constructed. In financial markets, value hinges on mathematical formulas (MacKenzie and Millo 2003; Rona-Tas and Hiss in this volume) and sometimes on speculative frenzies expressing the herding behavior of actors. In aesthetic markets, the assessment of value is the result of contingent judgments of aesthetic quality in the market field. In the case of products valued for their moral qualities, the social basis of their valuation is already part of the definition of the object studied. It is on the basis of these markets that certain mechanisms in the construction of value and price can be especially well depicted, allowing the researcher to identify

---

[17] For a recently published overview of the current state of economic sociology in France, see Steiner and Vatin (Steiner and Vatin 2009).

general mechanisms that can also be applied to markets for industrial goods and consumer goods more generally.

The types of markets investigated in sociological studies on valuation gain further empirical significance in contemporary economies. The financialization of the economy (Froud et al. 2009) has increased the importance of financial markets during the last 30 years. Increasing product differentiation in functionally saturated markets has also led to the growing importance of moral and aesthetic criteria in the marketing of products (Rössel 2007; Stehr 2007). Today we can also find elements of aesthetic or moral judgments as part of product valuation in many markets where the functionality of the product used to be paramount: telephones, refrigerators, electronic equipment—everything from television sets to mobile phones and Apple computers. This is an important historical transformation of the structure of the economy that will have crucial consequences for sources of future growth but is also associated with the emergence of new risks, which are social in character. Value that hinges largely on symbolic meaning structures is vulnerable because attachments of consumers and investors can shift rapidly.

The study of markets like the wine market, where the social construction of value is especially apparent, allows for the identification of general principles. The next step, however, would be to focus studies on core industrial markets, whose relevance for the economy is still paramount even if it is receding. Much of the economy consists of airplanes, power plants, pork bellies, screws, and workers.[18] A sociologically informed theory on valuation and pricing must aim at a general theory applicable to all market exchanges. Can the theoretical findings on value constitution, deduced from the study of wine, art, and finance, be applied to the study of other types of markets? Or do valuation processes differ systematically in different types of markets and, if so, how?

This broader empirical scope will also be necessary for advancing theory construction. The current state of research on valuation and pricing shows many interesting theoretical concepts. Among them are the notion of judgment devices, the distinction between standard markets and status markets, the concept of singularity, and the notion of heterarchy. Moreover, the existing research shows how different types of social structures such as networks, institutions, conventions, and cultural frames play a role in the valuation and pricing of products. Some research has also addressed the question of how these structures actually play out in the action process, hence focusing attention on social practices and laying the groundwork for a microfoundation of the sociological investigation of value. What is still missing is a general sociological theory of valuation and pricing of goods.

---

[18] For the investigation of valuation processes in the labor market, see the work by Eymard-Duvernay and Marchal (Eymard-Duvernay and Marchal 1997). Yakubovich, Granovetter, and McGuire (Yakubovich et al. 2005) studied pricing strategies within the American electricity industry in the early twentieth century.

The chapters of the volume provide empirical case studies as well as conceptual advances. The book begins by dealing with value in a broader sense: the first section is entitled "What is Valuable?," and the chapters by Fourcade, Karpik, Gourevitch, and Beckert discuss moral values, their formation, and the relations between economic and noneconomic values. The second section brings up the problem of valuation in aesthetic markets. The chapters by Garcia-Parpet, Mears, Velthuis, and Hutter all shed light on how value is created and established in markets for wine, fashion models, and art. The third section brings together texts that analyze financial markets. Rona-Tas and Hiss study the role of credit rating agencies, and Yenkey and Smith look at the formation of value in stock exchange markets. The final chapter by Ravasi, Rindova, and Stigliani connects the discussion of aesthetic value with organizational aspects of industrial production. The book ends with a comment from David Stark.

REFERENCES

Ahrne, G. and Brunsson, N. (2008). *Meta-Organizations*. Cheltenham: Edward Elgar.

Akerlof, G. A. (1970). The Market for "Lemons": Quality Uncertainty and the Market Mechanism. *Quarterly Journal of Economics* 84: 488–500.

—— and Kranton, R. E. (2010). *Identity Economics: How Our Identities Shape Our Work, Wages, and Well-Being*. Princeton, NJ: Princeton University Press.

Ansari, S. and Munir, K. (2008). How Valuable Is a Piece of the Spectrum? Determination of Value in External Resource Acquisition. *Industrial and Corporate Change* 17: 301–33.

Appudarai, A. (1986). *The Social Life of Things: Commodities in Cultural Perspective*. New York, NY: Cambridge University Press.

Aspers, P. (2001). A Market in Vogue: Fashion Photography in Sweden. *European Societies* 3: 1–22.

——(2009). Knowledge and Value in Markets. *Theory and Society* 38: 111–31.

——(2010). *Orderly Fashion: A Sociology of Markets*. Princeton, NJ: Princeton University Press.

——(2011). *Markets*. Cambridge: Polity Press.

—— and Beckert, J. (2008). Märkte. In A. Maurer (ed.), *Handbuch der Wirtschaftssoziologie*. Wiesbaden: VS Verlag.

Becker, H. (1982). *Art Worlds*. Berkeley, CA: University of California Press.

Beckert, J. (1996). What Is Sociological about Economic Sociology? Uncertainty and the Embeddedness of Economic Action. *Theory and Society* 25: 803–40.

——(1999). Agency, Entrepreneurs and Institutional Change: The Role of Strategic Choice and Institutionalized Practices in Organizations. *Organization Studies* 20: 777–99.

——(2009*a*). Koordination und Verteilung: Zwei Ansätze der Wirtschaftssoziologie. In S. Nyssen and G. Voruba (eds.), *Die Ökonomie der Gesellschaft*. Wiesbaden: VS Verlag.

——(2009*b*). The Social Order of Markets. *Theory and Society* 38: 245–69.

—— and Rössel, J. (2004). Kunst und Preise. Reputation als Mechanismus der Reduktion von Ungewissheit am Kunstmarkt. *Kölner Zeitschrift für Soziologie und Sozialpsychologie* 56: 32–50.
Benjamin, B. A. and Podolny, J. M. (1999). Status, Quality and Social Order in the California Wine Industry. *Administrative Science Quarterly* 44: 563–89.
Beunza, D. and Garud, R. (2005). *Securities Analysts as Frame-Makers*. Universitat Pompeu Fabra Economics and Business Working Paper No. 733. Barcelona: Universitat Pompeu Fabra.
—— and —— (2006). *Frame-Making: An Interpretive Approach to Valuation Under Knightian Uncertainty*. Working Paper. New York, NY: Columbia University.
Biggart, W. N. and Beamish, T. (2003). The Economic Sociology of Convention, Habit, Custom, Practice, and Routine in Market Order. *Annual Review of Sociology* 29: 443–64.
Binder, M. and Niederle, U. M. (2007). *Institutions as Determinants of Preference Change: A One Way Relation?* Paper on Economics and Evolution 0607. Jena: Evolutionary Economics Group, Max Planck Institute of Economics.
Boltanski, L. and Thévenot, L. (1991/2006). *On Justification, Economies of Worth*. Princeton, NJ: Princeton University Press.
Bourdieu, P. (1984). *Distinctions: A Social Critique of the Judgement of Taste*. Cambridge, MA: Harvard University Press.
——(1992/1996). *The Rules of Art: Genesis and Structure of the Literary Field*. Palo Alto, CA: Stanford University Press.
——(1983/2001). The Forms of Social Capital. In M. Granovetter and R. Swedberg (eds.), *The Sociology of Economic Life*. Boulder, CO: Westview Press, 96–111.
——(2005). Principles of an Economic Anthropology. In N. J. Smelser and R. Swedberg (eds.), *The Handbook of Economic Sociology*. Princeton, NJ: Princeton University Press, 75–89.
Brunsson, N. and Jacobsson, B. (2000). *A World of Standards*. Oxford: Oxford University Press.
Buchanan, J., Tollison, R., and Tullock, G. (1980). *Toward a Theory of the Rent Seeking Society*. College Station, TX: Texas A&M University Press.
Callon, M. (ed.) (1998). *The Laws of the Markets*. Oxford: Blackwell Publishers.
——(2002). Pour en finir avec les incertitudes? *Sociologie du travail* 44: 261–7.
—— Méadel, C., and Rabeharisoa, V. (2002). The Economy of Qualities. *Economy and Society* 31: 194–217.
—— Millo, Y., and Muniesa, F. (2007). *Market Devices*. Oxford: Blackwell.
Carruthers, B. C. and Ariovich, L. (2010). *Money and Credit: A Sociological Approach*. Cambridge: Polity Press.
Chamberlin, E. (1933/1948). *The Theory of Monopolistic Competition: A Re-orientation of the Theory of Value*. Cambridge, MA: Harvard University Press.
Deutschmann, C. (1999). *Die Verheißung des absoluten Reichtums: Zur religiösen Natur des Kapitalismus*. Frankfurt a.M.: Campus.
Dewey, J. (1938/1998). The Pattern of Inquiry. In *The Essential John Dewey*. Bloomington, IN: Indiana University Press, 169–79.
Diaz-Bone, R. (2005). Strukturen der Weinwelt und der Weinerfahrung. *Sociologia Internationalis* 43: 25–57.
Djelic, M.-L. and Ainamo, A. (2005). The Telecom Industry as Cultural Industry? The Transposition of Fashion Logics into the Field of Mobile Telephony. In C. Jones and

P. H. Thornton (eds.), *Transformation in Cultural Industries*. Amsterdam: Elsevier JAI, 45–80.

Dodd, N. (1994). *The Sociology of Money: Economics, Reason and Contemporary Society*. Cambridge, MA: Polity Press.

——(2005). Reinventing Monies in Europe. *Economy and Society* 34: 558–83.

Douglas, M. and Isherwood, B. (1979). *The World of Goods: Towards an Anthropology of Consumption*. London: Routledge.

Dubuisson-Quellier, S. (2003). Confiance et qualité des produits alimentaires: une approche par la sociologie des relations marchandes. *Sociologie du travail* 45: 95–111.

Durkheim, E. (1893/1984). *The Division of Labour in Society*. London: Macmillan.

——and Mauss, M. (1902/1963). *Primitive Classifications*. Chicago, IL: University of Chicago Press.

Elster, J. (1983). *Sour Grapes: Studies in the Subversion of Rationality*. Cambridge: Cambridge University Press.

Espeland, W. N. and Stevens, M. (1998). Commensuration as a Social Process. *Annual Review of Sociology* 24: 312–43.

Eymard-Duvernay, F. (1989). Conventions de qualité et formes de coordination: l'économie des conventions. *Revue Economique* 40: 329–59.

——(2002). Les qualifications des biens. *Sociologie du travail* 44: 267–72.

——and Marchal, E. (1997). *Façons de recruter: le jugement des compétences sur le marché du travail*. Paris: Editions Métailié.

Favereau, O. and Lazega, E. (2002). *Conventions and Structures in Economic Organization*. Cheltenham: Edward Elgar.

Fiss, P. and Kennedy, M. (2009). *Of Porkbellies and Professions: Market Framing and the Creation of Online Advertising Exchanges*. Presented at the Second International Conference on Institutions, Innovation and Space, Alberta School of Business, June.

Fligstein, N. (2001). *The Architecture of Markets: An Economic Sociology of Twenty-First-Century Capitalist Societies*. Princeton, NJ: Princeton University Press.

François, P. (2008). *Sociologie des marchés*. Paris: Armand Colin.

Froud, J., Leaver, A., Johal, S., Nilsson, A., and Williams, K. (2009). Narratives and the Financialised Firm. In J. Beckert and C. Deutschmann (eds.), *Wirtschaftssoziologie. Sonderheft 49 der Kölner Zeitschrift für Soziologie und Sozialpsychologie*. Wiesbaden: VS Verlag.

Garcia-Parpet, M.-F. (1986). La construction sociale d'un marché parfait: le marché au cadran de Fontaines-en-Sologne. *Actes de la recherche en sciences sociales* 65: 2–13.

Gibbs, M., Tapia, M., and Warzynski, F. (2009). Globalization, Superstars, and Reputation: Theory & Evidence from the Wine Industry. *Journal of Wine Economics* 4: 46–61.

Graeber, D. (2001). *Toward an Anthropological Theory of Value*. New York, NY: Palgrave.

Granovetter, M. (1974/1995). *Getting a Job: A Study of Contacts and Careers*, 2nd ed. Cambridge, MA: Harvard University Press.

——and Swedberg, R. (eds.). (1992). *The Sociology of Economic Life*. Boulder, CO: Westview Press.

Hay, C. (2007). Globalisation and the Institutional Re-Embedding of Markets: The Political Economy of Price Formation in the Bordeaux en Primeur Market. *New Political Economy* 12: 185–210.

——(2010). The Political Economy of Price and Status Formation in the Bordeaux en Primeur Market: The Role of Wine Critics as Rating Agencies. *Socio-Economic Review* 8(4): 685–707.

Healy, K. (2006). *Last Best Gifts: Altruism and the Market for Human Blood and Organs*. Chicago, IL: University of Chicago Press.

Ingham, G. (2004). *The Nature of Money*. Malden, MA: Polity Press.

Ingram, P. and Roberts, P. (2000). Friendship among Competitors in the Sydney Hotel Industry. *American Journal of Sociology* 106: 342–87.

Jagd, S. (2007). Economics of Convention and New Economic Sociology: Mutual Inspiration and Dialogue. *Current Sociology* 55: 76–91.

Karpik, L. (2000). Le Guide rouge Michelin. *Sociologie du travail* 41: 369–90.

——(2010). *Valuing the Unique: The Economics of Singularities*. Princeton, NJ: Princeton University Press.

Koçak, Ö. (2003). *Social Orders of Exchange: Effects and Origins of Social Order in Exchange Markets*. PhD thesis. Palo Alto, CA: Stanford University.

Lawrence, T. B. and Phillips, N. (2004). From Moby Dick to Free Willy: Macro-Cultural Discourse and Institutional Entrepreneurship in Emerging Institutional Fields. *Organization* 11: 689–711.

Leibenstein, H. (1950). Bandwagon, Snob, and Veblen Effects in the Theory of Consumers' Demand. *Quarterly Journal of Economics* 64: 183–207.

Lichtenstein, S. and Slovic, P. (eds.). (2006). *The Construction of Preference*. Cambridge: Cambridge University Press.

Lounsbury, M. and Rao, H. (2004). Sources of Durability and Change in Market Classifications: A Study of the Reconstitution of Product Categories in the American Mutual Fund Industry, 1944–1985. *Social Forces* 82: 969–99.

Luhmann, N. (1988). *Die Wirtschaft der Gesellschaft*. Frankfurt a.M.: Suhrkamp.

MacKenzie, D. (2010). *The Credit Crisis as a Problem in the Sociology of Knowledge*. Working Paper. Edinburgh: University of Edinburgh.

——and Millo, Y. (2003). Constructing a Market, Performing Theory: The Historical Sociology of a Financial Derivatives Exchange. *American Journal of Sociology* 109: 107–45.

Maletz, O. and Tysiatchniouk, M. (2009). The Effect of Expertise on the Quality of Forest Standards Implementation: The Case of FSC Forest Certification in Russia. *Forest Policy and Economics* 11: 422–8.

Malinowski, B. (1922). *Argonauts of the Western Pacific: An Account of Native Enterprise and Adventure in the Archipelagoes of Melanesian New Guinea*. London: Routledge.

Marchal, E. and Rieucau, G. (2010). *Le recrutement*. Paris: La Découverte.

Marshall, A. (1920). *Industry and Trade: A Study of Industrial Technique and Business Organization; and of Their Influences on the Conditions of Various Classes and Nations*. London: Macmillan.

——(1920/1961). *Principles of Economics* (9th variorum ed., 2 vols). Edited and annotated by C. W. Guillebaud. London: Macmillan and Co.

Marx, K. (1867/1977). *Das Kapital: Kritik der politischen Ökonomie*, Vol. 1, 12th ed. Berlin Dietz.

McCracken, G. (1988). *Culture and Consumption: New Approaches to the Symbolic Character of Consumer Goods and Activities*. Bloomington, IN: Indiana University Press.

Micheletti, M. (2003). *Political Virtue and Shopping: Individuals, Consumerism, and Collective Action.* New York, NY: Palgrave-Macmillan.

Moeran, B. and Pedersen, J. (eds.) (2011). *Negotiating Values in the Creative Industries: Fairs, Festivals and Competitive Events.* Oxford: Oxford University Press.

Musselin, C. and Paradeise, C. (2002). Le concept de qualité: où en sommes-nous? *Sociologie du travail* 44: 256–60.

Mützel, S. (2009). Koordinierung von Märkten durch narrativen Wettbewerb. In J. Beckert and C. Deutschmann (eds.), *Wirtschaftssoziologie. Sonderheft 49 der Kölner Zeitschrift für Soziologie und Sozialpsychologie.* Wiesbaden: VS Verlag.

O'Neill, J. (2009). Market. In J. Peil and van Staveren, I. (eds.), *Handbook of Economics and Ethics.* Cheltenham: Edward Elgar, 317–24.

Orléan, A. (1999). *Le pouvoir de la finance.* Paris: Odile Jacob.

——(ed.) (1994/2004). *Analyse économique des conventions.* Paris: PUF.

Podolny, J. M. (1993). A Status-based Model of Market Competition. *American Journal of Sociology* 98: 829–72.

——(2005). *Status Signals: A Sociological Study of Market Competition.* Princeton, NJ: Princeton University Press.

——(1994). Market Uncertainty and the Social Character of Economic Exchange. *Administrative Science Quarterly* 39: 458–83.

Powell, W. W. (1990). Neither Market Nor Hierarchy: Network Forms of Organization. *Research in Organizational Behavior* 12: 295–336.

Power, D. and Hauge, A. (2008). No Man's Brand—Brands, Institutions, Fashion and the Economy. *Growth and Change* 39: 123–43.

Richins, M. L. (1994). Valuing Things: The Public and Private Meanings of Possessions. *Journal of Consumer Research* 21: 504–21.

Robbins, L. (1935). *An Essay on the Nature and Significance of Economic Science.* London: Macmillan.

Rössel, J. (2007). Ästhetisierung, Unsicherheit und die Entwicklung von Märkten. In J. Beckert, R. Diaz-Bone, and H. Ganssmann (eds.), *Märkte als soziale Strukturen.* Frankfurt a.M.: Campus, 167–81.

Salais, R. (1989). L'analyse économique des conventions du travail. *Revue Economique* 2: 199–240.

——and Thévenot, L. (eds.) (1986). *Le travail: marchés, règles, conventions.* Paris: INSEE–Economica.

Scheper-Hughes, N. (2004). Parts Unknown: Undercover Ethnography of the Organs-Trafficking Underworld. *Ethnography* 5: 29–73.

Schnabel, H. and Storchmann, K. (2010). Prices as Quality Signals: Evidence from the Wine Market. *Journal of Agricultural and Food Industrial Organization* 8: 1–21.

Schneiberg, M. and Berk, G. (2010). From Categorical Imperative to Learning by Categories: Cost Accounting and New Categorical Practices in American Manufacturing, 1900–1930. *Research in the Sociology of Organization*: 31, 255–99.

Simmel, G. (1904/1971). Fashion. In D. Levine (ed.), *Georg Simmel on Individuality and Social Form.* Chicago, IL: Chicago University Press, 294–323.

——(1907/1978). *The Philosophy of Money.* London: Routledge.

Smith, C. (1989). *Auctions: The Social Construction of Value.* Berkeley, CA: University of California.

Spates, J. (1983). The Sociology of Values. *Annual Review of Sociology* 9: 27–49.

Spence, M. (2002). Signaling in Retrospect and the Informational Structure of Markets. *The American Economic Review* 92: 434–59.

Stark, D. (2009). *The Sense of Dissonance: Accounts of Worth in Economic Life*. Princeton, NJ: Princeton University Press.

Stehr, N. (2007). *Moral Markets: How Knowledge and Affluence Change Consumers and Products*. Boulder, CO: Paradigm Publishers.

Steiner, P. (2010). *La transplantation d'organes: un commerce nouveau entre les êtres humains*. Paris: Gallimard.

——and Vatin, F. (2009). *Traité de sociologie économique*. Paris: Presses Universitaires de France.

Stigler, G. and Becker, G. S. (1977). De Gustibus Non Est Disputandum. *American Economic Review* 67: 76–90.

Thompson, M. (1979). *Rubbish Theory: The Creation and Destruction of Value*. Oxford: Oxford University Press.

Trompette, P. (2007). Customer Channeling Arrangements in Market Organization: Competition Dynamics in the Funeral Business in France. *Revue française de sociologie* 48: 3–33.

Uzzi, B. and Lancaster, R. (2004). Embeddedness and Price Formation in the Corporate Law Market. *American Sociological Review* 69: 319–44.

Vatin, F. (2009). *Évaluer et valoriser: une sociologie économique de la mesure*. Toulouse: Presses universitaires Mirail-Toulouse.

Veblen, T. (1899/1953). *The Theory of the Leisure Class: An Economic Study of Institutions*. New York, NY: New American Library.

Velthuis, O. (2005). *Talking Prices: Symbolic Meanings of Prices on the Market for Contemporary Art*. Princeton, NJ: Princeton University Press.

von Weizsäcker, C. C. (2005). *The Welfare Economics of Adaptive Preferences*. Preprint of the Max Planck Institute for Research on Collective Goods 2005/11. Bonn: Max Planck Institute for Research on Collective Goods.

Walzer, M. (1983). *Spheres of Justice: A Defense of Pluralism and Equality*. New York, NY: Basic Books.

Warde, A. (1994). Consumption, Identity-Formation and Uncertainty. *Sociology* 25: 878–98.

Weber, M. (1922). *Wirtschaft und Gesellschaft: Grundriss der Sozialökonomik, III. Abteilung*. Tübingen: Verlag von J. C. B. Mohr.

——(1946). *From Max Weber: Essays in Sociology*. Ed. by H. Gerth and C. Wright Mills. London: Routledge.

——(1904–1905/1968). *The Protestant Ethic and the Spirit of Capitalism*. London: Unwin University Books.

——(1921–1922/1978). *Economy and Society: An Outline of Interpretive Sociology*. Berkeley, CA: University of California Press.

Welskopp, T. (2010). *Amerikas große Ernüchterung: Eine Kulturgeschichte der Prohibition*. Paderborn: Ferdinand Schöningh.

White, H. (1981). Where Do Markets Come From? *American Journal of Sociology* 87: 517–47.

——(2008). *Identity and Control: How Social Formations Emerge*. Princeton, NJ: Princeton University Press.

——and Eccles, R. (1987). Producers' Market. In J. Eatwell, et al. (eds.), *The New Palgrave: A Dictionary of Economic Theory and Doctrine*. London: Macmillan, 984–6.

Witt, U. (2001). Learning to Consume: A Theory of Wants and the Growth of Demand. *Journal of Evolutionary Economics* 11: 23–36.

Yakubovich, V., Granovetter, M., and McGuire, P. (2005). Electric Charges: The Social Construction of Rate Systems. *Theory and Society* 34: 579–612.

Yogev, T. (2010). The Social Construction of Quality: Status Dynamics in the Market for Contemporary Art. *Socio-Economic Review* 8: 511–36.

Zbaracki, M. J. (2004). *Pricing Structure and Structuring Price*. Philadelphia, PA: University of Pennsylvania.

Zelizer, V. (1979). *Morals and Markets: The Development of Life Insurance in the United States*. New York, NY: Columbia University Press.

——(2004). Circuits of Commerce. In J. C. Alexander, G. T. Marx, and C. L. Williams (eds.), *Self, Social Structure, and Beliefs: Explorations in Sociology*. Berkeley, CA: University of California Press, 122–44. http://www.appropriate-economics.org/materials/circuits_of_commerce_-_zelizer.pdf (accessed September 15, 2010).

Zick-Varul, M. (2009). Ethical Consumption: The Case of Fair Trade. In J. Beckert and C. Deutschmann (eds.), *Wirtschaftssoziologie. Sonderheft 49 der Kölner Zeitschrift für Soziologie und Sozialpsychologie*. Wiesbaden: Vs Verlag, 366–85.

Zuckerman, E. W. (1999). The Categorical Imperative: Securities Analysts and the Illegitimacy Discount. *American Journal of Sociology* 104: 1398–438.

Part I
What Is Valuable?

2 Price and Prejudice: On Economics and the Enchantment (and Disenchantment) of Nature

*Marion Fourcade**

Price and Prejudice: On Economic Valuation and Social Values

What are the social implications of using money as a medium of exchange? Classical political economists did not have much to say about it: they assumed that money is a commodity like any other, and that monetary exchange is not fundamentally different from barter—just more convenient. Others had a different opinion. Karl Marx, for instance, thought that his contemporaries' benign view was misguided: money, he argued, is a *social* relation. Far from being "just a veil,"[1] *monetary* exchange does things to things and, by extension, to people's relations with one another. For instance, we tend to think of the monetary value of commodities as the objectified expression of some intrinsic worth. But this is a delusion: the two do not coincide. The "real" value of a shoe, for instance, is not its price but the amount of labor "congealed" in it, *under a specific state of social relations*. In other words, it is because we have made things commensurable through abstract labor that they can be exchanged through money—it is not money as such that makes things commensurable. By using money to conduct our economic exchange, we are obscuring the social relations that made the process of abstraction possible. The commodity form that prevails in capitalism thus operates a vast deception

---

* Earlier versions of this chapter were presented at the Annual Meeting of the Society for the Advancement of Socio-Economics, Washington, July 8–11, 2004; the miniconference of the Theory Section, American Sociological Association Annual Meeting, San Francisco, August 14–17, 2004; and the Center for the Study of Law and Society, UC Berkeley, April 25, 2005. I acknowledge helpful comments on earlier versions or presentations of this work by Jens Beckert, Irene Bloemraad, Vicki Bonnell, Michael Burawoy, Bruce Carruthers, Craig Calhoun, Thomas Gieryn, Michael Hanemann, Michèle Lamont, Dawne Moon, Stanley Presser, Dylan Riley, Charles Smith, Sandra Smith, David Stark, and Viviana Zelizer.

[1] Note, however, that the concept of money as "a veil" was popularized by the neoclassical rather than the classical political economists. See Patinkin and Steiger (1989).

by turning the intersubjective and social relation between persons in the production process into an abstract relation between objects (or between people and objects), mediated by money. Money, then, serves to conceal "real" essences by allowing for the conflation of economic value (which is eminently social) with market price.

Money also bears a special status as a commodity. People want money for itself, they honor it and respect it. Most importantly, money conveys power—it allows people to change their standing as human beings, and to bind others to themselves. "I am ugly but I can buy for myself the most *beautiful* of women. Therefore I am not *ugly*, for the effect of *ugliness*—its deterrent power—is nullified by money" (Marx 1988: 138). With money one may debase beautiful or morally desirable things and sublimate ignoble ones. Money is the ultimate agent of social domination because it has the power to *overturn* any other form of worth.

Marx thus believed in an absolute, albeit socially contingent, order of value "behind the world of prices" (Heilbroner 1983: 267). Politically, of course, Marx's articulation was highly subversive—not to mention the fact that he also claimed to offer the only truly *scientific* approach to political economy. But there was already another contender in the debate over value, a contender that both sought to challenge Marx on the scientific merits of his approach and was more successful in mustering political support. In 1871, Manchester University professor Stanley Jevons proposed that the relative degree of satisfaction (or "utility")—not labor—should be considered the ultimate foundation of value. Jevons's views grew straight out of the dominant British philosophy of utilitarianism, and opened up a new—and soon to become influential—analytical model for political economy.[2]

The new economics that developed and flourished out of this so-called "marginalist" theory had implications for the relationship between value and price. One of the basic teachings of neoclassical microeconomics is that the utility a consumer derives from a good—let us say apples—is a decreasing function, with the quantity of apples consumed on one side and the market price of apples on the other. But there always comes a point where the additional satisfaction derived from spending more money on apples is actually not worth the price! In economic jargon, this means that in equilibrium *the subjective value, to the consumer, of the last unit of good* (its marginal utility divided by the marginal utility of money itself) *will equal the good's market price*. Mirowski (1990) notices that value and price are in fact often used as synonymous terms in the economics literature—as, for instance, in Debreu's classic *Theory of Value* (1959), where the only definition of value ever formulated is as "price times quantity."

What we may call the "subjective" concept of value has also been developed in a more sociological direction. On this analytical terrain, the concept is less

---

[2] Jevons' utilitarian views appealed to the most influential (and categorically non-Marxist) group on the British left at the end of the nineteenth century: the Fabians (Shaw 2006).

individualistic than its neoclassical counterpart (as Simmel [1978] points out, subjective value perceptions are always "socially constructed") and more critical of the narrow equation between subjective value and price. Sociologists have generally suggested that aesthetic, moral, and symbolic aspects are always paramount to understanding the formation of economic values, as are the particular microinteractional contexts in which value is supposedly determined (Smith 1989). Such aspects may affect both the very *possibility* and the particular *shape* of economic valuation: hence social taboos against the commercialization of love (Zelizer 2005) or human organs (Healy 2004) have generally prevented these "objects" from being *legally* incorporated into the monetary sphere, even though money continues to earmark intimate relationships in all sorts of ways and markets of "bodies for sale" continue to flourish unofficially.

Economic valuation processes are thus idiosyncratic and contingent on the particular historical settings and social relations they serve (Zelizer 1979, 1985). In their ambitious synthesis, Boltanski and Thévenot (2006) argue that there are different "economies of worth," with different philosophical bases, institutional supports, and social structures; consequently, the relationship between market price and other forms of worth is a moving target. This is especially true since sociologists acknowledge powerful feedback effects between subjective value and price: pricing changes people's motives so that the value they attach to an object may actually be *endogenously* connected to the monetary sacrifice they consented to when they bought it (Simmel 1978). This kind of logic is highly relevant to explain some of the pricing patterns observed on the arts market, for instance, where the product—art—is emotionally bound up with the people who produce and acquire it (Velthuis 2005) and is linked to their personal finances (Coslor 2009).

From Economic Markets to Economic Values

To sum up, the sociological critique of price economics, as well as some critical analyses within economics, have so far centered on three questions: the general disconnection between market prices and other forms of worth, whether objective (Marx) or subjective (Boltanski and Thévenot 2006); the sociological and economic factors that prevent the market mechanism from functioning as predicted in the standard model—so that prices remain sticky, are set monopolistically instead of competitively, or through mechanisms that have little to do with market equilibrium; and the further social and symbolic significance of prices once they have been set. In all these analyses, prices are always taken to be real entities, however deceptive they can be about worth. They exist out there, for us to study. Hence while we as sociologists do not buy the economists' account of the mechanisms that drive prices, we still buy into their general naturalization of the price system as something that just "is."

But what if we were to treat prices as artifacts? Not simply as artifacts of the market mechanism, but as technological artifacts, brought about by men and women working together to make prices a real thing? What if we shifted our analytical focus from the *meaning* (social, symbolic, cultural) of prices to the *technologies* that sustain the price system? And what if we analyzed these technologies for what they stand for—what is the price system supposed to achieve, for example? What makes it legitimate or acceptable? (Muniesa 2000).

Treating prices not as things but as technologies brings us back to a point perhaps first raised by Karl Polanyi (1944) in his critique of nineteenth-century market society but powerfully extended by Callon (1998, 2008) in his analysis of the "embeddedness of economic markets in economics." The real power of economics, Callon argues, is ontological: it is the power to "economicize" the material world through the imposition of a legitimate language and the proliferation of "calculative agencies." Economics produces (performs) a world (an economy) in which calculability is a key cultural competence, thereby reinforcing the applicability and performative power of economics itself. Furthermore, this back-and-forth movement between economy and economics is itself constitutive of the stable economic objects that we call "markets" or "prices."

MacKenzie and Millo (2003) have provided what may be one of the best empirical illustrations of this transformative power of economics. In their analysis of the development of the Chicago Board Option Exchange's derivatives market, they show that the celebrated success of the Black–Scholes formula of option pricing came not from its accurate *description* of the existing behavior of option prices but rather from the fact that financial market actors started *using* it to set option prices, thereby instigating a self-fulfilling prophecy by which the formula came, after some fluctuations, to reflect prices accurately. In the process, they argue, both modern finance *and* modern financial economics were born, mutually constituting each other.

Auction theory exhibits similar performative features. If the actors involved in highly complex auctions possess the material means to do so, they will *try actively* to learn how to play the auction game as defined by its designers, including by means of hiring economic consultants. Hence while these (usually corporate) actors may not have behaved according to the economic model prior to their entry into the auction market, their economic advisers will make sure to guide them toward the self-interested and calculative forms of agency posited by the model—ultimately making the theory "true." The spectacular economic "success" of the radio spectrum auctions in the United States and the United Kingdom (Guala 2001), as well as that of the "search phrase" auctions (Smith 2007), cannot be understood outside of this profound mechanism of economics feeding back into economic processes.

Smith (2007) adds an important point: the product often only gets *defined* through the very process and techniques of pricing—thereby turning markets into what he calls "definitional mechanisms." Thus, in the case of both the Black-Scholes formula and the spectrum or search phrase auctions, economic technologies served to create markets de novo. Certainly, the idea of options existed long ago, but no market could exist for them because no one knew how to price them. Similarly, no one knew how to establish property rights on something as immaterial as the radio spectrum. In other words, the products and their market came into being and were defined all at once.

Many pricing technologies, then, are tools (complex, highly sophisticated economic tools) that bring markets into existence. That is, they are technologies whose purpose is to construct a space of "tradability." Still, there are many goods that remain outside the space of market exchange. For instance, people and institutions care (or are made to care) about driving safe cars, breathing clean air, and eating foods that won't cause them to develop some long-term disease; they care about the country's safety, or about protecting the planet from climate change.

Economists reason that if people mobilize, express their concern, form associations, promote legal and administrative rules, and lobby governments, then the things that people use these means to defend *must have value*. Researchers further argue that if people are willing to spend their time, their tax dollars, or their charity contributions defending such goals, then the *economic* value of their preferences may be identified and indeed calculated quite easily. In other words, even though some goods are not traded and may not even be tradable, the *trade-offs* that people make to pursue them are a good enough indication of the monetary value they implicitly attach to them (Lohmann 2009). For instance, if people are willing to drive an extra 40 miles to reach an unpolluted beach, as opposed to one that is much closer but less clean, then the value of their enjoyment of the more remote beach corresponds at least to the extra time, plus the amortizing costs of the gas and car. Finally, since for economists preferences are presumed to be individual and not social (or interdependent), these preferences may be *aggregated*. The value of the remote beach, for instance, may be calculated by adding up the travel costs of all the people who make the effort to go there.

Economic valuation technologies are fundamentally mechanisms by which the things people care about (or *should* care about; more on this below) are turned into things with economic value. To be sure, we are not in the highly visible value realm of market-clearing mechanisms, where people's desires to buy and sell are exposed publicly (consider the strawberry auctions described by Marie-France Garcia [2008], for instance); but the more ambiguous realm of non-market goods is being routinely framed for calculative purposes too, through economic technique. What obscures the similarity between processes pertaining to market (e.g., strawberries) and non-market (e.g., wildlife) goods is that the role of politics is more obvious in the latter, which also involves a broader range of organizational settings and actors, sometimes with conflicting claims and purposes. Thus, non-market accounting has been crafted not only by administrative agencies interested in developing health, safety, or environmental standards but also by the corporate actors these standards seek to monitor and discipline; by executive departments weighing the pros and cons of different national security strategies; by civic organizations working to promote certain values and rights—such as biodiversity or gender equity; or by courts seeking to compensate individuals and communities for physical, psychological, or social "injuries." The production of monetary equivalents for things such as human life, health, scenery, or bald eagles is a techno-political affair.

The purpose of this chapter is to offer a reflection upon the kinds of valuation technologies that are being deployed in cases where markets do not exist *and* are not even sought (in contrast, for instance, to the spectrum auction cases, where a clear policy goal was to bring a market into existence). I suggest that even in such cases, the ultimate outcome is to increase the legitimacy and authority of the market logic. The reason is that since at least World War II, economists have been no less central to the valuation of non-market goods than they are to framing the processes that generate market prices. Economics operates by and large *as if* non-market goods were priceable (since they have subjective value, and price and value are deeply intertwined), that is, *as if* they were being traded on markets. The world of what David Stark (2009: 7) calls "Parsons' pact" (economists study value, sociologists study values) is long gone: from the point of view of economics, every object—tangible or not—every form of worth can presumably be subjected to an economic valuation process. (Social) values may be collapsed into (economic) value. The irony is that this narrowing down on the side of economics is at the same time surprisingly liberating on the side of sociology: it means that sociologists are now free to recover the values—and more precisely what Stark, again, calls the "accounts of worth"—that stand behind every "economic value" problem and are, indeed, "constitutive" of it (2009: 11). It further suggests that sociology's critique of economics must shift away from a focus on economic markets, in which the value problem remains confined to things that are effectively traded, to *a focus on economic valuation processes, where the value problem is much more general and encompasses everything that people care about* (or are believed and made to care about) (Figure 2.1).

What Marx and other critics (Ackerman and Heizerling 2004; Radin 2001) call "commodification" is thus not an abstract process. It is, instead, a very *concrete* one which (1) relies on technologies designed to make things comparable so that they *may* be thought of as exchangeable (Espeland and Levine 2002) and (2) uses money as the privileged medium of exchange. Note that the operation of many of our administrative, corporate, and legal institutions is dependent on such techniques of monetary commensuration. Think, for instance, about the expansion and rationalization of financial auditing to all sorts of organizations—from state agencies to corporate subunits, from museums to hospices, from international aid programs to charities (Power 1999). Think, also, about the no less remarkable expansion of "money judgments" in the court system—the increasingly complex use of money as an

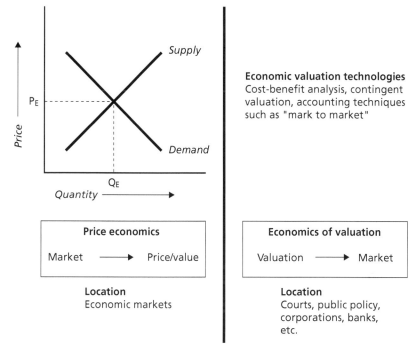

Figure 2.1 The two roles of economics

instrument to deter illegal behavior, compensate injury or breach of contract, and punish violators.

The Legal Production of Economic Values

The law ought to be especially interesting to us here as an important (yet often overlooked) locus of economic valuation. Much legal activity, through the central function of injury compensation, revolves around the question of the value of things that are typically hard to square with money: trust, health, the life of a loved one, or feelings of personal worth (as in discrimination cases). How do courts go about producing monetary equivalents in such cases?

At first glance, the process looks highly erratic. Levels of monetary compensation vary widely across socio-legal structures (civil vs. common law), across legal situations (jury vs. judge trials), and across comparable cases (for example the enormous variability of the value of a "statistical life" [Sunstein 2004]). Still, courts in the Western world have witnessed over time a considerable expansion and technical rationalization of monetized legal remedies. The United States especially stands out in this long-term historical movement, because of the comparatively extensive reach of money as a compensatory instrument in

American courts, and because of the comparatively heavy American reliance on all kinds of economic valuation experts—economists, accountants, statisticians, and others—to help calculate damage awards.

The legal system has long been recognized as a site of economic production in its own right, of course (Beckert 2008; Swedberg 2003; Weber 1978). A substantial literature in economic sociology analyzes the role of legal environments in shaping markets and organizational fields (Edelman and Suchman 1997). Furthermore, since the development of the law and economics movement in the United States, the constitutive power of the law on the economy has attained an extraordinary level of self-consciousness. Indeed, the credo of the law and economics school is that the law can be used to manipulate incentives in non-market as well as in market areas and can thereby be transformed into an instrument for the pursuit of economic efficiency (Mercuro and Medema 1997; Posner 1987). This position starts with the recognition that the law is more than a "context" that frames economic activity: it is fundamentally one of the locations where a whole set of economic outcomes is being produced, with powerful social consequences.

It is difficult to pinpoint when economics and the law became closely interconnected in the United States. As Fligstein (1990), Dobbin (1994), and others have shown, US courts took an interest in economic questions and got involved with the regulation of the market early on—if anything, economists followed the courts' movement toward antitrust rather than preceded or provoked it (Mayhew 1998). During the 1920s and 1930s, the legal community, notably under the impulse of realist scholarship, welcomed the incorporation of economic knowledge into the legal system as a way to promote certain chosen ends. Interwar economists, particularly the institutionalists, were greatly attentive to the economic impact of legal rules, wrote extensively on regulation, and, at least in a number of individual cases (J. R. Commons, for instance), were intensely involved with the courts, government commissions, and the drafting of legislation (Mercuro and Medema 1997).

Beginning in the 1930s, University of Chicago-based economists spearheaded an explicitly normative and pro-market turn of this literature.[3] After Ronald Coase (1960) offered a powerful argument for using markets to solve disputes over rights in his article on the "problem of social cost" (published in the first issue of the Chicago-originated *Journal of Law and Economics*), economists started to extend the price-theoretic framework to all sorts of legal issues; a number of legal scholars saw an opportunity too, and jumped on the bandwagon of the "economic analysis of the law" with the fervor of the newly converted (Medema 1998; Posner 1987).

Of course, the niche for economic expertise within the US legal system is not purely "supply-driven," to use an economic metaphor. The common legal culture of fact-finding and expert witnessing favors the incorporation of

---

[3] The roots of Chicago law and economics can be traced back to the 1930s (and specifically to Henry Simons's appointment to the School of Law in 1931).

rationalized forms of knowledge (Golan 2004; Jasanoff 1995); the competitive way in which professions are organized in the United States (Abbott 1988) paradoxically allows for a more natural turf overlap between professions; and the constantly evolving and ambiguous nature of the legal and regulatory environment prompts social actors (such as corporations, citizen groups, or government offices) to search for professionals who can help them formulate quantifiable standards to evaluate the impact of regulations, the realm of possible actions, and eventually to prosecute or defend their behavior in court (Dobbin and Sutton 1998; Jepperson and Meyer 1991).

For all these reasons, the American legal system has historically been uniquely open to economists and therefore constitutes a key arena where economic knowledge (meaning economic theories and methodologies) is being applied, developed, tested, contested, validated, and/or dismissed (by contrast, in other legal systems the law is more autonomous, and legal decisions do not need as much support—at least rhetorical support—from outside experts). Such assimilation of economics into the legal system is not, however, without important sociological consequences. In particular, it profoundly affects the way in which the law conducts its function of valuation.

Among other things, the discipline of economics supplies the legal system with sophisticated technologies for eliciting value where value is hard to establish or even to identify. Not only because economics is uniquely placed to do so—indeed Coase recognized long ago that what gives economists a great advantage over other disciplines is that they are able to use "the measuring rod of money" (1994:44)—but also because neoclassical economics connects money to the intangible and the immaterial through subjective value or "utility." The point, however, is that in doing so, economics is not merely "functional," providing the law with the kinds of techniques it needs to measure some immaterial prejudices that would have been identified prior to the valuation exercise. What I am suggesting instead is that *economics performs a "definitional" role: it participates in the very conceptualization of the things to be compensated and subjectively valued*. In other words, economics is also performative of legal categories themselves, and beyond them of the categories we ordinary citizens can legitimately rely upon to assess the worth of things around us.

This is true, I argue, because of the deep intertwining between monetary worth and other forms of worth that is at the core of economics. On the one hand, economists rely explicitly on (their perception of) many different types of worth when they design valuation methodologies—for all practical purposes, their goal is often to translate beauty, enjoyment, peace, or commitment into hard numbers. On the other hand, valuation methodologies give non-monetary forms of worth a particular focus and orientation. By institutionalizing (or "performing," see Callon 1998) acceptable and effective conceptualizations *within* the calculative tools themselves, economic valuation practices play an important "definitional" role (Smith 2007).

In the following pages, I rely on a well-known environmental case—the 1989 Exxon Valdez oil spill in Prince William Sound, Alaska—to illustrate economic valuation processes as they specifically pertain to the natural environment. Clearly, this example is highly specific, and deals with only one of the many techniques developed by economists and environmental accountants to elicit economic value where value is not revealed by an established, working market mechanism. However, the valuation of natural resource damages in the Exxon Valdez oil spill was such a turning point in the field that the case deserves special status. First, it provides a powerful illustration of the philosophy of value and the "epistemic culture" (Knorr Cetina 1999) within the discipline of economics, since the spill aftermath expanded the reach of economics into areas that were not an obvious part of its jurisdiction. Second, the case helps exemplify the unique role economists play in the legal system—specifically in the American legal system at the end of the twentieth century—and the consequences of this role on the social construction of value. Third, the case offers a compelling example of the complex processes involved in the framing of the relationship between monetary value (price) and worth (seen here, as if on a photo negative, through the "prejudice" occasioned by the spill).

The Day the Sea Died

A fairly recent phenomenon, tied to the growth of maritime oil transport and offshore oil exploitation, oil spills have been a not infrequent occurrence since the 1960s. Even as I am writing these lines, a broken pipe from the Deepwater Horizon platform is spewing oil into the Gulf of Mexico in amounts that are still widely disputed. Unlike nuclear waste spills, which are hidden from view and whose consequences take a long time to reveal themselves, oil spills represent an in-your-face, immediate, highly visible, malodorous, and observably destructive ecological catastrophe. Even in the most isolated place—a beautiful fjord in North America, say—they would be hard to miss: the "black tide" occasioned by the spill coming from a large platform or tanker will spread over hundreds of miles of coastline, easily accessible to television cameras and photographers.

This is what happened shortly after the supertanker Exxon Valdez ran aground on Bligh Reef in Prince William Sound near Valdez, Alaska, spilling 30,000 tons of crude oil (nearly 11 million gallons).[4] The Native Chenegans remember that day, March 24, 1989, as "the day the sea died" (Carver 1999).

---

[4] It was later demonstrated that the ship's captain who was supposed to supervise his pilot's maneuvers was drunk when the incident occurred, and that his drinking problem had long been known by the company.

Although the spill was not the worst such disaster suffered by the United States in terms of tonnage, its location in an area known and celebrated for its pristine wilderness caused it to have an enormous impact on the "collective conscience." The event was a public relations disaster for the Exxon Corporation and the oil industry in general; oil companies had little way of effectively countering the relentless broadcasting and publication of scores of vivid and heart-wrenching pictures of beautiful seabirds—murres, gulls, ducks, bald eagles—and endearing marine mammals—seals, sea lions, otters, dolphins, orcas, even a whale—all covered in oil and gasping for air.[5] News media interviews with the local population, many of them Alaska Natives, added to the sense of injustice and the enormous amount of public anger. The Alaskan state government was suspect, too, due to its close relationship with the oil industry. That industry in turn appeared to be solely driven by the pursuit of corporate profits (Engstfeld 1992). Moral outrage in the United States and elsewhere was so acute that it has been argued that the spill was a defining moment in framing the environmental consciousness of the nation (Birkland and Lawrence 2002).

There was a strong sense that something worthy (a beautiful, wild, quiet, innocent, productive "nature") had been harmed or irreparably lost. But what was this material and emotional devastation all worth? In particular, how did the law frame the value question, and how did it go about calculating an appropriate monetary response? Who had been injured? Who ought to be compensated? How and how much? Nature, of course, does not defend itself in a court of law. Wildlife does not sue the polluter. Only people have legal standing here, or governments acting in the name of a putative "public." It is the peculiarity of our age that our legal institutions will take advantage of these sentiments of public indignation and seek to translate them into legal and monetary terms. The sense of injury at the visible distress of the natural world (which is itself socially constructed and historically situated, of course) thus soon finds its way into legal categories and economic valuation procedures, for the purposes of damage compensation.

PASSIVE USE

So what did this mess cost? After a plea bargain with the US Justice Department failed, a federal grand jury in Anchorage indicted the Exxon Corporation and its shipping subsidiary on five criminal counts on February 27, 1990.[6] The Exxon Corporation spent more than $2 billion to clean up the area, and was ordered to pay $300 million in compensatory damages as well as $500 million

---

[5] The US Fish and Wildlife Service estimates mortalities directly related to the spill to be in the range of 350,000 birds and 3,500 sea otters (these are lower bound estimates, as reported by the National Oceanic and Atmospheric Administration in its case history of the Exxon Valdez oil spill). See http://www.akrrt.org/Archives/Response_Reports/ExxonValdez_NOAA.pdf (accessed May 12, 2010).

[6] The five counts included two felony charges under the 1972 Ports and Waterways Safety Act and the Dangerous Cargo Act, and three misdemeanors under the Clean Water Act, the Refuse Act, and the Migratory Bird Act. See Keeble (1999: 269).

in punitive damages to various local victims.[7] Most significantly, the spill was sanctioned by a rapid and large out-of-court settlement of $1.025 billion between the state and federal governments and Exxon as *sole compensation for environmental damage (or "damages to the public's natural resources")*. That figure, in other words, was deemed to represent public compensation for the injury suffered by the people's beloved "nature," as estimated and calculated through the legal-economic process.

Was this a "rational" number? It depends. On the one hand, the process looked very arbitrary: the round figure of $1 billion, for instance, was reportedly handpicked by the governor of Alaska at the time, after a political negotiation with the oil industry,[8] so the actual number had a certain arbitrariness to it. Yet the rationale behind the production of this particular monetary settlement was extremely elaborate. The background work had cost huge amounts of money and involved a large number of experts, including some of the most prominent names in the economics profession. How can we explain this discrepancy?

There was a feeling among public officials that the magnitude and visibility of the incident was such that only a very high monetary compensation would succeed in making the public "whole." And so legal officials went and searched for a valuation method that would somehow *help them argue* for what they felt would be an "appropriate" number. With this goal in mind, economists working for the state of Alaska suggested estimating not only the cost to restore the Prince William Sound environment to its previous "natural" state but furthermore the cost of a program that would prevent with certainty the eventuality of a similar incident in the future. But how should such an estimate be produced? One traditional possibility was to base calculations on actual, known costs for such programs. The economists, however, recommended a different route and proposed that a new method be considered, which in fact had never been implemented on such a large scale. It was (and still is) called "passive use" damage valuation. Here, a key litigator for the plaintiff in the case (the state of Alaska) describes how critical this methodological move was for the ultimate outcome:

When you actually would go look at real damages, [they were] sort of compensatory for the most part, like sports fishing I think we had valued [at] about $36 million. Tourism was like $18 million or something like that. We did [something] where we took individual species and tried to assign a value to the dead animals by looking at replacement costs or the costs they expended trying to rescue them, or something like

---

[7] This includes, for instance, economic losses paid out to fishermen and native tribes.

[8] What I call here the "$1 billion settlement" was actually a slightly higher number: it included a criminal fine of $25 million; criminal restitution of $100 million for the injuries caused to the fish, wildlife, and land; and a civil settlement of $900 million paid into a trust fund over ten years. Finally, the settlement included a provision allowing the state and federal governments to claim an additional $100 million in the future for natural resources restoration, should the money above prove to be insufficient. (In 2006, the governments filed a new suit for $91 million using this "reopener clause.")

that, that you could assign a value. And that came out to like $50 million. We had a few others we did. But when you start adding all those things together it's not a lot of money. But the way we got [the number] up was because the American courts allowed, or at least it had never been done before, but the rules were going to allow us to try the passive use damages. And the passive use damages came out at $2.4 billion [Note: the correct number is $2.8 billion]. But absent those passive use damages, the kinds of damages we could get were going to be very, very limited. Not limited, but they were going to be small compared to what actually has happened...

We immediately convened attorneys and policy makers who dealt with natural resource damages. And we just started brainstorming on the kinds of damages that might be available. And passive use very quickly came to the top as being something that might capture a lot of damages. So our next step was we immediately tried to hire the best passive use people we could find. We, in the state of Alaska, we were very fortunate in that this spill happened during our legislative session. And one of the first things that happened is that our legislature appropriated about $35 million for us to litigate with and to investigate with. So we had the funds to go out and hire people. And even then one person we tried to hire, we lost out to Exxon by about a day I think. A guy who was a Nobel laureate, an economist.[9]   (US #1, May 25, 2006)

The quote immediately begs the question: what is the providential technique that allowed the measurement of these "passive uses"? The approach starts from a simple idea: using "survey questions to elicit people's values for private or public goods or services, by determining what they would be willing to pay for specified changes in the quantity or quality of such goods or services or what they would be willing to accept in compensation for well-specified degradations in the provision of these goods or services" (Carson et al. 1992: 1–5). These economic values are determined by asking people to state their preferences through the medium of money, contingent on the qualitative or quantitative changes described in the survey (hence the name "contingent valuation" for the process). The valuation is "passive," because it focuses specifically on those resources that people are unlikely to use directly themselves. If people did use these resources, then values could be calculated through a more traditional analysis of consumer behavior, that is through *revealed*—rather than *stated*—preferences (for instance, how far people are willing to travel to lay their towels on a clean beach when the one they normally go to has been oiled). What passive use valuation typically does instead is estimate the utility people derive from *knowing* some unique natural spot exists that they could someday visit (but more likely will not); or knowing that some rare species of bird that lives in Far Eastern Siberia will be protected. For instance, I enjoy the fact of knowing that Yosemite Valley exists, that people like me can benefit from admiring its beauty, and I would

---

[9] *Note*: The economist mentioned here was Kenneth Arrow; the state ended up hiring Robert Solow, another Nobel laureate in economics.

probably oppose any plan to build a dam on the Yosemite River, even if I do not ever plan to visit the place. My personal use of Yosemite is passive, but the utility I derive from the existence of Yosemite is not zero.

Historically, the method has its sources in the development of cost–benefit analysis (CBA) in US federal agencies. Originally developed by the US Army Corps of Engineers, CBA was appropriated and expanded by economists in the postwar period (Hanemann 1994; Lohmann 2009; Loomis 2000; Porter 1995). More specifically, the creation of organizations devoted to the management and protection of the so-called "natural resources," such as the Ford Foundation-sponsored Resources for the Future (1952) and the federal Environmental Protection Agency (1970), prompted a surge of interest in the valuation of environmental goods as an extension of the CBA framework. A clean environment, for example, was conceptualized as a new "benefit" to be counted; conversely, the negative environmental impact of a public works or industrial project could now be factored in as a cost. It is thus in these institutions that many of the methodological developments in natural resource economics took place. These economic tools then gained prominence with the rationalization of legal rules surrounding environmental issues. The most important turning point here was in 1980, when in the aftermath of the Love Canal crisis, Congress passed a law known as CERCLA (or the "Superfund" law) that made the assessment of natural resources damages mandatory in cases of toxic spills and hazardous waste.

In choosing contingent valuation as the preferred method of valuation for the ecological damages caused by the spill, the environmental economists working for the state of Alaska were deliberately taking inspiration from the federal rules and practices established after CERCLA.[10] Less than two years after the spill and with funds released by the state and federal governments, a contingent valuation survey was designed and administered in four main locations across the United States, chosen to represent different segments of the American public (lawyers had determined earlier that the spill was of national significance, so that the lost passive use values at stake in this case were those of the whole country).[11] Respondents to the survey were presented with visual and oral information about the Prince William Sound, the transportation of oil in the area, the local wildlife, and how it had been affected by the spill. They were then briefed on a program of Coast Guard escort ships that would prevent another large oil spill with certainty, financed by income

---

[10] And in 1986, a milestone judicial decision (*Ohio v. United States Department of the Interior*) specified that non-use damages to natural resources could be calculated using the contingent valuation method in cases where use values were not measurable (Thompson 2002).

[11] There was some discussion about whether to include populations outside of the United States at the outset. However, this consideration was eliminated for three reasons: (1) Practically speaking, it eliminated the costs of multinational survey work; (2) the plaintiffs were trustees suing on behalf of Americans; and (3) this conformed to our [the contingent valuation researchers'] conservative principle of "when in doubt choose the course of action likely to produce a smaller value" (e-mail exchange with Stanley Presser, November 29, 2004).

taxes as well as a special tax on the oil industry; finally, they were asked whether they would vote for such a program, and how much they would be willing to pay for it if it was implemented (Carson et al. 1992).

META-ANALYTICS

There are several meta-analytical points worth discussing here. The first one is the individualist, consumer-oriented, privatist philosophy that inspires this method. By asking people to provide a monetary equivalent of a putative "utility" loss, and then aggregating these values, contingent valuation reconstructs the natural environment as an aggregation of *individual* preferences, each one disconnected from the preferences of other individuals and therefore from any relevant social context: in contingent valuation, everything happens *as if* any one of us could go, *independently from other individuals*, to the grocery store next door to buy a piece of Prince William Sound.[12]

Second, the whole process appears very artificial and can only be resolved thanks to an enormous work of "framing" (Callon 1998) that produces the calculating public. For instance, interviewers administering the survey were primed to elicit a response from people who said they were unsure, and repeatedly insisted that respondents provide one. Thus if the respondent expressed uncertainty or questioned the interviewer, the interviewer had to reply: "We want to know what *you* think. Take as much time as you want to answer this question. We find that some people say they would vote for, some against; which way would you vote if the program cost your household a total of $___?" (Carson et al. 1992: 3–58).

Third, the nature of the survey instrument itself was extremely confined and reflected a very particular political imagination. Questions about appropriate measures to repair damage and means of payment were closely controlled, and the realm of options was fairly narrow. For instance, interviewees could only vote on and express a willingness to pay for an escort ship program—closing Prince William Sound to tanker traffic was not an acceptable possibility; neither was asking the oil industry to pay for the *totality* (as opposed to just a part) of the program. The obvious methodological reason is that if such a possibility had been present, there would have been no point in asking people how much they were willing to pay *of their own money*. Conversely, the implication of such a framing was that if people were not willing to part with their dollars, they probably did not care much about Prince William Sound and its wildlife.

---

[12] As Sen argues, "The philosophy behind contingent valuation seems to lie in the idea that an environmental good can be seen in essentially the same way as a normal private commodity that we purchase or consume. [That idea] is itself quite absurd. The amount I am ready to pay for my toothpaste is typically not affected by the amount you pay for yours. But it would be totally amazing if the payment I am ready to make to save nature is independent of what others are ready to pay for it, since it is typically a social concern" (2000: 949). Also see Lohmann (2009: 522).

When all was said and done, the contingent valuation survey revealed that the median American household valued the Prince William Sound natural environment at $31. The figure of $31 per household, when multiplied by 91 million American households, gave a total willingness to pay (or utility loss) among US residents of $2.8 billion for the Prince William Sound environment, which was ultimately settled at $1 billion in 1991 dollars. Even reduced to that number, the settlement money was not insignificant and provided for a whole series of new policies, from the closer monitoring of supertanker traffic to the reservation of land or maritime areas for environmental protection, from ecological studies to the promotion of Native Americans' cultural heritage. In other words, the whole process "reassembled" the social world of Prince William Sound and arguably reorganized how we think about "nature" as well.

The adoption of the contingent valuation method served in the Exxon case to justify an unprecedented settlement, which—by the sheer amount of resources it liberated for ecological monitoring and restoration—had a dramatic impact both on the local setting and on environmental science and politics in general. By implementing the concept of "non-use" values, economists may have participated directly in the construction of new relationships between people and their environment. In this new framing, nature was not so much constructed as it was a "thing" with intrinsic value, an idea that people far away—in California, Ohio, Georgia—enjoyed, and which therefore had to be preserved, enhanced, and promoted as such. Paradoxically, the survey's forced process of abstraction and disentanglement from local relations and uses made the Prince William Sound stand for something bigger and more universal. Thus, although the economists' claims were about the economic value of the Sound and the Sound only, in their urge to elicit numbers they symbolically called upon much more—a pure, unspoiled, intangible "nature." The philosophy and outcome of the valuation process did, in a sense, participate in magnifying the symbolic worth of Prince William Sound.

The paradox is that all of this happened against a background of heavily controlled, technical commensuration. Prince William Sound was effectively commensurated with money and implicitly commodified, through the disaggregation of its economic value, into the personal utilities of the 1,000+ citizens surveyed, not to mention the 91 million US households these people supposedly stood for. The methods underlying the Exxon Valdez settlement were in fact playing on a dual symbolic register: on the one hand, they mobilized a powerful *collective* imagining of untouched, pure, and seemingly priceless Alaskan wilderness. Indeed, *their (economic) success depended on that mobilization*: as Kahneman and Knetsch (1992, see also Diamond and Hausman 1994) have suggested, in willingness-to-pay surveys it is hard to distinguish between economic value and the purchase of "moral satisfaction." On the other hand, Prince William Sound was likened to a vulgar commodity, whose value in the eyes of the putative *individual* consumers lay only in the price they were willing to pay. Finally, that very process of commodification was also the material condition of the Sound's further *sacralization*: by fetching a high number and allowing the near totality of the $1 billion settlement to be spent on further ecological activities in the area, it made the Sound even more renowned, precious, and special. It helped "[re]generate the shared meanings, understandings, mindsets and governing narratives intrinsic" to our relationship to that rare place that is Alaska.[13]

Cultural Ambivalence about the Measuring Rod of Money

Non-market valuation methods are profoundly dual, all at once objective and subjective. They thrive on inarticulate and eminently collective forms of worth but act *as if* none of these characteristics were relevant. They seek to make the ineffable concrete and calculable while at the same time maintaining some of its ineffable character. They long to reflect the unique character of Prince William Sound, but they can only do so through abstraction and commensuration. They imagine a market for goods whose most defining economic condition is to *not* have a market.

Duality does not mean neutrality, however. First, as countless critics have shown, people's responses in contingent valuation surveys are extraordinarily sensitive to survey manipulations. Because of this, the method is extremely versatile and can accommodate almost any type of politics. As debates surrounding estimates of the value of statistical life show, non-market valuation methods are never immune to political charges, precisely because the economic values they produce are always dependent on extensive framing work and are contingent on the configuration of political pressures (e.g., Fourcade 2009; Viscusi 2009). For all its complex design and rationalized procedures, the contingent valuation survey following the Exxon Valdez oil spill and, even more, the settlement itself were driven primarily by the *Realpolitik* goals of governments trying simultaneously to assuage the public's anger in an age of alert environmentalism and to tread carefully around the powerful oil industry. This is the first lesson: *economic methods are performative, but with qualifications*; both whether and how they "perform" their world is determined, in part, through the intervention of politics.

Second, for all its controversial epistemology, it is undeniable that the contingent valuation method has had a conservationist impact in the United States—helping make certain tracts of unspoiled nature more "valuable" as such. But—to go back to Marx's point with which we opened this chapter—does valuation under these terms simply amount to commodification? The answer is somewhat nuanced, and demands that we take into account the

---

[13] The quote is from Smith (2007: 2) and applies to market transactions.

method's complicated relationship to mainstream economics. One of the fundamental tenets of microeconomic theory is that the equilibrium price must be unique; otherwise, individuals would take advantage of arbitrage opportunities between several prices (this principle is usually referred to as the "law of one price"). Consequently—if microeconomics is logically consistent—the price an individual is willing to pay for one item (a pristine environment in the Prince William Sound, for example) must equal the compensation that same individual would be willing to accept to forgo the item (maximum willingness to pay equals minimum willingness to accept). Presumably, then, the "American nation" could be paid a certain price to let Alyeska or the Seven Sisters "spoil" the Prince William Sound, under controlled conditions. This evokes the logic of tradable emissions permits (such as carbon or sulfur dioxide emission rights): the measuring rod of money cuts both ways.

If we follow this logic, the virtual market of contingent valuation and the real market of pollution vouchers are conceptually equivalent: they represent *two sides of the same methodological coin of neoclassical environmental accounting,* as some critics (e.g., Hopwood 2009; Lohmann 2009) have pointed out. Thus the somewhat left-wing natural resources economics coming out of the environmental establishment would wrap around to meet the free-market economics of nature coming from Coase and Chicago. What an irony! But not so fast. As it turns out, resource economists have suggested that the willingness to pay and the willingness to accept may differ, and even widely diverge, in the case of truly unique public goods that have few or no substitutes, for instance the Grand Canyon (Hanemann 1991; Krutilla 1967; Shogren et al. 1994). And indeed empirical evidence from contingent valuation studies and experiments indicates large differences in people's responses between willingness to pay and willingness to accept, with the latter generally two to three times higher.[14] This is the second lesson: *sacralization and commodification do go hand in hand, but again with qualifications.*

Economics is never as powerful as when our societies, through the workings of their many institutions, such as the law, express and validate a "need" for *monetary* valuation in the first place. For proponents of the contingent valuation method, its great societal benefit is that it does manage to answer this need: it elicits economic values where all we obviously see are other forms of worth (in the sense of Boltanski and Thévenot [2006]). It is not so much that the "price" produced by this method measures some preexisting "prejudice" suffered by the public. Rather, this prejudice, and all the symbolic and legal baggage that goes along with it, becomes legible primarily through its realization as a price—that is, once this prejudice has been framed as a payment by the polluter or as a "willingness to pay" for the Sound's return to its pure and unspoiled natural state. Does this mean that other ways of expressing and compensating distress are being quietly hidden away? Not

---

[14] Most microeconomists disagree, however, and use the same empirical evidence to criticize the imprecise nature of the contingent valuation method.

necessarily. The possibility of a large-scale payment for nature "as such" also serves as a rallying point for other ways of framing and institutionalizing our relation to the non-human world, be they symbolic, legal, ecological, or political. This is the third lesson: *monetary worth and other forms of worth do not necessarily stand in a contradictory relationship* (or what Viviana Zelizer [2005] calls a "hostile worlds" relationship). What gives content—hostile or not—to the relationship is not only how money is extracted (Marx's point) but also what we do with it—how, to use another one of Zelizer's concepts, we "earmark" it (Zelizer 1994). Thus the fact that the Exxon Valdez settlement money was redistributed back to protect the particular nature of Prince William Sound obscured not only the economic philosophy that had made the settlement possible but also the process of oil extraction that goes on elsewhere in Alaska, through the intense and relentless exploitation of yet another "nature." This, after all, may be just one of the many cultural contradictions of capitalism in the United States—a country, let us not forget, whose most munificent philanthropists often came from the ranks of the most ruthless industrialists.

▪ REFERENCES

Abbott, A. (1988). *The System of Professions: An Essay in the Division of Expert Labor*. Chicago, IL: Chicago University Press.
Ackerman, F. and Heizerling, L. (2004). *Priceless: On Knowing the Price of Everything and the Value of Nothing*. New York: New Press.
Beckert, J. (2008). *Inherited Wealth*. Princeton, NJ: Princeton University Press.
Birkland, T. and Lawrence, R. (2002). The Social and Political Meaning of the Exxon Valdez Oil Spill. *Spill Science and Technology Bulletin* 7(1–2): 17–22.
Boltanski, L. and Thévenot, L. (2006). *On Justification: Economies of Worth*. Princeton, NJ: Princeton University Press.
Callon, M. (1998). The Embeddedness of Economic Markets in Economics. In M. Callon (ed.), *The Laws of the Markets*. Oxford: Blackwell, 1–57.
——(2008). What Does It Mean to Say that Economics Is Performative? In D. MacKenzie, F. Muniesa, and L. Siu (eds.), *Do Economists Make Markets? On the Performativity of Economics*. Princeton: Princeton University Press, 311–56.
Carson, R. T., Mitchell, R. C., Hanemann, W. M., Kopp, R. J., Presser, S., and Ruud, P. A. (1992). *A Contingent Valuation Study of Lost Passive Use Values Resulting from the Exxon Valdez Oil Spill*. Report to the Attorney General of the State of Alaska. San Diego, CA: Natural Resource Damage Assessment Inc. http://www.evostc.state.ak.us/pdf/econ5.pdf (accessed March 30, 2011)
Carver, T. (1999) Exxon Valdez Anniversary. Published on the BBC online network, March 25.
Coase, R. H. (1960). The Problem of Social Cost. *Journal of Law and Economics* 3: 1–44.
——(1994). Economics and Contiguous Disciplines. In *Essays on Economics and Economists*. Chicago, IL: University of Chicago Press, 34–46.

Coslor, E. (2009). Playing by the Rules: Competing Logics of Exchange in the Market for Contemporary Art. Presented at the Annual Meeting of the American Sociological Association, August. http://www.allacademic.com/meta/p306848_index.html (accessed March 24, 2011)

Debreu, G. (1959). *Theory of Value*. New Haven, CT: Yale University Press.

Diamond, P. and Hausman, J. (1994). Contingent Valuation: Is Some Number Better than No Number? *Journal of Economic Perspectives* 8(4): 45–64.

Dobbin, F. (1994). *Forging Industrial Policy*. Princeton, NJ: Princeton University Press.

——and Sutton, J. (1998). The Strength of a Weak State: The Rights Revolution and the Rise of Human Resources Management Divisions. *American Journal of Sociology* 104(2): 441–76.

Edelman, L. and Suchman, M. (1997). The Legal Environment of Organizations. *Annual Review of Sociology* 23: 479–515.

Engstfeld, A. (1992). *Das Alaska Syndrom*. Documentary film. Cologne: Engstfeld Filmproduktion.

Espeland, W. and Levine, P. (2002). Pollution Futures: Commensuration, Commodification, and the Market for Air. In A. Hoffman and M. Ventresca (eds.), *Organizations, Policy and the Natural Environment: Institutional and Strategic Perspectives*. Stanford, CA: Stanford University Press.

Fligstein, N. (1990). *The Transformation of Corporate Control*. Cambridge, MA: Harvard University Press.

Fourcade, M. (2009). The Political Valuation of Life. *Regulation and Governance* 3: 291–7.

Garcia, M.-F. (2008). The Social Construction of a Perfect Market: The Strawberry Auction at Fontaines-en-Sologne. In D. Mac Kenzie, F. Muniesa, and L. Siu (eds.), *Do Economists Make Markets? On the Performativity of Economics*. Princeton, NJ: Princeton University Press, 20–53.

Golan, T. (2004). *Laws of Man and Laws of Nature: A History of Scientific Expert Testimony*. Cambridge, MA: Harvard University Press.

Guala, F. (2001). Building Economic Machines: the FCC Auctions. *Studies in History and Philosophy of Science* 32: 453–77.

Hanemann, W. M. (1991). Willingness to Pay and Willingness to Accept: How Much Can They Differ? *American Economic Review* 81(3): 635–47.

——(1994). Valuing the Environment through Contingent Valuation. *Journal of Economic Perspectives* 8(4): 19–43.

Healy, K. (2004). Sacred Markets and Secular Ritual in the Organ Transplant Industry. In F. Dobbin (ed.), *The Sociology of the Economy*. New York, NY: Russell Sage, 336–59.

Heilbroner, R. (1983). The Problem of Value in the Construction of Economic Thought. *Social Research* 50(2): 253–77.

Hopwood, A. (2009). Accounting and the Environment. *Accounting, Organizations and Society* 34(3–4): 433–9.

Jasanoff, S. (1995). *Science at the Bar: Law, Science, and Technology in America*. Cambridge, MA: Harvard University Press.

Jepperson, R. and Meyer, J. W. (1991). The Public Order and the Construction of Formal Organizations. In W. Powell and P. DiMaggio (eds.), *The New Institutionalism in Organizational Analysis*. Chicago, IL: University of Chicago Press, 204–31.

Kahneman, D. and Knetsch, J. L. (1992). Valuing Public Goods: The Purchase of Moral Satisfaction. *Journal of Environmental Economics and Management* 22(1): 57–70.

Keeble, J. (1999). *Out of the Channel: The Exxon Valdez Oil Spill in Prince William Sound*, 2nd ed. Cheney, WA: Eastern Washington University Press.

Knorr Cetina, K. (1999). *Epistemic Cultures: How the Sciences Make Knowledge*. Cambridge, MA: Harvard University Press.

Krutilla, J. (1967). Conservation Reconsidered. *American Economic Review* 56: 777–86.

Lohmann, L. (2009). Toward a Different Debate in Environmental Accounting: The Cases of Carbon and Cost–Benefit. *Accounting, Organizations and Society* 34(3–4): 499–534.

Loomis, J. B. (2000). Environmental Valuation Techniques in Water Resource Decision Making. *Journal of Water Resources Planning and Management* 126(6): 339–44.

MacKenzie, D. and Millo, Y. (2003). Constructing a Market, Performing Theory: The Historical Sociology of a Financial Derivatives Exchange. *American Journal of Sociology* 109(1): 107–45.

Marx, K. (1988). *Economic and Philosophic Manuscripts of 1844*. Amherst, NY: Prometheus Books.

Mayhew, A. (1998). How American Economists Came to Love the Sherman Antitrust Act. In M. Morgan and M. Rutherford (eds.), *From Interwar Pluralism to Postwar Neoclassicism*. Durham, NC: Duke University Press, 179–201.

Medema, S. (1998). Wandering the Road from Pluralism to Posner: The Transformation of Law and Economics in the Twentieth Century. *History of Political Economy* 30: 202–24.

Mercuro, N. and Medema, S. (1997). *Economics and the Law: From Posner to Post-Modernism*. Princeton, NJ: Princeton University Press.

Mirowski, P. (1990). Learning the Meaning of a Dollar: Conservation Principles and the Social Theory of Value in Economic Theory. *Social Research* 57(3): 689–717.

Muniesa, F. (2000). Un robot walrasien: cotation électronique et justesse de la découverte des prix. *Politix* 13(52): 121–54.

Patinkin, D. and Steiger, O. (1989). In Search of the "Veil of Money" and the "Neutrality of Money": A Note on the Origin of Terms. *Scandinavian Journal of Economics* 91(1): 131–47.

Polanyi, K. (1944). *The Great Transformation*. Boston: Beacon Press.

Porter, T. (1995). *Trust in Numbers: The Pursuit of Objectivity in Science and Public Life*. Princeton, NJ: Princeton University Press.

Posner, R. (1987). The Law and Economics Movement. *American Economic Review* 77: 1–13.

Power, M. (1999). *The Audit Society: Rituals of Verification*. Oxford: Oxford University Press.

Radin, M. (2001). *Contested Commodities*. Cambridge: Harvard University Press.

Sen, A. (2000). The Discipline of Cost–Benefit Analysis. *The Journal of Legal Studies* 29(2): 931–52.

Shaw, G. B. (1915/2006). On the History of Fabian Economics. In E. Pease (ed.), *The History of the Fabian Society*. BiblioBazaar, 239–44.

Shogren, J. F., Shin, S. Y., Hayes, D. J., and Kliebenstein, J. B. (1994). Resolving Differences in Willingness to Pay and Willingness to Accept. *The American Economic Review* 84(1): 255–70.

Simmel, G. (1978). *The Philosophy of Money.* Boston, MA: Routledge Kegan and Paul.
Smith, C. W. (1989). *Auctions: The Social Construction of Value.* New York, NY: The Free Press.
—— (2007). Markets as Definitional Mechanisms: A Robust Alternative Sociological Paradigm. *Canadian Journal of Sociology* 32(1): 1–39.
Stark, D. (2009). *The Sense of Dissonance.* Princeton, NJ: Princeton University Press.
Sunstein, C. R. (2004). *Are Poor People Worth Less Than Rich People? Disaggregating the Value of Statistical Lives.* John M. Olin Law & Economics Working Paper No. 207. University of Chicago. http://papers.ssrn.com/sol3/papers.cfm?abstract_id=506142 (accessed March 24, 2011)
Swedberg, R. (2003). The Case for an Economic Sociology of Law. *Theory and Society* 32(1): 1–37.
Thompson, D. B. (2002). Valuing the Environment: Courts' Struggles with Natural Resource Damage. *Environmental Law* 32: 57–89.
Velthuis, O. (2005). *Talking Prices: Symbolic Meanings of Prices on the Market for Contemporary Art.* Princeton, NJ: Princeton University Press.
Viscusi, K. (2009). The Devaluation of Life. *Regulation and Governance* 3: 103–27.
Weber, M. (1978). *Economy and Society.* Berkeley, CA: University of California Press.
Zelizer, V. (1979). *Morals and Markets: The Development of Life Insurance in the United States.* New York, NY: Columbia University Press.
—— (1985). *Pricing the Priceless Child.* Princeton, NJ: Princeton University Press.
—— (1994). *The Social Meaning of Money: Pin Money, Paychecks, Poor Relief, and Other Currencies.* Princeton, NJ: Princeton University Press.
—— (2005). *The Purchase of Intimacy.* Princeton, NJ: Princeton University Press.

3 What Is the Price of a Scientific Paper?

Lucien Karpik*

What is the "price" of a scientific article? Is there only one single price? How is it determined? Does it vary with the article's quality? Is it different across different sciences? Does it allow for the calculation of profit? Can it be used to drive research policy? Books have a price that varies, but not according to quality. Scientists on the American academic market can be associated with an economic value that simultaneously measures the overall worth of their work and the intensity of the desire to lure them from one university to another. We should be able to link this value to the classical notion of price, but unfortunately it does not obey the law of supply and demand, and as a consequence cannot drive the rational allocation of scarce resources. This said, can we completely exclude such an affinity to the classical notion of price? Just as Bordeaux winegrowers anticipate the new Parker Guide and French chefs await the new Michelin Guide, researchers in English-speaking countries anxiously await the publication each year of a score that establishes the relative quality of their work (and thus the level of their remuneration).[1]

In fact, the *"price" of a scientific article* is a category that belongs to a completely different register: it is the product of the interaction between a new object of study, a new way of determining quality, and a new way of distributing research resources that has resulted from a new research policy implemented in France and elsewhere. To grasp the precise meaning of this category, we must consider it in conjunction with the broader changes brought about by the new research policy: the transformation of researchers into entrepreneurs; the extension of managerial vocabulary and practices to the research realm; the use of indicators and rankings combined with the apparent disappearance of peer review; new modalities of research resource distribution; a generalized individual competition; the creation of new control

---

* Translation by Scott Kushner.

[1] "Every September, a ripple of excitement passes through the scientific community as the Institute of Science Information (ISI) publishes its latest set of impact factors, in which some six thousand journals are ranked according to the number of citations they received in the previous year...For others (scientists), however, it represents something more serious, because their career prospects are increasingly affected by the impact factors of the journals in which they publish" (Jennings 1998); "The annual release of newly calculated impact factors has become a big event" (Simons 2008).

organizations; the emergence of upheavals, schisms, and conflicts within the research world; and changes in relationships between the state and science.

The *new system of scientific evaluation* ties all of these elements together. With some variations, it occupies a prominent position in a growing number of countries. It incessantly expands its circle of experts, devotees, cynics, and victims within each country. And it has provoked the development of a vast and diverse literature in statistics, management, economics, sociology, political science, and law, not to mention ideological and existential thought.

What can we add that has not already been said? I propose two contributions in one: a study that applies a new theoretical perspective to the development of a new national evaluation system facing strong constraints. On the one hand, I study the beginnings of research reform in France, reform that has a tortuous technical, social, and political history. On the other hand, I suggest that the standard interpretation of French research reform—which is supposed to link rational and self-interested individual action, indicators and rankings, incentive and sanction systems, and competition to the premises, concepts, and logic of neoclassical economics—be replaced by an approach that does not overlook the specificities of research activities and products. This is the case for applying *the economics of singularities*, which was developed to account for goods and services that present the same specific features as scientific goods and services (Karpik 2010).

The analysis is therefore focused on examining the concrete forms, conditions, and consequences of France's new system of scientific evaluation; the new forms of competition among researchers; and the global sociopolitical transformations without which research reform would remain unintelligible.

More precisely, the first section is devoted to the examination of three changes: the construction of a manual metric in France, which is "history in the making"; the discreet power shift taking place between the researchers who participate in the general management of research organizations and the researchers who are in charge of scientific journals; and a comparison between an old and new form of competition within the research system. The second and third sections deal with indicators and rankings as new modalities of judgment devices and with the new forms of competition that govern the relationships among scientists. The fourth section is devoted to studying the links between the new research policy, state strategies, and the social and political transformations that have marked the research world over the last two or three decades.

Research Reform in France

Over the last two or three decades, research reform has been considered the preferred method of increasing researchers' efficiency while simultaneously decreasing public expenditures, in order for the country to face ever-intensifying global economic competition. This confidence in reform explains the emergence of new research policies, first in Great Britain, Australia, and New Zealand, and more recently in the major European countries. Changing the system of scientific evaluation is at the center of these policies. In all these countries, to different degrees, measurement tools have replaced peer review, the practice that has allowed what is true to be separated from what is false throughout the history of modern science.

In France, the 2006 reform[2] opened the door to a system of scientific evaluation: the development and deployment of tools equivalent to the computerized ones used in English-speaking countries, a transfer of power from one set of peers to another, and the rise of a new form of scientific competition.

SCIENTIFIC VALUE AND MEASUREMENT TOOLS

Scientific evaluation practices can be divided according to whether or not they use bibliographic databases. This division leads us to distinguish between the *citation model* and the *committee model*. The citation model is defined by the use of bibliographic databases and the automated calculation of indicators. It is applied only to English-language journals. The committee model, which does not make use of bibliographic databases, works through discussion with tools equivalent to the computerized ones used in the first model and is applied to scientific literature in languages other than English, especially in the social sciences. France currently uses the committee model. In order to assess the particularities of the French system, I will first present the principal characteristics of the citation model.

The citation model or digitized metrics

The invention of digitized metrics was made possible by a technological-scientific development from the 1960s—an indexed bibliographic database called WoS (Web of Science), endlessly updated with pertinent information from nearly 9,000 scientific journals. This database represents the central element of the evaluation device for *articles* published in scientific journals. This makes possible the automated calculation of a range of indicators, and consequently (1) the drawing of various comparisons at will that separate or combine scientific disciplines, countries, and historical periods; (2) the ranking of articles and scientists according to the criteria used in calculating the indicators; and (3) the deployment of research policies based on researchers' relative scientific value.

The information is processed using two basic operations: (1) the counting of citations, by which it is possible to know how many times a given article has been cited in all other articles published over a certain period of time; (2) the

---

[2] Loi de programme pour la recherche du 18 avril 2006 (law no. 2006-450).

calculation of an *impact factor* for a journal that corresponds to the ratio of the number of citations in the current year to the source items published in that journal during the previous two years. This value is computed for each scientific journal every year.[3]

The calculation of the value of the *indicators* relies on three fundamental conventions: (1) the scientific value of a published article is tied to the scientific value of the journal in which it is published; (2) the scientific value of a journal is determined by its impact factor, which varies over time and is set each year based on the previous year; (3) to simplify the calculations, journals are divided into categories based on their impact factors. The two most widespread methods are also the simplest. In one method, journals are divided into two categories, with the so-called A-list or "selected journals" bringing a specific value to all articles they publish, unlike those journals that are not "selected." In the other method, journals are organized into A, B, and C categories, such that an article published in an A-level journal sees its score doubled with regard to an article published in a B-level journal, while a publication in a C-level journal counts for nothing.

Depending on the way they are constructed, the so-called quality indicators hew more or less closely to one of two poles: a *productivity indicator*, whose value corresponds to the absolute number of articles that a researcher publishes in "selected journals" over a given period, and a *performance indicator*, which is calculated so as to take into account the weighted values associated with the different categories of journal.

Compared to peer review, these metrics present indisputable advantages: an objectivity derived from the use of impersonal procedures, constantly updated global information, the rapid calculation of indicators, and relatively low operating costs. They also present biases, limitations, and adverse consequences (Académie des Sciences 2009; Adler and Harzing 2009; Adler et al. 2008; Espeland and Stevens 2009; Gingras 2008). Very generally, indicators are considered to be measures of an article's scientific quality. But this signification is problematic at best. Citations are sometimes associated with *quality*, but they can also be associated with *prestige, reputation*, or an "old boys' network." In fact, a citation does not carry just one meaning because it *measures the usefulness that an author accords to a text*, and there might be a wide range of reasons for an author to cite one article or another.[4] The quality indicator is easy to measure, but unfortunately the exact nature of what is being measured is not clear. To avoid misunderstandings, the quality indicator will henceforth be referred to as the "usefulness" indicator.

---

[3] The presentation is oversimplified: there are several databases and multiple indicators (see Archambault and Vignola-Gagné 2004; Kermarrec et al. 2007).

[4] The criticism of assessment systems is as vigorous among hard scientists (though it is often claimed that the new research policy should not affect them) as it is among social scientists.

The committee model or the manual metric

The research reform instituted by the 2006 law and supplemented one year later by the Law on the University is a complex entity but, *with regard to scientific evaluation*, its two basic elements are the advancement of bibliometric tools and the creation of the Evaluation Agency for Research and Higher Education (Agence d'évaluation de la recherche et de l'enseignement supérieur [AERES]), which will henceforth be called the *Agency*.

Members of Parliament saw bibliometric tools as a preferred alternative to peer review due to the tools' great virtues: objectivity, generality, and comparability. For these reasons, and because social science journals had no bibliographic database, the Agency, the "keystone of the evaluation system," had to develop measurement tools equivalent to those that existed under the citation model in order to create the possibility for international comparisons. This reform, which is in its development and implementation phase, encountered a number of obstacles.

Long before the 2006 law and the creation of the Agency, many lists of selected journals, sometimes covering all scientific disciplines, sometimes only the humanities and social sciences, or sometimes only a single discipline, were drawn up, proposed, and almost always rejected (Fridenson and Studies 2009). They represented a useful starting point for the development of new solutions.

During the first two years of its existence, the Agency seemed to devote itself exclusively to collective evaluation. Then, without any warning, the lists of social science journals were posted to the Agency's website on July 8, 2008. For each scientific discipline, a corresponding list grouped journals into four hierarchical categories: A+, A, B, and C. These new lists largely resembled the earlier lists. Researchers were shocked and furious. They unleashed withering criticisms. The list publication was a resounding failure. A year passed, and new lists of social science journals were posted on the Agency's website in 2009. The overall result was marked by the abandonment of a uniform model. In economics and psychology, the lists were structured differently from those in other social sciences such as sociology. Social scientists' reactions were more reserved this time. The decision to abandon the ideal of comparability most likely means that the Agency, which absolutely could not do without researchers' support, simply acceded to the propositions, which for the various scientific disciplines were just expressions of professional strategies anyway. This is the tool that has been used to grade, calculate, rank, and distribute research resources since 2009.

PEERS REPLACING PEERS

The vast and tumultuous debate over the choice between peer review and bibliometric tools hides another choice, seemingly smaller but no less important. Having become the "pillars" of scientific value, journals could only benefit from an ever-stronger demand for access: their prestige rose, their power grew, and their credibility increased. But scientific journals are usually based on peer review. This observation lets us put aside the purely imagined fear of peer review's disappearance.

But the fear that peer review could be outsourced remains. Research reform in France implied the synchronization of the decline of scientists' collegial power in certain research organizations, especially at the CNRS (Centre national de la recherche scientifique [French National Center for Scientific Research]) and the universities with the rise of those scientists who edit journals that use peer review to choose articles. So far, this goal has been only partially realized. Nevertheless, journal editors have come to play a central role in the ranking of researchers and, in turn, in the allocation of research resources.

How can the reallocation of power from "peer-run organizations" to "peer-run journals" be explained? Because public officials' criticisms of the former have grown incessantly over the last several years, should we conclude that the latter have better judgment? Or, more precisely, might we imagine that some people think so?

In any case, it is not through any knowledge of the operation of French scientific journals that we can craft a response. This is because we have no such knowledge. However, in the United States, there are some sociological studies on scientific journals. These studies give prominence to results that bear on the French case. Although the scientists who participate in the production of journals are generally highly qualified researchers who devote much time to journal activities despite the purely symbolic compensation, the overall selections made by publications are rather erratic. Journal policies show judgment errors. The most serious and most common of these are not decisions to publish things that should have been rejected but instead to reject things that should have been accepted. In various ways, these policies reveal a fear of novelty and of heterodoxy (Campanario and Acedo 2007; Lawrence 2003: 260). Other, more specific criticisms have been leveled (Campanario 1998). No journal has all of these flaws (one hopes), and there are probably some among them that have been able to avoid all of these pitfalls, at least for a time. There are hardly any reasons to think that the same results would not be observed in French journals. Thus, it is possible to conclude that neither facts nor arguments should lead us to attribute to "peer-run journals" the qualities that "peer-run organizations" lack (or are thought to lack).

This detour shows the paradox that characterizes the new evaluation systems in all countries: the development of the bibliometric tool emerges from a critique of peer review, but the reliability of the tool's results depends on the reliability of the "pillars"—the journals—that are usually exclusively governed by peer review! How can we not be astonished that researcher-run organizations are distrusted even though their discussions are subject to a certain public control, and yet absolute confidence is invested in those who run the journals? For the moment, let us simply observe that this contradiction has laid the foundation for the invasion of the research world by indicators and rankings.

A NEW FORM OF COMPETITION?

The form of competition that research reform has produced has been laid out several times, at least in its broad outlines, by Bernard Belloc, who is an economist at the Toulouse School of Economics, the former president of the University of Toulouse I, and the adviser on Higher Education and Research to French President Nicholas Sarkozy.

The title of one of his articles offers a good starting point: "Save the Scientists" (Belloc and Friebel 2004). Until the publication of this article, scientists did not know that they needed saving, and in their innocence, they did not even know that anyone was fighting for them. But from what (or from whom) must they be saved? In Belloc's view, they need saving from rules and norms, authority and hierarchy, bureaucracy, memberships, solidarities—from everything that holds them back and keeps them from realizing their potential to discover or rediscover the largely hidden truth of *homo economicus*. In short, they must be allowed to be like all humankind: calculating actors who are fundamentally and rationally motivated by the advancement of their personal interests.[5]

Only the state has the resources and the power to produce the moral, social, and legal disembeddedness that will free researchers to pursue the satisfaction of their individual interests and to distribute rewards according to performance. Any attempt to stop the introduction of this new form of competition would only serve to reproduce the traditional economic solution of eliminating professional groups' power to compete on the free market (Friedman 1962). But to increase researchers' efficiency, Belloc imposes one supplementary and enigmatic requirement: the "introduction of *competition*" (emphasis by the author). This does not mean that the author denies that competition exists among researchers but instead that a new form of competition should be linked to the *quality issue*, and therefore to a regulatory authority and to evaluation tools. This new reality has been developed around three decisions: (1) the concrete delimitation of a research product—the *scientific article*—which, for all intents and purposes, becomes the common benchmark; (2) general criteria of scientific quality that are no longer applied directly to the thing evaluated—as would be the classic solution—but instead to the thing that performs the evaluation: the journal; and (3) a unidimensional ranking of articles published by researchers. In other words, the new form of competition deals with the issue of scientific quality.

Paradoxically, the effects on the relationship between *homo economicus* and rewards, regulatory authority, measurement tools, and efficiency are

---

[5] "A simple and effective solution consists of introducing more competition. The most productive researchers should benefit from the best working conditions and the best professors must be rewarded...Of course, the introduction of competition must be accompanied by the creation of a regulation authority that will evaluate individuals and universities so that the highest-performing researchers and establishments are also the best funded" (Belloc and Friebel 2004).

only an extension of the market model to knowledge. In fact, the combination of competition and the new evaluation system is purely pragmatic and therefore not built on any relevant theoretical framework. Even more important, this reasoning necessarily demands that scientific activities and products are equivalent to economic activities and products. This proposition is rejected here.

Scientific Singularities

What do we mean when we speak of research? When we speak of researchers? Can we be satisfied with the everyday meanings of these words? Neoclassical economic theory has two ways of describing goods and services: on the one hand, differentiation, and on the other, the distinction between "search," "experience," and "credence" goods. None of these fits here. To break with an argument that is so general that it comes at the expense of products' specificity, we need to begin by constructing the concept of the "scientific article" and more generally of "research products" before we examine the consequences of this conception.[6]

A DEFINITION AND ITS CONSEQUENCES

Like a painting or a film, a scientific article is a *singularity* defined by three concurrent characteristics: multidimensionality, incommensurability, and radical quality uncertainty. *Multidimensionality* means that the scientific article is a configuration of qualities, that it is composed of heterogeneous and interdependent elements. *Incommensurability* refers to the absence of equivalents between symbolic worlds endowed with the same status, which in no way excludes a comparison from a particular point of view. And, just as the quality of a doctor or lawyer's services can only be known after paying for them, a *radical quality uncertainty* refers to the impossibility of predicting by any means (including probabilistic calculation) the emergence of a new scientific theory or a new interpretation of an old theory. Similarly, it is impossible to predict whether an article will be among those articles that are neglected upon their publication but become famous after a time or, conversely, whether it will be touted at first only to fade from memory later on.

All that is science is not singularity. Scientific reality, like artistic or legal reality, is heterogeneous, not only in the broadest sense but also for each discipline, for each field, and even for each researcher. This heterogeneity, which was foreshadowed by the notions of "paradigm," "scientific style," and

---

[6] This section briefly (and necessarily dogmatically) summarizes several developments drawn from *Valuing the Unique* (Karpik 2010: 1–128) that are useful to the analysis.

"knowledge regime," has been known for a long time: in no way does it rule out the application of the concept of singularity, since this concept accurately describes dominant research practices and since its specific effects can be observed in reality. Because they have to do with singularities, the comparison of scientific articles and the appraisal of their scientific value both encounter considerable difficulties that can only be overcome with some help.

In order for singularities to remain as singularities, any form of coordination must overcome two major obstacles: first, to create conditions where actors can make a reasonable judgment about or between singularities, and second, to maintain the primacy of quality competition over price competition. The judgment devices deal with the first obstacle, and the relationships between the symbolic and material orientations of action deal with the second.

JUDGMENT DEVICES AND THEIR EFFECTS

Because of the great quantity and complexity of scientific knowledge and because its volume grows very quickly, the researcher—as a producer and reader of new knowledge—is always threatened by the flow of information. The researcher needs a way to distinguish between what is relevant and what is not; this task cannot be accomplished alone. Help is found in research networks, criticisms, review essays, journals, books, sometimes in the mass media, and in the prizes and medals that single out great authors.

These cognitive arrangements constitute *judgment devices*. To be useful, these devices must offer focused, formatted, and credible knowledge. They are focused because the information is organized around certain criteria or a particular configuration of evaluation criteria, formatted because the presentation must satisfy the conditions of the passing of judgment, and credible because radical uncertainty can only be ended by instilling confidence. Judgment devices are guides for action, and their use reduces actors' ignorance of a subject.

These devices also perform a qualification operation on ideas and publications—the simplest forms would be "this theory is or is not interesting" or "this paper is to be read or ignored"—and they compete among themselves: the symbolic authority of judgment devices grows as their relative influence becomes stronger. Subtle balances and imbalances are changed, sometimes unintentionally and often suddenly, by the appearance of new devices, such as the lists of selected journals.

PRIMACY OF QUALITY COMPETITION

The primacy of symbolic value over economic value expresses the operating logic of markets of singularities as well as the actions of the individual actors who comprise them. Individual action, to start there, is no longer understood as a unique dimension characterized by the degree to which it maximizes utility, but as one that is characterized simultaneously—to appeal to the

Weberian tradition—by two analytically distinct principles: symbolic orientation and material orientation.

A researcher's *symbolic orientation* becomes apparent in the constellations of values, beliefs, and norms used. Some of these, such as originality, tenacity, ambition, and the joy of discovery, directly influence researchers' scientific practices in the context of a shared historical imagination populated by great scholars, great works, ideals like professional pride, and a commitment to individual and collective autonomy. All of this is more or less blended together, valorized, and transformed into existential forms of engagement. *Economic orientation* is defined in the classic fashion as the relations between means and ends. The researcher's concrete actions must be analyzed as the outcome, the more or less stable compromise between these two principles of action. The distinction between symbolic and economic orientation offers a good opportunity to give a more precise meaning to a researcher's effectiveness by distinguishing between the degree of *relevance* on the one hand and the degree of *efficiency* on the other.

In the universe of singularities, the symbolic orientation prevails over the economic orientation. This hierarchy expresses a logic whose persistence and evolution must be linked both to competition between mechanisms, which are intended to ensure the reproduction of singularities, and to the struggles among actors.[7] The essential influence on actors' forms of actions is produced by the judgment devices, which can generally be divided into two categories.

TYPES OF JUDGMENT DEVICES AND TYPES OF COMPETITION

Once networks are excluded, the extremely varied and quickly expanding universe of judgment devices can be divided into two broad categories: *substantial devices* and *formal devices*. The judgments of substantial devices deal with the specific content of the products, as with critics or guides, while the judgments of formal devices concentrate on rankings (the countless charts). The research system features the same divide, and research reform *consists fundamentally of removing substantial devices in favor of formal devices.*

With this definition, the previous results of the differential effects of substantial and formal devices can be put to the test: (1) formal devices favor a tendency toward conformity, which combines impoverishment (through the suppression of originality) and standardization (by the use of the smallest meaningful difference); (2) formal devices favor weak attachments to singularities and therefore tend toward desingularization (Karpik 2010: 242–9); (3) control of the formal devices bestows the power to control and guide users' choices (Karpik 2010: 175–9).

---

[7] The primacy of symbolic competition over material competition distinguishes markets and quasi markets of singularities from all other markets. See the concrete studies of markets for wine, music, luxury items, legal services, and other goods in Karpik (2010).

The Conflict between Two Forms of Neocompetition

Researchers' effectiveness is the new official imperative. But the term remains empty until one is able to distinguish among different forms of competition within the universe of singularities and discern the different criteria of judgment used in each of them. These distinctions allow us to see the *likely evolution* of the French research system.

EMULATION AND RIVALRY

As it is usually understood, research reform amounts to the extension of market competition within the research system. But the relation between price, supply, and demand does not apply in the research world, *making the notion of market completely irrelevant here*. The scientific struggles that occur between researchers are closer to those seen in the sports world (the World Cup, the Olympics, and others) and fall under the term of neocompetiton. Moreover, the distinction between substantial and formal judgment devices becomes the basis of two different forms of neocompetition: *emulation* and *rivalry*.

What research reform has really done is to build a new form of neocompetition into the research system that operates alongside emulation, the classic form of scientific neocompetition. Here, this new form of competition will be called rivalry.

Emulation and rivalry as ideal types can be systematically (and dogmatically) compared. Emulation is characterized by (1) the drive to make discoveries; (2) a competitive arena where all competitors are focused on the "same" problem; (3) the specific influence of substantial devices and scientific contents; (4) a focus on values (originality) and ideals (professional pride, autonomy); (5) different forms of success; (6) a strong attachment to scientific singularities.

Rivalry is the new form of neocompetition. It is characterized by (1) the drive to top the rankings; (2) a competitive arena defined by the scope of the rankings (in some cases, broad branches of science; in other cases, specific disciplines); (3) the specific influence of formal devices; (4) the erosion of traditional values and ideals resulting from the growing importance accorded to economic value; (5) a single path to success (the publication of papers in selected journals); (6) a weakening attachment to scientific singularities and the resultant tendency toward desingularization.

Under the new evaluation system and the increasing relative importance of economic considerations, it is possible to develop a simplified economic vocabulary for rivalry. Here, (1) the *product* is the article published in a scientific journal; (2) the *user* or consumer of the product is the scientist, through the intermediary of citation counting in countries where the citation model is used, or the scientific journal in countries where the committee model is used; (3) the *scientific value* of an article is based on the relative value of the journal category in which the article is published; (4) a *researcher's overall scientific value* is measured by the overall score that results from the multiplication of the number of articles published by the weighted value of the journals in which they were printed; (5) the *quasi price* of an article is based on the distribution of research resources as a function of the ranking of researchers;[8] and (6) the *quasi profit* is represented by the difference between the advantages received by the researcher and the advantages that would have been enjoyed had the researcher fulfilled the minimum requirements laid out by the Agency for "publishing" researchers. Taken together, these terms define a *quasi market* of singularities. It is in this quasi market that the price—or more precisely the *quasi price*—of a scientific article is meaningful.

By comparing emulation and rivalry, we can infer that scientific struggles should be stronger, more general, and more individualized under rivalry. But these logical inferences can take different concrete forms according to the types of indicators and rankings that are used.

RIVALRY AND TYPES OF RANKINGS

The Agency, like all similar agencies around the world, distinguishes among three main quality indicators: a productivity indicator, a performance indicator, and a measure for books. Each of these can be linked to observed and likely effects.

The *productivity indicator* and all its minor variants measure the number of articles published in the lists of selected journals. When this indicator is used to rank researchers and consequently to distribute research resources, the effects are easy to ascertain. Historical experience confirms this. In the 1990s, Australia initiated research reform based on an indicator where the absolute number of articles played an essential role. This policy was reinforced by the Australian universities. It took a long time to discover the double effect of this practice: a spectacular growth in the number of articles published and a no less spectacular reduction in the number of articles cited (Butler 2003). The number increased at the expense of quality, which led to the realization that the profit distributed was inflated to the same degree that the quality of the product was low. One can only be amazed by the astonishment among the affected parties at the time and wonder at the French official decision to use a productivity indicator for some social sciences. Can there be any doubt as to the effects of such an indicator? And can there be any doubt that these effects would be even worse in France, which, unlike Australia, had no way to track the consequences of such a choice over time?

---

[8] The quasi price varies with the value of the impact factor, the overall value of the distributed economic resources, and the inequality rule observed in the division according to rank. For an analysis of an analogous problem, see Steiner (2010: 194–231).

The French list of selected journals in economics offers a typical example of a *performance indicator* that is more heavily focused on quality than usual, because the absolute number of articles is effectively weighted according to the relative quality of the journal categories. Two features characterize this list: (1) the highest category (A+) is composed exclusively of a few American and British journals where the likelihood of a French scholar's work being published is very low; and (2) the French journals are relegated two levels lower, in the B category. There again, it is not difficult to identify several likely effects: (1) at best, only a handful of French scholars will be able to get into the main journals in the A+ category, and those who succeed will likely be those who have spent some time working in American settings; (2) the barriers to economic heterodoxy will become very high; and (3) French economics journals are devalued (Audier 2009).

The bibliographic databases were conceived from the starting point of a basic unit—the article—but this form of publication corresponded to the dominant practices of the exact sciences. In the social sciences, the picture changes, as several studies have shown that about half of the knowledge produced is published in book form (Larivière et al. 2006). Logically, this reality would have led either to changes in the bibliographic databases or the development of new methods that would incorporate books into the evaluations. But inertia won the day. In a charitable spirit, this lack of change was accompanied in France by the following solution: *independent of any evaluation, each book would count as much as one article.* It is not clear what would be worse: that the book be totally ignored or that it be scored with complete disregard for its content. In any case, with or without this practice, the use of quality indicators can only favor the decline of the book. How could a rational and self-interested researcher, which is what all researchers are now expected to be, begin such an undertaking anymore? Does the use of a subaltern technology justify the loss of the great treasures of social science knowledge?

THE LOGIC OF GLORY AND THE LOGIC OF EXCELLENCE

With the advent of research reform, rivalry should gradually replace emulation. But it is not enough to elaborate new tools, because these can still remain unused. This has not been the case in France, where the tools have already been put into use even though research reform was just implemented in 2009. It is difficult to delimit the present influence of these tools and even more difficult to predict their future deployment. Still, we can present an impressionistic assessment of their extent and the forces that drive them: the government and the researchers.

Government action has included (1) the creation of allowances and positions for "excellent" scientists; (2) the use of researchers' rankings to distribute a portion of available research funding at a few universities; (3) the Agency's internal use of the journal lists to deal in practice with the general distinction between "publishing" and "nonpublishing" researchers; (4) the present push in some quarters of the CNRS to extend the use of the excellence rankings and financial incentives.

But the strongest drive for the use of these devices is coming from scientists themselves. Some of them believe that the new system places more emphasis on talent than the previous system. Others are ideologically sympathetic to the new policy. But most of them use the excellence ratings in informal ways purely for reasons of convenience. To members of peer committees, the ratings device looks like such a useful tool that pressure is mounting in some quarters to use it in an official way. This is not surprising. On the quasi market of scientific singularities, just as on the market of singularities, rankings have the same attraction. It is convenient to use a ranking to judge a song. Or, for that matter, to judge a scientific article or a scientist.

Only a small fraction of researchers have been converted so far: we are far from any general agreement. The wholesale and uncontested replacement of one form of neocompetition by another, and all that they both imply, does not seem to be the least bit likely. Such a situation creates a conflict at the heart of the research system.

The research world is made up of several conceptions of science incarnated in people and institutions. This world is a pluralistic milieu, full of conflicts, that can defend itself when necessary. For example, the researchers' uprising of 2003–4 emptied the laboratories and was sufficiently powerful and productive to elaborate a true, written research policy. Also of note were the great uproar in 2008 about the lists of "selected" social science journals and the tenacious university strike in 2009. The diversity of values, ideals, commitments, situations, positions, ambitions, and career paths leads us to imagine that the new research policy will create a *dualistic* and conflictual neocompetition, but only after a long time and with some confusion along the way.

For social science disciplines that use any kind of productivity indicators and rankings, the "logic of excellence," that hallmark of reform, will take root in the near term in research whose originality (Guetzkow et al. 2004) and adventurousness are limited. As researchers struggle harder and harder, the results of their struggles increasingly favor conformity—an avoidance of risky fields, blind conformity in the subjects studied, formulaic articles—and opportunism. The more intense the competition, the more it tends to replace scientific stakes with professional stakes (Académie des Sciences 2009; Adler et al. 2008; Asari and Aziz 2005; Espeland and Sauder 2007; Segalat 2009). This evolution can become all the more powerful as economic value rises and breaks the moral foundation of research: the professional pride and freedom necessary for bold inventiveness (Bénabou and Tirole 2003; Osterloh et al. 2007). In sum, the logic of excellence governs a form of neocompetition based on more modest scientific ambitions, a more rapid rhythm of production, a more obvious economic orientation, and "performances" that lead to high quasi profits.

This evolution is indeed occurring, but it is difficult to imagine that it could tremendously weaken bold research, which demands inventiveness and persistence, and whose duration and results are marked by great uncertainty. It is difficult to believe that these changes could call into question classical science's emulation system, with its breakthroughs and its universities dedicated to research. Even more difficult to believe is that it could lessen the yearning for scientific prestige, the passion of discovery, the desire for greatness, the accepted importance of peer review, the appeal of scientific recognition, and the support offered by many institutions.

The increasingly strong internal tension between the primacy of the symbolic orientation and the strengthening of the economic orientation, between the privileged appeal to substantial devices or formal devices, should therefore provoke the growing rift between the two systems of research, two forms of neocompetition, and two overarching logics that we might call *the logic of glory* and *the logic of excellence*: "The scholarly search for the unique is different from the administrative search for excellence" (Waters 2005: 39).

Democratic Tyranny

If the urgent improvement of economic efficiency is the official explanation why the research system has been turned on its head, why have there not also been reforms at the *Grandes Écoles* to establish research-based education? And why have there not been widespread reforms at French corporations, where research is rather weak in comparison to foreign corporations?

In fact, it seems with research reform that the state is simultaneously pursuing two distinct goals, one official and widely known, the other more discreet but perhaps more important. To distinguish the essential from the peripheral, the reforms must be linked to the dynamics of public policy and the professional and social transformations that society has undergone over the last three decades. By tying these two threads together, it becomes possible to understand how the two projects are at once distinct from and wholly implicated in one another.

THE STRATEGIC STATE

Research reform is not an isolated operation with exceptional goals and means. It is part of a general and ambitious redefinition of the role of the state that has been underway for some time and whose origins can be found in the "crisis of governmentalism." The state's much-documented inability to transform French society and the repeated humiliation that has followed its attempts to do so are the ingredients of a major political question that has generated many committees and reports, as well as several reforms, that have been extensively studied by sociologists (Berrebi-Hoffman and Gremion 2009;

Bezes 2009; Bruno 2008; Garcia 2008; Hood 1995; Le Galès and Scott 2010; Vilkas 2009).

Under the influence of high-ranking civil servants and (usually foreign) consultants, the *New Public Management*, as this new art of government is called, has married a set of common organizational rules (the separation of management and production, the dismantling of administrations in favor of specialized single-function institutions, the use of indicators to conduct and measure the results of policies, reference to the neoclassical economic orthodoxy) to a new conception of the relationships between rulers and ruled that should allow for the coexistence of efficiency and civil peace. Two general methods can be distinguished: management/camouflage and the creation of delegates that cannot report to any higher authority.

The art of government takes a particular form in the management of collective action by way of devices whose most prominent feature is a concealment of the active role of the state. As already shown in the studies of public action, the research devices have four primary characteristics: they appear to be modest, their effects are indirect, their influence works closely on individuals' minds, and they influence individual decisions from afar. The goal is efficiency without conflict: the management of performance is inseparable from the management of consent.

The traditional grandeur of institutions has now been replaced by the discretion of single-function organizations. But above all, it is *procedure*, the way of conducting affairs, that is being substituted for public action, action that would otherwise be determined by the appropriateness of the means to the ends. Common sense imagines that procedure is less noble and less powerful than the law, which is the state's weapon in the sense that it is the incarnation of general rule and it rests on the power of the police and of justice. But the reverse is true. In effect, history shows that procedure is generally more durable than the law, and once procedure has been established, accepted, and entangled in a set of concrete measures, it quickly becomes invisible, resilient, and sprawling.

Coercion no longer takes the form of public rules that can be linked to specific authorities and specific consequences. Instead, it derives from competition. Far from trying to replace bureaucracy with the tournament (Lazear and Rosen 1981), government combines the two in order to establish a form of neocompetition, guided by influence, that is fused with a panoply of indicators and a system of incentives and sanctions.

Without any apparent violence, the competitive system pushes aside all who refuse to play by the rules by simply denying them the opportunity to succeed. The malleability associated with conformity literally *pays off*. By making individuals' quasi profits dependent on the relationship between fluctuating research resources and the relative scientific value of researchers as determined by the measurement tools, the evaluation system—inasmuch as it manages to legitimize the rules of the game under pretenses of freedom or independence—ultimately leads to *an unprecedented degree of interference in researchers' affairs*, specifically their preferences, choices, and motivations. The effectiveness of these forms of action is even more surprising because the devices allow the center to control the periphery without having to meet it. Acting through procedure, measurement tools, competition, and an official delegate should be enough to inhibit the formation of common interests and occasions for collective conflicts.

Taken together, through their forms and degrees of intervention in the affairs of researchers, these devices show a state that is both near and distant, omnipresent and elusive, a state that is all the more powerful when it avoids the tests by which its power might be measured.

The 2006 law created the Evaluation Agency for Research and Higher Education (Agence d'évaluation de la recherche et de l'enseignement supérieur, or AERES), which we have called the Agency, and assigned it the sole mission of evaluating all the research organizations that receive public funding. This amounts to about 140,000 people. To the French Parliament, the Agency represents the "keystone" of research reforms. One MP, who was not certain whether he should be proud or concerned, said "the existence of an independent agency wholly dedicated to evaluation has not been tried anywhere else in the world." The Agency was charged with developing the measurement tools: it was to draw up the lists of selected journals and define the indicators. We can finish our discussion of the Agency by considering two characteristics that are not necessarily its most prominent but are certainly meaningful.

The Agency is a QUANGO, a quasi-autonomous nongovernmental organization *(autorité administrative indépendante)* that does not fall under any superior authority. The director and the members of the council are named by the government, and the Agency's director in turn names the "scientific deputies" who see to the organization's operations. These deputies are researchers who work part time for the Agency: they are officially granted the status of *experts*. Such a semantic designation is hardly accidental: it sets them apart. The term "expert" designates a person who because of his status in the Agency has a specific competence and exercises a form of authority. The designation enforces a distance from other researchers and removes the threat of collegial power. In one fell swoop, the experts develop, apply, and enforce the Agency's policies and, by their very existence, create a fundamental split in the research world.

Aside from presenting official documents and guides to the preparation and presentation of collective evaluation results, the Agency's website is largely characterized by what is not there but ought to be. No discussions about the stakes and practices of the agency's policy; no information on the organization's everyday operations, committee meetings, and deliberations; no forums on contemporary trends in bibliometrics. The message is clear: the Agency is an administrative and expert authority that dislikes debates. It sets and enforces public policy. Its presentation and representation is organized around a denial of politics.

THE LOSS OF SOCIAL STATUS AND THE FALL FROM POWER

Over the last two or three decades, the relations between political leaders and scholars have changed. The clearest signs: the fleeting disregard expressed over the course of time and the invariable disdain for the research policy elaborated at the 2004 *Etats Généraux de la Recherche* meeting, for the reports from the major French and foreign scientific institutions, and the heavy criticism of reform that has come from researchers in the exact as well as the social sciences, from foreign countries as well as from France.

But the world has changed over this period. French and foreign scientists are no less knowledgeable today than they were in the past; they are no more or less wise. But three decades of flourishing financial capitalism have led to a *loss of social status* for the research world. The alliances between high political and administrative powers and the leaders of large banks and multinational corporations, as well as the concomitant rise of a collective passion for money, a growing disinterest in knowledge and culture, and the extension of anti-intellectualism, combine to explain easily why the scientific world has lost its social status. Research reform has hastened this evolution. It would be easy to show how each step has also resulted in the humiliation of those who want to maintain the emulation system and all its related values and practices.

The most significant expression of this evolution is the *sudden and strong decline of the participation of researchers in their organizations' management*. Certainly, scientists continue to play a role in scientific institutions. They continue to run them and see to their operations, but they no longer do so as formal or informal representatives of the scientific community. They are now named by the state and only hold power thanks to the state. Reform has led, in somewhat ostentatious fashion, to a *professional dispossession* in favor of centralized power and its appointees. The "profession's" ability to make an assessment and take action is no longer recognized, because for the strategic state attempting to consolidate power, nothing can get between it and those on whom it acts, certainly not professional forces that could only threaten the state's policies (Paradeise and Lichtenberger 2009).

It is in this light that we can understand the replacement of peer-run organizations by peer-run journals. While some would have us believe that this is the result of researchers' questionable practices (which do exist), it is in fact more the result of the desire to do away with an independent source of power: the organizational committees are at least partially composed of elected researchers, who claim to act in the name of their colleagues, who base the distribution of research resources primarily on peer review and do not hesitate to speak out in opposition to government policies when necessary.

The disdain and indifference on the part of the political and economic elites expresses the new social and political relationship imposed by the rulers on the scholarly world. And the interventionism that deeply affects the researcher's individual activities would probably not have gone so far if the social bedrock had not been so deeply eroded over the last two or three decades.

RETURN TO PEER REVIEW?

The status of peer review occupies a central place in reform.[9] Let us be clear. It is not surprising, shocking, or disgraceful (let alone scandalous) to use bibliometric tools so long as the tools measure what they are intended to measure. It is likewise not surprising, shocking, or disgraceful (let alone scandalous) to use peer judgment so long as conditions are met whereby the practices are fair and reasonable. Therefore, the only thing left to do would be to list the pros and cons and, after comparing them, to make a choice. These exercises have already been conducted and they still always leave out the most important point: the meaning of peer review is not limited to its technical value.

Peer review represents a subject that is too complex to be developed here and too crucial to be completely ignored. In France, the use of peer review as the primary method of publishing articles and books, evaluating careers, and distributing research funding has long drawn criticism from researchers at some institutions, such as the CNRS. Because of a lack of studies, it has never been possible to evaluate the nature and relative importance of the condemned practices. Proposed reforms were rarely adopted. This background noise was heard and amplified by political authorities, to the point of essentially discrediting the practice of peer review in France altogether.

If this criticism was so successful, it is also because many researchers, faced with the explosion of theses, committees, and journals, were not displeased at the arrival of measurement tools that allowed them to gain some precious time for their work. Other reasons have been given to explain why some scientists more or less abandoned the battle for peer review. But one fact should have made them take a closer look: *major American universities—the so-called research universities—have kept their distance from the new evaluation systems. At the heart of advanced capitalism, peer review has maintained its dominant position.* This should put an end to any simple explanations.

Peer review has three major characteristics. First, it consists of a singular relationship: the relationship between a singular reader and a singular work. The validity of the judgment can only be based on such a relationship. Next, because peer review is in theory irreplaceable, it grounds the legitimacy of scientific power. Only a singularity can judge another singularity in any worthwhile manner, and the contexts of this judgment may be eminently diversified. It is by the nature of the act—judgment in the universe of radical quality uncertainty—and the extended scope of its application that peer review establishes the necessity of individual and collective scientific power. Finally,

---

[9] "...Reaffirm the primordial value of the direct evaluation of scientific work beginning with original publications and, eventually, with hearings" (Académie de Sciences 2009: 3 [translation by the author]); "Peer review is...a bad system but the best one possible" (Joan Sieber as cited in British Academy 2007: 1).

I nearly forgot the most important point: *to judge work, you have to read it.* Not read everything: existing selection processes have proven themselves successful. This reading is certainly a demand that can become heavy, but it is also a matter of organization. In any case, it is important that the work be read.

In no way do these demands reduce the value of the criticisms leveled at peer review, which are particularly concentrated in the social sciences, especially because the plurality of theoretical points of view seems to inhibit any general agreement on scientific quality and, in turn, any ranking of work and/ or people. Fortunately, recent sociological work on the functioning of committees and juries has largely modified the validity of these arguments (Lamont 2009; Musselin 2005). This work shows three main results: (1) the diversity of theoretical perspectives is not an insurmountable obstacle to decisions based on scientific quality, because the pertinent evaluation criteria are produced and transformed in the course of the discussion process that leads to the decision; (2) the committee of peers, so long as it is properly constituted, is the nearest expression of the will of the research community; (3) these committees are the most direct expression of one of the main organizing principles of the world of science: *collegiality.*

No one claims that the conditions of the proper usage of peer review are easily met—though various solutions have been proposed[10]—and no one presently knows effective ways to limit, in research as elsewhere, the fascination sparked by ranking devices whose material and psychological benefits are obvious, as evidenced by the steady stream of top-ten lists. The force of these arguments should not prevent us from making two essential observations about the research world: on the one hand, it is the collective process, the confrontation of arguments, that allows for the best determination of the highest scientific quality; on the other hand, the renunciation of peer review carries with it the renunciation of scientific power, and therefore the renunciation of the scientific community's ability to participate in its own governance.

Conclusion

Through the economics of singularities approach, it has become possible to integrate research reform into a general theoretical framework. First, equivalent products have been replaced by scientific singularities and competition has been replaced by neocompetition. Second, the distinction between substantial judgment devices and formal judgment devices has offered a meaningful way to distinguish two different types of neocompetition

---

[10] The concrete solutions may not be the same for all types of evaluations: recruitment, promotion, selection of publications by journals and publishers, distribution of research funding, etc.

(emulation and rivalry), to compare them systematically according to the central researcher orientation (the race toward discovery priority versus the race toward a better rank on the excellence ranking) and the differential qualification effect of the two types of judgment devices. This allows us to define research reform as the attempt to replace substantial devices with formal devices—or, more precisely, to replace emulation with rivalry.

We can also make a realistic assessment and interpretation of the new policy's effects. But to reach such a goal, the type of neocompetition should be combined with the types of indicators and rankings in use. For the French social sciences, the combination of rivalry and a productivity ranking should result in the production of a large number of articles that could be thought to belong to "normal science," a science that would no longer be defined by the interval between two scientific revolutions but instead as a general and stable norm. In other words, the search for quantity will catalyze a refusal of originality, risk, the broad view, new questions, and changes of theoretical perspectives. To put it bluntly, the search for quantity results in a loss in quality and a step toward the desingularization of knowledge (Lawrence 2008).

If we add to this the devaluation of the book, then sociological analyses that aspire to understand and explain the world and to rally the public to such a goal (Gauchet 2009) will find themselves increasingly discouraged. Scientific passions and risky research undertaken with some institutional support will survive, but their relative importance will be affected by the fight against a dominant conception of science. In France, this history is just beginning: the future is not yet written. But the stakes are high.

It is difficult to justify such a research policy by the necessity of researcher efficiency, especially because the number of studies on these policies' effectiveness is scarce and the results are mitigated by caveats. One can invoke theoretical blindness, the democratic control credo, or the spread of neoliberalism (Foucault 2010; Power 1997). Here, I wish to relate these policies, with their tyrannical management of individual researchers both by stripping collegial power from them and by attempting to control and orient them through the systematic use of precise and specific judgment criteria, to the rise of a new political and economic elite that seeks to extend its power to scientific creation.

REFERENCES

Académie des Sciences (ed.) (2009). *L'évaluation individuelle des chercheurs et des enseignants-chercheurs en sciences exactes et expérimentales.* Paris: Académie des Sciences. http://www.academie-sciences.fr/presse/communique/rapport_080709.pdf (accessed March 31, 2011).

Adler, N. J. and Harzing, A. W. (2009). When Knowledge Wins: Transcending the Sense and Nonsense of Academic Rankings. *The Academy of Management Learning & Education* 8(1): 72–95.

Adler, R., Ewing, J., and Taylor, P. (2008). Joint Committee on Quantitative Assessment of Research: Citation Statistics. *The Australian Mathematical Society Gazette* 35(3): 166–88.

Archambault, E. and Vignola-Gagné, E. (2004). *The Use of Bibliometrics in the Social Sciences and the Humanities*. Report prepared for the Social Sciences and Humanities Research Council of Canada. Montreal: Science-Metrix.

Asari, M. A. and Aziz, N. (2005). The Use, Misuse, and Misconception of Impact Factor. *The International Medical Journal* 4(2): 102–3.

Audier, F. (2009). Évaluation et listes de revues: le cas de l'économie et de la gestion. Laviedesidees.fr. http://www.laviedesidees.fr/IMG/pdf/20090917_bibliometrie.pdf (accessed March 24, 2011)

Belloc, B. and Friebel, G. (2004, September 1). Libérons les chercheurs. *L'Expansion* 689: 32.

Bénabou, R. and Tirole, J. (2003). Intrinsic and Extrinsic Motivation, *Review of Economic Studies* 70(3): 489–520.

Berrebi-Hoffman, I. and Gremion, P. (2009). Elites intellectuelles et réforme de l'Etat: Esquisse en trios temps d'un déplacement d'expertise. *Cahiers internationaux de sociologie* 1: 1–126.

Bezes, P. (2009). *Réinventer l'état*. Paris: Presses Universitaires de France.

British Academy. (2007). *Peer Review: The Challenges for the Humanities and Social Sciences*. London: The British Academy Report. http://www.britac.ac.uk/templates/asset-relay.cfm?frmAssetFileID=6434 (accessed September 19, 2010).

Bruno, I. (2008). La recherche scientifique au crible du benchmarking: Petite histoire d'une technologie de gouvernement. *Revue d'histoire moderne & contemporaine* 55 (4bis): 28–45.

Butler, L. (2003). Explaining Australia's Increased Share of ISI Publications: The Effects of a Funding Formula Based on Publication Counts. *Research Policy* 32(1): 143–55.

Campanario, J. (1998). Peer Review for Journals as It Stands Today: Two-part Article. *Science Communication* 19(3): 181–211 and 19(4): 277–306.

——and Acedo, E. (2007). Rejecting Highly Cited Papers: The Views of Scientists Who Encounter Resistance to Their Discoveries from Other Scientists. *Journal of the American Society for Information Science and Technology* 58(5): 734–43.

Espeland, W. N. and Sauder, M. (2007). Ranking and Reactivity: How Public Measures Recreate Social Worlds. *American Journal of Sociology* 113(1): 1–40.

——and Stevens, M. L. (2009). A Sociology of Quantification. *European Journal of Sociology* 49(3): 401–36.

Foucault, M. (2010). *The Birth of Biopolitics: Lectures at the Collège de France, 1978-1978*. New York, NY: Picador.

Fridenson, P. (2009). La multiplication des classements de revues de sciences sociales. *Le mouvement social* 226(1): 5–14.

Friedman, M. (1962). *Capitalism and Freedom*. Chicago, IL: University of Chicago Press.

Garcia, S. (2008). L'expert et le profane: qui est juge de la qualité universitaire? *Genèses* 70: 66–87.

Gauchet, M. (2009). Vers une société de l'ignorance. *Le Débat* 156: 144–66.

Gingras, Y. (2008). La fièvre de l'évaluation de la recherche: du mauvais usage de faux indicateurs. *Bulletin de méthodologie sociologique* 100: 42–4.

Guetzkow, J., Lamont, J. M., and Mallard, M. (2004). What Is Originality in the Humanities and the Social Sciences? *American Sociological Review* 68(2): 190–212.

Hood, C. (1995). The "New Public Management" in the 1980s: Variations on a Theme. *Accounting Organizations and Society* 20(2–3): 93–109.

Jennings, C. (1998). The Wrong Impact? *Nature Neuroscience* 1(8): 641–2.

Karpik, L. (2010). *Valuing the Unique: The Economics of Singularities*. Princeton, NJ: Princeton University Press.

Kermarrec, A.-M., Faou, E., Merlet, J.-.P., Robert, P., Segoufin, L. (2007). What Do Bibliometric Indicators Measure? INRIA. http://www.irisa.fr/ipso/perso/faou/publis/indicateurv08_english.pdf (accessed September 19, 2010).

Lamont, M. (2009). *How Professors Think: Inside the Curious World of Academic Judgment*. Cambridge, MA: Harvard University Press.

Larivière, V., Archambault, E., Gingras, Y., and Vignola-Gagné, E. (2006). The Place of Serials in Referencing Practices: Comparing Natural Sciences and Engineering with Social Sciences and Humanities. *Journal of the American Society for Information Science and Technology* 57(8): 997–1004.

Lawrence, P. A. (2003). The Politics of Publication. *Nature* 422: 259–61.

—— (2008). The Mismeasurement of Science. *Current Biology* 17(15): R583–5.

Lazear, E. P. and Rosen, S. (1981). Rank-Order Tournaments as Optimum Labor Contracts. *Journal of Political Economy* 89(5): 841–64.

Le Galès, P. and Scott, A. (2010). A British Bureaucratic Revolution? Autonomy without Control or "Freer Markets, More Rules." *Revue française de sociologie* 51: 117–41.

Musselin, C. (2005). *Le marché des universitaires: France, Allemagne, Etats-Unis, Paris*. Paris: Presses de Sciences Po.

Osterloh, M., Frey, B. S., and Homberg, F. (2007). *Accountability in Research and Academia*. Unpublished Working Paper. Zurich: University of Zurich. https://www.uzh.ch/iou/orga/ssl-dir/wiki/uploads/Main/Accountability6_final.pdf (accessed September 19, 2010).

Paradeise, C. and Lichtenberger, Y. (2009). Universités: réapprendre la responsabilité collégiale. *La Revue du MAUSS* 33: 228–43.

Power, M. (1997). *The Audit Society: Rituals and Verification*. Oxford: Oxford University Press.

Segalat, L. (2009). Science et finance: mêmes symptomes, mêmes dangers. *Le Débat* 156: 186–91.

Simons, K. (2008). The Misused Impact Factor. *Science* 322(5899): 165.

Steiner, P. (2010). *La transplantation d'organes: un commerce nouveau entre les êtres humains*. Paris: Gallimard, 194–231.

Vilkas, C. (2009). Des pairs aux experts: l'émergence d'un "nouveaux management" de la recherche scientifique? *Cahiers internationaux de Sociologie* 1: 61–79.

Waters, L. (2005). *Enemies of Promise: Publishing, Perishing, and the Eclipse of Scholarship*. Chicago, IL: Prickly Paradigm Press.

4 The Value of Ethics: Monitoring Normative Compliance in Ethical Consumption Markets

*Peter Gourevitch**

Organic food sells well. So do items marked as coming from the rainforest, or having no pesticides, or using no child labor, or bearing the "Fairtrade" label, conveying compliance with FLO-CERT criteria and procedures. Consumers pay more for such products (Hiscox and Smythe 2009), since in many cases, if not most, these attributes do add to the cost of production. How do consumers decide if it is worth paying that higher cost to obtain the ethically made product?

The drive for ethical consumption raises fascinating issues about the construction of value and the determination of price (Henderson 2001; Vogel 2005). Ethical consumption has to do with the way a product is made: whether it pollutes, exploits children and women, hurts animals, and/or consumes too much energy. These are all characteristics of the production process, not the use value of the product. It is not about how the strawberries taste but how they were grown.

In this regard, ethical consumption resembles the dimension of "authenticity" in art. Originals have value beyond their appearance because of who made them: an attribution of production, not usage. As Karpik (2007) observes, authenticity as a value is an aspect of product "singularities." The social valuation of the ethical consumption movement thus partakes of processes common to all products whose value is symbolic and whose quality uncertain. Consumers of such products seek assistance in ascertaining key features of the production processes that they cannot observe by inspecting the products directly. With ethical consumption, they turn to NGOs who monitor and

---

* Thanks for comments on earlier draft to participants in the Menaggio conference of June 2009; to Michael Barnett, Suzanne Berger, Carew Boulding, Celia Falicov, Susan Hyde, Miles Kahler, David Lake, Kal Raustiala, Dan Posner, Michael Schudson, Janice Stein, Wendy Wong, and Dan Yankelovich. Earlier versions of this chapter were delivered at a conference, "Beyond Virtue," at UCSD March 20–1, 2009, funded by the Institute for Global Conflict and Cooperation, and to Fellows at the Bellagio Center for comments on a talk April 23, 2008, and at the Global Fellows Seminar at UCLA June 2008; and with assistance from the Rockefeller Conference Center Bellagio, Italy, April 10–May 8, 2008; the Monk Center at the University of Toronto, September 2008; and grants from UCSD Sabbatical Funds, the UCSD Senate, and the Panta Rhea Foundation.

evaluate producers and production processes. Fairtrade is among the most well-known labels performing this function. It is for all intents and purposes a brand that conveys social values. The valuation of Fairtrade coffee thus resembles the valuation of wine: social processes of consumption mix with economic attributes of production, refracted by the politics of rival evaluations of taste—from Parker, the American individual, to the French traditions of institutionalized expertise (see also Garcia-Parpet 2009 and in this volume).

Two elements of social construction arise in this type of valuation: the first concerns how these goals acquire importance—why do people want them? The second concerns how the production goals are verified—why do people believe the specific product conforms to their production process requirements? Societies vary substantially in assigning value to production goals. Europeans are much more worried about genetically modified organisms (GMOs) than are Americans. In the United States, the "blue" coastal states care more about these issues than do the more conservative "red" states. Ethical consumption values fit into other attributes of social standing, culture, employment, and education. Wealthy people can afford to pay the higher prices, but they can also afford to worry about these issues. Consumption of ethical goods confirms identity, as does engagement in the social movements associated with verification, as some people seek to be "verifiers" while others prefer to be "vigilantes" or protesters (Elliot and Freeman 2003).

It would be useful to situate this value system in a culture frame that explores the system's links to, as well as boundaries from, other social currents: antiglobalization, critique of markets, the environment, social justice, equality, and a range of social criticism. Buying fair trade is an indicator (Daviron and Ponte 2005; Jaffee 2007; Levi and Linton 2003; Murray et al. 2003), a marker that signals not only concern with ethical consumption but with other value systems, and defines one as different from free market or social conservatives in various ways. Ethical consumption/production could be a driver of these other value systems, or it could derive from them a reflection of other processes. European attitudes, for example, could be a vehicle for critique of US capitalism, or a critique of the value system involved in these products.

Interesting as these questions are, this chapter focuses on the second dimension noted above: not why these production considerations are valued, but how they are assessed. How do consumers learn which products actually fit their norms? In 2006, a *New York Times* story noted that over half the wild salmon sold in fancy New York retail markets was in fact farm raised. Recent press reports have featured unsafe products from China, such as heparin (an ingredient in blood thinner medication) and melamine (added to milk), and unsafe toys sold by Mattel. In 2007, Merck had to withdraw the painkiller Vioxx from the market, despite FDA approval, because of evidence that the drug contributes to heart attacks. The financial meltdown of October 2008 showed how unreliable are many standards of evaluation in that industry (most notably bond ratings and mortgages).

Consumers can be misled. They may think there is no child labor, just as a collector may be duped into a fake Picasso. Ethical consumption requires *accurate monitoring* to ensure the product conforms to our goals in where and how it was made. Accuracy in monitoring is not the same as *effectiveness* in stopping bad practices, because finding child labor does not stop people from buying the product anyway. But accuracy is surely a part of the solution in designing processes for effective limits in unethical behaviors. The issues of accuracy and efficacy impact the construction of price: if it costs more to achieve these goals, many of us will pay that extra price if we are sure that the product conforms in fact to the standard of production and we think that buying the approved product will achieve the desired social result.

Again, the comparison to authenticity in the art market is instructive. As considerable market value lies in who created the object, how is this ascertained? In art, expertise dominates verification. Expertise is identified through training, certification of training, recognition in the field, and previous experience in the field. Art is internally referential; there is no behavioral proof of authenticity as there might be in building codes or medical practice or medicines. The assessment of the value of a work of art is only based on the reputation of the expert, verified by the reputation of others. Art rises and falls in value according to taste, and so the expert makes a call, which the "mandate of history" may reject or accept. But the verification of authenticity is separate from the value of artist or the genre, and can be determined separately from the value of the artist or art; if the art is valued, authenticity will increase the value; if it is not valued, authenticity will not raise the price.

Verification by expertise lies at the core of many processes of valuation: efficacy in medicine, safety in cars, or energy use in appliances. In many of these processes, there is some objective information that can be invoked: the building stands up, the medicine cures, the car does not crash. In other cases, considerable judgment calls are required and these can only be made by experts: evaluating medical malpractice or water purity are some examples. It is impossible to legislate precisely what is prohibited. Governments delegate authority to professional groups of experts, peers from the target community, or often professional associations, who then develop guidelines of best practice and become the panels which review specific actions—an extensive chain of delegation which relies in part on norms of professional practice to reinforce the risk of scandal.

The expert model relies on the professionalization of expertise: the emergence of standards, training, and verification systems that are widely recognized and institutionalized. In some areas, like the quality of restaurants or fine wine, the authority is claimed but contested, and the criteria vary by country. The difference in criteria and method on the role of the expert vs. the consumer provides an interesting comparison among countries, as we lay the Michelin Red Guide alongside Zagat and Chowhound (Karpik 2000).

In the field of corporate social responsibility (CSR), these methods of determining expertise are problematic. The field lacks consensus on standards—

agreement on definitions of expertise, methods of training, and membership in professional associations. It is an arena where government regulation is relatively low, and where private firms control important pieces of information. CSR is a field with a low level of institutionalization: the formal rules regime is weak, professional standards are not well developed, and the profit motive is suspect as a guarantor of compliance with norms.

It is precisely these features that have drawn in NGOs. Many NGO websites suggest their reliability by specifying they are "nongovernmental" and "non-profit." As such, the NGOs claim to be beyond capture (the problem of governments) and beyond self-interest (the problem of profit-seekers). NGOs fault government either because it is absent (especially in many labor standards or environmental areas) or, if laws are on the books, ineffective because governments are "captured" by the targets of regulation and thus fail to sustain adequate standards or to enforce them. NGOs fault monitoring by for-profit firms, because the drive to maximize return squeezes against the cost of higher standards, and as a result firms become judges in their own cases—a conflict of interest.

NGOs aid consumers by monitoring compliance by firms with ethical production norms and then signaling what products are made in compliance with them. Many NGOs offer labels or brands—FSC (Forestry Stewardship Council, one of the pioneers in this field [Bernstein and Cashore 2007; Cashore et al. 2004]), Fairtrade, Fishwise, Leaping Bunny, MSC (Marine Stewardship Council)—as "shorthand" information cues to convey reliability (Lupia and McCubbins 1998; Popkin 1991). Many of these organizations are run by well-meaning people devoted to their cause. They work long hours for mediocre pay. They are virtuous, ethical, with high standards and a strong sense of obligation.

Is this enough? That organizations are virtuous in values does not establish that they are reliable in their monitoring. We cannot be sure from their virtue that they are using tough standards, or that the labels they use accurately describe the production processes of the contents. Two separate issues are raised: whether the standards are tough enough, and whether the standards are being met. The two interact: it is harder to meet tough standards, and harder to monitor compliance to tougher ones, than soft. The many stories about food, safety, environmental damage, the collapse of financial institutions, and the Madoff Ponzi scheme, all of these despite the monitoring work of many NGOs and private actors, give us pause.

NGO Incentives to Monitor

If private and public groups failed to detect error in the financial system when a powerful economic interest existed to do so, why should we have more confidence in NGOs dealing with ethical consumption issues? These areas may indeed be harder to monitor—they have less regulation behind them, lack of clear indicators, and ambiguity on results. If mistakes happen in private sector monitoring where the stakes are quite high, and measurement often clear, then we may have reason to examine whether NGOs are effective in areas where measurement can be quite difficult and the stakes less clear.

Thinking about the "stakes" gives us an important way to approach this: reliability is connected to the costs of being unreliable, the costs of being wrong (Gourevitch and Lake 2010). Actors can post a "bond" on their action, a price they will pay if they are proven wrong, such as the warranty on a product. This idea, stressed by Ronald Coase (1937, 1960), lies at the core of arguments about the ability of private arrangements to solve problems without formal government involvement; George Akerlof's Nobel Prize in Economics was based on exploring this logic (Akerlof 1970).

Lupia and McCubbins (1998) build on this idea with their analysis of "costly speech." In evaluating the reliability of a speaker—in our case the NGOs who are putting a label or brand on products—our confidence rises to the extent that we can: (1) observe "costly effort on the part of the speaker," (2) verify the speaker's statements, (3) apply a penalty to the speaker for lying, and (4) observe a convergence of interests between us and the speaker.

The first three points involve the measurement of cost and thus focus on the challenges of calculation, the process of measurement, and are thus rationalist in approach. The fourth point is more culturalist, as it involves understanding what drives the convergence of interests: religion, charisma, values, personality, networks. Trust has some element of construction: belief in the speaker, belief in the appropriateness of the speaker. The degree of acceptable risk varies across peoples and cultures and circumstances (Henrich et al. 2004).

NGOs can engage in actions to communicate credibility. They operate in a complex strategic environment, populated by diverse audiences for whom they "perform" and seek to persuade. It is these different audiences to which NGOs must be credible, and thus a major strategic challenge for NGOs involves strategizing how to manage the sometimes conflicting demands of these different audiences: these include targets, principals, the public, and other NGOs.

NGO Audiences

Targets: One essential audience for all NGOs is "targets," the actors whose behavior these NGOs hope to change. *Principals*: Principals are actors who delegate responsibility for particular tasks to NGOs and, in turn, have the ability to terminate that relationship once begun; principals have the power to hire and fire NGOs. *The Public*: NGOs exert pressure to comply with standards because they can mobilize purchases, votes, or volunteer efforts. In ethical consumption, consumers may want to buy products made in distinctive ways. The public thus comprises another important audience; those people whose actions are critical to success. *Other NGOs*: NGOs often care about the opinion of other NGOs, who together constitute a community of credibility. While maintaining a distinct identity, NGOs often work together on campaigns for social change, and as such seek acceptance by others in the form of partnerships.

Strategies that NGOs use to demonstrate or enhance their credibility with these different audiences include: (1) adopting autonomous governance structures, (2) developing autonomy in revenue sources, (3) increasing transparency, (4) professionalizing, and (5) expending costly effort. With these criteria in mind, we can explore through cases the issues that arise in assessing an NGO's ability to monitor compliance with standards in a credible manner.

These criteria are likely to influence price in that they shape consumer confidence in the NGO's evaluation of the production processes that comprise the normative part of what consumers seek in a product. To the extent that consumers are willing to pay higher prices for ethically produced items, they will seek confirmation that the items before them have been produced in the desired manner. In the absence of clear governmental enforcement or private-sector conflicts of interest, NGOs provide information so that the consumer's confidence in the product, and hence the price paid, is mediated through consumer confidence. In so doing, the evaluation from an NGO influences production valuation.

GOVERNANCE STRUCTURES

We can compare NGOs by looking at how much distance from the target of the monitoring is provided by the governance structures. We see several elements that shape distance—the degree of "arm's length"—such as composition of the NGO's board and fees and funding sources.

If the target is represented on the board, that compromises the NGO's objectivity. An example of a highly credible NGO is Underwriters Laboratory (UL), which inspects equipment for safety. Created when the use of electricity spread, UL was funded by insurance companies seeking to lower costs from fire claims and thus had a strong incentive for accuracy. UL is now controlled by an association that has no members on it from the "targets" of inspection (the makers of the machines). Its funds come from fees paid by those seeking inspection. It does not have legal authority, though some states require a UL label for anything purchased with public money; UL has no obligation to pay dividends to investors.

If the target of monitoring pays, the NGO's credibility goes down because the organization cannot afford to alienate its funder. The bond rating agencies in the United States, for example, are paid by the firms that seek classification of their bonds. Firms want high ratings and the agencies want to be paid, so both pay a cost for a negative rating: the firm wishing to attract customers to buy the bond, and the rating agencies hoping to keep the firms as clients (see also Rona-Tas/Hiss in this volume). The credibility of such ratings should therefore be low. They are used nonetheless because many investment vehicles (such as pension funds) legally require them.

The organizational issue of board membership plays a central role in the controversy over the Fair Labor Association (FLA) and the Worker Rights Consortium (WRC). The FLA arose to measure compliance with labor standards in the supply chain after bad publicity hit Nike (Locke and Romis 2007; Locke et al. 2007). At first Nike tried self-certification, inspecting labor standards internally; these actions failed to reassure the consumer activists. Nike realized it needed external verification from an organization whose autonomy signaled credibility. It needed an NGO—an important point, since the monitoring plays a role on both sides, the monitors and the monitored. The FLA was formed with the active involvement of the US Department of Commerce and includes firms on its governing board. In so doing, it gets some benefits: financial contributions, information about practices at each firm, access to information, and openness to inspections. But the firm representatives have influence over the workings of the FLA. They can shape the criteria of fair labor, weakening the standard; they can get weak inspection rules adopted (no unannounced visits, for example), etc. These interventions compromise the FLA, making it vulnerable to charges of "greenwashing." Having corporate board members weakens its signal to the outside world about the commitment to its goals. By contrast, the WRC, an organization that arose out of university campus bookstores in the United States, has no "targets" or corporations on its board. It claims greater credibility thereby, not just for having tougher standards but because of the composition of its board.

The "multistakeholder concept" used by the FLA is important in the system of social accounting. The companies realized they needed "third-party involvement" because their internal evaluations lacked credibility. By involving the various parties in the disputes, the organizations get "buy-in," or engagement. These parties include: the protesters—in campus book stores and various NGOs focusing on rights, working conditions, and equality; the monitoring organizations, or "verifiers" (Elliott and Freeman 2003); and the companies themselves, who are needed to provide information, access, and a commitment to respond. The government is not formally involved, but it does participate in the development of labor standards. In the Clinton administration, Robert Reich succeeded in some of his efforts to bring Labor Department engagement into line with these standards and helped to develop the FLA. But government regulations remain weak, and firms have light labor standards, so much of the monitoring depends on work by NGOs (Piore and Schrank 2008).

Does the FLA system work—is it valid, does it eliminate bad practice? Is it reliable, does it consistently find the same results? The FLA is strongly critiqued by the WRC, which argues that the FLA is deeply compromised by the participation of industry groups on its board. This participation by firms drives the FLA to have low standards and poor monitoring, and that leads to "greenwashing"—providing the appearance of compliance with good labor practices but not the reality of doing so. The WRC works with local NGOs to empower workers to report labor rights violations in order to assist colleges and universities in enforcing their codes of conduct. The FLA seeks to accredit apparel brands as being in compliance with FLA standards by requiring that companies adopt monitoring programs (Worker Rights Consortium 2009).

The WRC does not issue a certification or seal of approval. Certification, WRC documents argue, is misleading. It allows companies to "pass" an inspection, then revert to bad practices, using the seal to give the impression of approval. Inspection must be ongoing. Complaint documentation and resolution must be a constant process. The university group members receive reports and thereby reach their own conclusions on whether their standards are being met.

The WRC develops its own standards, compliance, and structure. On the question of standards, the WRC details more explicitly its view of bad labor practices, such as wages (it insists on the "living wage" standard), and addresses more directly the issue of women's rights (protection of pregnant women). On the question of procedures, WRC says it responds more to workers' complaints and does not rely solely on checklists, which factories can more easily evade (Esbenshade 2004). Instead of issuing a certification to a company, the WRC examines factories. It has a Designated Suppliers Program, which involves inspection of each factory according to a variety of criteria. The consortium then requires that campus bookstores source only from these factories.

As far as its structure, the WRC does not have industry people on its board. This is a quite visible contrast with the FLA, and it is stressed in WRC documents. The FLA voting system allows its firm representatives to veto any discussion of standards or investigation. The complaint procedure of the WRC requires the involvement of workers and, unlike in the FLA, the workers are interviewed in situations that protect their opinions from being observed by managers. In the FLA process, complaints are given to the executive director of the FLA and to the firm to resolve within 45 days, after which the FLA director can appoint another monitor. The reports on factories and firms are not made public by the FLA, whereas the WRC supplies these to the campus members.

Board composition is a good indicator of NGO monitoring capacity. Having a target's agent on the board does not prove bias but it strongly suggests the possibility. This bias has the advantage of being easily observable, so that different NGO groups can be better compared. This is a good "low-cost" indicator of challenges to credibility. In such a case, we would want to know more about implementation: the processes of complaints, of inspection, of follow-up. We would have to know more about money: without firm involvement, for example, the WRC raises less money than the FLA.

The contrast between the FLA and the WRC provides insight into the "multistakeholder" concept. Conflict of interest remains a substantial concern even if contending parties are represented. Having all the players around the table certainly provides advantages of some kinds: parties are able to work out areas of dispute, common cause, common agreement. There can be greater information exchange and more dispute-resolution mechanisms. Excluding the industry representatives certainly would cause some damage to that element of the system.

Conversely, excluding the firms may be essential for the goal of credibility and for valid and reliable monitoring. Here, it is important to sort out the standard from the monitoring. The lower the standard, the easier it is to meet it, and the fewer will be the disputes about satisfactory observation. Monitoring may be reliable and valid to the standard agreed on, but this may not be valid for the goals of many consumers. So the discussion comes back to values of the "ethical consumer." The presence of industry people will certainly mean lowering standards and thereby lead to charges of greenwashing.

The FLA and WRC present the consumer with the dilemma of "rival ethical brands"—two labels which both claim to signal "better" labor standards in the products that consumers seek to buy. How is the consumer to know which is "best?" With competition, does the bad (weaker standard) drive out the good (stronger standard), or is it the reverse (Cohen and Sabel 2006; Fung et al. 2001)? Branding is costly, and so is compliance (Singer 1998). The price rises with stronger standards, and we are back to what consumers will pay (Hiscox and Smythe 2009). One of the costs for consumers is the search for information. There is no way of escaping this: concerned consumers must do at least some research. They have to read up on the standards and decide which suit their values.

A key insight of the attention in monitoring procedures governance to an organization's autonomy from the target is skepticism about the United Nations Global Compact. The Compact has attracted considerable interest because of its international character (Keck and Sikkink 1998; Seidman 2007; thereby addressing the problem of diverse rules and process) and because of corporate involvement in the process.

The behavior of first-world companies in poor countries generated controversy: the chemical pollution by Union Carbide in Bhopal, India; the price of AIDS drugs in poor countries; issues of pollution, labor standards, and human rights. To create a framework for managing these controversies, UN Secretary-General Kofi Annan authorized efforts to create a UN Global Compact, which was then proclaimed in 1999. The compact enunciates ten principles (Ruggie 2004) dealing with human rights, labor, the environment, and corruption. Corporations sign up for compliance with these standards, as do NGOs and labor groups. Committees have developed within countries to help articulate the issues involved. New statements have been issued on topics such as corporate governance.

Critics of the UN Global Compact point out that there is no monitoring of adherence to the standards. There is no certification of whether companies comply with any of them. Corporate participation is entirely voluntary. A group called Global Compact Critics calls the UN program "bluewashing," meets regularly, and issues reports with criticism of specific corporate behaviors (Kell 2005). Defenders argue that the compact helps promote a culture of responsibility, a set of norms that over time gather force by changing the terms of discussion. These may acquire strength through legal processes, entering the norms used by judges and lawyers.

FUNDING

Following the logic of the board composition, the farther the funding from the target of the monitoring, the greater the credibility of the NGO. NGOs try hard thereby to get money from foundations, from members, and from donations, so as to avoid being tainted by corporations. Many of them charge fees for services like inspections. These fees could be cause for concern. Fees appear to make the NGO autonomous from financial dependence, but the distinction between fees and profit may be blurry. When NGOs depend on fees for their livelihood, they may be reluctant to question the behavior of a firm when that may entail losing the fee. If fees in bond ratings distort objectivity in measurement, fees in labeling for social consumption may be no different.

Monitoring is expensive. Someone has to pay. If the firm is compromised by doing the monitoring internally and chooses to go outside, it has to contract for this outside monitoring. The agency doing the monitoring must receive some kind of compensation from the firm so that it can continue to operate, whether this comes in the form of donations or from a fee in exchange for the monitoring service. The question posed is whether it matters for credibility if the recipient of the fee is a profit-making firm or a nonprofit organization.

The suspicion of a profit motive is that in the interests of making money, the monitoring will be compromised. The fees can make the monitor so dependent on the target of evaluation that the monitor cannot really afford to "blow the whistle." Deloitte & Touche, for example, offers consultancy services for corporate governance and enterprise risk management, and also offers outsourcing, all of which raise issues of costs, and benefits, connected to ethical production issues. Could the actual monitoring Deloitte does have credibility? The profit motive can be compatible with credible monitoring if we can identify the countervailing force, the economic motive for the high standard, as with the fire insurance example in UL. And we have seen examples of the profit motive failing as a guarantor of monitoring: the Toyota recalls in the winter of 2010 are a strong example.

Social entrepreneurship is a growing movement. A number of firms advertise a commitment to "triple bottom line" standards—"people, planet, profit." These firms face many trade-offs among these goals, which may make it difficult for consumers to evaluate their behavior (Elkington 1994, 1997). Similarly, nonprofit companies can be vulnerable to conflicts of interest that would compromise their credibility. Such conflicts could occur if the nonprofit is very dependent on the income from the fees to assure its own survival. Since monitoring costs money, the funds for it have to come from fees or gifts or grants. Some monitoring NGOs get gifts or grants from foundations or individuals committed to the cause.

Several firms offer an opportunity to explore these issues. Verité, based in Amherst, Massachusetts, is one such firm (Hirt 2007). Like the regular audit/accounting companies, Verité charges a fee; the only difference is that the company does not have shareholders who demand a profit. Verité does not make its reports public, and its income is based on fees from groups who could defect if their audit were negative. Verité prides itself on working directly with companies and local NGO groups to conduct the many factory audits it has completed. In its 2008 program catalogue, Verité writes that the company is "an international non-profit consulting organization specializing in training, social auditing, and research." Verité does both auditing and consulting: it helps train firms to do auditing and to improve corporate practices, as well as audits them for compliance with goals. Revenue information can be found in its tax filings, not so easily on its website. Ms. Allison Devore, Verité's Director of Development, states, "we've diversified our funding to remain independent and objective as a nonprofit organization with a balanced revenue stream from individuals, government, foundations, and corporations, both as clients and as sponsors" (Baue 2004). In 2006, over 95% of the company's income came from fees. In 2007, Verité received the prestigious Skoll Foundation Award for Social Entrepreneurs and a three-year grant of $1,015,000 to "strengthen partnerships with NGOs in dozens of countries and train 1,500 practitioners to replicate its [Verité's] model by the end of 2009" (Skoll Foundation 2007), thereby producing a dramatic increase in the share of Verité's revenue from grants, gifts, and donations.

Verité published its fee schedule and receipts in its *Monitoring and Supplier Assessment Services Pricing* for 2007, which gives estimates for Verité services such as Risk Assessments, Social Compliance auditing, Remediation Check-ups, Re-audits, and Worker Interviewer Packages (Hirt 2007). In 2002, Verité was commissioned by the California Public Employees' Retirement System (CalPERS) to do a detailed study on labor issues in the Chinese information technology sector. The company evaluated country labor policy in 27 countries based on 42 standards of compliance. As a result, CalPERS withdrew its investments from four countries because of labor rights violations.

Another fees-based firm is AccountAbility. This organization rates companies on how well they have developed responsible practices: "The AccountAbility Rating is a tool for measuring the extent to which companies have built responsible practices into the way they do business." Firms are given a score on how well they comply. AccountAbility pays the costs of monitoring by charging a fee, and company compliance is voluntary. The companies may therefore refuse to renew the service if they get a bad score. AccountAbility includes in its rankings whether the firm has used AccountAbility for training purposes, which adds further to the conflict of interest concern about fees and ranking.

Another mechanism that seeks to evaluate firms is the Social Responsibility Investment Funds: mutual funds which pick stocks that comply with some social standard. These allow people "to do well by doing good." The dilemma for CSR investment funds is that they need to advertise a good rate of return. There is much debate about whether this can be done, and whether the funds actually do the sorting among firms that consumers seem to want (Chatterji et al. 2007; Hawken 2004).

All of these cases of fee-based monitoring raise questions about independence of the monitor. These NGOs are formally autonomous from the groups they are monitoring, but their fee structures make them dependent on business from their monitoring targets: the monitoring organizations have to attract clients and make them come back. For all of these NGOs, we should explore the costs to them of finding a firm in violation of a standard, how often violations are found, how public they are made, and what happens to the firm when the violations are made public.

TRANSPARENCY OF PROCESS

If governance and funding are important signals to consumers about the credibility of NGO evaluation of ethical production processes, so too is information about NGO processes. NGOs can signal a commitment to objectivity in making public the information about their processes: in finance, on fees, income, taxes, expenditures; in organization, on the composition of their boards and the backgrounds and selection mechanisms of their board members. This information allows observers to estimate the possible conflicts of interest inside the monitoring process. The transparency itself is a costly "bond" to the community that signifies an NGO's commitment to these shared values; not providing the information can signal a reluctance to be transparent and thus lower credibility.

Similarly, the NGO sends signals by being transparent in its processes, conveying full information about how it verifies and what it finds. The Fair Trade organizations have a strong reputation in the CSR consumer community. Yet on some dimensions they are not transparent: FLO-CERT does evaluations of coffee-producing cooperatives, but it does not communicate information about its analyses of the internal workings of the groups it evaluates. Giving out such information would, it says, violate confidentiality arrangements that are commitments made in return for cooperation—another indicator of the challenge of voluntary participation in this system. Government regulation could coerce compliance, but the voluntary nature of the NGO system cannot.

Other NGOs are not transparent in their finances: while some post their tax returns on websites, listing donors and expenditures, many do not. Some list their boards of directors and internal decision-making rules, while many do not. A few NGOs note cases where a company has not complied with standards, but most NGOs do not: if no deviations are noted, it could either mean the targets of monitoring are all perfect or that the organization is unwilling to cause tension in its network with "accusations."

This verification by "process" tracing resembles evaluations in the world of art. Originality in an artwork is sometimes verified by a detailed history of the creation and then subsequent ownership. In the social consumption field, the equivalent is "chain of custody" accounting, tracking the handoff to the next person in the chain with careful notation of each step. With fish, for example, an area of the ocean is first examined and then approved as a sustainable fishery. Then all fish taken from that area is passed along the value chain, through to retail, with each step carefully noted and recorded. In this way, any deviation from the standard can be traced (Aguirre 2005; Owens 2007). This is the same process used in the Toyota supply chain or by any other manufacturer working to identify and prevent defects, and is similar to insistence on place-of-origin accounting in monitoring French wine appellation certification.

The verification process has itself become part of the construction of value, so the consumer builds a connection to the process and internalizes a ritual of verification and investigation. Consumers identify with the NGOs, with the activists, with the culture of being a "vigilante," or a "verifier," and thus with the performative aspects of verification—people chaining themselves around trees, the Rainforest Action Network capturing the microphone at Home Depot. These examples show substantial engagement in activities, which become ways of affirming participants' identity as movement activists.

How are we to evaluate the organization when we find an "error"—that is, something in the monitoring process that proves to be incorrect? KIVA is well known in microfinance for raising money via the web among prosperous people in the first world to help poor people in developing countries with small loans that help them develop their business: a bottom-up bootstrap method. KIVA has recently been criticized for misleading its donors (McIntosh 2010). Like many NGOs, KIVA uses Person-to-Person (P2P) methods: it has donors pick from among posted portraits of individuals, families, or groups, so that the donors sense that their money goes to that specific target. The process turns out to be more complex: the funds go to an intermediate organization with substantial funds, whose credit rating is the one you see; if needed, this intermediary pays the loan to KIVA of the smaller NGO; the money given by the donor is not likely to go to the specific donor picked, and the loan may have already been made before you offer the money.

And yet it is not clear this sort of misinformation bothers donors. Some of the critics suggest that if the donors knew the money did not actually go to that specific person they would back off. Do the distortions undermine credibility?

Is it the fact of an inaccuracy—if this fact is wrong, all facts connected to KIVA can all be wrong? Or is it the specific fact: that the personalist connection is not correct, and since the personalist connection is so powerful in fundraising—it is common to many organizations—jarring that connection with this specific fact is certain to undermine the system as a whole?

KIVA continues to raise substantial funds. This may tell something important about the construction of credibility and valuation. People are not surprised by imperfection; they know that organizations and individuals have limitations. They have some kind of hierarchy of significance in their minds, some way of evaluating the trade-offs: good works against small errors. People have a narrative in their heads about their role in the world, about what they can do or not do to make things better. Many have a sense of altruism and wish to help people. They are more likely to help those in a community, to whom they feel a connection. The Web helps build that connection. They cannot know the people in the many countries, but they can feel they know them. They respond to story. But the response is not literal. They do not really know the specific target; they imagine meeting someone like that. The NGO solves the connection problem of altruism. It is playing proxy in establishing who is worthy and reliable. Donors trust the NGO to get the money to someone like the person in the picture. Does the donor care which specific person it is? So long as it somehow fits the narrative, the donor is satisfied, delegating the KIVA "agent" to find the people who fit the narrative requirements. So long as KIVA is actually helping people by getting the money to someone in need, the donor is not so concerned about details.

The stronger the attachment to values, the stronger the common interest, the more tolerance of "small" errors. Acknowledging these criticisms, KIVA has altered its website to show a more complex process of linking donors to recipients: a gesture to transparency.

PROFESSIONALISM OF STAFF AND PROCESS

Another way of evaluating the credibility of an NGO lies in examining its skills and procedures. Having people with formalized skills such as accounting and financial management at the NGO conveys using resources for certain kinds of quality. A similar commitment to expending costs for quality lies in producing quality reports, websites, communication, and participation in meetings. These activities provide a kind of information shorthand to donors who want information about the quality of NGO activity but have difficulty evaluating it more directly. In the development field, for example, local NGOs provide valuable services that the international agencies wish to support. In sorting out which NGOs seem credible recipients, these agencies look at indicators of professionalism: educational level of the NGO employees, the quality of the reports, thoroughness of data, financial tracking, participation of staff in meetings of other NGOs and comparable professions (Boulding 2012).

This kind of information is an indicator, a substitute for evaluation of actual activities.

Another interesting example comes with Islamic Relief. This charity based in London faces problems with intelligence officials in Western countries who fear it can be used as a conduit of funds to terrorist organizations. To signal assurance of its insulation from this, Islamic Relief is assiduous in its professionalism: participating in meetings with other NGOs, using formalized accounting, generating well-prepared reports, doing all the things that make it like other credible NGOs, all helping to build an image of an NGO like any other (Thaut et al. 2010).

COSTLY EFFORTS IN OTHER FIELDS

Organizations facing criticism for their behavior in one arena of activity may compensate by undertaking costly activity in another. Fairtrade organizations in Guatemala working under FLO Fairtrade certification, criticized for various procedural irregularities in their procedures, stress the contribution they make to building schools and other infrastructure for communities. Community development is certainly a valid goal, but is it what the purchasers of Fairtrade coffee think they are doing when they pay a premium?

This sort of exchange is a familiar strategy of corporate philanthropy: earn a great deal of money and build goodwill by building hospitals, donations to orphanages, and the like. Wal-Mart provides an interesting example of this strategy in the CSR field. A huge retailer, Wal-Mart may be the largest target among NGOs in the ethical consumption world. It has been in the crosshairs of advocates of many causes: sustainable development, labor conditions, environment, human rights. Wal-Mart has frustrated the NGOs because the company's customer base is relatively unresponsive to the accusations thrown at the firm. Many Wal-Mart customers are low income, far more concerned about price than other social values, and not able to afford the costs that often come with sustainable products. Activists have trouble getting traction against Wal-Mart through consumer boycotts using the focused strategy developed in other campaigns.

Instead, the NGOs collaborated to develop a specific anti-Wal-Mart campaign. It attacked the company in different ways on a range of issues—dozens of pinpricks, stuck in many places: zoning battles to stop new stores; studies on employee use of welfare because of low wages and benefits; lawsuits on sexism, discrimination, and labor abuses; reports; books; films. The many media stories on these issues drove up Wal-Mart's negatives in the image surveys. Communities stopped issuing licenses to build. Expansion stopped, and sales fell flat.

At first, Wal-Mart responded with the familiar "ring the wagons" strategy: fight, deny, attack. This worked for a long time, but by the early years of this decade, sales went flat, media treatment got quite negative, expansion was blocked by denial of permits, legislation got passed requiring worker benefits, and Wal-Mart switched strategies. In the early 2000s, CEO Lee Scott started to meet critics, invite discussion, seek alliances, open up information, and ask critics to serve on committees and work with the company. Wal-Mart undertook environmentally friendly activities: efficient light bulbs, less packaging material, energy-efficient trucks, sourcing of organic food from China. It developed a health plan for workers. It held lots of meetings and worked with reporters. The negative publicity went down, and Wal-Mart picked up less negative press. When the recession of 2008 made consumers more price-sensitive, the company was one of the few firms to sustain sales during the 2009–10 period. There is still substantial criticism from labor and other sources, but the atmosphere has changed (Baron and Barlow 2006; Conroy 2007; Fishman 2006; Lichtenstein 2006; Spotts and Greenwald 2005).

McDonald's has done something similar by going to a respectable NGO, Conservation International, to develop plans for sustainable sources of fish for its restaurant (Jost 2009). For the CSR community, the advantage of involving McDonald's and Wal-Mart is market power: if these giant companies compel suppliers to conform, the results are enormous, far more powerful than regulation is likely to produce. This "Purchasing Power Partnership Model" (PPP) has attracted substantial attention as a stakeholder model. It is difficult to evaluate the impact of the PPP model on outcomes, as there is little clear evaluation of how it is able to affect the supplier's behavior separate from the activities that the company might have undertaken anyway.

Wal-Mart represents the strategies by firms that can make CSR monitoring difficult. With many dimensions to CSR, firms can make progress in one domain while ignoring another. The public may not notice or may have a different hierarchy of values. The public may not pay careful attention to the "types" of progress but think in more general terms.

To sum up, monitoring by NGOs can be quite effective when the incentives are clear: when the costs are being paid by the consumer, not the producer, the criteria and processes are transparent, and the costs of being wrong are visible. Private firms can monitor effectively within their own production system under similar conditions, viz., Toyota. Private bonding breaks down when the incentives are clouded: viz., bond rating agencies, accounting firms, or brokerage houses.

Conclusion

The "consumers" of ethical consumption products face a challenge similar to people in other markets where the process of production is an important component of quality and therefore of price. They need help in determining whether the specific process meets their desiderata. NGOs offer to provide that kind of information, as "verifiers" monitoring the process and as "vigilantes" in publicizing bad behavior.

The ethical consumer must take signals from many sources and invest a lot of energy in seeing if these sources are credible (Eiperin 2010). Since consumers are likely to be very busy, and there are many products and many standards, they will have to economize in their search costs—and thus rely on brands. Branding by NGOs becomes central. Branding can be credible when the quality is observable, but it can be more difficult to discern this credibility when the quality cannot be observed—and nonobservability is the essence of ethical production processes.

The system of NGO monitoring arouses considerable debate. Specialists in labor rights are especially doubtful that such monitoring can be accurate or effective. Global competition presses the firms to squeeze their suppliers, and this in turn forces evasion of standards. Many of those who work in the labor issue area dismiss the NGO approach as a kind of neoliberal distraction away from the hard tasks of government regulation, enforcement, and inspection. On the other side are the many well-meaning activists in these organizations, who find power in the virtue of the goals and dedication of their activism and in the edifice they have constructed.

The skeptics give little market value to the verification systems based on NGOs. Even if they are interested in the goals of the specific NGO, they may not purchase products it verifies or certifies—or they may suspend their skepticism and do it anyway. In the case of the skeptic, the accuracy of the monitoring is only one element in the social determination of the market price.

Consumers who want the information NGOs provide can use a variety of indicators to assure themselves about accuracy of monitoring. They can look at the incentives for the NGO to be accurate. These include organizational features, the autonomy the organization has from the targets of the monitoring, funding sources that provide distance from the targets, professionalism among the staff and in the procedures, and transparency in processes and procedures.

From the perspective of the NGO community that is focused on CSR, the state is not reliable. Yet the NGOs operate in the shadow of the state. They rely on rules of the state. At the same time, states face limits on what they can do without the involvement of civil society (Culpepper 2003; Herrigel 2007; Levy 1999). It is not one or the other but how these all fit together. NGOs and firms need each other. The firm needs the NGO to sanction its behavior, to legitimate it, to verify compliance. The NGO needs the firm to sustain its activity, through money, cooperation, and visibility. Both organizations need the state to set rules and a structure of enforcement within which private activity can operate effectively.

Monitoring by NGOs, as well as by governments, relies on a long chain of trust (Cook et al. 2009; Levi and Stoker 2000). There will never be enough information to be sure about the efficacy of any kind of monitoring, be it by the government, by NGOs, or by any other third party. We are too busy to track down all the information sources and references. At some point, we have to rely on cheap information indicators, and therefore on some intermediary we trust. And so there are processes of trust formation that need to be integrated into the calculus of evaluating the costs and benefits of effective monitoring. In this regard, the ethical production/consumption system provides an important field for studying the social construction of markets. Prices and markets in ethical consumption are perhaps not quite as sharply different from those where there is "use" value. Many social influences shape the definition of use and what is acceptable, as they do for "ethical" use, and use may not be so easy to ascertain. Understanding price and value formation in the ethical consumption field requires breaking down a number of analytic barriers.

REFERENCES

Aguirre, T. (2005). *Sustainable Seafood and Corporate Social Responsibility*. IR/PS CSR Case 05-01. School of International Relations and Pacific Studies, UC San Diego. http://irps.ucsd.edu/assets/020/8414.pdf (accessed March 29, 2011).

Akerlof, G. (1970). The Market for "Lemons": Quality Uncertainty and the Market Mechanism. *Quarterly Journal of Economics* 84(3): 488–500.

Baron, D. (2006). *Wal-Mart: Nonmarket Pressure and Reputation Risk (A)*. Case No. P52A. Stanford University Case Studies.

Baue, William. (2004, December 2). Gap-Verité Collaboration Exemplifies Award-Winning Practice on Social Responsibility. Sustainability Investment News. http://www.socialfunds.com/news/article.cgi/1581.html (accessed March 29, 2011).

Bernstein, S. and Cashore, B. (2007). Can Non-state Global Governance Be Legitimate? An Analytical Framework. *Regulation & Governance* 1(4): 1–25.

Boulding, C. (forthcoming, 2012). Dilemmas of Information and Accountability: Foreign Aid Donors and Local Development. In P. Gourevitch, D. Lake, and J. G. Stein (eds.), *Beyond Virtue: Evaluating the Credibility of Non Governmental Organizations*. New York: Cambridge University Press.

Cashore, B., Auld, G., and Newsom, D. (2004). *Governing Through Markets: Forest Certification and the Emergence of Non-State Authority*. New Haven, CT: Yale University Press.

Chatterji, A. K., Levine, D. I., and Toffel, M. W. (2007). *How Well Do Social Ratings Actually Measure Social Responsibility?* Working Paper 33. Social Responsibility Initiative. Harvard University, John F. Kennedy School of Government.

Coase, R. P. (1937). The Nature of the Firm. *Economica* 4(16): 386–405.

——(1960). The Problem of Social Cost. *Journal of Law and Economics* 3: 1–44.

Cohen, J. and Sabel, C. F. (2006). Global Democracy? *NYU Journal of International Law and Politics* 37(4): 763–97.

Conroy, M. (2007). *Branded: How the Certification Revolution Is Transforming Global Corporations*. Gabriola Island: New Society Publishers.

Cook, K. S., Levi, M., and Hardin, R. (eds.) (2009). *Whom Can We Trust? How Groups, Networks, and Institutions Make Trust Possible*. New York: Russell Sage.

Culpepper, P. D. (2003). *Creating Cooperation: How States Develop Human Capital in Europe*. Ithaca, NY: Cornell University Press.

Daviron, B. and Ponte, S. (2005). *The Coffee Paradox: Global Markets, Commodity Trade and the Elusive Promise of Development*. London: Zed Books.

Eiperin, J. (2010, May 3). Environmental Certification Becoming Increasingly Crowded and Contested Field. *Washington Post*, 4.

Elkington, J. (1994). Towards the Sustainable Corporation: Win-Win-Win Business Strategies for Sustainable Development. *California Management Review* 36(2): 90–100.

—— (1997). *Cannibals with Forks: The Triple Bottom Line of 21st Century Business*. Oxford: Capstone.

Elliott, K. A. and Freeman, R. B. (2003). *Can Labor Standards Improve Under Globalization?* Washington, DC: Institute for International Economics.

Esbenshade, J. L. (2004). *Monitoring Sweatshops: Workers, Consumers, and the Global Apparel Industry*. Philadelphia, PA: Temple University Press.

Fishman, C. (2006). *The Wal-Mart Effect: How the World's Most Powerful Company Really Works—and How It's Transforming the American Economy*. New York, NY: Penguin.

Fung, A., O'Rourke, D., and Sabel, C. F. (2001). *Can We Put an End to Sweatshops?* Boston, MA: Beacon Press.

Garcia-Parpet, M.-F. (2009). *Le marché de l'excellence: les grands crus à l'épreuve de la mondialisation*. Paris: Editions du Seuil.

Gourevitch, P. and Lake, D. (forthcoming, 2012). Credible Ethical Action. In P. Gourevitch, D. Lake, and J. G. Stein (eds.), *Beyond Virtue: Evaluating the Credibility of Non Governmental Organizations*. New York: Cambridge University Press.

Hawken, P. (2004). *Socially Responsible Investing*. Sausalito, CA: Natural Capital Institute. http://www.naturalcapital.org/docs/SRI%20Report%2010-04_word.pdf (accessed August 5, 2009)

Henderson, D. (2001). *Misguided Virtue: False Notions of Corporate Social Responsibility*. London: Institute of Economic Affairs.

Henrich, J., Boyd, R., Bowles, S., Camerer, C., Fehr, E., and Gintis, H. (eds.) (2004). *Foundations of Human Sociality: Economic Experiments and Ethnographic Evidence from Fifteen Small-Scale Societies*. New York, NY: Oxford University Press.

Herrigel, G. (2007). Corporate Governance: History Without Historians. In G. Jones and J. Zeitlin (eds.), *Handbook of Business History*. Oxford: Oxford University Press.

Hirt, D. (2007). *Verité: Auditing Labor Standards*. IR/PS CSR Case #07-17. School of International Relations and Pacific Studies, UC San Diego. http://irps.ucsd.edu/assets/021/8425.pdf (accessed March 29, 2011)

Hiscox, M. J. and Smythe, N. F. B. (2009). *Is There Consumer Demand for Improved Labor Standards? Evidence from Field Experiments in Social Product Labeling*. Department of Government, Harvard University. http://www.people.fas.harvard.edu/~hiscox/SocialLabeling.pdf (accessed August 2, 2010).

Jaffee, D. (2007). *Brewing Justice: Fair Trade Coffee, Sustainability, and Survival*. Berkeley, CA: University of California Press.

Jost, L. (2009). *Conservation International and the Credibility of the Purchase Power Partnership Model*. IR/PS CSR Case #09-01. School of International Relations and Pacific Studies, UC San Diego. http://irps.ucsd.edu/assets/033/10581.pdf (accessed March 29, 2011)

Karpik, L. (2007). *L'économie des singularités*. Paris: Gallimard.

—— (2000). Le Guide rouge Michelin. *Sociologie du travail* 42: 369–90.

Keck, M. E. and Sikkink, K. (1998). *Activists Beyond Borders: Advocacy Networks in International Politics*. Ithaca, NY: Cornell University Press.

Kell, G. (2005). The Global Compact: Selected Experiences and Reflection. *Journal of Business Ethics* 59: 69–79.

Levi, M. and Linton, A. (2003). Fair Trade: A Cup At A Time? *Politics & Society* 31(3): 407–32.

——and Stoker, L. (2000). Political Trust and Trustworthiness. *Annual Review of Political Science* 3: 475–507.

Levy, J. (1999). *Tocqueville's Revenge: State, Society, and Economy in Contemporary France*. Cambridge, MA: Harvard University Press.

Lichtenstein, N. (ed.) (2006). *Wal-Mart: The Face of Twenty-First-Century Capitalism*. New York, NY: New Press.

Locke, R. and Romis, M. (2007). Improving Work Conditions in a Global Supply Chain. *MIT Sloan Management Review* 48(2): 54–62.

——, Qin, F., and Brause, A. (2007). Does Monitoring Improve Labor Standards? Lessons from Nike. *Industrial and Labor Relations Review* 61(1): 3–31.

Lupia, A. and McCubbins, M. (1998). *The Democratic Dilemma: Can Citizens Learn What They Need To Know?* New York, NY: Cambridge University Press.

McIntosh, C. (forthcoming, 2012). Monitoring Repayment in Online Peer-to-Peer Lending. In P. Gourevitch, D. Lake, and J. G. Stein (eds.), *Beyond Virtue: Evaluating the Credibility of Non Governmental Oraganizations*. New York: Cambridge University Press.

Murray, D., Raynolds, L. T., and Taylor, P. L. (2003). *One Cup at a Time: Poverty Alleviation and Fair Trade Coffee in Latin America*. Fair Trade Research Group, Colorado State University. http://www.colostate.edu/dept/Sociology/FairTradeResearchGroup/doc/fairtrade.pdf (accessed August 2, 2010)

Owens, M. C. (2007). *Sustainable Seafood Labeling: An Analysis of the Marine Stewardship Council*. IR/PS CSR Case # 07-02. School of International Relations and Pacific Studies, UC San Diego. http://irps.ucsd.edu/assets/021/8419.pdf (accessed March 29, 2011).

Piore, M. and Schrank, M. J. (2008). Toward Managed Flexibility: The Revival of Labour Inspection in the Latin World. *International Labor Review* 147(1): 1–23.

Popkin, S. (1991). *The Reasoning Voter*. Chicago, IL: University of Chicago Press.

Ruggie, J. (2004). Reconstituting the Global Public Domain: Issues, Actors, and Practices. *European Journal of International Relations* 10(4): 499–531.

Seidman, G. (2007). *Beyond the Boycott: Labor Rights, Human Rights, and Transnational Activism*. New York, NY: Russell Sage Foundation Press.

Singer, P. (1998). *Ethics into Action: Henry Spira and the Animal Rights Movement*. Lanham, MD: Roman and Littlefield.

Skoll Foundation. (2007, March 14). *Ten Innovative Social Entrepreneurs Receive Million-Dollar Awards from the Skoll Foundation*. Press release. http://www.skollfoundation.org/ten-innovative-social-entrepreneurs-receive-million-dollar-awards-from-the-skoll-foundation (accessed March 31, 2011)

Spotts, G. and Greenwald, R. (2005). *Wal-Mart: The High Cost of Low Price*. New York, NY: Disinformation Company.

Thaut, L., Barnett, M., and Stein, J. G. (forthcoming, 2012). In Defense of Virtue: Credibility, Legitimacy Dilemmas, and the Case of Islamic Relief. In P. Gourevitch, D. Lake, and J. G. Stein (eds.), *Beyond Virtue: Evaluating the Credibility of Non Governmental Organizations*. New York: Cambridge University Press.

Vogel, D. (2005). *The Market for Virtue*. Washington: The Brookings Institution Press.

Worker Rights Consortium (2006/2009). *The Designated Suppliers Program*. http://www.workersrights.org/dsp/ (accessed March 29, 2011)

5 The Transcending Power of Goods: Imaginative Value in the Economy

Jens Beckert*

What do we value? All market exchange involves a sacrifice of scarce assets, usually money. An actor is only willing to make this sacrifice if he attributes value to the good he receives in return. If the exchange is voluntary, its occurrence presupposes that the buyer has a desire for the good he is purchasing, a desire that prevails over the money he must pay in exchange for it. For economies to grow, producers must attract customers to the products they offer.

Large parts of the world are underdeveloped, and people in these places cannot satisfy even their most basic needs. In affluent countries, by contrast, purchasing power is high, and most people have satisfied their basic needs. One hundred years ago, households in OECD countries spent 80% of their incomes on the basic needs of food, clothing, and housing. This figure has dropped to 30–40% today (Adolf and Stehr 2010: 3). In this situation of affluence, we must wonder why there is no saturation of markets, and why people continue to purchase ever more goods, instead of saving their money or working less. "Consumers do not automatically use surplus income to satisfy new wants" (Campbell 1987: 18). In advanced capitalist economies, market saturation and decline of demand are constant threats to markets (Fligstein 2001: 17). But how do we understand why actors desire the things whose value they reveal in the purchase? What is it that goods must promise so that actors form preferences for owning them and are willing to make sacrifices to obtain them?

In this chapter, I address the question of what attracts customers to the goods they purchase. In the first part of the chapter, I introduce a distinction between three sources of value. First, goods can be valued for the difference they make in the physical world. Second, they can be valued for the differences they make in the social world when they position actors in the social space. Third and finally, they can make a difference in the consciousness of the

---

* For helpful comments on earlier versions of this chapter I would like to thank Patrik Aspers, Christoph Deutschmann, Edward Fischer, Chris Hann, Kai-Uwe Hellmann, Jörg Rössel, Wolfgang Streeck, and the members of my research group at the Max Planck Institute for the Study of Societies.

individual who owns or consumes them, in the form of the fantasies that they evoke, and hence make a difference in the imaginative world. I designate these three respective types of value as physical, positional, and imaginative. Positional and imaginative value form the central concern of this chapter. They are the most critical to understanding the creation of value in affluent consumer economies, because positional and imaginative value have much higher potential for growth than goods valued only for their physical performance (Reisch 2002: 227; Hutter in this volume). They also provide a foundation to explain why demand grows despite affluence.

While the creation of positional and imaginative value is in principle limitless, at the same time this value rests on shaky ground, since it is entirely anchored in the intersubjective recognition of symbolic qualities attached to the goods. Success "goes together with quick failure, as when the space for dreams associated with a particular brand no longer resonates with the symbolic needs of a large enough group of customers" (Djelic and Ainamo 1999: 628). This holds true not only for consumer markets but also for financial markets and real estate markets, as can be seen from the dot-com crash in 2000 and the sudden devaluation of derivatives, sovereign debt, and housing prices in the crisis that started in 2007.

In the second part, I discuss the positional and imaginative sources of value with special reference to the work of Emile Durkheim. Durkheim has dealt with issues of value and price in the economy in his early work on the division of labor (1984) and the posthumously published lectures *Professional Ethics and Civic Morals* (1992).[1] The most informative concepts to address the question of valuation of goods, however, come from his *The Elementary Forms of the Religious Life* (1965), even though this book does not deal with the valuation of economic goods.[2] The suggestion made here is that this book can be read not just as a sociology of religion but also as a sociology of valuation. I therefore follow approaches that connect market phenomena and religion (Deutschmann 2009a; Isenberg and Sellmann 2000). Based on Durkheim, I argue that value emerges from the symbolic connections made between goods and the socially rooted values, as well as the aesthetic ideals held by the purchaser. By arguing that the imaginative value of goods is closely linked to social values, I suggest that the valuation of goods is poorly understood if it is seen as the expression of a hedonistic individualism. Instead, valuation is in many ways connected to the social and moral order of society (Fischer and Benson 2006; Richins 1994; Stehr et al. 2006); it expresses, reinforces, or challenges this order, and is anchored in social practices.

In the third part, I build upon Durkheim's analysis of totemistic religions to explore how the connection between material objects and values is created and

---

[1] See also Beckert (2002).
[2] There are some marginal remarks to be found in the book that relate vaguely to the economy, but they receive no systematic treatment.

maintained. The final part of the chapter discusses the issue of change in the symbolic valuation of objects, a phenomenon not observed in the sacred objects of religion. The conclusion discusses the implications of the argument for investigating the valuation of goods on markets.

The Performance of Goods: Physical, Positional, and Imaginative

The objects exchanged on markets are commodities. Commodities can be goods or services.[3] A good, to use a definition by George Shackle, is "an object or an organization which *promises* performance" (1972: 178). For the good to have value, its purchaser must have a positive view of what he expects the good to perform: the good "makes a difference" for the owner through its (potential) performance. Goods comprise different types of value at the same time. This does not refer to differences such as the difference between a table and a chair but rather means that goods provide different types of performance for their owners. The distinction proposed in this chapter is that the quality of a good can make a difference in the physical world, the social world, or the imaginative world. Accordingly, I speak of the physical, positional, and imaginative value of goods. Note that this is not an essentialist distinction between goods, but between the sources of value that goods have; two or all three types can be—and often are—simultaneously present in any concrete good.

1. Qualities of goods that make a difference in the physical world alter a physical state in one way or another. A shirt covers a part of the body and keeps it warm. A car has value because it can bring the owner from place A to place B. A house provides shelter from the weather. A machine allows one object to be transformed into another object which can be sold on the market for a profit. The list of examples of how objects make a difference in the physical world can be extended indefinitely. It can also be expanded to take into account differences in quality within one category, in order to distinguish goods of the same type. A car can be faster, safer, or more comfortable than another car; a shirt can be warmer or more durable; one machine is more cost-efficient or time-effective than another. All of these are differences of a good with regard to its performance in the physical world. In the literature, the physical performance of goods is often referred to as "functional value" (Valtin 2005) or "utilitarian value" (Richins 1994), terms that are misplaced if they imply that objects can be valued without

---

[3] In this chapter, I focus only on goods. This focus is chosen for reasons of simplicity. All arguments made here, however, are also applicable to services.

being functional, or that the function of goods is limited to their physical performance. This is not the case.

While the *physical performance* of a good is objective, in the sense that it is a quality of the object itself, the valuation of a good's physical qualities depends on the user's cognitive understanding (Witt 2001: 27). Only by knowing the "how-to" of using the good can value be ascribed to it. The knowledge required for the physical performance of a good implies that this type of performance cannot be distinguished from the other types of object performance based on the concept of meaning. The qualities are valued based on the knowledge of the potential purchaser, and differences in valuation can stem from the different meanings the recognized qualities of the object may have for different actors.[4] There is no value without knowledge, and value differs between actors with different knowledge—a point famously analyzed by George Akerlof (1970).[5]

2. The investigation of *positional performance* in sociological scholarship has been just as important as that of physical performance, if not more so. Here, the value assigned to the product does not depend on its assessed (promised) transformative power in the physical world but on its capability to position its owner within the space of a differentiated social world: Products routinely co-occur with certain types of people and social occasions, thereby allowing the members of a given society to infer, albeit often unconsciously, the positions and memberships of others (see Ravasi, Rindova, and Stigliani in this volume).

The positional performance of goods requires that there is agreement on their meaning within the relevant group (Miller 1998; Reisch 2002: 232; Witt 2010). Although there can be variation in the way an object is interpreted, a complete lack of agreement would make it impossible to use the object as a signifier of social status and social belonging. So positional value does have an objective basis, but this objectivity is not anchored in the physical qualities of the product; instead, it depends upon

---

[4] This is well known from the observation made in innovation studies that at times the innovators of a new product themselves do not understand the possible physical performances of their innovation. A familiar example of this is the Post-it notes that were invented by the 3M company (Garud and Karnoe 2001). The company happened to invent a "glue that did not glue" that was worthless to anyone until someone had the idea that this glue could be used for the sticky notes that today are used by millions of people.

[5] Akerlof's analysis, however, implies that the problem is one of distribution of knowledge and not of the social constitution of qualities. Following Akerlof, once the qualities of goods are known to everyone, there is an objective basis for judging one good and comparing it to all others. This individualistic assessment fails to take into account that the criteria used to evaluate product qualities are based on social conventions, that is, that judgments of quality are socially constructed. These devices might be objective in the assessment of physical qualities which can easily be measured (such as the different chemical compositions of oil), but the object might be so complex that qualities could not be objectively established, or the qualities might be aesthetic. In this case, qualities are not only measured through judgment devices but established by them. We can see this at work when critics' ratings of a wine (e.g., Parker) influence how consumers assess its quality.

what meaning, in terms of social identity, is ascribed to the product in the actor's social environment.[6]

The positional value of goods has been meticulously described in sociological and anthropological accounts, especially by Thorstein Veblen (1973), Georg Simmel (1919), and Pierre Bourdieu (1984). The early sociology of consumption emphasized the hierarchical stratification that occurs through possession and exhibition of luxury goods, the social dynamics that develop out of attempts by lower social classes to imitate the consumption patterns of the upper classes, and the reactions to these imitations by the upper classes. More recent accounts of the social performance of goods place less stress on the element of status and class differentiation and focus more on the multilateral constitution of heterogeneous lifestyles based on different consumption patterns (Arnould and Thompson 2005). Differentiated lifestyles, which find expression in specific consumption patterns, constitute and express parts of the social identities of actors. Consumers construct a wide range of narratives of identity associated with certain kinds of products offered in the market, a process that can be interpreted as democratization of symbolic value creation (Djelic and Ainamo 2005: 8).

3. The *imaginative performance* of goods has in common with positional performance that the goods are valued for symbolic qualities; in both cases, the value of the good is based on ascribing qualities to it that transcend its materiality. "People buy things not only for what they can do, but also for what they mean" (Levy 1959: 118). Meaning is not detached from the materiality of the product, since material qualities can themselves acquire symbolic meanings.

The common feature of symbolic qualities explains why the positional and imaginative qualities of goods are frequently treated as one category (Levy 1959). However, this intermingling ignores important differences in the way the symbolic comes into play. Imaginative qualities make a difference—and are valued—because they arouse images that alter the state of consciousness of the owner. The objects evoke fantasies based on symbolic associations with desired events, people, places, or values (Campbell 1987; d'Astous and Deschênes 2005; Holbrook and Hirschman 1982; McCracken 1988: 104ff.; Ullrich 2006: 45ff.). The good performs as an arbitrator or bridge between the subject and a desired but intangible ideal. Part of the value of a good derives from the way it affects the mind. This can take place independently from the recognition of the ascribed value by others, but not independently from the assessments of the purchaser. Imaginative performance comes into play when the owner sees the good as a "connection" to espoused ideals symbolically represented in the object.

---

[6] As Durkheim (1965: 261) remarked with regard to totemistic emblems: the value "assumed by an object is not implied in the intrinsic properties of this latter: it is added to them." See also Marshall (2010: 64).

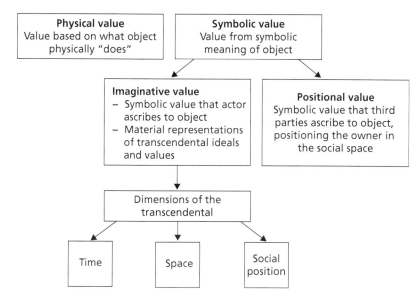

Figure 5.1 Typology of value

The distinction between positional and imaginative value partly follows the distinction between forms of symbolic consumption introduced by Marsha Richins (1994). *Positional performance* of a good is public, in the sense that a third party must attribute symbolic meaning to the good, which forms the basis to classify the owner by bestowing a certain social identity upon him. This happens independently from the owner himself. The owner might be aware of the positional effects of his purchasing choices and take them into consideration, but the positional effects depend on the meanings ascribed to the good *by others*. In the case of *imaginative value*, it is the purchaser himself who must ascribe symbolic meaning to a good. This is a private act, though the symbolic meanings reflect moral values and orientations that are socially constituted (Fischer and Benson 2006; Richins 1994). Hence the social positioning of the owner by others, via the possession of objects, is not identical to the "bridging of displaced meaning" (McCracken 1988: 104) through the imaginative performance of goods.[7] The distinctions between the three types of value are depicted in Figure 5.1.

---

[7] An example to help clarify the difference can be taken from gambling. The possession of a lottery ticket does not lead to a social repositioning. For the owner of the ticket, however, it can be a bridge that allows him to imaginatively transform his social position.

The Totemistic Qualities of Goods

By what mechanisms do actors become attracted to the qualities of goods, if not by the physical performance of these goods? To address this question, I refer to Emile Durkheim's study on *The Elementary Forms of the Religious Life* (1965). I argue that this work can be read as a sociology of valuation. The aim is to understand the attraction to goods not as a simply hedonistic urge that has its psychological cause "in a desire for the pleasure which it brings" (Campbell 1987: 80), but rather to interpret it as a specific form of orientation toward the realization of values shared in social groups and as confirmation of membership in a moral community. This follows Durkheim's intuition that secularization does not imply the extinction of the sacred in society but goes hand in hand with the emergence of secular forms of the sacred. While Durkheim demonstrated this social transformation primarily with regard to the expansion of rights granted to the individual (Joas 2000), I am arguing here that it also provides a model to analyze the valuation of goods in the economy (see also Belk et al. 1989).

In his treatment of totemistic religions in Australia, Durkheim deals with the role of religious practices in the social integration of these societies. The central insight Durkheim arrives at is that the moral influence of society over its members is not primarily based on felt obligations and fears of sanctions but instead on a positive binding of the members of the clan to the values of the social group. People feel *attracted* to the religious regulations (Durkheim 1965: 240ff.). The notion of attraction is crucial for analogies to economic valuation, because if exchange is voluntary, demand for goods only emerges if the goods have a positive appeal, that is, they provoke in others a desire to own them.

Based on this insight, Durkheim questions where this attraction to the values of society originates. He investigates the ritualistic practices of the Australian clans and the role of sacred objects in these practices, starting from the observation that the world of tribal society is strictly divided into two spheres, the sacred and the profane. Objects that symbolically represent the clan—usually an animal and its representation in artifacts (the totem)—are separated from other objects through a strict set of rules on how to engage with them. These regulations are associated with the belief in the power—or *mana*—of these objects. This power of the totem is of course not inherent in the object itself but attributed to it by the believers. Durkheim, however, insists that the power deriving from the sacred objects and felt by the clan members is not purely illusory but can in fact be analyzed as the power of the moral community of the clan (1965: 236). The symbolic qualities of sacred objects are "imaginative bridges to the transcendental" (Tappenbeck 1999: 50), in which the moral community finds a collective representation.

In his analysis of symbolic representation, Durkheim identifies a specific human capacity at the core of religious beliefs. I will argue that this capacity also lies at the heart of attributing symbolic value to goods in the economy:

namely, the faculty to attribute to objects qualities that exist only in the imagination and have no objective material correlate in the object itself. "[C]ollective representations very frequently attribute to the things to which they are attached qualities which do not exist under any form or to any degree" (Durkheim 1965: 259ff.). The quality is *symbolically* represented in the object, "yet the powers which are thus conferred, though purely ideal, act as though they were real; they determine the conduct of men with the same degree of necessity as physical forces" (1965: 260). In this sense, the specific quality attributed to the object is fictitious and real at the same time. The fictitiousness of meanings does not imply that they are arbitrary, but neither are they determined by the objects themselves nor by the neurological structures of the brain. Instead, they emerge from the cultural and social context of the actors.

One implication of these collective symbolic representations in objects is the possibility of *positional value* of goods. The capacity of goods to *position* their owners in the social space runs parallel to Durkheim's analysis of the (mysterious) power of the totem: actors experience that the association with specific objects constitutes a specific recognition of the person. Goods bestow identities and signal membership in a social group in the same way that the totem constitutes the identity of the clan member. Consequently, a change in consumption patterns also leads to a change in social identity. The categorization (classification) of a person follows the classification of the objects he consumes. In this way, the objects exercise power over the individual.[8] If the (potential) owner desires the social identity associated with the good, the good has an attraction that is independent from its physical performance and that is based on symbolic meanings.

The positional performance of goods is one important source of symbolic value. Yet it is not convincing to attribute the desire for a good that goes beyond the attraction of its physical qualities to *only* its status and identity effects. A second implication of the collective symbolic representations in objects is the possibility of *imaginative value*. The same way the totem is the symbolic representation of the moral rules (values) of the clan, goods can become symbolic representations of secular values of the moral community. Durkheim (1965: 251) brings up the example of the flag as a material representation of the nation that is respected (valued) as a symbol standing for the values of the nation. The flag is a sacred object, representing the moral community and at the same time "being" this community. This is why, as Durkheim observes, soldiers in war will risk their very lives to defend their

---

[8] This is not to say that identities are completely created and maintained through consumption patterns, but all social groups make some demands on their members with regard to their consumption patterns, and deviation from group norms is sanctioned. Groups differ widely with regard to their tolerance for deviations, however, and group membership in most cases involves other elements in addition to consumption patterns.

flag—a flag which matter-of-factly is no more than a piece of fabric that can be replaced cheaply (1965: 251ff.).[9]

The analogy Durkheim makes between religious phenomena and military or political action can be extended to the valuation of material goods exchanged on markets, provided we show that the sacred can also be symbolically represented in commodities and can serve as a "bridge" to the transcendental.[10] To develop this point, which extends Durkheim's sociology of religion to a sociology of valuation, I will start with a quote from a book by an expert on wine who reports on his experience when drinking a bottle of very old wine:

> The oldest red wine I have drunk was an 1811 Chambertin. Imagine what this evokes: you're at the height of the Napoleonic era, this becomes a heavy symbol, and moreover, it's the year of Halley's Comet, which isn't even yet called Halley's Comet. To have a comet in your cup, that's straight from the history books!
> (Audouze 2004, quoted in Garcia-Parpet in this volume)

The value of the bottle of wine consumed—the price must have been several thousand euros—stems from the year it was produced, which for the person making this statement symbolically represents two important historic events. It is not just the rarity of the wine and certainly not its taste which makes it valuable but the possibility of an imagined association with events that took place long ago. The wine has the evocative force of connecting the person who consumes it to a distant time and to the events that were going on then. Because of their extraordinary character, the events—Napoleon's power over Europe and the passing of Halley's Comet—have the aura of the sacred. The same way the totem stands for the moral community of the clan and the flag stands for the nation, the bottle of wine symbolizes a cherished historical event and is a means to associate the purchaser with this event. The object gives a material shape to a transcendental meaning by embodying this meaning. This connection presupposes the imaginative, because the object and its meaning are discontinuous: their unity exists only as a mental construction (see Tappenbeck 1999: 104).

Objects can be inscribed with meanings that conjure up mental images. In the case of religious symbols, these meanings remind the believer of the force of the community, while in the case of the consumer, they allow for an association with intangible ideals. The symbolic meaning transforms the object into an arbitrator, arousing mental sensations in the owner of the object that connect him to these ideals. This magical power of objects is a source of value because it provides the experience of pleasurable or even intoxicating

---

[9] These phenomena of secular but sacred entities have also informed later discussions of civil religion (Bellah 1967; Luckmann 1967).

[10] See also Belk et al. (1989). Durkheim himself pointed to the fact that collective representations can "out of the commonest object...make a most powerful sacred object" (1965: 260). Yet he did not apply his insights from the analysis of totemistic belief systems to the economy. This is striking, because Durkheim showed in his earlier work an intense interest in matters of valuation and price formation in the economy (Beckert 2002: 98ff.).

sensations.[11] But this is not an individual process. Durkheim emphasizes that the attraction to the ideals symbolically represented in the objects emerges from the community; the imaginative attributes of an object only have "power" to the extent that their perception is shared among members of a social group (Durkheim 1965: 238). Thus, the imaginative value of goods, though individually experienced, is a social phenomenon.

Our taste for luxuries, for goods beyond our conventional buying power, is not simply greed, not only self-indulgence. It is also attributable to our need, as groups and as individuals, to reestablish access to the ideals we have displaced to distant locations in time or space (McCracken 1988: 116).

Three Dimensions of the Transcendental

We can find unlimited instances where economic value is constituted based on symbolic associations and the images these symbols arouse. Analytically, the transcendent power of goods can be ordered along three dimensions: the *time dimension*, associating the owner of the good with a distant past or a desired future state; the *space dimension*, connecting the owner of the good to (momentarily) unreachable desired places; and the *social dimension*, linking the owner of the good to people and social positions that are desired but factually out of reach. All three dimensions have in common that they transcend the "here and now" and allow the owner of the good to associate himself with intangible values or aesthetic ideals.

1. Examples of transcendence in the time dimension are the purchase of old wine and, more generally, the purchase of antique objects. The ownership of the objects allows a symbolic connection to the cultural or political values of specific periods or historic people. Investments, on the other hand, as objects bought in the present with an imagined future value, extend the grasp of time into a period that has not yet arrived and extend the role of imaginative value from the demand side of the market into the supply side. The production of goods for the market evokes images of profit. But an orientation toward the future can also be related to the demand side. One example is Viviana Zelizer's analysis (1979) of the emergence of the life-insurance industry in the United States in the nineteenth century. Zelizer showed that life insurance found demand—became

---

[11] The mystical and quasi-religious appearance of commodities is also an important part of Marx's analysis of commodity fetishism (Marx 1977). However, Marx attributes the exchange-value of commodities to the employment of labor power in the production process, and he defines as fetishism the actors' perception of the exchange of goods as a relationship between goods, rather than a relationship between the actors themselves. In the analysis developed here, the mystical character of goods is located in the attribution of symbolic value. Hence, value is understood not from the side of the production process but from the perspective of market exchange.

valuable to consumers—only once it was conceived as representing espoused values of caring for the family. The value of the good emerged from the imagining of social recognition after death.

2. The *space dimension* of the imaginative value of goods is represented by products marketed based on their regional origin and traditional production methods. These products are valued because they carry meanings of place, which evoke in the consumer images of proximity and of partaking in this desired local environment. Examples are products with an AOC label (or another label of distinct regional production), which associates the products with images of locality. Fair trade products connect purchasers to an otherwise geographically and socially distant world and allow them to imagine "doing good" for people in a specific country. The value created lies not in the physical qualities of the product but in the opportunity it offers the consumer to put value convictions into practice. The same way that symbolically charged products allow for transcendence of time, they also allow for transcendence of place, and thereby connect their owners to the ideals they associate with that particular location.

3. The *social dimension* of the transcendent power of goods partly shows in the "contact charisma" that objects can attain. An accessory like a handbag, if carried by an idealized celebrity like Madonna, becomes "infected" through this contact. Owning the same handbag creates images of proximity to the idealized person and becomes a way of partaking in her identity. The aura of the singer is transferred to the purchaser of the handbag and becomes a quality that creates value in its own right.[12] The parallel to a religious phenomenon is obvious: in the same way that everything touched by the prophet becomes part of the sphere of the sacred (Durkheim 1965: 254), the handbag, touched and carried by the idealized charismatic person, becomes a symbolic representation of the charismatic power of this person; the object becomes a second-class relic.

The social dimension of the transcendent power of goods, however, does not require that the object come into direct contact with a charismatic person. Djelic and Ainamo (2005: 39) provide an example of this in Charles Frederick Worth, a pioneer of women's haute couture in the nineteenth century, who made deliberate references in his fashions to "aristocratic ways of life." Through these references, he created symbolic representations of lifestyles of the upper class that allowed his customers an imaginative link to this social group.[13] The imaginative transformation of social class can also be based on an imagining of future wealth. Lottery tickets, which contain the remote possibility of a radical transformation of social position, conjure up fantasies of being part of the world of the rich. The tickets are

---

[12] See also Durkheim (1965: 243ff.).
[13] The values that actors aspire to are socially differentiated; they need not be identical for everyone (Bourdieu 1984).

not valued as a prudent investment but rather for their ability to summon these imaginings (Beckert and Lutter 2007, 2009). In the harsh light of day, such a ticket is no more than a colorful piece of paper, worth not more than half of what has been spent for it, but it can provoke sensations that allow its purchaser vicarious participation in the world of the rich. Speculative investments in financial products are likewise motivated by images of a changed social position through future profits and wealth (Buchanan and Vanberg 1984; Keynes 1964). Joseph Schumpeter (1912) puts images of immortality at the root of entrepreneurial activity when he ascribes the motivation of the entrepreneur to a desire to found one's own dynasty.[14]

Goods can be attractive because of their ability to summon images based upon what the goods symbolize in the three dimensions discussed; their value goes beyond their physical and positional performance. "[M]any of the cultural products offered for sale in modern societies are in fact consumed because they serve as aids to the construction of day-dreams" (Campbell 1987: 92). As is the case with the positional performance of goods, imaginative performance has a magical quality to it: it offers access to past historical events, distant regions, espoused aesthetic or moral values, or unreachable social positions by making the object a symbolic representation of the otherwise intangible. On the strength of the mental images they arouse, goods can be vehicles to transcend time as well as physical and social space, allowing actors to participate vicariously in otherwise unreachable realms.[15]

This value of the good is *not purely illusory*. Indeed, when goods become material representations of otherwise abstract or distant events, values, and ideals, they offer a mental realization of the desired. The symbolically charged good evokes sensations that virtually embody the realization of the desired state. Drinking the Chambertin from 1811 evokes the sensation of actually being part of this time. Holding a lottery ticket in the hand allows the gambler to summon fantasies of being rich, which transforms the situation of being rich into an accessible state in the present. In this sense, the symbolically charged object is not only a representation of the desired event, value or ideal but also an essential part of what it represents by participating in the reality that it represents (cf. Tillich 1986: 5).[16] Schumpeter (1912: 164) observes that from the moment the entrepreneur begins to seriously realize a new combination, its existence becomes perceptible in a very real sense. If a desired state

---

[14] Images of future monetary wealth, evoked by lottery tickets, investments in financial markets, or entrepreneurial activities, are symbolic associations with infinite wealth and thereby provide parallels to religious rituals aiming at closeness to God (Deutschmann 1999).

[15] A new form of this transcendence through imagination can be seen in virtual worlds. "Digital theaters" (Molesworth and Denegri-Knott 2007) are games in which the players transcend their actual historical, spatial, and social identities. Virtual worlds are also markets where the "electronic equipment" for the aspired identities must be purchased. Conceptually, however, these products do not differ from the fictions in novels or films that evoke pleasurable fantasies in the reader or viewer.

[16] This is also indicated in neurological studies in which brain activities are observed while the test subject is reading a story. The studies show that the "brain regions involved in reading action words are some of the same regions involved in performing analogous actions in the real world" (Speer et al. 2009).

is attainable, at least in theory, then striving for it by taking practical steps to achieve it can provoke sensations that are similar to what would be experienced if the goal had already been achieved. Striving and attaining are not strictly separate from each other:

> When we become sure that some desired good is actually to be ours or that some desired event is definitely going to happen...we experience the well-known pleasure of savoring that future event in advance...This savoring, this fusion of striving and attaining, is a fact of experience that goes far to account for the existence and importance of noninstrumental activities. (Hirschman 1986: 150ff.)[17]

The Role of Practices

How do these transcendent qualities of imaginative value become attached to the objects that represent them? In general terms, the meaning of a good and hence its value derives from socialization, repeated interaction with the good, and participation in shared activities, as well as from corporate marketing (Richins 1994). I argue, however, that answering this question requires special attention to practices in the market field (see Warde 2005). Here again, a reference to Durkheim's work is illuminating, because he identified the sources of attachment to religious and political symbols by looking to ritualistic religious *practices*. Durkheim observed that social life in the tribal communities fell into periods of everyday activities on the one hand, and periods of ritualistic festivities, during which the members of the clan assembled, on the other. These festivities would usually take place in physical proximity to the totem of the clan. The passion and exaltation experienced through dance, music, fires, the darkness of the night, and the use of drugs would provoke a collective effervescence in which the clan members experienced a state of transcendence of their own consciousness. Since the totem was the center of these festivities, the clan members would attribute this experience of self-transcendence to the power of the totem (Durkheim 1965: 252).

At first glance, the reference to ritualistic practices might seem far-fetched for understanding the imaginative value of goods, but we can observe corresponding examples in contemporary economies. The positive aura surrounding a good associated with a charismatic celebrity like Madonna might derive from experiences of collective effervescence, for instance what might be experienced attending one of her concerts. A reference to "extraordinary" experiences can also hold true for the transcendent power of objects associated

---

[17] Hirschman connects this insight to religious experiences by quoting Pascal: "The hope Christians have to possess an infinite good is mixed with actual enjoyment...for they are not like those people who would hope for a kingdom of which they, as subjects, have nothing; rather, they hope for holiness, and for freedom from injustice, and they partake of both" (Pascal, Pensée 540, quoted in Hirschman 1986: 150ff.).

with places. The regional product consumed while one is living in a given region or staying there on vacation might become associated with treasured memories of the place. High jackpots in the lottery lead to mass public ecstasy that parallels the intoxication described by Durkheim and increases demand for tickets. New models of cars or consumer electronics products are presented to the public in theatrical performances at fairs that show obvious similarities to the ritualistic practices described by Durkheim. In these kinds of cases, practices generate wants rather than wants generating practices, a point already made by Alfred Marshall (1961).

Durkheim mentions a second practice needed to keep the "mana" of religious symbols alive. The passions created in the moments of collective effervescence lose their impression on the individual clan members over time. To avoid such deterioration, religious groups and political movements alike assemble their members in meetings regularly to revitalize the values and beliefs of the community (Durkheim 1965: 240). The church service or the party convention brings together the congregants and reminds the believers in ritualistic practices to cherish the values of the community.

Similar connections between the stabilization of imaginative value of goods and group practices can be observed on markets. Markets in which the symbolic value of products plays an important role typically have a social organization that brings consumers and experts into communicative exchange to discuss the objects for sale. In the art market, for example, galleries will start a show with an opening, where potential buyers, the seller, the artist, fellow artists, and art experts come together in a ritualistic affirmation of the quality of the objects to be sold. Museums and art critics also form part of the community of communication in the art world that reaffirms the value of the product and its sacred qualities and sets standards for the assessment of quality in communicative practices (Becker 1982; Beckert and Rössel 2004; Velthuis 2005). In the lottery market, syndicate play leads to higher participation rates (Garvía 2007). In the car market, the symbolic value of the car is established and reaffirmed communicatively through advertisements and car magazines, visits to the car dealership, car races, and private communication among lay "believers" who have faith in the qualities of the object. Post-sale advertising can remind customers of the transcendent qualities of the car, protecting them from the danger of disillusionment. Vintage car owners form clubs and assemble regularly in ritualistic club meetings to admire the old cars they possess and thereby reconfirm their value. Consumer electronics firms—Apple is the most prominent example—organize the release of new products by creating scarcities that bring the most dedicated customers together to wait (sometimes overnight) in a long queue to be among the first to buy the product once the store opens. This creates a group experience of like-minded people. Group experiences can also be organized virtually, leading to para-social interaction (Horton and Wohl 1956), the illusion of face-to-face interaction through mass media. Consumers of Nespresso coffee, for instance, become members of a

"Nespresso Club" and receive a magazine with regular updates about the product and its users. Magazine ads and television commercials remind potential customers of symbolic qualities of the products being advertised that would otherwise fade from consumer consciousness.[18]

Imaginative valuations are fragile constructs of the mind that need constant reaffirmation in communicative practices if they are to be maintained.[19] Following Hirschman's analysis (1986) of the utopian element experienced in idealistic political practices, the value an actor places on an object will increase with the intensity of his personal engagement with it. For the person who is ignorant about wine, a Chambertin from 1811 might not have any specific significance (value!). It is the aficionado or expert who is deeply committed to the product for whom it has an intoxicating quality and superior value. This intoxication, however, must be constantly revitalized through reaffirmations of the symbolic content in social practices.

The Dynamics of Imaginative Value

This opens up the question why the symbolic value of goods changes at all. While it is quite obvious that the physical value of a good changes with innovations, which add new and superior physical qualities, the dynamics of the symbolic qualities of goods are not as easily understood. It is here that the greatest difference from Durkheim's analysis of religion emerges. Durkheim pointed out that religious symbols remain stable: "While the generations change, [the totemic emblem] remains the same; it is the permanent element of the social life" (1965: 252). Looking at monotheistic religions, it is certainly the case that the significance and meaning of specific sacred objects changes in the course of history and might remain theologically contested. Religions, however, do not exchange their sacred objects continuously. This is contrary to the dynamics of symbolic values in the economy; in capitalist economies, it is even a constitutive element of their existence, because the alteration in symbolic value attributions is a source of growth. But what mechanisms are responsible for these varying dynamics of symbolic value in the market sphere?

1. The first mechanism is the logic of differentiation, described by Georg Simmel (1919) and referring to the positional value of goods. If the purpose of consumption beyond the physical qualities of goods is to signal higher social status through the exclusivity and novelty of the products consumed,

---

[18] In this sense, advertising is not just manipulative, as a long tradition of cultural criticism maintains (Adorno and Horkheimer 2002; Galbraith 1958), but constitutive of the symbolic content of goods.

[19] Alan Warde (2005) has recently suggested basing the sociology of consumption on a theory of practice.

goods lose value once they become popular and are consumed by lower social classes, or are diffused into the mainstream, beyond the margins of a defined social group. This means that ever more novel objects must be defined as symbolic representations of distinction, a mechanism that finds expression in continuous processes of valuation and devaluation.
2. The second mechanism stems from the process of appropriation itself, which leads to a devaluation of the acquired object. This relationship between appropriation and devaluation has also been examined in part by Georg Simmel. In his *Philosophy of Money* (2004) Simmel analyzes value as emerging from a distance between subject and object:

We desire objects... in terms of [their] distance as something not-yet-enjoyed, the subjective aspect of this condition being desire... The object thus formed, which is characterized by its separation from the subject, who at the same time establishes it and seeks to overcome it by his desire, is for us a value. The moment of enjoyment itself, when the separation of subject and object is effaced, consumes the value. Value is only reinstated as contrast, as an object separated from the subject. Such trivial experiences as that we appreciate the value of our possessions only after we have lost them... (Simmel 2004: 66)

A similar idea of disillusionment is advocated by Colin Campbell (1987). For Campbell, however, it is not the loss of the distance between subject and object as such which leads to the devaluation but rather the disappointment that stems from the discrepancy between the perfection in which the object was imagined and the imperfections visible once it is in the owner's possession. "Since reality can never provide the perfected pleasures encountered in day-dreams... each purchase leads to literal disillusionment, something which explains why wanting is extinguished so quickly" (Campbell 1987: 90). Hence it is not the closing of the distance to the object itself which produces disillusionment but more precisely the closing of the distance to the imaginative.

Both authors are right in pointing to a process of disillusionment associated with the appropriation of goods. Nevertheless, we reach a different perspective on the cause of this disillusionment if we compare economic goods to the totem: the disillusionment is specific to the *commodity*. Goods sold on the market hold the promise that possessing them will indeed lead to the appropriation of the espoused dimensions symbolically represented in the object. The (potential) purchaser sees in the object the embodiment of the transcendent, which can be appropriated through the purchase. It is this reifying illusion which at the same time constitutes the attraction of the goods *and* is the source of their devaluation once they are actually possessed.

We can see this in a comparison to religious symbols. The religious ideals always remain physically unattainable for the faithful, and therefore distanced. While the totem allows the follower to achieve *spiritual* closeness to the sacred through proximity to the sacred object, its possession is in no way thought to be a possible realization or appropriation of the espoused ideals. The significance of religious objects does not go beyond representation; their possession serves only to remind the member of the community of the values that the community stands for and of his or her membership in the community. This difference is also expressed in the strict regulation of, and restrictions on access to, the sacred object. Followers might not be allowed to touch or even see the totem except during special religious festivities. The secular good, by contrast, maintains this distance from the consumer only until it has been purchased. The sacrifice made with the purchase allows the object to be appropriated and used, that is, carried into the world of the profane. This possession at the same time reduces the good's imaginative value, because the object "is now an incipient part of the 'here and now' and to this extent vulnerable to contradiction" (McCracken 1988: 112). While the object appears to be *part* of the transcendental quality it represents, this is at the same time logically and empirically impossible; this fact is experienced once the object has been purchased and appropriated.

On the one hand, the promise of appropriating the transcendental qualities through the purchase of the good is indispensable to inducing the purchaser to pay for it. On the other, this promise triggers disillusionment, because once the object is possessed, the imaginative space shrinks, and the purchaser attains only the immanent (profane) qualities. Here, the reification of values in commodities reaches its limit. The communicative efforts of producers, as described in the previous section, attempt to reduce and defer this disappointment—by reconfirming the transcendental qualities of the good through post-sale communications, or by creating new symbolic values for the object, for instance applying the time dimension to turn a used car into an antique. The consumer can postpone the disillusionment by postponing consumption of the good (not drinking the Chambertin from 1811, for example) or restricting the use of the product (wearing a new suit only for special occasions), keeping it symbolically within the realm of the sacred. Belk et al. (1989: 30) distinguish four distinct ways of maintaining the sacred status of goods: "The separation of the sacred from the profane, ritual, bequests, and tangibilized contamination."[20]

The only exception, where this process of disappointment and devaluation does not apply, is in the accumulation of money. Since money is devoid of any of the concrete characteristics of a good and at the same time offers the freedom to buy any good with it (Parsons 1963), in a way it is the most perfect material representation of the sacred, one that withstands the disillusionment of appropriation. Money cannot be contradicted by experience, because

---

[20] It would be an important question to investigate which types of products are more vulnerable to disillusionment than others. One hypothesis would be that products which can also be defined as investment goods (art, real estate, jewelry, etc.) are less vulnerable because they can evoke fantasies of increased wealth after their purchase. See also the paragraph on money.

money is an abstraction (Deutschmann 2009*b*; Parsons 1963; Simmel 2004). The only threat to the imaginative value of money is its devaluation through inflation. One can see the special attraction of money in its duality: having no concrete qualities itself, money still allows for the potential to obtain any qualities desired. At the same time, it makes the question of why actors purchase goods even more puzzling, because consumer goods must have a higher value than the perception of the potentiality embodied in the money not spent (Ullrich 2006: 59ff.).

The described limits of the reified representation of values in goods also trigger the *dynamics* of imaginative value. The symbolic representation of the sacred in the object must be projected onto new objects each time a new good is appropriated. While the owner is invariably disappointed with the promised value once an object has been purchased, this promise remains in other objects not yet possessed. Once imaginative goods are appropriated, "the individual must swiftly transfer 'bridge' status from the purchased object to one that is not now owned" (McCracken 1988: 115). One can speak of a specifically human vulnerability that stems from not only our ability to create fiction (see below) but also from our "need for fiction" (Iser 1991).[21] In an economic system that depends on the willingness of consumers to desire more and newer products, human fiction-ability creates a demand for products that are independent of the difference the product makes in the physical world. In advanced economies, this is an ever more important source of economic growth, and it remains a source of motivation even if the consumed products do not lead to heightened levels of satisfaction (Frank 1999: 64ff.). The paradox evolving is that it is "absolutely essential for us never to receive what it is we want" (McCracken 1988: 116).

It is here that the supply side of production comes together with the demand side. Producers, who are dependent on the marketability of their products, invest in associating their products with consumers' espoused ideals: through advertisements, and marketing activities more generally, producers attempt to find out and construct what consumers value. This is a necessarily dynamic process for two reasons. First, the constant disappointments following the purchase of goods create an unending demand for new products. The shift in imaginative associations is possible because, as Durkheim argued, the symbolic qualities can in principle be attached to any object. And second, the charging of products with symbolic value is contested between competing producers. Producers compete to attach consumers to their products and to detach consumers from the products of their competitors (Callon et al. 2002). While the charging of products with imaginative value is manipulative and

---

[21] The most comprehensive treatment of the role that fantasies of a desired, better world play is probably Ernst Bloch's *The Principle of Hope* (1995). While Bloch focuses on the utopian political potential anchored in the human ability to imagine a better future, he explicitly also discusses the experience of consumers who daydream of new identities when (window-)shopping. The transcending, that is, utopian, force of human imagination forms the core of Bloch's analysis.

reifies the desires of actors to "appropriate" transcendent values, it also promises an imaginative salvation by providing access to intangible ideals.[22] Because of the mechanisms described, this salvation is never achieved in full. But the manner in which producers' needs to sell their products correspond to consumers' aspirations to find symbolic representations of their transcending desires shows how imaginative value can significantly contribute to the system integration of the economy *and* the social integration of society.

Conclusion

Investigations of the economy in political economy and economic sociology focus primarily on the supply side of markets. Market sociology, too, puts much more emphasis on firms and their coordination in competition than it does on the demand side. Such a productionist bias does not do justice to contemporary economies. In advanced economies, where many consumer needs are satisfied, consumers' motivation to buy products cannot be taken for granted. One precondition for markets to function is that consumers value the products being offered and are willing to make sacrifices in order to possess them. Where does this willingness stem from? The distinction between the physical, positional, and imaginative value of goods provides a tableau of different value sources in the economy. The focus of the chapter is on the imaginative performance of goods as a source of value and economic growth.

Durkheim's sociology of religion provides important insights into the construction of imaginative value. Durkheim's work is read here as a sociology of valuation: his claim that the totem emblem is respected as the symbolic representation of the values of the social group is transposed to the valuation of secular goods in contemporary societies. While the role of imaginative value has been the subject of treatments in the investigation of consumption (Campbell 1987; d'Astous and Deschênes 2005; McCracken 1988; Ullrich 2006), these studies are limited in part because they use a psychological desire for newness or other individual traits to explain imaginative value (d'Astous and Deschênes 2005). Contrary to their explanation, I have argued that the imaginative performance of goods is based on the charging of these goods with values and ideals prevailing in the social field. These can be aesthetic or normative ideals that find a symbolic representation in the object. In "the aesthetically valued object there resides the principle of the True and the Good" (Gell 1992: 41).

---

[22] We can speculate that this need is less acute for people who are engaged in artistic, intellectual, or entrepreneurial activities. Such creative activities provide an illusory access to the sacred (creating beauty, finding the truth, creating the new) that satisfies the needs that other actors project onto objects. This would explain also why these groups are often snobbish, cynical, or morally opposed to consumerism (cf. Adorno and Horkheimer 2002; Arendt 1958).

One implication of this claim is that markets, instead of being the expression of an unbound individualism, become more integrated into the moral fabric of society as the basis of valuation shifts to the positional and imaginative performances of goods in affluent economies. This corresponds to claims of a "moralization" (Stehr 2007) and "aesthetization" (Rössel 2007) of markets. Moreover, it provides evidence in the sphere of the economy for a claim that Emile Durkheim has made with regard to social development in general, namely that processes of secularization do not lead to the elimination of the sacred but to the emergence of secularized forms of the sacred. One way in which the sacred finds expression in modern societies is through consumption practices. In this chapter, I take issue with the assertion that the sacredness of an object becomes contaminated when that object is brought into the sphere of market exchange. Instead, I argue that symbolically charged commodities are also representations of value—not just in the economic sense but also in the moral sense of the term (see Fourcade-Gourinchas 2009).

The reference to Emile Durkheim makes it possible to conceptualize the social practices through which goods become charged with imaginative value and through which actors in the field attempt to maintain (or destroy) this value. Experiences of collective effervescence are one source of imaginative value. The communication between consumers, experts, producers, and critics is meant to keep the imaginative value alive and shield it from the disappointment that sets in once the product is actually possessed. The communicative practices surrounding the construction of imaginative value are part of socialization (*Vergesellschaftung*), and thus part of the fabric of society. At the same time, the mental representation of intangible ideals in objects and the striving to realize these ideals through the purchase of these objects entail a utopian element, whose contribution to the understanding of social dynamics goes far beyond the sphere of consumption. Both entrepreneurial action and intergenerational strategies of wealth accumulation (e.g., maintaining an inheritance for one's children) show very similar characteristics to the striving for a utopian state (Schumpeter 1912: 164ff.). As in Max Weber, this connection to utopianism hints at transcendental motivations underlying rational economic action. Unlike Weber's view, however, this new outlook identifies the nonrational core of economic action in the tendency by consumers and investors to project the sacred onto objects attainable on the market, rather than seeing it in the disciplinary effects of religious doctrines. What do we value? When it comes to imaginative value, the answer may be straightforward: We value our values.

REFERENCES

Adolf, M. and Stehr, N. (2010). Zur Dynamik des Kapitalismus. In A. Kabalak, K. van den Berg, and U. Pasero (eds.), *Capitalism Revisited: Anmerkungen zur Zukunft des Kapitalismus*. Marburg: Metropolis, 15–38.

Adorno, T. W. and Horkheimer, M. (1944/2002). *Dialectic of Enlightenment*. Stanford, CA: Stanford University Press.

Akerlof, G. A. (1970). The Market for "Lemons": Quality Uncertainty and the Market Mechanism. *Quarterly Journal of Economics* 84: 488–500.

Arendt, H. (1958). *The Human Condition*. Chicago, IL: University of Chicago Press.

Arnould, E. J. and Thompson, C. J. (2005). Consumer Culture Theory (CCT): Twenty Years of Research. *Journal of Consumer Research* 31: 868–82.

Becker, H. S. (1982). *Art Worlds, Berkeley and Los Angeles*. Berkeley, CA: University of California Press.

Beckert, J. (2002). *Beyond the Market: The Social Foundations of Economic Efficiency*. Princeton, NJ: Princeton University Press.

——and Lutter, M. (2007). Wer spielt, hat schon verloren? Zur Erklärung des Nachfrageverhaltens auf dem Lottomarkt. *Kölner Zeitschrift für Soziologie und Sozialpsychologie* 59: 240–70.

——and—— (2009). The Inequality of Fair Play: Lottery Gambling and Social Stratification in Germany. *European Sociological Review* 25: 475–88.

——and Rössel, J. (2004). Kunst und Preise: Reputation als Mechanismus der Reduktion von Ungewissheit am Kunstmarkt. *Kölner Zeitschrift für Soziologie und Sozialpsychologie* 56: 32–50.

Belk, R. W., Wallendorf, M., and Sherry, J. F., Jr. (1989). The Sacred and the Profane in Consumer Behavior: Theodicy on the Odyssey. *Journal of Consumer Research* 16: 1–38.

Bellah, R. N. (1967). Civil Religion in America. *Dædalus, Journal of the American Academy of Arts and Sciences* 96: 1–21.

Bloch, E. (1995). *The Principle of Hope*. Cambridge, MA: MIT Press.

Bourdieu, P. (1984). *Distinctions: A Social Critique of the Judgement of Taste*. Cambridge, MA: Harvard University Press.

Buchanan, J. M. and Vanberg, V. J. (1984). The Market as a Creative Process. In D. M. Hausman (ed.), *The Philosophy of Economics: An Anthology*. Cambridge, MA: Cambridge University Press, 379–98.

Callon, M., Méadel, C., and Rabeharisoa, V. (2002). The Economy of Qualities. *Economy and Society* 31: 194–217.

Campbell, C. (1987). *The Romantic Ethic and the Spirit of Modern Consumerism*. Oxford: Basil Blackwell.

d'Astous, A. and Deschênes, J. (2005). Consuming in One's Mind: An Exploration. *Psychology & Marketing* 22: 1–30.

Deutschmann, C. (1999). *Die Verheißung des absoluten Reichtums: Zur religiösen Natur des Kapitalismus*. Frankfurt a.M.: Campus.

——(2009*a*). Capitalism and Religion: An Unorthodox View. In D. Junker, W. Mausbach, and M. Thunert (eds.), *State and Market in a Globalized World: Transatlantic Perspectives*. Heidelberg: Universitätsverlag Winter, 135–46.

——(2009*b*). *Soziologie Kapitalistischer Dynamik*. MPIfG Working Paper 09/5. Cologne: Max Planck Institute for the Study of Societies.

Djelic, M.-L. and Ainamo, A. (2005). The Telecom Industry as Cultural Industry? The Transposition of Fashion Logics into the Field of Mobile Telephony. In C. Jones and P. H. Thornton (eds.), *Transformation in Cultural Industries*. Research in the Sociology of Organizations, Volume 23. Amsterdam: Elsevier/Jai, 45–80.

—— (1999). The Coevolution of New Organizational Forms in the Fashion Industry: A Historical and Comparative Study of France, Italy, and the United States. *Organization Science* 10: 622–37.

Durkheim, E. (1912/1965). *The Elementary Forms of the Religious Life.* New York, NY: The Free Press.

—— (1893/1984). *The Division of Labour in Society.* London: Macmillan.

—— (1957/1992). *Professional Ethics and Civic Morals.* New York, NY: Routledge.

Fischer, E. F. and Benson, P. (2006). *Broccoli and Desire: Global Connections and Maya Struggles in Postwar Guatemala.* Stanford, CA: Stanford University Press.

Fligstein, N. (2001). *The Architecture of Markets.* Princeton, NJ: Princeton University Press.

Fourcade, M. (2009). Price and Prejudice: Economic Technology as Cultural Practice. Unpublished manuscript. Berkeley, CA: University of California, Berkeley.

Frank, R. H. (1999). *Luxury Fever.* New York, NY: The Free Press.

Galbraith, J. K. (1958). *The Affluent Society.* New York, NY: Houghton Mifflin.

Garud, R. and Karnoe, P. (2001). Path Creation as a Process of Mindful Deviation. In R. Garud and P. Karnoe (eds.), *Path Dependence and Creation.* Mahwah, NJ: Erlbaum, 1–40.

Garvía, R. (2007). Syndication, Institutionalization and Lottery Play. *American Journal of Sociology* 113: 603–53.

Gell, A. (1992). The Technology of Enchantment and the Enchantment of Technology. In J. Coote and A. Sheldon (eds.), *Anthropology, Art, and Aesthetics.* Oxford: Clarendon Press, 40–66.

Hirschman, A. (1986). *Rival Views of Market Society.* New York, NY: Viking Press.

Holbrook, M. B. and Hirschman, E. C. (1982). The Experiential Aspects of Consumption: Consumer Fantasies, Feelings, and Fun. *Journal of Consumer Research* 9: 132–40.

Horton, D. and Wohl, R. R. (1956). Mass Communication and Para-social Interaction: Observations on Intimacy at a Distance. *Psychiatry* 19: 215–29.

Isenberg, W. and Sellmann, M. (eds.) (2000). *Konsum als Religion? Über die Wiederverzauberung der Welt.* Mönchengladbach: Kühlen.

Iser, W. (1991). *Das Fiktive und das Imaginäre: Perspektiven literarischer Anthropologie.* Frankfurt a.M.: Suhrkamp.

Joas, H. (2000). *The Genesis of Values.* Cambridge, MA: Polity Press.

Keynes, J. M. (1936/1964). *The General Theory of Employment, Interest, and Money.* London: Macmillan.

Levy, S. J. (1959). Symbols for Sale. *Harvard Business Review* 37: 117–24.

Luckmann, T. (1967). *The Invisible Religion: The Problem of Religion in Modern Society.* New York, NY: Macmillan.

Marshall, A. (1920/1961). *Principles of Economics* (9th variorum ed., 2 vols.). Edited and annotated by C. W. Guillebaud. London: Macmillan.

Marshall, D. A. (2010). Temptation, Tradition, and Taboo: A Theory of Sacralization. *Sociological Theory* 28: 64–90.

Marx, K. (1867/1977). *Das Kapital: Kritik der politischen Ökonomie* (Vol. 1, 12th ed.). Berlin: Dietz.

McCracken, G. (1988). *Culture and Consumption.* Bloomington, IN: Indiana University Press.

Miller, D. (1998). *A Theory of Shopping.* New York, NY: Cornell University Press.

Molesworth, M. and Denegri-Knott, J. (2007). Digital Play and the Actualization of the Consumer Imagination. *Games and Culture* 2: 114–33.

Parsons, T. (1963). On the Concept of Political Power. *Proceedings of the American Philosophical Society* 107: 232–62.

Reisch, L. A. (2002). Symbols for Sale: Funktionen des symbolischen Konsums. In C. Deutschmann (ed.), *Die gesellschaftliche Macht des Geldes*. Wiesbaden: Westdeutscher Verlag.

Richins, M. L. (1994). Valuing Things: The Public and Private Meanings of Possessions. *Journal of Consumer Research* 21: 504–21.

Rössel, J. (2007). Ästhetisierung, Unsicherheit und die Entwicklung von Märkten. In J. Beckert, R. Diaz-Bone, and H. Ganßmann (eds.), *Märkte als soziale Strukturen*. Frankfurt a.M.: Campus, 167–81.

Schumpeter, J. (1912). *Theorie der wirtschaftlichen Entwicklung*. Berlin: Duncker & Humblot.

Shackle, G. L. S. (1972). *Epistemics & Economics: A Critique of Economic Doctrines*. Cambridge, MA: Cambridge University Press.

Simmel, G. (1908/1919). Die Mode. In Georg Simmel (ed.), *Philosophische Kultur*. Leipzig: Kröner, 25–57.

——(1978/2004). *Philosophy of Money* (3rd ed.). London: Routledge.

Speer, N. K., Reynolds, J. R., Swallow, K. M., and Zacks, J. M. (2009). Reading Stories Activates Neural Representations of Visual and Motor Experiences. *Psychological Science* 20: 989–99.

Stehr, N. (2007). *Moral Markets: How Knowledge and Affluence Change Consumers and Products*. Boulder, CO: Paradigm Publishers.

——Henning, C., and Weiler, B. (eds.) (2006). *The Moralization of the Markets*. New Brunswick, NJ: Transaction Publishers.

Tappenbeck, I. (1999). *Phantasie und Gesellschaft: Zur soziologischen Relevanz der Einbildungskraft*. Würzburg: Königshausen und Neumann.

Tillich, P. (1986). *Symbol und Wirklichkeit*. Göttingen: Vandenhoek & Ruprecht.

Ullrich, W. (2006). *Habenwollen: Wie funktioniert die Konsumkultur?* Frankfurt a.M.: Fischer.

Valtin, A. (2005). *Der Wert von Luxusmarken: Determinanten des konsumentenorientierten Markenwerts und Implikationen für das Luxusmarkenmanagement*. Wiesbaden: Deutscher Universitätsverlag.

Veblen, T. (1899/1973). *The Theory of the Leisure Class*. Boston, MA: Houghton Mifflin.

Velthuis, O. (2005). *Talking Prices*. Princeton, NJ: Princeton University Press.

Warde, A. (2005). Consumption and Theories of Practice. *Journal of Consumer Culture* 5: 131 53.

Witt, U. (2001). Learning to Consume: A Theory of Wants and the Growth of Demand. *Journal of Evolutionary Economics* 11: 23–36.

——(2010). Symbolic Consumption and the Social Construction of Product Characteristics. *Structural Change and Economic Dynamics* 21(1): 17–25.

Zelizer, V. (1979). *Morals and Markets: The Development of Life Insurance in the United States*. New York, NY: Columbia University Press.

Part II
Aesthetic Markets

6 Symbolic Value and the Establishment of Prices: Globalization of the Wine Market

*Marie-France Garcia-Parpet**

The goal of this article is to show that the representations, uses, and values attributed to a product constitute essential factors in the process of establishing its price. Indeed, the battles over the classifications that define products constitute a key element in setting the rules of the market, and there are many examples of these battles in the literature (among these see Bonneuil and Thomas 2009; J. Bourdieu 2003). However, most of the work that informs the thinking on quality is primarily focused on distorting effects caused by opportunistic actors and/or information asymmetry, or the question of the norms and formal investment necessary for the proper functioning of market institutions (Akerlof 1970; Eymard-Duvernay 1989; Thévenot 1995). All too often, such work assumes that there is consensus on the meanings attributed to quality. Our goals here are to present the different worlds of meaning and see which social actors are willing and able to bridge these different worlds. These are the very foundations for any agreement on the meaning attributed to the quality of the products that are to be examined, a precondition to the possibility of adjusting supply and demand by the free fluctuation of prices.

The analysis of the wine market, where value is being radically redefined through the globalization process, can show what is needed for a healthy market when the product has a strong symbolic component. By extension, such an analysis can shed light on all the challenges that must be confronted so that competition can play out solely in terms of price.[1] We seek to demonstrate that the issues motivating market participants are not limited to production costs, variations in winemaking techniques, corporate structure, or even investment strategies. These issues can only be fully understood if we also consider the battles over wine classification, the cultural wars over the criteria of excellence, and the struggles over the selection of expert juries. Can a

---

* Translation by Scott Kushner.

[1] Lucien Karpik underlines the blind spot of neoclassical economic theory, which only considers prices as a differential feature, and he also attempts to account for the economic coordination of cultural goods that cannot be reduced to homogeneous or differentiated goods (Karpik 2010).

product as diverse as wine submit to a single scale of symbolic value on the international stage? Who gets to define excellence? How can we reach an agreement on the principles of evaluation?

The story of Aimé Guibert shows the importance of classifications in the formation of prices. Guibert is a winemaker who enjoys a global reputation today. He has accumulated the means to produce an excellent product, but he was once at odds with the established French institutions. What constraints hemmed in this peerless producer? The question of a given product's market in the age of globalization lies at the heart of the debate between economics and the social sciences. To respond, it is essential to situate producers and consumers—as well as the full range of actors who participate in the reconfiguration of the wine supply and the institutionalization of the market—socially and historically.

A Winegrower Takes on the System

A former glove manufacturer from Millau who had once been president of the Chamber of Commerce, Aimé Guibert, struggled through the crisis that struck the French leather industry in the 1960s. He then reinvented himself as a winegrower, where he proved he had a talent, though there was nothing in his background that suggested this would be the case. A Protestant who studied political science in college, Guibert married a woman from a noble family who was an amateur archaeologist. In the early 1970s, he bought a farm in the Hérault[2] with an old Gallo-Roman mill that had traditionally been used for mixed farming. With the help of a friend who was a professor of geography at the University of Bordeaux and was known for his expertise in winegrowing soils, he discovered that a portion of his property boasted soil exceptionally well suited for wine production that had been known to yield a grand cru. Emboldened by this prestigious knowledge, Guibert thought he might be positioned to produce what wine professionals and oenophiles call "grands vins."

He was short on capital during this difficult period. But he still had sufficient connections and possessed a deep knowledge of bank operations from his long years in business. This allowed him to secure the loans he needed. The son of an industrial family that had supplied the Court of England for several generations, Guibert understood the demands of the luxury goods market. He transferred his business talents to winegrowing, adopting the most refined techniques: grape varieties (especially those used in the Bordeaux region), small yields, choice harvests, and a deferral of immediate profits. He

---

[2] A French department in the Languedoc, this region was traditionally devoted to the mass production of wine, as we will see below.

retained Émile Peynaud, the era's most respected Bordeaux oenologist, who had advised well-known producers such as Château Margaux, to guide him in his winemaking endeavors.

If we reason that prices are formed according to a logic of production factors, Guibert would have been expected to experience an unqualified success when he brought his products to market. However, when he presented his wines to different French merchants, he was met with complete rejection. No wholesaler of quality wines would taste a wine from a region that was so stigmatized. The only hope of success lay in escaping the grip of the classifications that had historically been used: the *Appellations d'Origine Contrôlée* (AOC, or the legal rules that have regulated production since 1935 and created privileged geographic zones) and the methods in which judgments (in the form of awards) were institutionalized.

Thankfully for Guibert, the wine critics in Great Britain and North America offered him a different fate. In the face of financial pressure, he was able to build value in his wines because of the international—and specifically English—dimension of his earlier businesses and the corresponding social capital. Not finding any success with French wholesalers and collectors, he felt that in order to deal with his financial troubles he would have to make use of the address book he had developed in the leather business. With the help of an English restaurateur who moonlighted as a wine merchant, he established himself in the British and American markets among trendsetters, putting his wines on the same level as Château Lafite (the highest rated Pauillac wine in the Médoc). He jumped to the top of the hierarchy of French wines in terms of geographic origin and prestige class.[3] Discussed by the most well-regarded critics in England and the United States, his wines were the subject of articles, book chapters, and even a book by the head of the Christie's wine department (Mackenzie 1995). Recognition by a prestigious wine professional acted as a trigger, and all the well-known trendsetters mentioned his wine. Still, Guibert's "worldwide reputation" was fragile since he still lacked any recognition in France, a country which despite the impressive advances in quality in New World wines had maintained its dominance in "grands vins". He would have to wait eight years before the success he had achieved in American and British circles had a boomerang effect on the leaders of French thought, when the *Revue des vins de France* dedicated an issue to Guibert's wines, ranking them among "the aristocrats of the great estates of Bordeaux, Burgundy, or Champagne" (*Revue des vins de France* 1993).

What are the perceptions of a product (legally guaranteed or otherwise) that allow for such different evaluations? Guibert's unusual itinerary invites us to reflect on the diversity of reactions to products that result from particular

---

[3] Château Lafite is an AOC name but was also included in the 1885 classification scheme that was developed by Chamber of Commerce members for the Universal Exposition and is still in use today. This classification only applies to wines of very high quality.

forms of institutionalization[4] and market regulation. His rise also pushes us to consider the dynamics of markets that emerge from a morphologic evolution of the social composition of demand. In France, it is a natural conception of wine, linked to the privileging of certain geographical areas historically devoted to its production, which has solidified an opposition between ordinary wine and quality wine.

The "Terroir": Estates and Artificial Scarcity

Guibert's operations are in the Languedoc. This French region was known several centuries ago for its fine vineyards,[5] but it came to be seen as a mass production region in the nineteenth century. Standardization was considered a *sine qua non* condition for the conquest of emerging markets. Increasing "industrialization" of certain aspects of the winemaking process followed the concentration of production. Meanwhile, the search for "reliable types" of wine was pursued under pressure from the international market, the rise of cooperative cellars, and mass production in France (Stanziani 2005: 78). However, at the beginning of the twentieth century, bolstered by political strength that came from the size of their parliamentary representation in Third Republic France, vineyard owners took comfort in a business model that meshed with a resistance to capitalism and industrial standards. The major estates and merchants in Guibert's home region acted as a counterweight and the parliamentary representatives took up the cause of the estates, which were then small peasant winegrowing properties. Putting an end to a difficult period that set growers and merchants against one another, the Law of 1935 effectively favored vineyard owners,[6] an artisanal mode of production, a natural conception of wine, and a production circumscribed by the borders of designated communes: the AOC. This eliminated a standard of quality obtained by blending wines from different origins, which was a manufactured style of wine that was made by merchants.[7] This structuring of competition

---

[4] Sidney Mintz (1985) shows that in the United Kingdom, sugar was once a luxury good that was reserved for kings and the bourgeoisie. Later, it lost its luster and became a sweetener for tea, coffee, or chocolate, taking its place as an essential component of working-class cuisine due to its high caloric content.

[5] At the beginning of the nineteenth century, the wines of Saint-Georges-d'Orques, Vérarques, and Saint-Christol were classified by André Julien in a category equal to that of the wines of Saint-Émilion (Bordeaux) and Mercurey and Givry in Burgundy (Julien 1816).

[6] The 1935 legislation was the culmination of several laws established in the late nineteenth and early twentieth centuries that regulated the wine market. For an analysis of the writing and repercussions of these laws, see Jacquet and Laferté (2006), Sagnes (1992), and Stanziani (2005).

[7] This is what Gilles Laferté has called "republican control of the market" (2006), a reference to Neil Fligstein (1990), who speaks of financial control (and later of control tied to the value of investments in contemporary American capitalism) in order to describe the imposition of a norm on the market through political means by a social group.

was due in great measure to the intervention of the state, which, far from merely playing the role of a judge charged with keeping order and guaranteeing confidence, is an essential player in the construction of supply and demand.[8]

The AOC system functions as a gatekeeper by limiting the number of appellations and the amount of winegrowing land that can be established in a given territory based on existing reputations. Decrees of recognition, handed down by expert commissions and approved by the National Committee, establish barriers to entry into the quality wine production market and, by extension, allocate opportunities to make a profit. The Institut National des Appellations d'Origine (National Institute of Appellations d'Origine, or INAO) forces estates to operate within territories that have characteristics specified by the institution. It also grants authorizations to plant in order to ensure a favorable development of the market or, more recently, to meet the needs of social policy.[9]

This historic construction led to a system of economic organization that obeys two specific logics. On the one hand, there is a state-organized mass wine market, subject both to structural imbalances between supply and demand and to a constrained market structure that relies on limiting supply through obligatory stockpiling and distilling, characteristic of the European regime. On the other hand, the creation of the AOC system turned terroir names into guaranteed income for reputable vineyards, a form of corporatism in which professionals came to control the conditions of access to the labels without any direct state intervention in the organization of the market. This duality was evident in the commercial wines distributed in France and persisted until the beginning of the 1980s (Bartoli and Boulet 1990: 7–38; Boyer 1990: 39–76).

These two forms of market institutionalization have since evolved. The differences between them have diminished (because of an increase in the number of appellations, an expansion of the cultivated acreage, an extension of the AOC system to products other than wine, a stronger state presence in the INAO, the creation of intermediate categories between AOC and table wines), but these two separate institutionalizations of production have persisted as a hierarchy among products.

Excluded from privileged production zones, Guibert's wines were also cut off from all the marks of quality (such as prizes, awards in the specialty press, and the major winemaking organizations, especially in France). These marks enforce the opposition between "table wines" or "vins de pays" and "AOC wines" as well as the impossibility of drawing a comparison between wines

---

[8] As far as the wine market is concerned, such state intervention in favor of certain social groups has manifested itself on several occasions. The most famous consisted of a set of measures intended to topple direct competitors to producers in the Gironde, known as the Bordeaux privilege (Pijassou 1980: 299–300).

[9] For more information on the functioning of the Appellations d'origine contrôlée, see Garcia-Parpet (2009).

of different appellations. It is among the AOC wines that we find the most prestigious categories, such as the Village Appellation, Premiers Crus, Crus Bourgeois, etc. "Vin de pays" and "vin courant" producers are penalized straightaway in competitions. Regardless of the true quality of the wine, experts, wine professionals, and consumers tend to place a higher value on AOC wines. The French press reinforces this distinction, and the impact is magnified by the importance of mass distribution that has come to dominate retail sales of wines and which is used by the various stores to promote the products. The *Guide Hachette de vins*, for example, the best-selling wine guide in France, defines AOC wines as "the royal class, that of all great wines."

The institutionalization of the AOC system is inspired by the geography of Paul Vidal de La Blache, which constructed the nation based on the history of small parts that became elements of a larger unit (Thiesse 1991). In this view, excellence can only be recognized within a given appellation, as is seen when the Mâcon Prize is awarded or at the Salon général de l'Agriculture, to name only the most prestigious competitions. A Saint-Emilion, for example, can only be compared to another Saint-Emilion. What awards could Guibert's wines have won if they could not even be entered into competition? We see here that the right to compete precedes the problem of price formation.[10]

A Natural Conception of Wine: Aristocratic Elites and Vintages

The AOC, a legally mandated symbolic construction that valorizes a natural conception of wine in the name of peasant values, does not contradict a conception of the product that was established in the eighteenth and nineteenth centuries.[11] As with all other products, the properties of wine can be only completely defined in relation to objective, natural, and technical characteristics and the habitus that structures the perception and appreciation of the product (here wine). This defines the real demand with which producers

---

[10] The idea of a social construction of competitions is present in the work of Max Weber (as cited in Swedberg 2003: 119), but it was also proposed in 1924 by John R. Commons, who wrote that "the theory of free competition developed by economists is not a natural tendency toward equilibrium of forces but is an ideal of public purpose adopted by the courts, to be attained by restraints upon the natural struggle for existence" (as cited in Steiner 2005: 64). But the idea of economic efficiency as a social construction was largely developed by Pierre Bourdieu (2005) and Neil Fligstein (1990, 2001). These authors understand markets as eminently political and conflictual, where cognitive frames and schemes define legitimate economic models and the most powerful groups use culturally acceptable rules to perpetuate their power.

[11] This is not to say that there is no competition among regions and appellations. The aristocratic model privileges Bordeaux and Champagne, emphasizing châteaus, coats of arms, and noble titles. It coexists and competes with commercial products that play on folklore in order to seduce bourgeois tastes with a popular aesthetic that valorizes the wine artisan. The comparison never surfaces in competitions; the differences emerge in usage (minor and major ceremonies, ordinary meals, etc.).

must contend. Wine's capacity to hold and gain value over time and the relative values of vintages developed in light of the encounter between Bordeaux producers—whose noble origins provided access to necessary technical and financial means as well as to powerful merchants—and an aristocratic British clientele for whom this product became an excellent marker of social distinction. The bottling process is very closely linked to the aristocratic mode of consuming wine that developed in the eighteenth century among a minority of privileged birth and great wealth.

Just like wigs, attire, or servants, it [wine] is a necessary element of distinction, which, in a society whose order is decomposing, is maintained by appearances and behavior... Because birth no longer counts and wealth remains unstable, other indicators are sought in order to define the drinking elite: manners that include knowing how to drink, taste which is good taste. From this moment on, we speak of wine lovers, indeed of connoisseurs, for whom good manners include knowing how to drink, and these wines of the aristocratic and bourgeois elite accumulate and grow old in cellars, are displayed on tables, and become associated with delicacies. (Garrier 1998: 136–255)

From "clarets," light wines from Bordeaux, the English aristocracy came to appreciate the "New French clarets," darker wines from the Médoc that were called "black wines," differentiated by vintage and often sold at auction (Pijassou 1980: 402). British buyers were very particular about origin and vintage and in this regard had a more complete and precise lexical range than the French.[12]

Interested in adopting aristocratic practices in the hope of climbing the social ladder, the upper bourgeoisie in France adopted this luxury too (Elias 1983). In the nineteenth century, as we see in Balzac's novels,[13] the petty bourgeoisie pleased itself by imitating aristocratic tastes, including the consumption of wine. In our time, the petty bourgeoisie that aspires to this refined taste is driven by the press and by self-help books, which never fail to report on the habits of celebrities.[14]

The value of wines tends to grow with time, and then, unlike legitimate works of art whose value stabilizes, it tends to come back down as the wine loses its gustatory properties, especially its fruit, and eventually becomes vinegar.[15] Increases in value are linked to wine's ability to stand up over time and improve in quality. These characteristics are associated with the

---

[12] Gilbert Garrier notes that the term *growth* was roughly equivalent to the French term "cru" in that era, while the latter predates the former by a century (Garrier 1998: 148).

[13] In *The Lesser Bourgeoisie*, an unfinished novel by Balzac, Madame Thuillier invites city employees to dinner in order to promote her youngest son's career. She has glasses put out for Champagne and Bordeaux, as well as small glasses for Malaga, but she does not know in what order to serve the wines.

[14] The wide range of appellations, the related prices, and the variable age of the wines ensure that the valuing of vintages is within reach of more or less wealthy consumers.

[15] Pierre Bourdieu and Yvette Delsaut draw a comparison between the evolution of the value of artistic goods and the length of time that they have been regarded as minor works of art, as in the cases of haute couture or legitimate works of art (P. Bourdieu and Delsaut 1975).

specific climate conditions of a given year, which is to say the vintage. Distinctions are generally made among wines that are ready to drink young (within one to three years), wines with moderate aging potential (good to drink after five years), wines with significant aging potential (to be drunk after ten or 20 years), and rare wines, those which are meant to be held several decades. In a general sense, the older that wines are, the more they are esteemed, but the increase in value over time is offset by specific climate conditions that change over the years, ensuring (or not ensuring) the gustatory quality of the wines.[16]

Wine's increase in potential value (oenological, symbolic, and financial) as a function of time has effects on the significance and the manner in which one goes about purchasing wines and on the associated strategies for purchase.[17] For example, the *Guide Hachette* declares,

> The purchase of wines to drink or wines to keep does not follow the same logic. Different goals lead to different choices. Wines intended for immediate consumption should be ready to drink, which is to say de primeur wines... Wines to be held are bought young, with the intent of letting them age. Always choose the best bottles in a big year, wines that not only will stand up over time, but will increase in quality as the years go by. (Guide Hachette des vins 2003: 23)

Starting a collection gives rise to the constitution of capital whose relation to the market (the possibility of transforming it into money, or even into a financial instrument, or conversely into an unalienable good) varies as a function of its composition, the mode of its acquisition, and the social characteristics of its owner. The purchase of wine with the intent of future consumption is the anticipation of moments of pleasure inextricably linked to strategies of presentation of the self, the family, or the political group to which the individual belongs. At the same time, it offers the possibility of profit, at least in the case of the rarest wines, which can be converted into cash.[18] The owner of a Paris wine cellar, to whom individuals entrust the storage and care of their wine in exchange for compensation, expressed the attitude of his clientele by saying: "It's a way of saving, but unlike opening a bank account, this lets them drink from time to time. It's a living product, like antique cars. It's because of tradition, and for the pleasure of using it from time to time and sharing it with friends. There is a social aspect that is important with wine..."

---

[16] According to the ratings in *La Revue des vins de France* (2002: 185), a 1989 Château Lafite Rothschild is worth €180, while a 1984 bottle is only worth €87, a 1982 is worth €417, and a 1981 is worth €117.

[17] Here, we only consider purchases by individuals. Purchases by professionals, brokers, and wholesalers are the result of much speculation regarding a wine's future maturity.

[18] Similarly, the viticultural business, the raising of horses, and racing stables constitute forms of economic capital with a strong symbolic dimension (Pinçon and Pinçon-Charlot 1998). In Chile, José del Pozo (1998) studied the establishment of "French vineyards" near Santiago in the nineteenth century. An economic and political elite made these the site of the production of luxury and high-society functions.

The existence of sections like "Investment Fun" in magazines such as *Figaro-Magazine, Les Échos*, and *La vie Financière* testifies to the widespread nature of these savings, investment, and speculation practices.[19] But it is in publications aimed at a bourgeois audience that has a close relationship with financial capital in which we see reports directly comparing wine's profitability to that of other investments. An article in *La Vie Financière* entitled "Capital Gains in a Bottle" compares the performance of the CAC 40 stock market index, which went up 76% in ten years, to the price of Grands Bordeaux wines, which rose 190% in the same period (Placements vins 2002: 73) (Figure 6.1).

Transactions involving wines for aging and rare wines take place through the intermediaries of brokers and specialized trading houses, through classified ads in specialty publications like the *Revue des Vins de France*, and more recently on the Internet, especially on eBay, which is mostly used for small quantities and occasional purchases because of the complexity of the sales. These sales are supplied by professionals who specialize in the rare wine business or by individuals who, suffering from liquidity problems, seek revenues from cellar sales, even from bottles that they have inherited, in order to stay afloat. In each case, we see that a "good cellar" supposes financial stability, bourgeois manners, and a knowledge of wine. All of this conspires to associate consumption or possession of grands crus with professional and financial success.

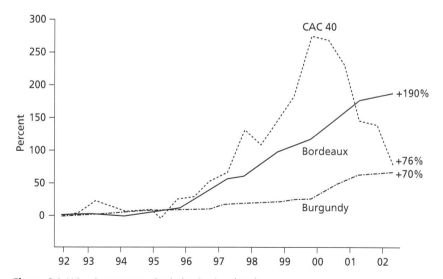

Figure 6.1 Wine investment: Capital gains in a bottle

[19] Equally noteworthy are the practices of counterfeiters, just as with works of art. There have been court cases linked in particular to the falsification of 1900 Margaux et Lafite.

Vintages and History in the First Person

A vintage not only designates an exceptional harvest but it also serves to define life's moments. The vintage on its own can signal the significance that one attributes to a friendship or an event. In a novel where he recounts the life of a Bordeaux broker, the writer and former Château Margaux proprietor Bernard Ginestet stages an encounter between his protagonist, who has just put his emotional and business affairs in order, and one of his colleagues in a club where "chartrons" (Bordeaux wine brokers and professionals) often meet for lunch. The colleague immediately senses that something remarkable has happened in the life of the broker when he orders a 1953 Palmer. The colleague exclaims: "You're too kind! What are we celebrating that you're ordering such a vintage?" (Ginestet 1998).

The value of a vintage increases all the more when it coincides with an important social event. The year 1811 is an emblematic example in this regard. In *Les dynasties bordelaises de Colbert à Chaban* (1991), Paul Butel reports that the English placed substantial orders with the large commercial houses due to that year's passing of Halley's Comet. François Audouze, an expert on rare wines, explains this phenomenon in *Les Carnets d'un collectionneur de vins anciens* (Audouze 2004): "The oldest red wine I have drunk was an 1811 Chambertin. Imagine what this evokes: you're at the height of the Napoleonic era, this becomes a heavy symbol, and moreover, it's the year of Halley's Comet, which isn't even yet called Halley's Comet. To have a comet in your cup, that's straight from the history books!"

Finally, the vintage corresponding to an individual's birth year is often sought. In an interview, a wine broker who is an expert in rare wines said that the most sought-after wines right now are those from the years 1945 to 1965 (for people between 50 and 60 years old). He claims that this demand is present above all in business circles and that the symbolic meaning is often privileged over the organoleptic qualities of the vintage in question.

Bottles that have belonged to famous people are all the more sought after.[20] The Hôtel Drouot auction of François Mitterrand's cellar, which had been kept in his rue Bièvre home, demonstrates the importance of the identity of a wine's owner. The event was reported in the press (notably in a *Paris-Match* article entitled "Great Men: *sic transit gloria*" [Grands hommes 2005: 12]), on the radio, and on television. The number of television networks and journalists who were present testifies to the interest generated by personalized objects that recount history. The press, which was waiting when the Drouot opened its doors, left

---

[20] When wines are prestigious and those who have owned them are famous, it is not only the monetary value that changes with a wine's age and rarity but also the vocabulary used to describe a product. We speak less of bottles than of flasks. Once "pleasing" or "young," the wines now become "complex" or "dazzling." At the same time, the site and modes of sale change. "Great cellars" and "grands vins" are sold in cellars found in Paris's refined neighborhoods or at auctions run by auctioneers who deal in the most highly esteemed artworks.

immediately after the last bottle belonging to the French president had been sold, even though, according to professional opinion, the subsequent sales were much more interesting from an organoleptic point of view. The bottles whose labels mentioned that they had been given as gifts to the former president or his wife sold at prices ten times higher than expert estimates, while other bottles were sold at prices much closer to these original evaluations. Of 43 lots bearing no mark of their former owner, 16 were sold for prices within the range estimated by the expert, or perhaps 15% higher than these, while 27 fetched higher prices that still did not reach double the initial estimate.[21]

Collectors participating in the Mitterrand auction seemed to be difficult to track, since a good number of them made their purchases by telephone through the intermediary of a broker, which is a regular practice among oenophiles. We could speculate that the secrecy of the purchases, in these specific cases, could be related to the financial hardship of the family. In light of the expected media attention, the necessity of the cellar sale put the interested family members in a delicate situation. The only buyer that we were able to interview was a socialist activist, a small business owner in the Périgord. He came specifically from his home region to buy wines and give them to his grandfather, a childhood friend of Mitterrand. Having obtained the catalogue a few days beforehand, and doubtless expecting that the wines that had been explicitly given to Mitterrand would fetch a higher price than he would be able to pay, he decided to bid on a lot of German wines, described in the *Paris-Match* article as "having probably been given by Helmut Kohl," but which had no special features mentioned in the catalogue. The lot, estimated at between €150 and €180 by the expert, was sold for €150. The day after the sale, once he had returned to the Périgord, he told me by telephone that he had sensed a certain bitterness from a German journalist who interviewed him on the subject: she had not expected that the lot of bottles, which bore no official trace of their prestigious ownership, would only sell at its oenological value, and that this final price was even less than that, since those present at the auction had no particular interest in German wines. The buyer in question was able to fulfill his second wish and buy himself two bottles of 1971 Monbazillac Château Le Caillou, an unexceptional vintage that only had meaning for him: it came from the year he was born.

Bottles that belonged to Thomas Jefferson are legendary. They fetch record bids because of the confluence of three factors: the quality of the vintage, the historic year of US independence, and the fact that the wine belonged to a very famous oenophile[22] who contributed so much to this historic event. These wines are consumed less and less frequently and become little more than trophies, displayed like crown jewels.[23]

---

[21] The only wine with a dedication on the label whose value did not increase was an Algerian wine.
[22] Jefferson lived for many years in France. He developed a wine classification system that is very close to the Bordeaux classification.
[23] Here, an analogy can be drawn to the trading of jewels in the Western Pacific in the Kula ring. The necklaces and bracelets are objects that gain prestige through their histories and the importance of

Through these various examples, it is clear that the ways of collecting and drinking wine are constitutive principles of its economic and symbolic value. It can never simply be reduced to the conditions of production. Yuna Chiffoleau and Catherine Laporte's analysis of the price formation of Burgundy wines shows that producers who have no access to the best appellations and have weak exports calculate prices as a function of production costs, which denotes a certain remove from the regular functioning of the wine market (Chiffoleau and Laporte 2004). The social identity of the person who holds the wine and the conditions in which it is kept combine with the social identity of the person who decides to drink it and chooses the circumstances of the drinking. Together, these factors are just as decisive as cultural and wine-making practices.

Other Worlds, Other Wines

Wine production in the so-called "New World" (the United States since the 1970s, and later Australia, South Africa, Chile, Argentina, and New Zealand) has developed outside of the criteria that dominate French wine production. In the United States, wine consumption and production grew more intense thanks to Italian immigrants who consumed young wines with friends and family.[24] Prohibition, which was in effect from 1920 to 1933, disrupted production but did not destroy it. It was against a background of fraud, perceptions of the product based on alcohol content, and confusion over standards of quality that wine production had to regain its footing in the 1930s. As many table grapes were produced as grapes for wine production. "Riesling" (a varietal traditionally used in Alsace) was produced, even though this varietal was not used in its composition. "Sauterne" and "Burgundy" were made using neither the varietals nor the methods from the regions to which the names referred. Fine wines, consumed by elites, were imported from

---

those who owned them. However, they are sometimes too heavy or cumbersome to be used by Trobrianders during ceremonies. Similarly, rare wines are drunk less and less frequently and become mere trophies to be displayed like crown jewels. This is the case with certain bottles that have acquired all the criteria of legitimacy and are held as part of a collection (Malinowski 1922: 89; see also Appadurai 1986).

[24] Although winegrowing had existed since the eighteenth century, when it was introduced by Spanish Franciscan missionaries, commercial production of wine did not begin until around 1830, through the efforts of a Bordeaux native named Louis Vigne. Production increased rapidly from the 1860s through the 1880s. Prohibition dealt a difficult blow to winegrowing, although it did not wipe it out entirely: consumption was allowed in religious ceremonies and Italian immigrants were allowed to drink among themselves. Some wines were produced illegally. When Prohibition was repealed in 1933, a group of producers who had survived the storm created the Wine Institute to strengthen the industry: it established standards of production, pushed for the simplification of laws that had hindered commerce, supported research, and introduced wine to Americans.

Europe, especially France, or came from California where few producers ensured quality production.[25]

The pace of quality production that developed in the context of liberal policies (with regard to cultivated acreages, production techniques, and varieties used in mass production[26]) led to a homogeneous product made using winemaking practices that were based on sophisticated technologies developed at the oenology laboratories at Berkeley and Davis and did not hew to restrictions imposed by the weight of tradition. The production of wines from a single varietal, a practice introduced by a merchant in 1939, gained considerable ground in the 1970s, doubtless a response to a desire for the clarification of quality criteria.[27] The varietals used evoke, in entirely legitimate ways, French production and its different regions (Cabernet-Sauvignon and Merlot correspond to Bordeaux, Syrah to Côtes du Rhône, Pinot Noir to Burgundy, and Riesling to Alsace). A classification based on prices was developed that established a price hierarchy consisting of five categories.[28] This conception of quality was also adopted in Southern Hemisphere countries.[29]

Wine Novices, the Media, and the Market

Table manners vary with the social structure of a country, its history, its religious and cultural differences, and its position in the world geopolitical system. Elites in "dependent" countries tend to adopt the cultural values of the dominant countries. Wine lovers outside of France and Italy originally came mostly from a cosmopolitan elite that was familiar with French culture and its geographic and gastronomic specificities. Over the last several decades, however, in an increasing number of countries wine has come to be consumed not only by a privileged bourgeoisie but as a relatively common beverage among the middle class, a substitute for tea, beer, or liquor in ceremonies and at

---

[25] Notable among them were German immigrants like Charles Krug, Jacob Beringer, Charles Wetmore, and Karl Wente, who founded prestigious estates that still exist today in the Napa Valley or have been sold off, and French immigrants in Santa Clara County, especially Etienne Thee, Charles Lefranc, and Paul Masson.
[26] According to a study by Marie Claude Pigouche, in 1998, seven companies each owned more than 2,000 hectares of vineyards (Pigouche 1999).
[27] American production had long used French appellations as generic categories, such as "Chablis," "Champagne," and "Burgundy," even though the Burgundies often included Carignan, a varietal that is not used in Burgundy, and even though they were often the target of lawsuits brought by the Institut National des Appellations Contrôlées that aimed at stemming the abusive usage of appellations.
[28] Less than $5 for basic wines, between $5 and $7 for premiums, between $7 and $14 for super premiums, between $14 and $50 for ultra premiums, and more than $50 for icons.
[29] For the largest developments related to the countries of the Southern Hemisphere, see Garcia-Parpet (2009).

gatherings of friends. Consumption has increased in countries that are not traditionally wine producers, while it has decreased in Mediterranean countries that have traditionally been producers. The rate of wine consumption in France continues to be the highest in the world, but as in Italy and Spain, it is decreasing overall. China, on the other hand, has broken the record for growth, increasing from 273.4 to 1158.6 million liters over the same period. The increase in consumption is just as strong and steady in the United States (7.7 liters per year per resident in 2000, compared with 4.9 in 1970) and in the countries of northern Europe. These figures, which reveal neither the quality of the wines nor the specific demographic profiles of the consumers aside from their national identity, hide a change in consumers' social and cultural profiles. These profiles may be related to consumption practices that are essential for understanding market dynamics. In the United States, this increase in wine consumption among the middle class is related to the characteristics of two emblematic wineries (Ernest & Julio Gallo and Robert Mondavi[30]), through which we can trace the history of American winemaking. Although they are positioned differently in the quality spectrum, these two wineries have been dominated by a constant attention to marketing that they have deployed in different manners: Gallo has launched enormous radio and television ad campaigns, while Mondavi has organized festivals and established an association for artisanal wine tasting. They have counted on growing demand in the middle class, which has not traditionally consumed a lot of wine and has little knowledge of wine and refined gastronomy in France. The demand for inexpensive, highly alcoholic wines consumed by the pitcher doubled between 1968 and 1972 (Torres 2006). In the 1970s, a growing number of consumers began to appreciate wines that achieved a high degree of quality. These wines were produced according to a logic that was modeled on the French system but still lost most of its specificity.

The entry of the middle class, which usually did not have well-developed tastes, into the game of oenological distinction brought with it such things as the anxiety that accompanies value judgments from friends or others about one's tastes. This growing number of new wine enthusiasts is the basis for a supply of oenological advice (reviews, books, prizes, television programs, and wine-tasting courses): in a sense a market-within-a-market that, far from being a mere cog in the traditional wine machine, has done much to throw its assumptions into question.

---

[30] Brothers Ernest and Julio Gallo, the sons of an Italian immigrant, founded their winery in 1933. Today, it is the largest winemaking enterprise in the world, with more than 3,240 hectares of vineyards. It played a large role in the period following Prohibition. Occupying the most prestigious spot in American winemaking from the start of its operations in 1966, and described by Hugh Johnson in the *Modern Encyclopedia of Wine* as aiming to produce high-quality wine at an industrial scale, Robert Mondavi is the third-largest American producer. Although Robert Mondavi owns many estates, the company buys wines from other producers and markets them under its own brands.

At once an index of and an instrument for increasing wine consumption, the growth of the oenological press first developed in nonproducing countries that are culturally close to France, like England, or in more recent entrants to the wine production market, like the United States. While it is possible to point to the appearance of a certain number of wine guides in the United States and England beginning in the 1960s,[31] in France these books and reviews only became popular in the 1980s, with the translation of English-language texts.[32] This accelerated in the 1990s and original French publications began to take up more space on the booksellers' shelves.[33]

Robert Parker, a former lawyer who was born in Maryland, began his career as a critic in 1978 with a bimonthly newsletter called *The Wine Advocate*. He later published books on the wines of Bordeaux, the wines of Burgundy and Beaujolais, the wines of the Côtes du Rhône region, and general books on the wines of France (Parker 1994a, 1994b, 1997a, 2001). He is doubtless the most mythical figure in wine criticism. His assessments have reputedly had devastating or magical effects on the fate of wines that he includes in his rankings.[34] Parker's power over the value of wines revealed itself on numerous occasions as we conducted our field research. Winegrowers who were interviewed mentioned time and again the exorbitant power of reviews Parker had published and affirmed that he "sets the market." One of them expressed the influence Parker held over the demand for his products:

Two years ago, I don't know why, Parker chose one of our wines. There were six wines selected by Parker. In America, he's the master! In the frenzy that followed, Japan [meaning a Japanese client]... Japan hadn't looked at the map and he didn't stumble upon us by accident. It's because we'd been chosen by Parker. Last year, we won a gold medal at the agricultural fair; we had to get it certified... The Parker... there are those who are for it, and those who are opposed...

A certain number of producers tend to "Parkerize" their wines in order to give them a woodier flavor, since this is a quality that Parker appreciates. On November 21, 1997, *Le Figaro patrimoine* reviewed the new edition of the

---

[31] In the case of the American wine press, see work by John Storm (1955), William Edman Massee (1961), and *The Pleasures of Wine: A Guide to the Wines of the World* (1963). For Great Britain, see Wildman (1972) and Busselle (1986).

[32] Paul de Cassagnac's *Les vins de France* and the *Revue des vins de France*, which was originally known as *La Revue du vin de France*, are exceptions to this rule. Only 100 copies of Cassagnac's book were printed on heavy stock, of which 70 were reserved for the author and were not intended for sale; a first edition of 100 numbered copies was also issued. The *Revue du Vin de France*, founded in 1927, was not at first a periodical wholly consecrated to tastemaking. It was also intended for wine professionals.

[33] Among the French publishers offering books about wine are Assouline, Calman-Levy, Fayard, Flammarion, Hachette, Laffont, Larousse, Rivage, Solar, Stock, and Seuil.

[34] Pierre-Marie Chauvin (2005) draws attention to the fact that Parker, based on his reviews of Bordeaux wines, is not the iconoclast that his overly rapid judgments would lead one to believe. But it's doubtless due to the fact that Parker pays more attention to the wines of this region and thereby imposes an uneven treatment (e.g., skimping on opinions on other regions of France) that Parker breaks with the French mode of thinking that had always held that regions and appellations ought not to be compared to one another.

Guide Parker in the following terms: "*Guide Parker des vins de France*, new edition by Robert Parker. The new bible from the American wine messiah has arrived. With his anathemas and panegyrics, this 1,104-page brick contains the tastings and opinions of the uncontested expert who brings prices to a boil and lends mystique to wines when his ratings surpass 90 percent."

Foreign critics who have begun to produce review books are endowed with a world of possible comparisons that is larger than those used by the competition juries in France. In publications like *Wine Spectator*, a highly respected American periodical among wine professionals, wines are constructed such that all red, white, and sweet wines can compete in each category. The critics undertake blind taste tests and report the results, indifferently matching up wines from Bordeaux, New Zealand, or Chile, annihilating in one fell swoop the differences that have been built up by the history of production and social wine consumption in France. This new selection method for wines of quality has been imitated in Switzerland and France, where the "World Pinot Noir Competition," the "World Chardonnay Competition," and the "World Rosé Competition" have been held.

Even when they respect the overall French classification scheme, foreign publications make comparisons between different appellations that were unthinkable according to the criteria traditionally used in France. For Hugh Johnson, wines from Bourgueil and Chinon constitute "a type of Bordeaux that will stupefy you with its charm and vitality," while Cabernet Franc offers "a sort of pastel sketch of a great Médoc." Furthermore, the 1855 classification system plays a role (even if it is not explicitly invoked by the *Guide Hachette des vins*). The French *Guide Parker* creates a hierarchy among the different wine-producing regions. In the introduction to the section dedicated to Bordeaux, Parker offers a paean replete with superlatives:

> Bordeaux estates, which are generally called chateaux, produce the greatest number of wines with aging potential... The Bordeaux region always produces wines at a higher level than those from anywhere else in the world. Among the world's best Cabernet Sauvignon and Cabernet Franc makers, Bordeaux remains the benchmark. (Parker 1997*b*: 127, 143)

He seems not to note lesser valued regions, such as the Loire Valley, which is a manner of establishing a hierarchy. Foreign authors also distinguish themselves from their French counterparts by their tendency to award scores and comment on a wine's organoleptic qualities instead of discussing the vineyards and the winemakers.

It is in this context that Guibert's wines, which "accidentally" found their way into the hands of a prestigious English expert, were judged equivalent to the finest French grands crus. These wines, which before could barely find a buyer, soared in value to fetch very high prices. This spectacular reversal of fortunes, which was only made possible by a change in the structure of the market at the international level of the social composition of supply and demand and the corresponding methods of assessment, was the first step in questioning an institutionalization that had stabilized and routinized the markets for over 50 years. Irreproducible, this dazzling trajectory was nevertheless at the root of a new understanding of the possibilities of quality production that were offered by the region where Guibert kept his vineyards.

New Beliefs, New Practices, and the Rejection of Legal Constraints

In the face of a market environment shaped by law and entrenched thinking, the vast majority of winegrowers, who do not enjoy AOC recognition, see themselves as having no option for fighting against their marginalization except conforming to the rules set forth in the legislation, even if, as the last ones into the castle, they stand to realize profits far lower than producers benefiting from preexisting fame.[35]

Like many production zones in France that aspired to quality production, Languedoc-Roussillon did acquire its AOC designation,[36] but the price was redevelopment accompanied by a difficult process of social differentiation. The profits tied to the recognition of appellations have often been limited. The AOC price advantage was entirely relative, tied to limited yields but above all to the image of popular wines attached to the region. The AOC regulations were often perceived as a "legal constraint" and the entire process was seen as an attempt to "import the social realities of Bordeaux." Having nothing to lose in a system where everything contributed to their marginalization, the producers of Languedoc-Roussillon did not hesitate to break with an orthodoxy that had far too often failed to live up to its promises of economic and symbolic profits. Having finally overcome the obstacle that hindered the progress of vineyards in the "Winegrowing South,"[37] an institutional invention gave the wine producers the objective

---

[35] The 1935 legislation allowed the extension of estates and an increase in the number of appellations following agreement by the expert committee of the INAO. The strong presence of state representatives on the committee allowed for a significant growth in appellations as a function of social preoccupations and attention to rural areas.

[36] A small number of new appellations have been recognized, notably Fitou, Faugères, Saint-Chinian, Corbières, Coteaux du Languedoc, and Coteaux du Minervois.

[37] The region's other nickname, the "Red South," evokes the social movements led by winegrowers against the large property holders and the state in the hopes of getting better prices.

conditions required to generalize quality production. This generalization of quality is, in great part, at the root of the transformation of a forgotten region into a pioneering region and is the driving force behind the marked improvement of its reputation.

Guibert's success, which provoked a new perception of the quality of wines from the region, led merchants who had survived the transformations that had taken place in the production and distribution of viticultural products to establish new classification systems, trusting that consumers would have a different understanding of excellence. Robert Skalli, the son of an Algerian vineyard owner, now owns a 217-hectare estate in Corsica and one in the Pope Valley in California. He is chairman of the board of an important food services company and as a wine dealer in Languedoc has become the leader of the effort to increase the prestige of the region's wines. It is his knowledge of the international market, and especially the American market, that has allowed him to predict the potential of Languedoc-Roussillon. As the leader of a core group of large brokers and estates, he enjoyed the support of local leaders (the president of the departmental young farmers' league and the president of the departmental section of the National Federation of Agricultural Workers' Union [FNSEA], among others). He gave a decisive push to an effort that had been underway since the early 1970s to increase the value of table wines. This first allowed the enactment of legislation prohibiting blends with imported wines and advocating the use of recommended varietals (local varietals Grenache, Syrah, and others) and the varietals of the great French AOC zones that have become "international standards" (Cabernet Sauvignon, Merlot, etc.). "Vins de pays" were created in 1968, and in 1981 the Pays d'Oc designation was established. Finally, in 1987, the names of the varietals used were allowed to be indicated on the label. This new way of imagining the product, marrying a rigorous production process to an interpretative framework that was meaningful to consumers who were used to distinguishing wines by varietals, allowed for a direct response to the demands of the foreign market, especially the American market.

In a January 1995 interview in the *Revue Vinicole Internationale*, Skalli insisted that the key to this Schumpterian innovation was the consumer's point of view:

Some used to consider quality as being exclusively reserved for AOC wines, but they see today that it can be found elsewhere... You only need to look around the world over the last 15 years to see the proof... The success of Californian or Australian wines [among new consumers] is based on their simplicity: you only need to understand and retain about a dozen words (Chardonnay, Merlot, etc.) to make sense of these wines. The success of such an approach depends on a rigorous production process that ensures consistent quality, productivity, agroalimentary efficiency, and specificity of the varietal and wine type on a global scale. (Académie d'Agriculture de France 1993)

The same year that the Vin de Pays d'Oc denomination was created, Skalli established the "Fortant de France" brand for export and the "Fortant" brand for the French market, relying on the production of single varietal wines with a good price-to-quality ratio. His main markets were exports (60% of sales) and mass retail (72% of French sales). This exceptional production in Languedoc-Roussillon by a charismatic producer, along with the legitimation of new categories of quality linked to varietals, led to a transformation of the social morphology among regional producers. Local brokerage houses, conscious of the need to offer wines that would satisfy the new demands of their clientele, and the producers' associations that had been created with state support saw an opportunity to succeed in this new manner of conceiving of quality wines. There was widespread adoption of the new classification.

Cooperatives and producers' associations saw significant changes in terms of their size, their relationship to the land, the quality of their product, and their relation to cultural and commercial practices. Two of the cooperatives became large international groups, while a handful distinguished themselves through the quality of their products. Most of them encountered enormous difficulties in confronting new market demands, as the producers were deeply attached to the production methods associated with the excessive maximization of quantities and a political effort that put pressure on the government to obtain price controls. As many of the cooperatives faced difficulties, a certain number of winegrowers sought to become winemakers. Companies (most notably Duboeuf, the largest French viticultural group), merchants, and producers from established regions (traditional winemakers from Burgundy, including Antonin Rodet and Michel Laroche, as well as renowned producers from the Bordeaux region such as Mouton Rothschild), foreign interests (notably BRL Hardy, an Australian winery), individuals (the descendants of wine producers both from the region and from elsewhere) all came to set up shop in the region, attracted by the low cost of land and the new promises the region had to offer.

In the 1990s, Pays d'Oc wines represented the largest portion of "vin de pays" production (60%), of which 80% was exported, mostly to the United States. The wines gave a boost to the region and attracted the attention of wine professionals in France, which was made clear by articles with suggestive titles like "Pays d'Oc Wines: Masters of the Universe?" in the industry press.[38]

---

[38] See for example: Vins de cépage, la déferlante (1993); Dossier: Vins de cépages: prêts, partez? (1995); Les vins de cépage ont la cote (1996); and Les vins de pays d'Oc: maîtres du monde? (1998).

According to Étienne Montaigne et al., Pays d'Oc prices increased by a factor of two or three, depending on the varietal (1999).

If the runaway success of varietal wines from Languedoc has been met with obstacles thrown up by foreign competitors from "New World" countries planting more and more Merlot, Chardonnay, Cabernet Sauvignon, and Shiraz, this production of entry-level "varietal wines" in Languedoc-Roussillon has nevertheless allowed a certain number of producers there to benefit from the advantages of a different classification, which in turn obligates them to redirect their efforts toward making high-quality products. Bulk sales have progressively decreased in favor of bottles of handcrafted wines or those from high-quality estates. Moreover, Guibert's products and the production of varietal wines have sparked the production of upscale wines that, although not produced in accordance with the AOC system, combine rigorous cultural and winemaking practices and appropriate soils.

Among winegrowers who produce both AOC wines and vins de pays, it is most often the latter type of wine that acts as the entry-level product. An analysis of wines produced between 1998 and 2003 shows that even if the modal value of AOC wines is higher than that of vins de pays (the first falling between €8 and €11 and the second between €5 and €8), the highest prices were found among vins de pays.[39] The AOC rules had been questioned with such vigor that the most spectacular performances were realized by producers who chose to adopt other rules of production, even though these same producers were located in recognized AOC regions. This is the case with Daumas Gassac, a Guibert operation, whose upscale "Emile Peynaud" reserve sold at an ex-cellar price of €91.50 in 2003. Another example is found in the Grange au Père, an estate run by a former cooperative member and his son, who "learned at the knee" of Burgundy winemakers after having studied physical therapy. In 2002, their wine sold for €53 per bottle, according to the *Guide des vins du Nouvel Observateur*.

The transformation of Languedoc-Roussillon from an afterthought to a leader serves to remind us of deep changes in the wine market that had until now gone more or less unnoticed due to the market's extensive reach, the diversity of actors, and the ambiguity of those who contributed to the change through ambivalent practices.[40] This transformation acted as a trigger and drew reactions from producers in the most prestigious regions who were more susceptible to the effects of international competition and the significant

---

[39] To address the lack of data concerning many producers and to underline productive potential, we have chosen the highest priced wine between 1998 and 2003 from the range of products in a given year.

[40] In *Le marché de l'excellence: les grands crus à l'épreuve de la mondialisation* (Garcia-Parpet 2009), we found that a certain number of French businesses, which benefited from AOC legitimation but controlled brands endowed with great symbolic capital, did not hesitate to change the rules of the game and extend their production into new territory, validating practices that had previously been seen as heretical.

increase in the number of AOC wines that threatened institutionalized scarcity. The questioning of the "French model" has spread progressively from marginal regions. As renowned a region as Bordeaux saw a certain number of producers demand the right to print the varietal on the label and choose cultivation and winemaking practices that were forbidden by French law. The debate around production norms has reached the highest levels of wine professionals in France and is now being discussed among cabinet ministers and in Parliament.

The analysis of a product's global market through the particular career of one winemaker and the changing valuation of his products pushed us to reflect on shifts in consumer preferences. Except for the fact that this national model had been legitimated by international demand over the course of the previous centuries (which actually led us astray), nothing guaranteed the universalism of the values on which the supremacy of the AOC model rested. Without considering the historical and social specificity of a hierarchy legitimated by the state or by producer and consumer practices, one can sink into the universalization of criteria of excellence that are bound up in very specific modes of existence. Sociological and historical analysis must reconstruct the particularity of the agents and social configurations where classification schemes hold authority. To understand the process of valorization of wine market dynamics, we must move beyond neoclassical economic analysis, which holds that the market and actors are neither historically nor culturally situated, and analyze the complex connections between individuals' preferences at the national and international levels. Karl Polanyi showed that the national market is not the mechanical result of the gradual extension of local exchanges but instead the effect of mercantilist state policies aimed at increasing domestic and foreign commerce (1944: ch. 5). In the same way, the emergence of the global market cannot be the mechanical result of an extension of the national market. The evolutionary sequence—from local to regional to national to global market—completely undoes the order observed by historians and classical economists and certainly resets our understanding of the connections between fluctuations in national and international prices by taking into account the perceptions of producers and consumers.

REFERENCES

Académie d'Agriculture de France (1993). *Compte-rendu de l'Académie d'Agriculture de France: les vins fins et leur appellation* 70(1).

Akerlof, G. (1970). The Market for "Lemons": Quality Uncertainty and the Market Mechanism. *Quarterly Journal of Economics* 84(3): 488–500.

Appadurai, A. (1986). *The Social Life of Things: Commodities in Cultural Perspective*. New York, NY: Cambridge University Press.

Audouze, F. (2004). *Carnets d'un collectionneur de vins anciens: ses conseils, ses dîners, ses classements*. Paris: Michalon.
Bartoli, P. and Boulet, D. (1990). Régulation et spécificités sectorielles: la sphère viticole. *Cahiers d'Economie et de Sociologie Rurales* 17: 7–38.
Bonneuil, C. and Thomas, F. (2009). *Gènes, pouvoir et profits: la recherche publique dans les transformations de régime de production des savoirs en génétique végétale, 1884–2004*. Paris: Editions Quae.
Bourdieu, J. (2003). Normes et classifications à l'épreuve de la vache folle. In A. Stanziani (ed.), *La qualité des produits en France (XVIIIe–XXe siècles)*. Paris: Belin, 195–216.
Bourdieu, P. (2005). *The Social Structures of the Economy*. Trans. C. Turner. Cambridge: Polity.
——and Delsaut, Y. (1975). Le couturier et sa griffe: contribution à une théorie de la magie. *Actes de la recherche en sciences sociales* 1: 7–36.
Boyer, R. (1990). Les problématiques de la régulation face aux spécificités sectorielles. Perspectives ouvertes sur la thèse de Pierre Bartoli et Daniel Boulet. *Cahiers d'Economie et de Sociologie Rurales* 17: 39–76.
Bussele, M. (1986). *The Wine Lover's Guide to France*. London: Pavilion.
Butel, P. (1991). *Les dynasties bordelaises: de Colbert à Chaban*. Paris: Perrin.
Chauvin, P.-M. (2005). Le critique et sa griffe: ce que fait Robert Parker (aux vins de Bordeaux). *Terrains et travaux*. 9 (2005/2), 90–108.
Chiffoleau, Y. and Laporte, C. (2004). La formation des prix: le marché des vins de Bourgogne. *Revue française de sociologie* 45(4): 653–80.
Commons, J. R. (1934). *Institutional Economics: Its Place in Political Economy*. Madison: University of Wisconsin Press.
del Pozo, J. (1998). *Historia del vino chileno*. Santiago: Editorial Universitaria.
Dossier: vins de cépages: prêts, partez! (1995, June). *Revue Vinicole Internationale*.
Elias, N. (1983). *The Court Society*. Trans. E. Jephcott. Oxford: Blackwell.
Eymard-Duvernay, F. (1989). Conventions de qualité et pluralité des formes de coordination. *Revue économique* 2: 329–59.
Fligstein, N. (1990). *The Transformation of Corporate Control*. Cambridge, MA: Harvard University Press.
——(2001). *The Architecture of Markets: An Economic Sociology of Twenty-First Century Capitalist Societies*. Princeton, NJ: Princeton University Press.
Garcia-Parpet, M.-F. (2009). *Le marché de l'excellence: les grands crus à l'épreuve de la mondialisation*. Paris: Editions du Seuil.
Garrier, G. (1998). *Histoire sociale et culturelle du vin*. Paris: Larousse.
Ginestet, B. (1998). *Les chartrons: Edouard Menton, courtier bordelais*. Paris: Acropole.
Grands hommes: sic transit gloria. (2005). *Paris Match*.
Guide Hachette des vins. (2003). Paris: Hachette.
Jacquet, O. and Laferté, G. (2006). Le contrôle républicain du marché: vignerons et négociants sous la IIIe République. *Annales HSS* 5: 1147–90.
Julien, A. (1816). *Topographie de tous les vignobles connus*. Paris .
Karpik, L. (2010). *Valuing the Unique: The Economics of Singularities*. Trans. N. Scott. Princeton. NJ: Princeton University Press.
Laferté, G. (2006). *La Bourgogne et ses vins: image d'origine contrôlée*. Paris: Belin.

Les vins de cépages ont la cote (1996, December). *Rayon Boissons.*
Les vins de pays d'Oc: maîtres du monde? (1998). *Viti* 226: 46.
Mackenzie, A. (1995). *Daumas Gassac: The Birth of a Grand Cru.* London: Segrave Foulkes.
Malinowski, B. (1922). *Argonauts of the Western Pacific: An Account of Native Enterprise and Adventure in the Archipelagoes of Melanesian New Guinea.* London: Routledge.
Massee, W. E. (1961). *Wines and Spirits: A Complete Buying Guide.* New York, NY: McGraw-Hill.
Mintz, S. (1985). *Sweetness and Power: The Place of Sugar in Modern History.* New York, NY: Viking.
Montaigne, E., Laporte, J. P., Perez, V., and Galeote, X. (1999). Les mutations du négoce des vins tranquilles en France. *Actes du colloque Société française d'économie rurale sur la grande distribution alimentaire.* Montpellier: INRA, 122–35.
Parker, R. (1994a). *Les vins de Bordeaux.* Paris: Solar.
—— (1994b). *Les vins de Bourgogne et du Beaujolais.* Paris: Solar.
—— (1997a). *Wines of the Rhone Valley.* New York, NY: Simon & Schuster.
—— (1997b). *Guide Parker des vins de France.* Paris: Solar.
—— (2001). *Guide Parker des vins de France.* Paris: Solar.
Pigouche, M.-C. (1999). *Les vins de cépage: une production mondiale en plein essor.* Lattes: Comité économique des vins du Languedoc-Roussillon (CEVILAR).
Pijassou, R. (1980). *Un grand vignoble de qualité: Le Médoc,* Vol. 1. Paris: Jules Taillandier.
Pinçon, M. and Pinçon-Charlot, M. (1998). *Grand Fortunes: Dynasties and Forms of Wealth in France.* Trans. A. L. Secara. New York, NY: Algora.
Placements vins: de la plus value en bouteille. (2002 22–28, September). *La Vie Financière.*
Polanyi, K. (1944). *The Great Transformation.* Boston, MA: Beacon.
Revue des vins de France (1993, November).
Revue des vins de France (2002, November).
Sagnes, J. (1992). Viticulture et politique dans la première moitié du XXe siècle: aux origines du statut de la viticulture. In *Les recontres de Béziers: La viticulture française aux XIXe et XXe siècles. Colloque national d'histoire, Béziers le 30 mai 1992.* Montpellier: Presses du Languedoc.
Stanziani, A. (2005). *Histoire de la qualité alimentaire.* Paris: Editions du Seuil.
Steiner, P. (2005). *La sociologie économique.* Paris: La Découverte.
Storm, J. (1955). *Invitation to Wines: An Informal Guide to the Selection, Care, and Enjoyment of Domestic and European Wines.* New York, NY: Simon & Schuster.
Swedberg, R. (2003). *Principles of Economic Sociology.* Princeton, NJ: Princeton University Press.
Thévenot, L. (1995). Des marchés aux normes. In G. Allaires and R. Boyer (eds.), *La grande transformation de l'agriculture.* Paris: INRA/Economica, 33–51.
Thiesse, A.-M. (1991). *Ecrire la France: le mouvement littéraire régionaliste de langue française entre la Belle Epoque et la Libération.* Paris: PUF.
Torres, O. (2006). *The Wine Wars: The Mondavi Affair, Globalization, and "Terroir."* Trans. K. Smith. New York, NY: Palgrave.

Vins de cépage: la déferlante. (1993, November 11). *L'Express*.

Waldo H. (1963). *The Pleasures of Wine: A Guide to the Wines of the World*. New York, NY: Crowell-Collier Press.

Wildman, F. S. (1972). *A Wine Tour of France: A Convivial Wine Guide and Travel Guide to French Vintages and Vineyards*. London: Vintage.

7 Pricing Looks: Circuits of Value in Fashion Modeling Markets

Ashley Mears

Introduction

What makes one face a highly valued commodity amid an enormous pool of relatively "worthless" competition in the fashion modeling industry? Consider the case of a young male model from London, whom I will call JD.[1] By most measures, JD had a very successful first year as a model. A university student modeling part-time, his first photo shoot was a fashion campaign that paid £10,000 for one day's work. He was 20 years old and earning more in a month than he had earned all his life in part-time retail jobs.

Initially, JD measured a job's worth in monetary terms alone, and he could not get his head around working for "free." Upon booking a shoot for *Dazed and Confused* magazine in London, he refused the job upon learning that it was unpaid: "*Dazed and* what?!" he recounted. *Dazed and Confused*, it turns out, is a leading fashion magazine celebrated around the world as a launching pad for famous designers, musicians, and models.

In addition to snubbing *Dazed*, JD turned down scores of prestigious magazines and advertising campaigns. The jobs he did accept with glee paid high day rates and boosted his reputation among his friends and family back in Manchester, but detracted from his status in the business:

But then when I got *Sportswear Now* I was like, "Yeah man, *Sports Now!* My boys can see me in the window! Yeah!" It's just a [stupid] sporting goods store, but for me back in Manchester village everyone's like, "Yeah man, you did *Sports Now!*" And I'm like turning down *Vogue*. That's why I made a mistake. Because I turned down really big jobs.

Taking JD's statement into closer consideration, we might ask what counts as a "big job" in fashion modeling. Two years ago, JD thought the obvious: a big job paid big money. In this belief, we can see JD's mistake: not so much in turning down work but in not being able to discriminate different types of worth beyond immediate cash value. By overvaluing money and undervaluing fashion elites, JD was unable to see the long-term payoffs beyond short-term

---

[1] All names of respondents are pseudonyms.

profits. He was blind to symbolic rewards, seeing instead only economic ones. JD's problem, in short, was his illiteracy of the fashion field and its particular logics.

Fashion models sell their "look" to fashion clients in the modeling market, and agents, called "bookers," broker the trade. Although the term "look" seemingly refers to a fixed set of physical attributes, in fact looks are the flexible outcomes of social processes in which bookers and clients attempt to assign objective value to a symbolic product. Why are some looks, like JD's, sometimes worth thousands of pounds and other times paid little or nothing at all? How do bookers and clients determine the value of something so ambiguous for market exchange?

Such questions address key issues in economic sociology concerning processes of valuation and the construction of order in markets. Based on ethnographic data and in-depth interviews with modeling agents and fashion clients in New York and London, this chapter develops a framework to trace the social production of value in the aesthetic goods market. I argue that the look accrues value within a cultural production field stratified into two distinct yet overlapping spheres known as "editorial" and "commercial" fashion.[2] These two spheres are personified in JD's short career: there is *Dazed and Confused* on the editorial end and *Sportswear Now* on the commercial end, and between them there exists a status gulf. The people who work predominantly on each end constitute bounded networks, what Viviana Zelizer would call "circuits of commerce" (Zelizer 2004). Within their respective circuits, market actors form relationships and share mutual understandings of value, taste, and specific logics and routines when it comes to trading looks. By tracing the social construction of value on a seemingly anomalous good—a model's look—this study contributes to circuit-based analyses of markets in the cultural economy and beyond.

Value in the Aesthetic Economy

Models must meet basic physical criteria of attractiveness, height, and size. For women, these are typically heights of at least 5 ft. 9 in. (175.3 cm) and measurements close to 34–24–34 in. (86.4–61–86.4 cm); for men, a height of 6 ft.–6 ft. 3 in. (183–190.5 cm) and a waist of 32 in. (81.3 cm) are expected.

---

[2] A field, as Bourdieu defined it, is a distinct social universe with its own rules, logics, and capitals that function independently of—even opposite to—those of the economy (1993: 162). There are many such social configurations, from political and economic fields to industrial fields, each one guided by an internal logic and competition for localized capitals. Within the field of cultural production, there are loosely distinct fields of photography, literature, art, and so on. Even within fashion, the high-fashion modeling field is distinct from child, art, and glamor (erotica) modeling, because each has its own principles of operations and orienting logics of play.

Beyond these physical specifications, models' assets are sized up according to personal tastes and external evaluations of their appeal. This subjective appraisal is known in the market as a model's look (Mears and Finlay 2005). Like service workers, models perform "aesthetic labor" to achieve the look; that is, they project a desirable, cheery personality in addition to presenting an attractive physique (Entwistle and Wissinger 2006; Witz et al. 2003). Bookers and clients must then assess a model's worth and agree on the model's fees, typically in the form of an hourly or day rate.

Fashion modeling is structured like other markets in the growing cultural (Scott 2000) or "aesthetic economy" (Aspers 2005; Entwistle 2009), where culture, creativity, and aesthetics intertwine with commerce to sustain urban and, increasingly, global economies (Currid 2006). Like art, music, television, and other goods in the cultural economy, looks have fluid and unpredictable value (Scott 2000). The people who work in markets such as fashion face high stakes of unpredictability, in which "all hits are flukes" and "nobody knows" what will sell, or at what price (Bielby and Bielby 1994; Caves 2000).

Fashion modeling is a case of uncertain economic action in the aesthetic economy. Given the arbitrariness of aesthetic evaluation, bookers never know which looks will be desired by which client, nor can clients know which looks will appeal to their consumers. To add to the instability, the fashion market is constantly in flux, with new looks that are "hot" one season and forgotten the next, and agencies who continually tap into global networks of scouts in the search for "fresh faces." Furthermore, modeling does not require extensive investments such as education or training, so the entry criteria are low, and meanwhile the job is considered "cool" (Neff et al. 2005). This results in overcrowding, with a great deal of competition for any one model looking to secure work.

While competition is fierce, success is enormously skewed. So extreme is success that economists call these "winner-take-all" markets, in which a handful of "winners" reap lucrative and visible rewards, while the bulk of contestants fail (Frank and Cook 1995). According to the US Occupational Outlook Handbook, models earned an estimated median income of $27,410 in 2008,[3] a year in which three fashion models made it into *Forbes* magazine's "Celebrity 100" list of the world's most powerful celebrities: Gisele Bündchen with $35 million, Heidi Klum with $14 million, and Kate Moss with $7.8 million (Miller 2008). Though there are enormous disparities in models' economic worth, market participants are unable to account for the characteristics that distinguish "winners" from the rest. The underlying quality differences that separate a Gisele Bündchen from thousands of her physically comparable competitors are unknown to models, bookers, and clients alike (Godart and Mears 2009).

---

[3] Because the US Department of Labor surveys combined characteristics of demonstrators, product promoters, and models, these figures should be taken as rough estimates.

The tastemaker's dilemma—economic calculation under uncertainty—goes straight to one of the central problems of economic sociology: How does economic exchange happen in the absence of perfect information? What do we do when we do not know what is best to do? (Beckert 1996). Uncertainty, a situation in which actors cannot anticipate the outcome of a decision and cannot assign probabilities to the outcome, poses a distinctly sociological problem. Economists usually try to redefine uncertain scenarios into risky ones, from unknowable to calculable courses of action (Knight 1957). Such abstractions do little good for the booker and fashion client, neither of whom can rely on standard measurable characteristics to discriminate worth between models' looks. As Aspers has noted, markets in fashion are best conceptualized as "status markets," since they lack standard rubrics to measure product quality (Aspers 2009). Pricing is therefore a particularly troublesome endeavor for cultural producers, because in these contexts there is no clear correlation between price and quality.

Sociologists argue that prices, like other commensuration systems (Espeland and Stevens 1998), are outcomes of social processes, rather than mysterious quantities that emerge from some set of preexisting laws "out there" (White 2002). Prices and payments are tied to organizational constraints and to the moral worth and status positions of those getting paid (Podolny 2005; Velthuis 2005). Because status and moral worth are relational outcomes, prices are intimately tethered to the kinds of social relations that underlie markets.

To examine such relations within the fashion modeling market, I employ the concept of "circuits of commerce," introduced by Viviana Zelizer, who examines the social connectivity in settings such as gift giving, life insurance, and consumption. By "commerce," Zelizer (2004) invokes the old sense of the word, when commerce meant conversation and mutual exchange. A circuit is a type of social network organized around economic activity, but it is not *just* a network, because it contains specific understandings, practices, information, obligations, rights, symbols, and media of exchanges.[4] Sociologists have uncovered such webs of relationships in markets throughout the cultural economy, from the advertising (Nixon 2003), magazine publishing (Crewe 2003), and pop music (Negus 1999) industries to the art market (Plattner 1996; Velthuis 2005) and the fashion industry (Aspers 2005; Entwistle 2009: 51–74; Skov 2002).[5]

---

[4] While plenty of sociological research documents social ties in fashion markets (e.g., Godart and Mears 2009), this chapter is concerned with the *contents* of these networks—the shared practices, understandings, and meanings among them that constitute a circuit of social relations.

[5] In her analysis of the aesthetic economy of fashion modeling, Entwistle (2009: 51–74) use the term *circuits of value* to describe the interplay of editorial and commercial fashion production that valorizes looks into high-demand products. But whereas Entwistle draws mainly on Bourdieu and more recently actor-network-theory to outline the structure of the aesthetic economy, she overlooks the interpersonal connections and conventions crucial to the process. This study picks up where Entwistle leaves off, and examines the role of social interaction, relationships and shared conventions among and between actors within the circuits.

Broadly speaking, circuits of commerce contain within them specific understandings of how participants should do business. That is, their members abide by specific conventions—habits, routines, and norms—which are shared ways of doing things that enable participants to meet each other's expectations. Such coordination is necessary for an art world like fashion to happen at all (Becker 1982). The everyday assumptions and routines bookers and clients use throughout their working days may seem inconsequential, but conventions both enable and constrain economic activity (Beckert 1996; Biggart and Beamish 2003; Podolny 2005; Storper and Salais 1997). Conventions exert inertia on a set way of doing things, reproducing a structural order in worlds which might otherwise have infinite possibilities of arrangements (Becker 1995). While seemingly mundane, conventions in the aggregate result in huge wins or losses for bookers and the clients they service; conventions are therefore key to understanding how a look attains economic value.

In addition to conventions, members of a circuit share a sense of boundaries—an understanding of who is in and who is out of the right to participate. As Podolny has demonstrated, the status of producers in a market is a powerful boundary marker which producers use to their own advantage; a firm's high position in the status order lends higher profits (2005). Following Podolny, Godart and Mears have argued that fashion designers strategically choose models with an interest in positioning their design houses favorably in fashion's status hierarchy (2009). If the field of fashion, like other markets, is structured along status boundaries, circuits are a way to access the processes through which status is generated, contested, and reproduced in the field. Circuits give sociologists access to the dynamic, meaningful, negotiated interactions that sustain economic transactions; such a focus can reveal the cultural work of producers that sustains, and potentially reworks, the structure of a market.

Methods and Data

Data for the following analysis comes from participant observation and interviews with employees at two modeling agencies, Mode Models in New York City and Stella Models in London, and a snowball sample of 40 fashion clients.[6] I started this project in January 2004 as a participant observer at Mode Model Management, also known as Mode. After initially being introduced to Mode through a scout, the managers agreed that I could conduct an ethnographic study of the agency, and they later arranged my collaboration with Stella Models in London. Bookers arranged for me to experience the full

---

[6] Names of organizations have been changed to protect confidentiality.

range of modeling work in both New York and London, including five Fashion Weeks, hundreds of castings, and dozens of jobs in every type of modeling work over the course of two and a half years.

Throughout my participant observation, I sat beside bookers at their desks in the office and also attended castings and immersed myself into networks of fashion clients in both cities. Near the end of the participant observation phase of the research, I interviewed a snowball sample of agency workers in New York and London, speaking to a total of 33 employees: 24 bookers and seven business and account managers, and two bookers' assistants. Twenty of these employees were located in New York, and 11 worked in London. Bookers were recruited for interviews through referrals from participants.

Because a model's value emerges from the interaction between booker and client, I also interviewed a snowball sample of 40 clients: four fashion designers, 11 photographers, seven magazine editors, six stylists, two hair/makeup artists, and ten casting directors. Clients were recruited at castings, backstage at fashion shows, and during photo shoots I attended. My findings come primarily from the interview data, with supplementary use of the participant observation data. Interviews lasted between 45 and 90 minutes, and were tape-recorded, transcribed, and coded inductively using ATLAS.ti software, which allows for the emergence of broad themes.

The interview sample reflects the attribute of fashion as an industry with high proportions of white gay men in decision-making positions (McRobbie 1998; Wilson 2005). Sixty percent of the clients were men (25), half of whom identified as gay men, and none of the female clients identified as lesbian. Among bookers, half of the sample was male, among whom four identified as gay men, while just one of the ten female bookers identified as lesbian. Most bookers and clients (54) attended college for at least a year, and most (51) had an arts-related background from previous careers within the creative economy, typically as visual artists, fashion journalists, and actors.[7]

Mode and Stella are ideal research sites because they both are well-established medium-sized "boutique" agencies, each with a handful of supermodels and a broad representation of commercial and high-fashion models. They book models in all sectors of the fashion industry: commercial print advertising, magazine editorial, catwalk shows, catalogues, and fitting work, for which the agency receives a standard 20% commission. The two agencies earned nearly equal gross profits, both clearing between $4 and $6 million in 2004. While structurally similar, the agencies differ in size, a fact that reflects in part their respective locations in the fashion industries of London and New York.

---

[7] Only two bookers were former models, attributable to the career ladder of fashion models, who generally exit the field by aging out and transitioning into acting or similar creative industry sectors with low education requirements.

These two cities are well suited for the research project because although they are both global cities and fashion capitals, they vary in their type of fashion market. As a result of industrial developments along post–World War II trajectories, London fashion is a weak commercial enterprise with a stronghold in creativity and artistic concerns of "fashion for fashion's sake," while New York is widely regarded as a business center for fashion commerce (Moore 2000). In the modeling economy, the divide between fashion-as-art and fashion-as-commerce acts as a means of stratifying models into the two general categories of looks known in fashion parlance as the editorial and the commercial.

The Structure of the Modeling Market

Producers preface any discussion of their work with an explanation of which market they serve, the editorial or the commercial, a division similar to the art world's split between avant-garde and commercially successful art (Bourdieu 1993). Editorial and commercial models have different types of looks and audiences, earn inversely related amounts of prestige and income, and face unequal levels of risk, as outlined in Figure 7.1 (see also Mears 2010).

Modeling agencies tend to differentiate their models into separate "boards" of editorial and commercial looks, each connected to a loosely distinct network of bookers and clients. This happens explicitly at Mode, which is divided into Editorial, Women (also called "Commercial" and "Money"), and Showroom boards, each with its own seating arrangement within the agency and its

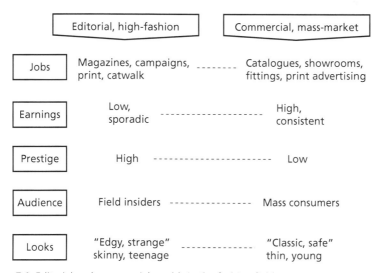

Figure 7.1 Editorial and commercial worlds in the fashion field

own page on the agency's website. At Stella, models and bookers are not explicitly separated, but informal differentiations are made between editorial and commercial bookers and models.

Editorial and commercial fashion can be analyzed as circuits because actors in each production world share distinct measures of success, good taste, and appropriate payments. They each share separate ideas about what counts as a valuable "look."

THE LOOKS

Apple Pie. Yoga Fit. The Belgians. The Drug Addict. Producers could endlessly name typologies such as these to describe the varieties of models' looks. But not all looks are equally valued. There is an economy to this jumble of looks, and it follows an anti-economic logic (Bourdieu 1993).

An editorial model is typically described as having an unusual—or to use a term that comes up often in the business—an "edgy" look. Bookers define edgy as meaning an "atypical" or "off-kilter" kind of look, perhaps not immediately recognizable as valuable to field outsiders:

> An editorial model generally has a more, um, strong look... at school she was probably considered very ugly by her classmates.
> —Fria, London, Editorial Head Booker, 26 years[8]

Bookers and clients are always on the lookout for edgy looks to push the envelope in fashion. Edgy models differ from the conventionally attractive models sought after for commercial work, whom bookers describe with terms like "wholesome" and "all-American."

These two looks, the edgy editorial and the "classic" commercial, are presumed by bookers and clients alike to resonate with separate classes of consumers. At the commercial end, bookers imagine the girl or boy next door will make sense to a mass middle market. Intelligible and relatable, this look sells by appealing to the everyday consumer. The editorial look, however, will not make sense to the masses; it will be considered "priceless" by elite photographers and designers. By way of example, several Mode agents invoked the successful editorial model Devan, a skinny Puerto Rican woman with a shaved head and tattoos:

> If you were a buyer from Neiman Marcus in Dallas, you would be scared by Devan!... Plus, some of my clients are really tame, like St. John's for example. You cannot put Devan in a St. John's knit suit and expect somebody to buy it.
> —Bre, NYC, Showroom Head Booker, 11 years

---

[8] Respondents are noted in text by pseudonym, market location, position held, and years of experience at the time of the interview.

Of course, as Raymond Williams points out, "There are in fact no masses; there are only ways of seeing people as masses" (Williams 1958). Bookers *imagine* catalogue and showroom consumers to be conservative middle-class people with mainstream taste, a process of "imagining the consumer" (Blaszczyk 2008). Based on their generalized interpretation of this unknown mass of people, bookers can imagine that an edgy look like Devan's will not go over well. A model like Devan will, however, resonate with consumers of the editorial circuit, which is to say, she will resonate with other producers within the editorial fashion circuit. The head editorial booker at Stella explained the audience difference in terms of the limited imaginations of those who book commercial models, as compared to the high-end clients whose tastes are perceived as more fashion-forward:

Well there's—there's your classic kind of all around, just beautiful girl. And that, you know, is preferred for television commercials and the kind of less forward-minded clients, you know, people that aren't really pushing the envelope for any job that they do. —Damien, London, Editorial Booker, 12 years

Bookers expect that "everybody," meaning all clients and their consumers, will understand the commercial look, but that only those with elite cultural knowledge will recognize the value of an editorial model like Devan. Upon determining for which circuit a model's look is best suited, bookers can then size up how much money he or she is likely to earn.

THE PAYMENTS

A defining feature of a circuit of commerce is localized media of exchange. In fashion modeling, acceptable payments vary between editorial and commercial circuits; some models will be paid in cash while others will receive clothes, pictures, and other perks in place of legal tender (see Table 7.1 for an overview of varieties of payments).

In the editorial circuit, "edgy" models either win big or they do not win anything at all. This board is by far the least profitable, but also the most prestigious, type of modeling work. Rates are low (on average $150/day for magazine shoots), work is sporadic, and many jobs pay in gifts and "perks," like offerings of clothes, shoes, and handbags. Editorial work can potentially lead to luxury brand campaigns, the industry jackpot. This is the highest echelon of success in the industry, only reached through the risky route of editorial work and only reached by a few. Campaigns can pay upward of a million dollars, depending on the exclusivity rights and length and region of use; exclusive worldwide, multi-year campaigns, like Kate Moss for Calvin Klein, are the most lucrative.

Such deals are rare, however, and more money is likely to flow into an agency from the commercial board. Catalogues, showrooms, and commercial print advertisements provide the bulk of any model's income. Catalogue work

Table 7.1 Range and averages of models' earnings per job

Job type	Earnings by women models		
	Min.	Average	Max.
Luxury brand campaign	40,000	100,000	1,000,000
Fragrance campaign	100,000	100,000	1,500,000
TV commercial	15,000	50,000	100,000
Low catalogue	1,000	2,500	5,000
Average catalogue	2,500	3,000	7,500
Top-level catalogue	7,500	10,000	20,000
Commercial advertisement	10,000	30,000	50,000
Showroom/hour	150	250	500
Showroom/day	400	1,000	2,000
Fashion show	0	1,000	20,000
Editorial shoot	0	100	225

Note: These average estimates come from interviews with models and interviews with bookers and accountants in both cities.

is the "bread and butter" of a modeling career, with rates that begin at $1,000 a day for new models, peak at $20,000 a day for top models, and average about $3,000 a day for most.

Mode has another commercial board called the Showroom board, which specializes in informal showroom modeling and fittings. It is consistently high volume work with small rates, on average about $200/hour, but for several hours, days, and weeks at a time. Some of the established showroom models have rates up to $2,000 per 8-hour day. This adds up to lucrative sums. In fact, the Showroom board brings in well over half of all earnings to Mode. A final type of commercial job is the television commercial, which is very lucrative—up to $100,000 per commercial shooting plus monthly residuals—but also sporadic.

Commercial work pays the bills for models and bookers alike, but at a cost: this is by far the least prestigious type of work. Commercial models with steady above-average earnings are valuable economic assets to the agencies, yet they are symbolically worthless. They do not accumulate the symbolic status required to book campaigns, and a model who becomes "known" for commercial work is essentially out of the running for the jackpot. The hidden cost of steady commercial work, then, is its toll on symbolic capital, which in the long run hinders financial gain. Joanne Entwistle documents this process in her study of the aesthetic economy, tracing the valorization process from editorial to commercial spheres, and Patrik Aspers has found a similar trade-off among fashion photographers in Sweden (Aspers 2005; Entwistle 2009).

Consider for example *Dazed and Confused* magazine in London, one of the most sought-after editorial jobs that JD, the model who led this inquiry, was quick to turn down early in his career—because, he scoffed, *Dazed* does not pay models for a day of shooting. It does not cover taxi fare, nor does it cover the cost of the magazine, about £3, which models must purchase for the "tear sheets"—pages torn from the magazine that are featured in their portfolios to showcase their work. In the end, models *lose* money by working for *Dazed*. In contrast, a day of catalogue work, say J.C. Penney, starts at about $2,500 minimum for a woman, and an hour of showroom work pays $150, with a minimum of 4 hours, or $600. Yet agents prefer to book their models in *Dazed* magazine over either option, because agents hedge their bets that the *Dazed* shoot will boost a model's profile with symbolic capital such that, in the long run, he will hit the campaign jackpot, and eventually his campaign earnings will far surpass those forgone catalogue or showroom earnings. The highest paid models at both Mode and Stella in 2005 were editorial superstars, booking over $2 million worth of jobs each (just over £1 million at Stella).

But this is a risky bet, bookers admit, and prestige, accountants are quick to remind, does not pay the bills. Commercial work offers safe and predictable earnings compared to the alluring but unlikely jackpot of fame and riches to be had in the more risky editorial market. In addition to making less money, editorial models have less time in the game. With the rapid turnover of "fast fashion," a model's editorial popularity can be as brief as two or three seasons before her bookings "fall off," as one booker put it. Commercial looks can maintain steady work for lengthier periods of up to ten years, such that the lifetime earnings of a showroom or catalogue model will likely surpass those of her editorial counterpart. The colloquial term "girl" somewhat accurately describes the majority of women editorial models, who range in age from 13 to 22, significantly younger than commercial models who are typically at least 18 and progress into their thirties and beyond.

This variety of payments may not make sense to outsiders, or indeed, to industry newcomers, those who have yet to be socialized in the anti-economic logic of the editorial circuit. Newcomers must go through a socialization process to gain editorial literacy, to learn, for instance, that *Dazed and Confused* is no simple magazine like any other. Such socialization appears in a variety of cultural goods markets; in the art market, for example, Velthuis documents a "semiotic socialization" process through which artists and dealers learn the appropriate meanings of art prices (2005). Prices are, after all, symbols; they hold different meanings for different actors, and within the editorial and commercial circuits, prices have particularized meanings such that "real money" is just one mode of payment.

THE PERKS

Editorial models also work for gifts and "perks," such as designer clothing. But like any gift, a model's perks are embedded in a system of exchange.

Most people tend to see legal tender, such as paper bills, as "real money," while non-monetary exchanges like "gifts" and "trades" are the extras, mere "perks," on the margins of serious economic transactions. Non-monetary payments are in fact central in the aesthetic economy, just as Zelizer has noted that they are also central markers of worth in household economies and organizations (Zelizer 1994). In fashion, perks are recognized media loaded with symbolic meanings. Market actors share an awareness of the proper matching of media, transactions, and status; appropriate matches are important to maintain because they represent social relations and hierarchies.

Gifts of clothing are most frequently given in place of monetary payment during Fashion Week, where many designers pay in "trade," which denotes a system of paying models in clothes. Designers of all levels, from bare budget start-ups to established retail giants, *can* pay in trade, but generally only new designers in the early stages of their careers barter with last season's leftover samples when hiring models.

This mode of payment would never be acceptable coming from catalogue clients. Precisely because they enable greater access to prestige and high-status names in fashion, editorial clients are able to forgo the monetary payments expected of their commercial peers. Thus, the perk marks the client's high social status. Clients may or may not come through on promises of barter, because they have already paid models with the opportunity to appear in coveted catwalks and shoots. Just as perks mark the prestige of editorial clients, they also signify the low status of novice models. Whereas top models command tens of thousands of dollars per catwalk appearance, newcomers must accept any payment. Frequently, new models are even hired to work in designer showrooms in exchange for vouchers of store credit at the retail shops.

THE RISKS

Throughout my interviews, bookers and clients constantly bemoaned a flooded market, claiming that there are more models and fewer jobs today than ever before, largely due to the Internet and the globalization of fashion. Mode bookers estimated that anywhere between 3,000 and 5,000 models flock to New York during a Fashion Week show season. This means they face enormous competition to sell any one model to a client, and clients face an enormous pool from which to choose. But given the limited appeal, rapid turnover, and ambiguous nature of edgy looks, bookers and clients face a more heightened sense of uncertainty when brokering editorial models than when using commercial ones.

Agencies in particular hedge big bets on their editorial boards. Editorial jobs are important for generating image and status, which are vital to secure catalogue clients and high-end advertisements like fragrance and cosmetic campaigns. While editorial models generate status, they rarely add to (and often detract from) their agency's financial books. Because editorial models are initially paid in intangible "perks," like pictures, clothing, and exposure, their agencies front the cost of their models' careers, covering expenses such as visas, plane tickets, apartment rentals, composite cards (business cards featuring a sample of pictures), pictures, and pocket money, along with other unforeseen expenses like health emergencies—all of which are "advanced" by a model's agency *before* that model secures a first job. Debt can pose a dangerous gamble, a Mode accountant explained:

What happens is once you've got a model in that much debt, the booker—sometimes you see it—well maybe the model's not gonna make the money. You don't want to cut your losses at $15,000, you want to get that model a couple of jobs that will recoup the agency that debt. You end up going deeper and deeper into the hole. It's like when do you cut the string, you know?   —Joe, NYC, Accountant, 5 years

This is especially dangerous for smaller agencies like Mode and Stella, which cannot afford to incur too many financial losses. During my research, Mode represented 300 models, about 60 of whom had debts ranging from a few hundred to upward of several thousand dollars. Stella had fewer models in the red and kept models' debts to well under £2,000, with rare exceptions creeping up to £3,500. Hedging is especially enticing for editorial bookers, who chase the volatile high-stakes prize of the winner-take-all contest. At Mode, bookers told stories of a recent flop who had cost the agency upward of $15,000, all because a persistent editorial booker had a "hunch" that a model's look was going to catch on to become a winner. It did not, for reasons no one could explain. Such stories irritate commercial and showroom bookers, who are far more market-sensitive. With less at stake, they play it safe and simply drop the models that clients do not "rent." Editorial fashion production is thus a higher risk endeavor than commercial work for models, agencies, and clients alike.

THE ECONOMIC WORLD REVERSED

Prestige therefore is recognized as a form of currency. Prestigious clients *know* that they do not have to pay their models much, if anything at all, because they provide models with valuable symbolic capital to jump start any modeling career, and bookers are aware of this:

Armani can turn around and build a girl's career or build a guy's career, there's a relationship between the client and the model hopefully, that mutually benefits both of them. Whereas nobody builds their career on the Pepsi ad.
—Ivan, NYC, Booker, 10 years

Brand-name fashion, as opposed to brand-name soda, adds value to a model's reputation and, hopefully, to his or her lifetime earnings. Likewise, editorial jobs generate prestige for the agency, which is vital to secure catalogue clients and high-end advertising like fragrance and cosmetic campaigns. Compared to catalogue and showroom boards, however, editorial work returns paltry profits. Explained Damien, an editorial booker in London for 12 years:

I would love to make more money, sure, everyone wants to make more money, but I bring in something else to the agency, I bring in the image, which is equally important.

While Podolny (2005) shows that firms accrue higher profits by virtue of their status positioning, firms in aesthetic markets complicate this straightforward correlation between status and profits. No agency can afford to have too many purely high-status editorial types, because they are a financial liability; rather, agencies must strike a balance between economic and symbolic capital (Entwistle 2009).

Perhaps inevitably, a subtle sense of disregard sometimes creeps upon the commercial booker, whose reliable stream of showroom and catalogue revenues is overshadowed by socially priceless but economically worthless (at least in the short term) editorial prestige:

Showroom, it's more body oriented, more about the height, you have to show the clothes. It's, I guess, less *"prestigious"* than the other boards... But also of my division, the girls are more commercial-looking. They might be more mainstream pretty, but less interesting perhaps, less *editorial*, whatever [rolls eyes].

—Bre, NYC, Showroom Head Booker, 11 years

Mode's Showroom board is quietly referred to among other agents as the "B-level" models, because their portfolios feature tear sheets from "down-market" magazines like *Parade* and *Redbook*. But without the Showroom's earnings, the agency would not survive. Commercial bookers are essentially the life support of any agency, yet their work simultaneously damages an agency's image. Bre's comments suggest she both knows and resents this.

This is not lost on the commercial models whose wages finance the prestige contest which excludes them. At Mode, an old office joke poked fun at one woman who made a good living as a showroom model but was continually requesting appointments to *Vogue* so she could get the editorial kudos she thought she deserved. She was mocked around the agency with the nickname "Supa-*star*." Such behavior baffles commerce-oriented accountants:

And there was one girl you know, she wanted to do the shows and that, but she's five foot seven, you know, and she did really well commercially and made a lot of money. But she's always moanin', "Oh, I'm not doing any shows," and that. You know they don't pay, why would you want it anyway?   —James, London, Accountant, 5 years

Accountants at both agencies, frustrated by the anti-economic logic of editorial jobs, repeatedly told me they could not understand why all models do not exclusively work for catalogues. The tension between the accountant's straightforward commercial logic and the agency's orientation toward symbolic rewards was especially clear one afternoon during an interview at Mode, when bookers suddenly erupted into applause and cheers after a booker shouted that his model has just booked a major magazine spread with a famous photographer. I was interviewing an accountant at the time, who paused to watch the celebratory display over a job that would result in less than $200 on the payroll. He then shook his head and shrugged, looking exasperated. As his heavy sigh suggested, it is not easy being an accountant in an economic world reversed.

The Social Art of Pricing

Having mapped out the structure of the modeling field into editorial and commercial circuits, each with a particular set of looks, risks, and rewards, we can now investigate how producers forge economic value from these two cultural worlds. How do bookers determine models' fees, and how do clients decide whether to accept these amounts? In fashion modeling, social relationships, structured along the editorial–commercial spheres of production, take center stage to construct the look's value.

Bookers play matchmaker between the model and client, mobilizing bodily capital to sell to clients and strategizing social relationships, all toward the end goal of sealing a deal, in which a client agrees to select a brooker's model and pays an agreed-upon price. One booker described her job as a "glorified telemarketer," in the business of packaging and selling people. Bookers do not just sell models; they also sell themselves and their social connections when making "sales pitches" to clients. Bookers are constrained by practical limitations, such as their clients' budgets, but they enjoy a substantial degree of autonomy in promoting and pricing models.

Bookers do not sell models according to some standard market index, since none exists. Models' wages have little to do with market research, consumer demographics, and sales; instead, they emerge from bookers' and clients' negotiations and, crucially, their social ties. Bookers always begin the transaction by naming the highest maximum fee they think they can justify on behalf of their model, and negotiations ensue. Explained Missy, a men's booker at Mode for eight years:

I think it's all in how you negotiate, if you just accept the rates that are offered, or if you try to get more. I was told when [I] first started: always ask for as much as you can justify. Like if you ask for something, be prepared to back up why you're asking for that.

Negotiations are an expected, and even welcome, part of naming a models' fee, such that the booker and client engage in a series of social interactions before a price is confirmed. Bookers negotiate fees in lively and creative ways. Several bookers put on a performance in order to "connect" with clients over the phone. Many bookers have a stock of favorite words they use to promote their models, descriptions like "hot," "fierce," and "a-*maz*-ing."

Bookers essentially play the circuits off each other. A model with some symbolic capital from editorial work can fetch a greater fee in her commercial work. Bookers justify their prices based on the model's existing editorial prestige, or *potential* for prestige, known as "buzz." Bookers actively inflate a model's value by "building the buzz," that is, spreading gossip in hopes of building excitement and creating a self-fulfilling prophecy. As Missy offered:

"We have this amazing new guy, you have to see him, everyone is talking about him, everyone is calling us about him, emailing us about him!" And sometimes you're lying, you're creating a little buzz... Nobody wants to be the one to miss out. They don't want their boss to say, "Well how come you didn't book this guy?"

Buzz can therefore translate into a higher price tag. The opposite process is at work for participants in the commercial sphere: too many close associations with commercial work can detract from a model's social standing. To protect their models' work biographies, editorial bookers carefully consider which kinds of images will boost models' profiles, in attempts to preserve the sacredness of the model's look from the commercial character of the trade. An editorial male model, for instance, explained that he booked catalogue only once in his two-year career, and it was a catalogue for Halloween costumes in which his booker demanded the model's face be partially hidden for all shots (at $2,000 for the day, it was one of the best-paying jobs he ever landed).

Bookers enhance their buzz-building capacity by being "in the know" about current fashion trends. They constantly browse fashion magazines and websites, and they "hang out" with one another and with clients at lunches, parties, and even weekly karaoke nights. Bookers must be enmeshed in dense social networks in order to sharpen their "eyes"—their ability to make fine distinctions—to see subtle differences in looks that they can pitch as valuable.

As bookers negotiate, they activate their social ties with clients, calling in favors with old friends and pushing the boundaries of clients' payment histories to their advantage. Erica, a London booker of four years, explained how her work-related friendships often help her to raise the price tag on her models:

You know how much they want the girl, not necessarily from what they've said, but from what they've done in the past, what they've said in the past and how they work and everything. That's when it's good to have relationships with people because you know well how far you can go before they crumble and go, "Okay, fine, take all my money!"

Central to Erica's bold play is the social connectedness and shared history she has with her clients. Value is negotiated between bookers and clients on the basis of reciprocity, trust, and shared understandings. Social ties and relationships enable bookers to catch and exploit their clients' attention. As one booker put it, "Models trade on our relationships with our clients."

Just as bookers work to establish relationships with their clients, clients too are socially connected to the pulse of fashion. Despite the abundance of models and agencies in New York and London that offer a variety of rates, clients are willing and even eager to pay premiums for fashion models who have been socially defined by bookers and by competing clients as valuable commodities. To account for this seemingly irrational behavior, in interviews clients appealed to the same kinds of buzz that bookers work hard to construct. In the high-end segments of advertising, clients are eager to score the hottest new look, the best fresh face with the most buzz and the greatest editorial promise. Clients are looking to bookers and to each other to keep on top of the trends, to be in the know, and to pick the most exciting new looks.

Like the bookers, the clients gossip to get informed. They hang out with one another, talk with each other, and share tips on upcoming hot new models.[9] One NYC casting director explained that when he bumps into other casting directors on the street in Soho, they routinely inform each other which models they each have their eyes on for upcoming photo shoots and catwalks.

By spreading the buzz, clients expect to hear buzz in return, which simplifies their work of finding the hot editorial models. Since there are no guarantees as to what makes a good look, clients tend to rely on imitation. This is especially the case in the high-risk editorial market, where fleeting aesthetic preferences can quickly snowball to make—or break—a model's career. Several bookers explained that fashion is a "follower," and that people within the industry are "sheep." This can often work to the bookers' advantage, since they can push their models based on past successes:

In fashion, a lot of people do pay attention to what the girl has done, and who she has shot with, and things like that. Just to be safe, they follow…I would tell the client, "Well she did this and she did that, she did that," you know, that would get a higher rate for her.   —Christoph, NYC, Editorial Booker, 7 years

As in other creative markets, imitation means that "the rich get richer," resulting in a cumulative advantage effect whereby successful goods accrue more success, such that small differences in product quality lead to large differences in popularity and create the large gaps in earnings between models (Frank and Cook 1995; Salganik et al. 2006).

Importantly, clients enjoy being a part of the buzz; they share a passion for fashion and a respect for edgy looks. They find excitement and pride in producing editorial fashion, and they relish the chance to take part in the collective redefinition of edginess each season. As Bandelj notes, the relational nature of all economic exchange generates affect; hence all economic action is "emotionally embedded" as well as socially embedded (Bandelj 2009). This is clearly demonstrated in how Rayna, a casting director of 17 years in New York, talks about her work:

I'll call a few key photographers that we work with, like, "You should see this kid!" Because it's exciting and it also, you know, everyone is looking—our business is

---

[9] For a structural account, see Godart and Mears (2009).

entertainment. We're essentially looking to get excited, and to be a part of something new.

In the aesthetic market, excitement generated through social interaction molds clients' preferences, playing a vital role in how much clients are willing to pay for a look.

While a hierarchy between editorial and commercial production stratifies clients and models from high to low status, this structural plane of the market does not directly determine prices. Status is a boundary marker drawn loosely around networks of editorial and commercial producers, with those participants associated with the commercial circuit deemed less artistic, and thus of lower status, than those associated with the editorial circuit. And yet, status is not static. It is not automatically determined by one's structural position. Rather, status is produced and contested through ongoing social interactions between clients and bookers.

Consider the efforts of a New York casting director of eight years, Kelly, who works for a low-status commercial teen fashion magazine in New York. Throughout our interview, she explained the difficulty of trying to book edgy editorial models given her position near the bottom of the status hierarchy, as bookers are reluctant to allow their editorial models to appear in her publication and risk threatening their rising reputations. She resorts to "snooping" to find models, which involves activating her social ties to call in favors from other casting directors:

I'm really friendly with the girl that works at [a prestigious magazine]. If I'm at a loss, I'll say, "Who have you seen recently who you think is amazing?" And also the fact that she's at [a prestigious magazine], she sees a different type of girl than I do, because, just how I was saying, people sort of try and maintain this level. And so I'll ask her, "Who have you seen?" And then I'll call their agencies and stalk them!

For Kelly, her relatively low status position demands constant maneuvering; as she put it, "It's so like high school." And just as in high school, the pecking order can be navigated through strategic socializing. By maintaining relationships with editors and casting directors at higher status magazines, Kelly is able to access a pool of editorial models from which she would otherwise be excluded. However, to actually hire an up-and-coming editorial model, Kelly will have to pay a premium to compensate for her lower position:

There's like a hierarchy of models in magazines as far as who they'll let do what... A lot of times since [bookers] are managing a girl's career, they'll sort of say, well you know what, she can't do your magazine... So they'll hold back sometimes. And either I'll have to beg or just sort of sweeten up the deal to try to get who I want.

To "sweeten up the deal," Kelly gives agents incentives to accept her job, such as increasing the number of pages on which to feature the model, or guaranteeing that the model will be appearing solo on a set number of pages, rather than having to share the page with another model. In effect, she pays a premium, in the form of additional "perks," to secure editorial models. As Kelly's work illustrates, status is a boundary marker, loosely segregating models, bookers, and agents along editorial and commercial ends of the market, but within this structural scaffolding, participants work out a sense of fairness and consensus on cultural worth.

The individualized negotiation of price means that, necessarily, some models earn more than others for doing the same amount of work. Such differences are to be expected, both among models from the same agency and between models from different agencies. To bookers, this earnings gulf poses its own set of problems, especially when models discuss rates while working with other models, which frequently leads to wounded egos and complaints:

If our girl is making less than another girl, yeah, she'll complain. And sometimes we can call the client and negotiate for higher... Sometimes we'll call up the agency of the girl who blabbed about her big rate and say, "Hey, you need to tell your girls not to talk—and also, how did you guys get more money than we did?"

—Sal, NYC, Showroom Booker, 6 years

As Sal notes, while bookers hope models from different agencies with different rates *don't talk*, they also welcome interagency help in determining rates. When unsure of what to negotiate for a job, bookers turn to their fellow bookers for advice, even if this means calling up a rival agency to seek advice and saying something along these lines:

Look, you guys are not getting this job. I am. It's already been determined. However, what do you think is fair? This is what I'm thinking, this is why I'm thinking. —Ivan, NYC, Men Booker, 10 years

Because this market is so unstable, bookers imitate and look to each other and to clients for signs of what is going to sell and at what price: What is a fair rate? What did they charge last year? As a result of imitation among high stakes, wages can become "locked in" to conventions, in which anyone who deviates from the convention risks being perceived as unfair, thereby breaking client trust and losing the job (Dimaggio and Powell 1983). Because everyone in fashion is networking and imitating each other, it becomes risky for bookers and clients to go against convention. The social work of building consensus on models' cultural worth thus lends a structural order to pricing through conventions:

You're always gonna charge the going rate. I mean, they pay what they can get away with paying and we bill what we can get away with billing. It all goes to what the market rate is, like anything else. —Joe, NYC, Accountant, 5 years

As the accountant suggests, a model's value is set by the "market rate," which is at once an economic calculation and also a product of social relationships and personal feelings. Bookers use these conventions just as art dealers draw from what Velthuis has identified as "pricing scripts" in the art market; such scripts are a set of routines that function as a cognitive manual for the variety of pricing decisions dealers make on behalf of their artists (Velthuis 2005: 117). Pricing scripts, like any convention, lend structure and predictability to the otherwise wildly fluctuating and socially sensitive price mechanism in the realm of aesthetics.

Conclusions

Prices tell rich stories about the social relations between buyers and sellers within any given market (Velthuis 2005). In fashion, a model's fee tells the narrative of her booker's social work and recognized eye, her position within the structural field of cultural production, and the social ties that bind her booker and clients together. In this chapter, I have used an analysis of two bounded social circuits, the editorial and the commercial in the fashion modeling market, to capture the rich social interaction that enables and sustains the economic exchange of looks. In the absence of standard measures to assess quality, producers in the aesthetic economy construct a social order from relationships as their antidote to uncertainty. A model's price, I have argued, is rooted in the interplay between prestige and profit—symbolic and economic capitals—and bookers and clients carefully balance each in their search for value among fashion models.

This chapter draws two lessons for sociologists on processes of value formation. First, firms and actors in aesthetic markets strategically balance high-status activities with low profits to be successful. This is a more nuanced picture than existing sociological accounts, which have suggested that firms accrue higher profits by virtue of their high-status positions (Podolny 2005). In fact, in the aesthetic economy, in keeping with Bourdieu's cultural production analysis (1993), high status yields higher earnings only after a time delay; that is, low-paid and high-status jobs accrue profits in the long run. Actors in aesthetic markets must carefully balance economic and symbolic capitals—too much high-status work for an agency could potentially mean economic disaster, just as too much lucrative commercial work could endanger the firm's reputation.

To comprehend the variety of payments in the aesthetic economy requires immersion in the field and socialization into the logics of the editorial—a socialization that JD, the young male model working in London, had yet to acquire at the start of his career. Today, JD has found his footing on the editorial and commercial circuits. In fact, he has completely reversed his attitude toward low-money jobs. When asked if he would shoot an editorial in *Dazed and Confused*, he nearly leaps out of his seat: "Ohmygod yes!" He explains, "basically, like a rate on *Dazed and Confused* is probably nothing, but I like fashion... and I would love to be in a picture... just to be part of it."

While JD emphasizes the symbolic rewards of working for high fashion for high fashion's sake, he also now recognizes the implicit economic value in "freebies" like pictures and affiliations with prestigious names.

Second, this research suggests that prices do not follow automatically from status positions or market structure but emerge through interactions within webs of cultural meanings patterned along status positions. By studying these webs, or circuits of value within markets, sociologists can capture the dynamic work it takes to arrive at consensus around social value. Circuits are a fruitful means to access the culture of a market, because shared values, norms, and conventions emerge within these bounded networks.

Thus, a status hierarchy provides the structural scaffolding in which editorial prestige confers advantages and buzz. These may be translatable into profit, but it is the social relations—and the negotiations, interactions, and shared understandings they enable—that allow status to manifest and carry weight. Prices are not reducible to status, as structural analyses of markets would suggest (Podolny 2005), but status is rendered meaningful, and contested, as market actors relate to each other.

Social ties within the fashion modeling market are crucial to the formation of prices, and while these ties tend to fall along status lines, status hierarchy alone does not determine them. In other words, culture, as well as structure, enables market actors to reach consensus, to find common meaning in the look.

Trading looks is at once an exercise in meaning-making and an economic calculation. The payment symbolizes consensus around cultural value. Economic value thus emerges from a shared *culture of production* that bookers and clients make with each other. Over time, through repetition, producers learn the bundles of conventions necessary to coordinate action and to give the otherwise turbulent market a common and coherent context. It will be important for sociologists to attend this intertwining of culture and commerce as the creative and soft-knowledge-intensive industries expand, a task well suited to analyses of circuits.

REFERENCES

Aspers, P. (2005). *Markets in Fashion: A Phenomenological Approach*. London: Routledge.
——(2009). Knowledge and Valuation in Markets. *Theory and Society* 38: 111–31.
Bandelj, N. (2009). Emotions in Economic Action and Interaction. *Theory and Society* 38: 347–66.
Becker, H. S. (1982). *Art Worlds*. Berkeley, CA: University of California Press.
——(1995). The Power of Inertia. *Qualitative Sociology* 18: 1573–7837.
Beckert, J. (1996). What is Sociological about Economic Sociology? Uncertainty and the Embeddedness of Economic Action. *Theory and Society* 25: 803–40.
Bielby, W. T. and Bielby, D. D. (1994). All Hits Are Flukes: Institutionalized Decision-Making and the Rhetoric of Network Prime-Time Program-Development. *American Journal of Sociology* 99: 1287–313.

Biggart, N. W. and Beamish, T. D. (2003). The Economic Sociology of Conventions: Habit, Custom, Practice and Routine. *Annual Review of Sociology* 29: 443–64.

Blaszczyk, R. L. (2008). *Producing Fashion: Commerce, Culture, and Consumers.* Philadelphia, PA: University of Pennsylvania Press.

Bourdieu, P. (1993). *The Field of Cultural Production: Essays on Art and Literature.* New York, NY: Columbia University Press.

Caves, R. E. (2000). *Creative Industries: Contracts between Art and Commerce.* Cambridge, MA: Harvard University Press.

Crewe, B. (2003). *Representing Men: Cultural Production and Producers in the Men's Magazine Market.* Oxford: Berg.

Currid, E. (2006). New York as a Global Creative Hub: A Competitive Analysis of Four Theories on World Cities. *Economic Development Quarterly* 20: 330–50.

Dimaggio, P. J. and Powell, W. W. (1983). The Iron Cage Revisited: Institutional Isomorphism and Collective Rationality in Organizational Fields. *American Sociological Review* 48: 147–60.

Entwistle, J. (2009). *The Aesthetic Economy of Fashion: Markets and Values in Clothing and Modeling.* Oxford: Berg.

——and Wissinger, E. (2006). Keeping Up Appearances: Aesthetic Labour in the Fashion Modelling Industries of London and New York. *Sociological Review* 54: 774–94.

Espeland, W. N. and Stevens, M. L. (1998). Commensuration as a Social Process. *Annual Review of Sociology* 24: 313–43.

Frank, R. H. and Cook, P. J. (1995). *The Winner-Take-All Society: How More And More Americans Compete for Ever Fewer and Bigger Prizes, Encouraging Economic Waste, Income Inequality, and an Impoverished Cultural Life.* New York, NY: Free Press.

Godart, F. and Mears, A. (2009). How Do Cultural Producers Make Creative Decisions? Lessons from the Catwalk. *Social Forces* 88: 671–92.

Knight, F. H. (1957). *Risk, Uncertainty and Profit.* New York, NY: Kelley & Millman.

McRobbie, A. (1998). *British Fashion Design: Rag Trade or Image Industry?* London: Routledge.

Mears, A. (2010). Size Zero High-End Ethnic: Cultural Production and the Reproduction of Culture in Fashion Modeling. *Poetics* 38: 21–46.

——and Finlay, W. (2005). Not Just a Paper Doll: How Models Manage Bodily Capital and Why They Perform Emotional Labor. *Journal of Contemporary Ethnography* 34: 317–43.

Miller, M. (2008, June 11). The Celebrity 100. *Forbes.* http://www.forbes.com/2008/06/11/most-powerful-celebrities-lists-celebrities08-cx_mn_0611c_land.html. (accessed March 24, 2000)

Moore, C. M. (2000). Streets of Style: Fashion Designer Retailing within London and New York. In P. Jackson, M. Lowe, D. Miller, and F. Mort (eds.), *Commercial Cultures: Economies, Practices, Spaces.* Oxford: Berg, 261–77.

Neff, G., Wissinger, E., and Zukin, S. (2005). Entrepreneurial Labor among Cultural Producers: "Cool" Jobs in "Hot" Industries. *Social Semiotics* 15: 307–34.

Negus, K. (1999). *Music Genres and Corporate Cultures.* London, New York, NY: Routledge.

Nixon, S. (2003). *Advertising Cultures: Gender, Commerce, Creativity.* London: Sage.

Plattner, S. (1996). *High Art Down Home: An Economic Ethnography of a Local Art Market.* Chicago, IL: University of Chicago Press.

Podolny, J. M. (2005). *Status Signals: A Sociological Study of Market Competition.* Princeton, NJ: Princeton University Press.

Salganik, M. J., Dodds, P. S. and Watts, D. J. (2006). Experimental Study of Inequality and Unpredictability in an Artificial Cultural Market. *Science* 311: 854–6.

Scott, A. J. (2000). *The Cultural Economy of Cities: Essays on the Geography of Image-Producing Industries.* London: SAGE.

Skov, L. (2002). Hong Kong Fashion Designers as Cultural Intermediaries: Out of Global Garment Production. *Cultural Studies* 16: 553–69.

Storper, M. and Salais, R. (1997). *Worlds of Production: The Action Frameworks of the Economy.* Cambridge, MA: Harvard University Press.

Velthuis, O. (2005). *Talking Prices: Symbolic Meanings of Prices on the Market for Contemporary Art.* Princeton, NJ: Princeton University Press.

White, H. C. (2002). *Markets from Networks: Socioeconomic Models of Production.* Princeton, NJ: Princeton University Press.

Williams, R. (1958). *Culture and Society, 1780–1950.* New York, NY: Columbia University Press.

Wilson, E. (2005, December 8). In Fashion, Who Really Gets Ahead? *The New York Times.* http://www.nytimes.com/2005/12/08/fashion/thursdaystyles/08FASHION.html (accessed March 24, 2011)

Witz, A., Warhurst, C., and Nickson, D. (2003). The Labour of Aesthetics and the Aesthetics of Organization. *Organization* 10: 33–54.

Zelizer, V. (1994). *The Social Meaning of Money.* New York, NY: BasicBooks.

—— (2004). Circuits of Commerce. In J. C. Alexander, G. T. Marx, and C. Williams (eds.), *Self, Social Structure, and Beliefs: Explorations in Sociology.* Berkeley, CA: University of California Press, 122–44.

8 Damien's Dangerous Idea: Valuing Contemporary Art at Auction

*Olav Velthuis**

Introduction

This chapter studies the devices through which prices are produced in the contemporary art market. Prices, I will show, are not established by means of neutral market devices that economic agents select in order to serve their own interests, or which emerge because of their efficiency in equilibrating markets, as neoclassical economics has either implicitly or explicitly assumed. Prices are themselves embedded in the meaning structures of markets, in the preexisting institutional frameworks of these markets, and in the shared values of the agents who populate these markets. Any theory that is to be successful in understanding the emergence and persistence of pricing devices in empirical markets should therefore incorporate wider considerations than just efficiency or self-interest. Also, in order for some of these devices such as auctions to become operational, a market order including status hierarchies and standards of value needs to be established.

In particular, this chapter seeks to understand why new works of art have almost invariably been sold through posted prices. This accomplishment is remarkable: a rich literature in economics suggests that for unique, expensive goods with an uncertain value such as art, auctions are the optimal price mechanism. Secondly, the chapter studies four rare cases in the history of modern art markets in which auctions have been used in order to produce prices for art. I show that the reasons agents have deviated from the norm of posted prices are hardly related to the arguments proposed in the economics literature. Indeed, if we are to understand this deviation and the norm itself, we need to look at pricing devices in social as well as cultural terms. These devices are, to put it in Viviana Zelizer's terms, intricate parts of circuits of commerce (Zelizer 2004).

---

* Thanks to Michael Hutter, Jens Beckert, Patrik Aspers, and participants of the conference on "Valuation and Price Formation on Markets," Villa Vigoni 2009, for their extremely helpful comments.

In the first section of this chapter, I briefly review economic literature on price mechanisms. In the second section, I argue how it is that art dealers have sold new works of art by means of posted prices rather than auctions. Because of their public character, auctions fail to produce social goods such as exclusivity and club membership, which art dealers provide to their buyers. In addition, turning the neoclassical economic argument on its head, auctions may be avoided as long as the "identity"—to put it in Harrison White's terms—of a piece of art and its maker has not been established (White 2002). The dense interactions between art dealers and their clients in the gallery space may enable the establishment of such standards in a way that the relatively anonymous interaction of auction sales does not.

In the remainder of the chapter, I study the rare use of auctions on the contemporary art market. Impressionist painters, for instance, organized auctions to sell their work because they were refused access to the dominant, established channels of marketing and valuing art in the nineteenth-century Paris art world (Section 3). Much closer to home, auctions are used for American charity events because of the status value these auctions produce (Section 4). In the emerging art markets of China and India, auctions are considered legitimate because they fit into preexisting institutional settings and with framings of contemporary art as an investment good (Section 5). Finally, in September 2008, the British artist Damien Hirst managed to sell his work successfully at auction because it was part of a wider event-driven and celebrity-oriented circuit within recent Western art markets (Section 6).

The material that this chapter draws on is eclectic. For the French art market, I make use of existing art historical studies as well as written accounts by friends of the impressionists who attended the auctions. For the charity auctions, I refer in part to the many guidelines regarding these events that have been drawn up by artists' associations in the United States and Canada, in popular online forums where artists discuss business practices, and in media reports. I attended a major charity art auction in the Netherlands, which took place at Sotheby's in May 2009 and raised funds for the art institutions De Appel in Amsterdam and Witte de With in Rotterdam, and I conducted interviews with two of the organizers and three of the artists involved. The sections on the Chinese and Indian art market and on Hirst's one-man auction draw on media reports exclusively.

Economic Literature on Pricing Mechanisms

In modern retail markets, three mechanisms exist to set prices, as well as many hybrid forms in which elements of these three mechanisms are combined. First of all, in cases of private negotiations (haggling, direct bargaining), individual sellers and buyers negotiate the details of a transaction including the price, which has not been fixed in advance. The mutual bargaining power of parties willing to exchange a good is in other words measured on the spot, with the price level as the main outcome of the process. Private negotiations predominated in pre-modern economies and still do in the bazaar economies that have been documented in detail by economic anthropologists (see Alexander and Alexander 1991; Fanselow 1990; Geertz 1979).

The second mechanism to set prices is through auctions. In the simplest form of this mechanism, buyers and sellers of a good convene at a specific place and time. During the auction, an auctioneer calls prices in order to find the equilibrium price where supply and demand meet; in other words, supply and demand interact directly in order to establish the price.[1] Auctions are used for a wide range of goods, including perishables like fruit, flowers and fish, cattle, agricultural products, primary metals, and financial assets such as government bonds (Okun 1981: 134). Recently, Western governments have used auctions to privatize companies, to sell mobile phone licenses, or to operate liberalized electricity markets (Klemperer 2004). On retail markets, however, auctions are rarely used: works of art, rare books, wine, antiques, or other collectibles are the few categories that are mentioned in the literature. More recently, this has changed to some extent through online auction houses such as eBay (see e.g. Lucking-Reiley 2000).

The third most prevalent mechanism to establish prices in modern retail markets is the use of fixed or posted prices: before the sale takes place, the seller sets a price and posts it, after which a sale is made once a customer agrees with this posted price. Posted, fixed prices are a relatively recent phenomenon, having been introduced in the early nineteenth century, when the exchange of everyday commodities became increasingly impersonal (Carrier 1994; cf. Fanselow 1990).

A rich literature in economics has emerged since the 1980s that has aided understanding of which price mechanism is being used. One drawback is that this literature focuses on wholesale markets, while retail markets get relatively little attention. Moreover, most contributions have a normative angle. Empirical studies of the emergence and institutionalization of a price mechanism on specific markets are rare.

Which normative arguments have been proposed to understand the occurrence of one price mechanism rather than another? First of all, as Preston McAfee and John McMillan argue in a review of auction literature, monopolist sellers who do not know the buyer's willingness to pay should prefer to sell by auction, because doing so forces all buyers to reveal this willingness. Second, auctions are optimal when there are only a few units of a good to sell, since

---

[1] Textbook economic theory, with its supply and demand graphs, implicitly assumes that prices for all goods are set by means of an auction mechanism. This happens with the help of an imaginary "Walrasian" auctioneer (named after one of the founding fathers of neoclassical economic theory, the nineteenth-century economist Léon Walras), who calls off prices until an equilibrium price is established (see Smith 1989).

each buyer is forced to reveal his willingness to pay.[2] Third, auctions should be used if widely accepted standards of value are lacking; and fourth, if the goods are expensive. Finally, auctions are preferred when market-clearing prices are highly unstable, for instance because supply and demand for goods such as flowers fluctuate on a daily basis or because the quality of the individual goods offered for sale, such as cattle, varies (McAfee and McMillan 1987; Milgrom 1985: 18; Phlips 1988: 89; cf. Smith 1989: 16).

The downside of auctions is however that they are relatively expensive to organize (Carlton 1991). This has changed somewhat with the Internet: David Lucking-Reiley argues that "as Internet technology lowers the cost of running an auction relative to using other pricing mechanisms, we might expect to see new types of goods be auctioned" (Lucking-Reiley 2000: 232).

Posted prices are expected for standardized goods, especially in complex selling organizations. If a company employs many sellers, it would be expensive to provide detailed instructions on when to bargain, with which customers to bargain, and how to do so. Also, principal–agent problems might arise because the sellers and the buyer have an incentive to collude, sell the work for a lower sum than the customer's willingness to pay, and share the difference. Therefore, if monitoring is expensive, posted prices will be preferred to haggling (Milgrom 1989). Another advantage for sellers is that information and transaction costs are relatively low: whereas it takes a long time for both an auction and a bargaining process to arrive at the price, posted prices enable instant sales (Fanselow 1990; Riley and Zeckhauser 1983). Thus, if opportunity costs to consumers are high because of their income level, posted prices may be expected.

Economists have little more to say on private negotiations than that these are "best avoided" because they are likely to result in "disagreement and inefficiency" (Milgrom 1989: 19). Or as the anthropologist Gretchen Herrman has argued more forcefully: bargaining "is considered irrational or pre-rational, something practiced by the essentialized exotic Other" (Herrman 2003: 239). Negotiations combined with fixed, posted prices do occur regularly on modern retail markets, however, giving a seller opportunities to discriminate prices on the basis of bargaining power and the seller's estimate of the buyer's willingness to pay (see e.g. Goldberg 1996; Ayres and Siegelman 1995).

Clear-cut as the arguments summarized in Table 8.1 may be, their predictive power is limited. The historical and geographical variation in price mechanisms used is much greater than economic theory can account for, as economists themselves have acknowledged. Moreover, on many markets, more than one selling mechanism is used simultaneously (cf. Arnold and

---

[2] This notion has been criticized by Charles Smith, however, who has convincingly argued that auctions deviate significantly from the economic model. Contrary to economic theory assumptions, the estimates of bidders are based on collective opinions that are highly subject to modification. As a result, prices do not reflect a simple composite of individual evaluations but rather complex, collective evaluations that are subject to intra-group influences (Smith 1989).

Table 8.1 Summary of conditions determining the use of price mechanisms

Condition	Auction	Posted price	Haggling
Characteristics of goods			
Standards of value are lacking	X		X
Supply is limited	X		
Market-clearing price is unstable	X		X
High-status value	X		
Characteristics of seller			
Complex organization		X	
Seller is monopolist	X		
Monitoring problems	X	X	
Characteristics of buyer			
High income (high opportunity costs)		X	
Differences in willingness to pay	X		X

Lippman 1995). Also, on the basis of the aforementioned arguments, it is hard to account for the dominance of posted prices in modern economies. As Arthur Okun has argued: "It is much easier to document empirically the widespread nature of cost-oriented prices than to provide an analytical foundation for those practices and attitudes" (Okun 1981: 154).

Why There Are No Auctions on the Primary Art Market

Applying neoclassical economic arguments to the primary art market, the case for auctions could not be stronger: artists are monopolists; they only have a relatively small number of units to sell; the value of each of these selling units is high, albeit uncertain. Furthermore, anecdotal information indicates that artists and their dealers have difficulties estimating their clients' willingness to pay (Velthuis 2005*b*). Indeed, in many gallery exhibitions, artworks remain unsold and are later returned to the artist's studio. In the rarer cases of very popular artists, shows are sold out even before opening, with art dealers developing waiting lists for new works to appear. Both cases indicate that the art dealer's price discovery by means of posted prices is far from perfect, and that auctions might arrive at better results. Moreover, the principal–agent problems cited by economists in favor of posted prices are hardly relevant for art markets since it is the principal/owner of the gallery who almost invariably closes the sales (Velthuis 2005*b*).

In short, one would expect auctions to predominate in the production of prices. The reality of art markets is different, however. Auctions are exclusively used on the secondary or resale market for art. On the primary market, they are by and large avoided. When for a previous study I asked art dealers in New York and Amsterdam whether they would consider organizing an auction at the end of a gallery show in order to sell the works on display, they either did not understand the question, responded disapprovingly, or even reacted with outrage. This hostility toward auctions also surfaced when the British celebrity artist Damien Hirst announced that he would auction 223 of his works at Sotheby's in September 2008. Art-world pundits considered his idea dangerous, since it might destabilize and further commercialize the art market. *The Economist* noted that with the sale Hirst was "breaking the art market's traditional rules" (The Economist 2008). Art critic Roger Bevan warned: "The final frontier protecting contemporary art galleries from the relentless encroachment of the auction houses has been emphatically breached... Now that Damien has demolished the moral barrier of using auctions for distribution and profit, other artists will follow suit" (Bevan 2008).

The reasons auctions are avoided on the primary market are fourfold: first of all, as Jens Beckert has argued, in order to master radically uncertain environments, economic agents "rely on social 'devices' that restrict their flexibility and create a rigidity in the responses to changes in an uncertain environment" (Beckert 1996: 819). In other words, auctions would only add to rather than stabilize the radically uncertain nature of the artistic and economic value of contemporary art.[3] Posted prices, by contrast, render these values to some extent predictable, especially since they are based on a set of pricing rules.

This predilection for the rigidity of posted prices can be further understood by taking the signaling function of prices into account: artists (and their dealers) fear that the volatility of auction prices may destabilize the artists' market because of negative price signals. For instance, when prices fail to achieve record levels set at a previous auction, collectors and other members of the art world may infer from these lower prices that the artist has a reputation in decline, a career that is not developing, or work that is deteriorating in quality (cf. Velthuis 2003). Instead, posted prices provide the artist and his dealer with control over the price levels and thereby—at least partially—over the signals these prices send out. By increasing prices only piecemeal and by avoiding price decreases and hence volatility, they seek to stabilize the market.

Second, before exchange can take place, a market order needs to be established, including the identity and status of the producers involved and the standards of value by which the works of art should be appreciated (cf. Aspers 2001*a*, 2009). It is questionable whether auctions manage to establish such order, status hierarchies, and standards of value. To understand why, one needs to take into account that price mechanisms are not only economical or technical devices that enable agents to produce prices. They are also social

---

[3] For the uncertain, socially constructed, and rapidly fluctuating value of art, see for example Moulin (1987, 1994), Plattner (1996), Bonus and Ronte (1997), and Beckert and Rössel (2004).

devices that imply specific types of social interaction. In particular, the relatively anonymous and short-lived type of interaction between sellers and buyers at auction by and large excludes the dense interactions, rich exchange of information and gossip, and continuing conversations that are a prerequisite for status hierarchies and that allow standards of value to emerge (see e.g. Aspers 2001a; Klamer 1996).

Third, auctions are considered illegitimate for cultural reasons. They present new works of art in a blatantly commercial context, which contradicts what Pierre Bourdieu has called the rules of art and the denial of the economy in particular (Bourdieu 1993). In other words, actors within the art world seek to frame contemporary works of art as cultural goods rather than commercial commodities. Hirst's partnership with the auction house Sotheby's has derailed such attempts at "decommodifying" contemporary art. As one artist remarked on a popular art market blog: "You simply cannot truly experience complex artworks in an auction house. It's just about selling, and nothing else." Instead, the artist continues, "It's also important to actually look at the stuff, yourself, out of the studio, in a clean white space, and present your ideas to the world."[4]

Finally, the democratic nature of auctions means that they fail to produce a social good that is highly valued on art markets: access to the exclusive social club of artists and collectors that forms around art galleries. Selling art through posted prices provides some degrees of freedom to art dealers to sell desirable pieces to collectors of the dealers' liking. As Michael Hutter put it: "dealers in markets for goods with communication potential not only sell commodities, but also actively create and provide a club good—namely membership in the community which adheres to the dealer's aesthetic style—which they sell jointly with the object" (Hutter et al. 2007: 249). The auction mechanism, in which the selection process of agents is only on the basis of willingness to pay and not on the basis of the agent's status within the art world, cannot produce this club good.

Auctions in the Modern Art Market of Nineteenth-Century France

If hostility toward auctions as a market device is steep in the primary art market, they have nevertheless been used at specific moments, within distinct geographical locations or particular segments of primary art markets. But even in these cases, the reasons for economic agents to choose auctions over posted

---

[4] http://edwardwinkleman.blogspot.com/2008/09/soul-searching.html (accessed September 5, 2010).

prices have little to do with the arguments proposed by economic theory. In the remainder of this chapter, I will discuss four such cases.

The first case is in the Parisian art market of the second half of the nineteenth century. At the time, auctions were regularly used as the sales mechanism of choice for new works of art. As the art historian Simon Kelly writes: "The auction house was at the centre of the Parisian art market in mid-nineteenth-century Paris" (Green 1987; Kelly 2003: 34). Among other auction pioneers were two painters of the Barbizon school: Theodore Rousseau and Narcisse-Virgile Diaz de la Peña. Like Damien Hirst, Rousseau and Diaz organized one-man sales at which they sold paintings directly out of their studios. Rousseau did so in 1850, 1861, and 1863, at the Hôtel Drouot, then as now Paris' main auction venue. Diaz organized 11 one-man auctions between 1849 and 1868. In order to cultivate interest in these among collectors, he and other artists published illustrated auction catalogues, for which he commissioned texts from art critics. Like Rousseau, Diaz made sure that friends would be present at the sale in order to bid up the works in case collectors' interest was absent.

The success of both artists' one-man sales varied. Some auctions were well received among critics, but a failure in economic terms: the majority of paintings did not sell, leaving one or the other painter in debt because of the costs he had incurred in organizing the auction. Other sales, however, were successful in economic terms as well, resulting in prices that were considered elevated by the standards of those days (Kelly 2003).

The impressionists, who organized two auctions in the 1870s, were less fortunate. After a first very badly received exhibition, at which the impressionists had shown together in 1874, Pierre-Auguste Renoir took the initiative to put on one of these auctions. It took place in the spring of 1875 and included, apart from Renoir's own paintings, those of Claude Monet, Alfred Sisley, and Berthe Morisot. The journalist and art critic Théodore Duret, one of the early friends of the impressionists who attended the sale, considered it a disaster (Duret 1910). The artists had to buy back many of the paintings themselves—72 in total. Friends or family members bought other works in order to protect the artists. Many paintings failed to raise more than 100 francs, in those days a meager sum (Bodelsen 1968). Moreover, the public rioted during the sale and ridiculed the works on display. The police had to be called in to break up the fights (Katz and Dars 1999).

In 1877, the impressionists tried one more time. Renoir and Sisley were the only painters represented in the first sale to participate; besides their paintings, the auction included works by Gustave Caillebotte and Camille Pissarro. Again, the painters were ridiculed. The audience passed on their paintings upside down through the auction venue (Duret 1910). The sale was so humiliating that the impressionists refrained from further attempts to sell their work at the Hôtel Drouot.

The dramatic results of the two impressionist sales did not prevent later artists from trying their luck. Most notably, the post-impressionist painter Paul Gauguin made an attempt. In 1891, Gauguin auctioned off his own works in order to quickly generate cash to travel to Polynesia (see e.g. Rewald 1986a: 79–80).[5] To his friend the essayist and poet Charles Morice, Gauguin explained: "The experience I won at Martinique was decisive. There and there only did I feel that I really was myself. That's why I want to go to Tahiti. I need money, about ten thousand francs. I think that a well-prepared sale of about thirty pictures from Martinique, Brittany and Arles could get them" (Hanson 1954: 193–4).

The art critic Mirbeau wrote an essay for the auction catalogue. The sale was covered by the media, and stirred wider interest in Gauguin's work. As was common at the Hôtel Drouot, fellow artists attended the sale, including Edgar Degas, who bought several works. In total, the auction revenue from the 30 paintings was over 9,860 francs (Hanson 1954: 195), which was close to what Gauguin had projected. One of Gauguin's first biographers characterized the auction as a "moral success" (Rotonchamps 1925: 88). In 1895, during a brief visit to Paris, the artist held another one-man auction in order to finance his prolonged stay in Polynesia. This later auction was much less successful; after deducting expenses, the artist netted only 500 francs from the sale (Hanson 1954: 245).

The last noteworthy example of auctions on the primary market in nineteenth-century France concerns posthumous sales, where the contents of an artist's studio would be sold after his death. These took place after the deaths of artists such as Delacroix (1864), Millet (1875), Courbet (1881), and Manet (1884). Manet even requested in his will that "an auction of the paintings, sketches, and drawings in my studio [be] held after my death" (Bodelsen 1968; Watson 1992: 93). The sale was preceded by a retrospective exhibition of Manet's work, again based on the contents of his studio, in the prestigious École des Beaux-Arts (Duret 1910: 194).

The question of why auctions were used legitimately on the primary market in nineteenth-century France does not have a single straightforward answer. One reason, no doubt, was that the artists involved were in dire straits. Rousseau and Diaz faced the collapse of the art market of the late 1840s. Gauguin had to raise money quickly in order to sail off to Tahiti. One of the few dealers who supported the impressionists, Paul Durand-Ruel, was on the verge of bankruptcy. The Salons, where the official, government-sanctioned exhibition and sale of contemporary art took place, had already refused the impressionists (Mainardi 1993). This left the artists with few options. Here it should be noted that historically, the auction has been the market device employed by the art market's outsiders. In the seventeenth century, merchants who were unable to secure membership in the artists' guilds organized auctions to sell their inventory. The guilds, in turn, attempted to forbid these auctions in order to prevent the market from becoming flooded with paintings of lower quality (see e.g. De Marchi 1995; Montias 1988; Prak 2003).

---

[5] Apart from single artists, some dealers such as Durand-Ruel and Boussod & Valadon also auctioned part of their stocks of new works of art (Gee 1981: 23; Rewald 1986b: 21; see also North 1992: 90; Watson 1992: 91).

The use of auctions should moreover be seen in light of the preexisting institutional structure of the nineteenth-century Paris art market. Whereas many art dealerships had originally been luxury stores, printing shops, and the like, the experts and appraisers of contemporary art were to be found at the auction houses (cf. Green 1987). Some of these experts, most notably Durand-Ruel and Georges Petit, combined their role at the Hôtel Drouot with dealerships themselves. In other words, the antagonism between the auction houses and the art dealers that prevails nowadays was absent in late nineteenth-century France. Leading art critics were writing texts for auction catalogues, which bestowed further cultural legitimacy on the auctions, as did their strong connection to retrospective exhibitions in prestigious cultural venues (Jensen 1994: 119).

Some of the nineteenth-century artists were also uncertain about the economic value of their work, and saw the auction as a way to find this out. Rousseau, for instance, used one of the one-man auctions to sell a new body of work, made in a new style that had not been appreciated by his existing collectors. Note, however, that some standard of value existed: Rousseau had already established a name for himself. Without his reputation, the auctions would probably have failed, like the impressionists' auction a couple of decades later.

Apart from artists' economic necessity, organizational configurations, and lack of access to other commercial devices at hand to sell their work, the legitimacy of some primary market auctions in nineteenth-century France also lay in moral values. The auctions provided fellow artists and friends with an opportunity to express care for an artist: it was common for these colleagues to appear at auction and to start bidding when nobody else did, in order to save the reputation of their companion. Those acquisitions were, in other words, infused with gift or charity elements. Also, the auctions that followed the retrospective exhibitions after the artist's death provided a last chance for the artist's colleagues and beloved to pay tribute. These sales had, as Michael Jensen put it, "an altruistic character" (Jensen 1994: 116).

Finally, art historians have argued that auctions could be used on the primary market because they were embedded in a wider speculative culture that prevailed in mid-nineteenth-century France. For instance, one art critic and frequent visitor to the Hôtel Drouot, which was located close to the Paris stock exchange, noted of the auction house that "its success corresponded to that financial surge which for ten years made the Bourse a speculator's paradise" (Green 1987: 62; see also Jensen 1994).

Charity Art Auctions

The second example of auctions being used systematically for the sale of contemporary art is the charity art auction. For these auctions, nonprofit organizations or an agent working for them invite contemporary artists to donate one or more works from their studios. The works are auctioned at a special fundraising event that sometimes requires the purchase of tickets for admittance. Although silent auctions are used for cheaper items, the charity art auction is usually an English, open-cry sale. After the costs are subtracted, the benefits of the auction go to the nonprofit organization. These proceeds may range from several thousand dollars for a local auction in which artists without a widely recognized reputation participate to $42 million for the most successful charity art auction ever: the Red auction organized in the spring of 2008 at Sotheby's New York. Famous artists such as Jeff Koons and Tracey Emin contributed work to the latter of these, and celebrities attended. The proceeds went to the Geneva-based Global Fund to Fight Aids, Tuberculosis, and Malaria.[6] The show was organized by Damien Hirst and the rock star Bono. The seven works that Hirst himself donated to the auction fared extremely well, raising almost half of the total auction revenue.

No systematic data regarding the history, frequency, or average sale revenue of charity art auctions exists.[7] Anecdotal information suggests that they are more frequent in the United States than in Europe, presumably because of the comparatively small government contributions to nonprofit organizations. "In an economy that has become less than friendly to many non-profit organizations, the fundraising auction has emerged as a popular, effective, and ethical income source," two experts on charity auctions write (Miller and Miller 1996: 95).[8] In the media, New York galleries say they get several requests per week to contribute works. Artists complain of being "inundated" with requests, resulting in charity auction fatigue. That a cottage industry has emerged of American companies that organize charity art auctions for non-profit organizations (often with their own inventory of artworks at the disposal of the client) also attests to the popularity of this type of sale.

If the public, overtly commercial character of regular art auctions is deplored in the contemporary art world because it violates the rules of art, to use Bourdieu's terms, it is this very public character which lends legitimacy to the charity art auction. Resembling the potlatch rituals of Indian societies, buyers at these auctions establish status by paying more than fair market value for a work of art. Thus, the charity art auction is infused with elements of gift transactions, with the surplus value (the auction price minus the fair market value of the artwork) exchanged for status.

---

[6] This section is partially based on newspaper and magazine articles on charity art auctions retrieved through a systematic search on Lexis Nexis (1990–2009). The key articles retrieved are: CBC News (2008), McEntire (1995), Lim (2000), Vaughan (2003), Greadell (2008), Walker (1997), and Kino (2006).

[7] In 2007, Sotheby's reportedly participated in more than 300 charity auctions, generating total revenue of $150 million. See Crow (2008).

[8] For instance, the number of press reports that can be retrieved through the electronic media archive Lexis Nexis about charity art auctions in the United States far outnumbers those in Europe.

Another reason why auctions are used for these fundraising events is that the bidding process creates moments of collective effervescence, which makes the events spectacular or pleasurable in themselves; to put it in terms of Randall Collins, the charity art auction comprises a set of interaction rituals that result in emotional energy (Collins 2004; cf. Miller and Miller 1996; Webber 2003: 123). Or as the anthropologist Heidy Geismar notes, "the auction is a theatrical production of price" (Geismar 2001: 43). Conversely, when the emotional energy is lacking, the charity auction may fail spectacularly. One observer recounted a time when artists were embarrassed and even shed tears when hardly anybody bid on their work.

In short, the auction mechanism is ingrained in these fundraising events. It simply would not make sense to substitute the bidding for private negotiations or posted prices. This does not mean, however, that charity art auctions are considered legitimate by all the actors that are directly or indirectly involved. Three arguments are frequently invoked against the institution. First of all, dealers see the charity auction as a form of competition that may result in loss of revenue. Likewise, and even more astutely given their low average income, artists wonder why they should be obliged to give away works of art which are in their eyes highly valuable. As the Canadian Artists Representation writes in its *Guidelines for Professional Standards in the Organization of Fund-Raising Events*: "Artmaking is a profession like any other, yet most Canadian artists find it difficult to make a living wage from their artwork. At the same time, community groups continually approach artists to donate portions of their inventory for fund-raising projects. No artists should be expected to donate works of art outright to any organization for fund-raising purposes."[9]

Secondly, artists complain that charity art auctions harm the development of their career because the prices established there are frequently lower than the prices that artists can fetch in the gallery, meaning that the latter pricing structure is hampered. The lower auction price, in other words, sends a negative quality signal to the audience. "What happens to the credibility of this carefully constructed pricing structure when, as is very often the case, 300 well-to-do citizens at a charity auction witness an artist's painting, which they had all heretofore believed to be worth a couple of thousands of dollars, fail to find a buyer at a couple of hundred dollars?" wonders an art appraiser and former organizer of these events.[10]

---

[9] Similar advice is given by the Philadelphia/Tri-State Artists Equity Association in its "Fundraising & Art Auction Guidelines"; available at http://www.artistsequity.org/auction_guideline.html (accessed September 5, 2010).

[10] Therefore, the Professional Guidelines of the Society of North American Goldsmiths regarding fundraising auctions state: "Every artist should maintain control over the selling prices of his or her work...Since auctioned artwork often sells far below retail price, maintaining control of pricing is impossible. The ultimate result of this discounted selling price is that the value of an artist's work and the ability of a gallery to command full retail prices for the entire body of an artist's work is adversely affected."

Finally, artists complain that the charity art auction entails an unwelcome diversion from the established path of a work of art, to put it in terms of the anthropologist Arjun Appadurai (Appadurai 1986). Since the auctions generally attract a public of art world outsiders, artists' work ends up in the hands of buyers who spend money during these events for social rather than aesthetic reasons. As one artist complains: "Most of these auction-goers are noncollectors. They are inexperienced in the art world, cannot appreciate the value... A bunch of doctors and researchers are more likely to bid up a scuba-diving excursion. You get the idea."

Auctions in Emerging Cultural Economies

The third instance of art auctions on the primary art market is in emerging cultural economies. Since the late 1990s, markets for contemporary art have emerged or expanded rapidly outside of Europe and the United States (see e.g. Artprice 2008; McAndrew 2008). In 2008, the size of the auction market for contemporary art in China, for instance, surpassed that of France, the country that until World War II was the center of the international art market. Although these emerging markets are integrating into a global market rapidly and adopting institutional configurations of Western art worlds, they have simultaneously maintained and developed local patterns of organizing exchange. Indeed, in China and to a lesser extent in India, new works of art have been sold at auction since the inception of a market for contemporary art.

In China, these auctions are embedded in a wider speculative culture, which has been developing ever since the country liberalized its economy and integrated into the global financial and commodity markets. Although the main customers at the auction houses are Western, a new class of Chinese collectors buy contemporary art in order to make a quick profit. As one expert on the Chinese art world notes: "There are charges that Chinese collectors are using mainland auction houses to boost prices and engage in widespread speculation, just as if they were trading in stocks or real estate" (Pollack 2008: 118).

Second, the overtly commercial commodity context of the auction house that Western art dealers and artists do not consider appropriate for contemporary art is considered legitimate in China. In more general terms, the "denial of the economy," according to Bourdieu one of the central features of Western art worlds, is hardly characteristic of China's art capitals, Beijing and Shanghai (Bourdieu 1993). As one observer notes: "If you're suddenly purging anticapitalism from every other part of life, why not from art too—which, after all, prides itself on being at the social forefront" (Vine et al. 2007: 50). Indeed, internationally successful artists like Zhang Xiaogang, Yue Minjun, and Zeng Fanzhi, whose works have sold regularly for more than a million dollars each and who are represented by prestigious Western art dealers, hardly feel ashamed of their financial and artistic success. Unlike their Western peers, they ostentatiously show off their wealth by driving in luxury cars made by Lexus and Mercedes Benz and buying opulent houses.

The auction house may be less appropriate for the anticommercial ethic of the Western art world than for this hedonistic ethic that characterizes key circuits within the Chinese art world. The long-term focus of Western art dealers and their artists on building a solid career also contrasts with the short-term focus of Chinese artists. "There's an instinctive urge to capitalize immediately on any fleeting opportunity before it disappears... Everything in their experience has taught them that it's foolish to bet on the long run," according to an art critic who specializes in Chinese contemporary art (Vine et al. 2007: 52). Whereas Western art dealers are concerned about the volatility of auction prices, which may harm the long-term pricing structure of the gallery, Chinese artists may have a higher discount rate for future prices and therefore prefer to capitalize on strong demand, even if it is short-lived, by means of auctions.

Buyers of contemporary art in China and India share this predilection to contextualize art as a public, commercially inspired commodity. The public character of auctions in these countries makes transparent the creation of artistic and economic value for a category of goods that hardly existed a couple of decades before. Says Georgina Adam, editor of the art market's main trade paper, the *Art Newspaper*: "new buyers tend to be more comfortable at auction: they see it as more transparent, and other people bidding reassures them" (cited in Carver 2008; cf. Vine et al. 2007). Moreover, auctions in Asia provide status conscious collectors with the opportunity to show off their wealth. Whereas art dealers may offer their Western collectors discretion and secrecy, the new middle classes of emerging economies may look for the exact opposite: opportunities to "flaunt their status by paying record prices," as art writer Barbara Pollack puts it (Pollack 2008: 123).

Auctions in China also enjoy legitimacy by default, just like those of the impressionists in nineteenth-century France: at least in the 1990s—the early days of the Chinese market for contemporary art—they were one of the few official art institutions. Hardly any museums or other cultural institutions existed that could establish the reputations of artists. "For the majority of [young Chinese artists], the search for patronage was a constant struggle," writes Michael Sullivan, one of the authorities on modern Chinese art. While artists who were sanctioned by the government got occasional commissions, professorships at universities or showroom sales, avant-garde artists were denied such opportunities. "They were lucky if they could show their work in hastily arranged 'salons,' private viewings, and cocktail parties in the hotel rooms or apartments of foreign diplomats and journalists. So desperate was their scramble for notice that some would not only bribe television stations and magazines to feature their work but pay critics to attack them. Any attention was better than none" (Sullivan 1996: 278; see also Clunas 1997; Vine et al. 2007: 49).

When the Chinese government began granting auction licenses in 1993, they became the first method of filling this institutional void.[11] In those days, only a handful of art dealers had opened their doors—not until the late 1990s would the gallery scene in Shanghai and Beijing start growing exponentially. By that time, however, artists were so used to selling works directly out of their studios and occasionally dealing with auctions that they frequently refused to buy into the Western practice of exclusive relationships with dealers (Vine et al. 2007). The auction remained an institution where reputations of young artists could be created, contextualizing them in a sale amidst the work of more established, recognized artists (Carver 2008).

The Hirst Sale

The final auction case is the sale that the British celebrity artist Damien Hirst organized in the fall of 2008. The previous examples show that his use of this type of sale was much less unique than media reports suggested.[12] Indeed, the similarity between some of the retrospective exhibitions preceding the one-man posthumous auction sales in nineteenth-century France and the museum-like retrospective show of Hirst's work that Sotheby's put up in its London offices on the eve of the sale is striking. Also, it is not farfetched to imagine that the highly successful Red charity auction, which Hirst co-organized and contributed to in the spring of 2008, inspired him to organize his own one-man sale. Sotheby's moreover, which hosted the sale, had by that time become familiar with the Chinese practice of using auctions on the primary market, and may have been willing to test the waters in the West as well.

For the artist and the auction house, the sale was an overwhelming success: the 223 works, auctioned off in separate sales on two consecutive days, brought in $200.7 million, which was 14% more than Sotheby's highest estimate. The top lot, *The Golden Calf*, a bull in formaldehyde with golden hooves, horns, and a gold disc on top of its head, sold for $18.6 million.

How did Hirst manage to get away with this experiment in spite of strong resistance within the art world? First of all, it needs to be noted that the value of Hirst's work and his own reputation within the art world had been firmly established before the event took place. At auction, his work consistently raised high prices, while at galleries a waiting list existed for the most popular

---

[11] In Japan, by contrast, auctions have historically been taboo on the primary as well as the secondary market and were for a long time even prohibited by law (Havens 1982: 119). Only when the Japanese economy integrated globally and Japan developed an interest in Western modern and contemporary art was this taboo eroded.

[12] *The Economist*, for instance, claimed that "such a sale has never been attempted before" (The Economist 2008).

works within his oeuvre. The sale in other words reinforces the argument made above that auctions may only be used once status and identity have been established, and not when standards of value are entirely absent. The auction was used to determine the exact value of individual—sometimes radically different—pieces, not to determine the value of Hirst's oeuvre or the reputation of the artist as such: the latter had long been established.

Second, Hirst anticipated the moral criticism of his enterprise—that it would lead to a further commercialization of the art world—and legitimated the endeavor by embedding the sale in another set of values. In the press release announcing the sale, he defended himself by calling auctions "a very democratic way to sell art." Posting prices in galleries, he argued, would be unfair because, as *The Economist* learned, Hirst "is irked by their [dealers'] habit of making potential new buyers prove themselves by waiting before they are allowed to purchase a work of art" (The Economist 2008). Instead, through an auction, every potential buyer could have access.

Third, Hirst succeeded because the sale fit into a superstar era in the art market (cf. Velthuis 2005*b*). This era started in the early 2000s, and was characterized by excessive attention to the lives and work of a small number of superstar artists such as Hirst, Jeff Koons, and Tracey Emin; steeply rising prices for contemporary art; the influx of new money; the participation of celebrities; and the emergence of an event culture. This culture was exemplified by the rise of art fairs, with their refined status machinery consisting of exclusive parties and VIP openings in which the global cultural and financial elite mingled. The Hirst sale was another such event.

Taking place on the same day as Lehman Brothers filed for bankruptcy, Hirst's auction also marked the end of this era. Prices for contemporary art have more than halved since then, celebrities have stopped visiting art fairs, and the newly rich collectors have at least temporarily dropped out of the art market. It is therefore unlikely, as a journalist for the *Wall Street Journal* and many others have speculated, that the Hirst sale was "a pivotal moment, like the end of the studio system in movies or the continuing decline of the record labels in the music business. Could the gallerist's traditional role as mediator between the contemporary artist and his market be passé?" (Kaylan 2008). No Western artists have subsequently imitated Hirst's attempts. Attesting to the changing climate within the art market, auction houses have followed the opposite strategy: aware that collectors do not want to be seen selling pieces, or afraid that public sales may result in disappointing price levels, they have ventured into private dealing. In the first half of 2009, Christie's turnover of contemporary art through private sales was higher than through auctions. And while sales at Sotheby's totaled $2.8 billion in 2009, compared to $5.3 billion in 2008, private sales were up 27%.[13]

---

[13] *Sotheby's Announces 2009 Fourth Quarter and Full Year Results* (2010).

Finally, Hirst's one-man auction was legitimate because it was perceived as an artistic enterprise in itself, made by an artist who is keenly aware of the art world's conventions and who knows how to increase his reputation by playing with these conventions and subverting them. In this sense, the sale could be considered a work of art in itself, which fits in to a much longer tradition of artists such as Marcel Duchamp, Yves Klein, or Jeff Koons using economic devices reflexively in their work to comment on the (cultural) economy (see Velthuis 2005*a*). Indeed, the auction can be seen as the sequel to another high-profile work that Hirst had made a year before: *For the Love of God*, a platinum cast of a skull covered with 8,601 diamonds. The artist claimed in the media, no doubt with tongue firmly in cheek, that the work had been bought by a consortium of investors, including himself (Byrne 2007).

Conclusion

This chapter contributes to a rich and rapidly growing sociological and anthropological literature showing that prices do not follow mechanically from the forces of supply and demand interacting. Instead, price setting is a social activity (Prus 1985) which involves noneconomic values such as fairness (Bolton et al. 2003; Frey 1986; Kahneman et al. 1986) and a wide range of cultural meanings (Velthuis 2005*b*). Pricing schemes are invariably socially constructed (Yakubovich et al. 2005), while in turn social structures (Uzzi 2004), status factors (Aspers 2001*b*), and power relations (Zafirovski 2000) must be taken into account to understand the outcome of the pricing process. Furthermore, as Marion Fourcade shows in this volume, national repertoires, institutional traditions, and diverging roles of experts may result in the production of different prices for elusive assets such as environmental goods. Finally, price itself may not be seen as a homogeneous entity. Instead, economic agents produce different types of prices in various commercial settings, of which the market price, that is the price against which a commodity is actually traded, is only one (Caliskan 2007).

Whereas most existing studies have focused on the production of prices per se, this chapter has studied the devices that are used to produce these prices. It has developed a number of arguments to come to terms with the wild historical and geographical variation of pricing devices encountered in empirical markets. Certainly, neoclassical economic theory has failed to do this: it cannot explain why fresh fish is auctioned in wholesale markets in Japan but sold through a combination of posted prices and private negotiations in the United States (Graddy 2006), why some expensive houses are auctioned but others are sold through posted prices, why art auction houses themselves decide to administer private negotiations in times of recession, or why haggling over the price tags of specific classes of retail goods is legitimate and even expected in some countries but unthinkable in others.

To understand this variation, I have argued first of all that we need to recognize that price mechanisms are not only economic devices directed at producing prices and enabling exchange but also social devices that produce values such as privacy and exclusivity (in the case of posted prices) or transparency and accessibility (in the case of auctions). Moreover, price mechanisms imply a specific type of interaction between economic agents, from the dense interaction of private negotiations in bazaar economies (Geertz 1979) to the anonymous settings of sealed-bid auctions. I therefore expect the occurrence of a specific device in empirical markets to be codependent on the preexisting social structure of that market.

Second, I have argued that pricing devices can only become operational once some form of market order, including status hierarchies, identities of the agents involved, and standards of value, is at least temporarily stabilized. The absence of auctions on the primary art market is partially because this order has not yet been established for the upcoming artists whose work is sold in this segment. Instead, one of the reasons that art galleries have managed to monopolize the primary art market is that they have effectively forged alliances with reputation-building agents such as art critics and curators. Further research should reveal if a similar connection between the construction of market order and pricing devices exists in other empirical markets.

Third, to understand the variation in pricing devices encountered, one needs to recognize that these devices never operate in and of themselves but require a wider institutional framework. In the case of art auctions, the museums, art dealers, and system of art criticism that we have become so used to in the West were by and large absent in the mid nineteenth-century French art market or in the Chinese art world of the 1990s. Indeed, historically auctions have been associated with outsiders who were excluded by the establishment from the official venues, whether guilds or salons (De Marchi 1995). Likewise, the local community artists that charity auctions frequently rely on are excluded from the official art world and its tastemaking machinery. The auctions have some legitimacy for these artists by default. This means that these auctions are not only an economic means of pricing and allocating goods but also a cultural means of gaining visibility and establishing reputations.

Finally, the chapter has argued that pricing and valuation, which are so frequently conflated, need to be disentangled. Pricing devices themselves need to be considered legitimate in order to become and remain operational, and in order to be considered legitimate, the shared values of the economic agents that work with these devices must be taken into account. The Hirst auction, for instance, worked because it was part of a wider era in the art market centered around superstar and celebrity values. In China, auctions are considered legitimate for new art because the art market is more firmly embedded in a speculative culture. I expect therefore that the historical variation in pricing devices is also related to the local cultures that predominate in each of these respective markets.

In short, with this chapter I am contributing to a growing literature on circuits of commerce, where forms of exchange are accompanied by specified morals, manners, symbols, and rituals, each of which in turn has shared meanings for actors within a circuit (Collins 2000; Fourcade and Healy 2007; Zelizer 2004). Pricing devices, with the patterned social interactions they at once presuppose and reproduce, and the cultural values and meaning structures they are embedded in, are an intricate part of these circuits.

■ REFERENCES

Alexander, J. and Alexander, P. (1991). What's a Fair Price? Price-Setting and Trading Partnerships in Javanese Markets. *Man* 26: 493–512.

Appadurai, A. (1986). Introduction: Commodities and the Politics of Value. In A. Appadurai (ed.), *The Social Life of Things: Commodities in Cultural Perspective*. Cambridge: Cambridge University Press, 3–63.

Arnold, M. A. and Lippman, S. A. (1995). Selecting a Selling Institution: Auctions versus Sequential Search. *Economic Inquiry* 33: 1–23.

Artprice (2008). *The Contemporary Art Market 2007/2008: The Annual Report*. Lyon: Artprice.

Aspers, P. (2001*a*). A Market in Vogue: Fashion Photography in Sweden. *European Societies* 3: 1–22.

——(2001*b*). *Markets in Fashion: A Phenomenological Approach*. Stockholm: City University Press.

——(2009). Knowledge and Valuation in Markets. *Theory and Society* 38: 111–31.

Ayres, I. and Siegelman, P. (1995). Race and Gender Discrimination in Bargaining for a New Car. *American Economic Review* 85: 304–21.

Beckert, J. (1996). What is Sociological about Economic Sociology? Uncertainty and the Embeddedness of Economic Action. *Theory and Society* 25: 803–40.

——and Rössel, J. (2004). Kunst und Preise: Reputation als Mechanismus der Reduktion von Ungewissheit am Kunstmarkt. *Kölner Zeitschrift für Soziologie und Sozialpsychologie* 56: 32–50.

Bevan, R. (2008, August 1). Damien Hirst Is Rewriting the Rules of the Market. *The Art Newspaper*. http://theartnewspaper.com/articles/Damien-Hirst-is-rewriting-the-rules-of-the-market-1)/8665 (accessed September 13, 2010)

Bodelsen, M. (1968). Early Impressionist Sales, 1874–1894 in the Light of Some Unpublished "Procès-Verbaux." *Burlington Magazine* 110: 331–49.

Bolton, L. E., Warlop, L., and Alba, J. W. (2003). Consumer Perceptions of Price (Un)Fairness. *Journal of Consumer Research* 29: 474–91.

Bonus, H. and Ronte, D. (1997). Credibility and Economic Value in the Visual Arts. *Journal of Cultural Economics* 21: 103–18.

Bourdieu, P. (1993). *The Field of Cultural Production: Essays on Art and Literature*. Cambridge: Polity Press.

Byrne, C. (2007, September 31). Hirst's Glittering Price Tag Loses None of the Shine. *The Independent*. http://www.independent.co.uk/news/uk/this-britain/hirsts-glittering-price-tag-loses-none-of-its-shine-463675.html (accessed September 9, 2010)

Caliskan, K. (2007). Price as a Market Device: Cotton Trading in Izmir Mercantile Exchange. *Sociological Review* 55: 241–60.

Carlton, D. (1991). The Theory of Allocation and Its Implications for Marketing and Industrial Structure: Why Rationing is Efficient. *Journal of Law and Economics* 34: 232–62.

Carrier, J. G. (1994). Alienating Objects: The Emergence of Alienation in Retail Trade. *Man* 29: 359–80.

Carver, A. (2008). Are Auction Houses Moving Onto Gallery Turf? *Bidoun Magazine: Art and Culture from the Middle East* 13. http://www.bidoun.org/magazine/13-glory/are-auction-houses-moving-onto-gallery-turf-by-antonia-carver/ (accessed September 7, 2010).

CBC News (2008). Bono's Charity Art Auction Nets $42 Million. *CBC News*. http://www.cbc.ca/arts/artdesign/story/2008/02/15/bono-hirst-auction.html (accessed September 9, 2010)

Clunas, C. (1997). *Art in China*. Oxford: Oxford University Press.

Collins, R. (2000). Situational Stratification: A Micro-Macro Theory of Inequality. *Sociological Theory* 18: 17–43.

——(2004). *Interaction Ritual Chains*. Princeton, NJ: Princeton University Press.

Crow, K. (2008, February 1). Bono Inc. Expands to Art. *The Wall Street Journal*, W4.

De Marchi, N. (1995). The Role of Dutch Auctions and Lotteries in Shaping the Art Market(s) of 17th Century Holland. *Journal of Economic Behavior and Organization* 28: 203–21.

Duret, T. (1910). *Manet and the French Impressionists: Pissarro, Claude Monet, Sisley, Renoir, Berthe Morisot, Cézanne, Guillaumin*. London: G. Richards.

Fanselow, F. S. (1990). The Bazaar Economy or How Bizarre Is the Bazaar Really? *Man* 25: 250–65.

Fourcade, M. and Healy, K. (2007). Moral Views of Market Society. *Annual Review of Sociology* 33: 285–311.

Frey, B. S. (1986). Economists Favour the Price System: Who Else Does? *Kyklos* 39: 537–63.

Gee, M. (1981). *Dealers, Critics, and Collectors of Modern Painting: Aspects of the Parisian Art Market Between 1910 and 1930*. New York: Garland Publishing.

Geertz, C. (1979). Suq: The Bazaar Economy in Sefrou. In C. Geertz, H. Geertz, and L. Rosen (eds.), *Meaning and Order in Moroccan Society*. Cambridge: Cambridge University Press, 123–225.

Geismar, H. (2001). What's in a Price? An Ethnography of Tribal Art at Auction. *Journal of Material Culture* 6: 25–47.

Goldberg, P. K. (1996). Dealer Price Discrimination in New Car Purchases: Evidence from the Consumer Expenditure Survey. *Journal of Political Economy* 104: 622–54.

Graddy, K. (2006). The Fulton Fish Market. *Journal of Economic Perspectives* 20: 207–20.

Greadell, C. (2008, February 19). Art Sales: Bono Breaks the Mould. *The Daily Telegraph*. http://www.telegraph.co.uk/culture/art/artsales/3671284/Art-sales-Bono-breaks-the-mould.html (accessed September 13, 2010)

Green, N. (1987). Dealing in Temperaments: Economic Transformation of the Artistic Field in France During the Second Half of the Nineteenth Century. *Art History* 10: 59–78.

Hanson, L. E. (1954). *Noble Savage: The Life of Paul Gauguin*. New York, NY: Random House.

Havens, T. R. H. (1982). *Artist and Patron in Postwar Japan*. Princeton, NJ: Princeton University Press.

Herrman, G. M. (2003). Negotiating Culture: Conflict and Consensus in US Garage Sale Bargaining. *Ethnology* 42: 237–52.

Hutter, M., Knebel, C., Pietzner, G., and Schäfer, M. (2007). Two Games in Town: A Comparison of Dealer and Auction Prices in Contemporary Visual Arts Markets. *Journal of Cultural Economics* 31: 247–61.

Jensen, R. (1994). *Marketing Modernism in Fin-de-Siècle Europe*. Princeton, NJ: Princeton University Press.

Kahneman, D., Knetsch, J. L., and Thaler, R. (1986). Fairness as a Constraint on Profit Seeking: Entitlements in the Market. *American Economic Review* 76: 728–41.

Katz, R. and Dars, C. (1999). *The Impressionists Handbook*. New York, NY: Sterling.

Kaylan, M. (2008, August 23). Hirst's Marketing End Run. *The Wall Street Journal*. http://online.wsj.com/article/SB121943624138364443.html (accessed September 13, 2010)

Kelly, S. (2003). "This Dangerous Game": Rousseau, Diaz and the Uses of the Auction in the Marketing of Landscapes. In F. Fowle and R. Thomson (eds.), *Soil and Stone: Impressionism, Urbanism, Environment*. Aldershot: Ashgate, 33–48.

Kino, C. (2006, May 28). Donating Work for Charity has a Downside for Artists. *The New York Times*. http://www.nytimes.com/2006/05/28/arts/design/28kino.html (accessed September 13, 2010)

Klamer, A. (1996). The Value of Culture. In A. Klamer (ed.), *The Value of Culture*. Amsterdam: Amsterdam University Press, 13–28.

Klemperer, P. (2004). *Auctions: Theory and Practice*. Princeton, NJ: Princeton University Press.

Lim, A. (2000, April 10). A Gift of a Price, but Do Artists Lose? *The Australian*, 18.

Lucking-Reiley, D. (2000). Auctions on the Internet: What's Being Auctioned, and How? *Journal of Industrial Economics* 47: 227–52.

Mainardi, P. (1993). *The End of the Salon: Art and the State in the Early Third Republic*. Cambridge: Cambridge University Press.

McAfee, R. P. and McMillan, J. (1987). Auctions and Bidding. *Journal of Economic Literature* 25: 699–738.

McAndrew, C. (2008). *The International Art Market: A Survey of Europe in a Global Context*. Helvoirt: The European Fine Art Foundation.

McEntire, F. (1995, September 3). Art For a Cause: Fund-Raisers for Charity Help... and Hurt. *Salt Lake Tribune*, E1.

Milgrom, P. R. (1985). The Economics of Competitive Bidding: A Selective Survey. In L. Hurwicz, D. Schmeidler, and H. Sonnenschein (eds.), *Social Goals and Social Organization: Essays in Memory of Elisha Pazner*. Cambridge: Cambridge University Press, 261–89.

——(1989). Auctions and Bidding: A Primer. *Journal of Economic Perspectives* 3: 3–22.

Miller, H. B. and Miller, W. A. (1996). Fundraising Auctions: The Professional Approach. *New Directions for Philanthropic Fundraising* 12: 95–107.

Montias, J. M. (1988). Art Dealers in the Seventeenth-Century Netherlands. *Simiolus* 18: 244–56.

Moulin, R. (1967/1987). *The French Art Market: A Sociological View*. New Brunswick, NJ: Rutgers University Press.
——(1994). The Construction of Art Values. *International Sociology* 9: 5–12.
North, M. (1992). *Art and Commerce in the Dutch Golden Age*. New Haven, CT: Yale University Press.
Okun, A. M. (1981). *Prices and Quantities: A Macroeconomic Analysis*. Washington, DC: Brookings Institution.
Phlips, L. (1988). *The Economics of Imperfect Information*. Cambridge: Cambridge University Press.
Plattner, S. (1996). *High Art Down Home: An Economic Ethnography of a Local Art Market*. Chicago: Chicago University Press.
Pollack, B. (2008). The Chinese Art Explosion. *ARTNews* 107: 118–27.
Prak, M. (2003). Guilds and the Development of the Art Market during the Dutch Golden Age. *Simiolus* 30: 236–51.
Prus, R. C. (1985). Price-Setting as a Social Activity. Defining Price, Value, and Profit in the Marketplace. *Urban Life* 14: 59–93.
Rewald, J. (1986*a*). *Cézanne: A Biography*. New York, NY: Harry Abrams.
——(1986*b*). *Studies in Post-Impressionism*. New York, NY: Harry Abrams.
Riley, J. and Zeckhauser, R. (1983). Optimal Selling Strategies: When to Haggle, When to Hold Firm. *Quarterly Journal of Economics* 98: 267–89.
Rotonchamps, J. D. (1925). *Paul Gauguin, 1848–1903*. Paris: G. Crès.
Smith, C. W. (1989). *Auctions: The Social Construction of Value*. New York, NY: Free Press.
Sotheby's Announces 2009 Fourth Quarter and Full Year Results, March 1, 2010 (2010). Press release. http://files.shareholder.com/downloads/BID/1017310186x0x353324/e21610be-04a6-4269-afd1-5e2db16d88ff/BID_FINAL.pdf (accessed March 31, 2011).
Sullivan, M. (1996). *Art and Artists of Twentieth Century China*. Berkeley, CA: University of California Press.
The Economist (2008, September 11). The Shark's Last Move. *The Economist*: 89–91.
Uzzi, B. (2004). Embeddedness and Price Formation in the Corporate Law Market. *American Sociological Review* 69: 319–44.
Vaughan, R. M. (2003, December 20). O Come All Ye Rich (and Shameless) Collectors. *The Globe and Mail*, R8.
Velthuis, O. (2003). Symbolic Meanings of Prices: Constructing the Value of Contemporary Art in Amsterdam and New York Galleries. *Theory and Society* 31: 181–215.
——(2005*a*). *Imaginary Economics*. Rotterdam: NAi Publishers.
——(2005*b*). *Talking Prices: Symbolic Meanings of Prices on the Market for Contemporary Art*. Princeton, NJ: Princeton University Press.
Vine, R., Phillips, C., and Pollack, B. (2007). Money Talks Mandarin. *Art in America* 95: 49–56.
Walker, H. (1997, September 9). Out of Context. *Santa Fe New Mexican*, 8.
Watson, P. (1992). *From Manet to Manhattan*. New York, NY: Random House.
Webber, D. (2003). Understanding Charity Fundraising Events. *International Journal of Nonprofit and Voluntary Sector Marketing* 9: 122–34.
White, H. C. (2002). *Markets from Networks: Socioeconomic Models of Production*. Princeton, NJ: Princeton University Press.
Yakubovich, V., Granovetter, M., and McGuire, P. (2005). Electric Charges: The Social Construction of Rate Systems. *Theory and Society* 34: 579–612.

Zafirovski, M. Z. (2000). An Alternative Sociological Perspective on Economic Value: Price Formation as a Social Process. *International Journal of Politics, Culture and Society* 14: 265–95.

Zelizer, V. A. (2004). Circuits of Commerce. In J. C. Alexander, G. T. Marx, and C. L. Williams (eds.), *Self, Social Structure, and Beliefs: Explorations in Sociology*. Berkeley, CA: University of California Press, 122–44.

9 Infinite Surprises: On the Stabilization of Value in the Creative Industries

Michael Hutter

Introduction

There is a category of goods that are desired for their ability to generate surprises. The category is old—as old as drama, epics, pictures, and songs. Such goods were part of societies before the rise of markets, but they became the products of crafts and industries once they could be sold. The sector producing and distributing such goods has only recently been expressly identified as the "creative industries." Besides markets for theater performances, books, paintings, and works of music, the sector includes goods like museum visits, video and computer games, fashion, and even advertising services. All the experiences enabled by these products are, to at least a small degree, novel. There is surprise in rediscovering traditional weaving patterns, going on city tours, listening to piano recitals, reading the news, playing against programmed monsters, seeing next year's fashion collection, or being unexpectedly captivated by an advertising campaign.

Novel products can be described, and so can the excitement or dismay experienced during a tour, a concert, an exhibition, or a video game. But the descriptions are difficult to compare with each other or among different speakers, and they are even more difficult to compare over long spans of time. And yet, in all the product categories of the creative industries, from works of music and art to design objects and television series, there exist stable ranges of valuation. Some of the goods have gained reputations that make their reproduction, variation, or simply the access to them particularly valuable. Even among new goods, there exist large differences in value. How is such value established when the "utility" of the goods lies in the uncertain effects of a subjective, mental experience, in feelings of unexpected elation and disappointment? How do such valuations gain stability even though the goods are singular and vary widely in their composition?

The first section of this chapter analyzes the characteristics of surprise-generating products. The second section discusses two mechanisms for anchoring valuations: the infinity relation of "praise value" and the equivalence of "price value." The third section examines evidence on the use of "infinity operators" in the contributions of creators, producers, amateurs, and critics along the value chain of creative industries' products.

The Surprise Economy: Features of an Emerging Sector

CONSTRUCTING THE CREATIVE INDUSTRIES

The notion of the creative industries has a fairly precise origin in the documents of a governmental agency.[1] In 1998, the British Department for Culture, Media and Sport (DCMS) published the *Creative Industries Mapping Document* (1998: 9), which delineated a sector called the "creative industries." The delineation had administrative and economic consequences because it rearranged the statistical account of the country's economic product, measured in market prices. The new structure combined the classic branches of cultural production, from the performing arts to literature, with commercial branches like advertising and video game software.[2] These statistical indicators have been used to demonstrate that the creative industries sector is not only the third-largest economic sector in the United Kingdom but holds equal economic importance in other industrially developed countries as well, such as Germany (Söndermann et al. 2009). A recent study by the United Nations Conference on Trade and Development (UNCTAD), using a more systematic definition of the creative industries, demonstrated that the share of creative industries' products in the trade balances of developing countries is growing at rates far above the average (UNCTAD 2008).[3]

The reasons for the rearrangement are clearly political. Products that contribute some degree of novelty seem to play a prominent role in contemporary economies. Their value is not primarily dependent on physical characteristics but is self-generated by those who invent, make, and use the products. When, as is the actual global situation, the diffusion of major technological innovations drives the cost of processing and storing information down, the perceived gain is even more pronounced. Goods in the creative industries may well become a major driver of economic growth.

Some authors attribute an even larger, "systemic" role to the sector: it distributes "new knowledge" which then increases the value of production in

---

[1] See Schlesinger (2009: 17).
[2] The branches included in the DCMS definition are the markets for art, music, performing arts, books, film, broadcasting, design, architecture, print, advertising, and video game software.
[3] The report distinguishes four major sectors: Heritage, Arts, Media, and Creative Services. Creative services include design, fashion, architecture, and advertising. See UNCTAD (2008).

all branches of an economy, thus turning it into a "creative economy."[4] The argument resembles the positive externality argument for education and research: dissemination of knowledge generates increases in productivity that cannot be attributed to single factors of production. But there is a twist to the externality argument, because the "new knowledge" diffused by creative industries products is clearly of a different kind than that generated by, say, new chemical products—it is less definitive, more playful, less certain, more contingent. This particular kind of "information" is contained in Shakespeare plays as well as in Tarantino movies, in Versace suits, and in Lucky Strike advertisements. What kind of information is it?

INFORMATION AND SURPRISE

The common characteristic of creative industries' products lies in being different, in being new. The experience of newness comes with the emotion of surprise: expectations are not met; they are either exceeded or disappointed. Surprise overwhelms expected certainties.[5] Spontaneous, involuntary utterances are indicative. Surprise happens only in a world of uncertainty. But the goods and devices that respond to the uncertainty are not intended to reduce it, as in the case of surveillance or of scientific research that uncovers hidden certainties. "Surprise goods" generate positive uncertainty, a kind of uncertainty that is desired by users because of the strong and positive emotions it generates in each of them.

The notion of surprise seems close to the notion of *Erlebnis*, or experience, which Gerhard Schulze identified as paradigmatic for the orientation of contemporary Western societies. Schulze points out that experiences connect organic body and mental consciousness. In fact, "the subject consists of experiences" (Schulze 1992: 735). Reflection about experiences constitutes a further desired type of experience. Schulze recognizes that expectations about experiences can be disappointed, but he does not recognize the positive sensation of surprise. Beckert (in Section 1 of his chapter in this volume) develops a distinction between the physical, positional, and imaginative value of goods. Certain goods, ranging from old wine to fashionable handbags, "arouse images that alter the state of consciousness of the owner."[6] Beckert is interested in the cultural and social context that allows the owner to ascribe symbolic meaning to a good. One can now add that new meaning always contains surprise—the surprise of something that has never been said, shown, or performed in quite the same way.[7]

---

[4] See Potts and Cunningham (2008). Other authors apply the term "creative economy" to the particular sector rather than to the entire economy. See Howkins (2001).

[5] The French and Middle English roots of "surprise" refer to being overwhelmed; the German "Überraschung" has the same meaning, with reference to being overtaken at great speed.

[6] Beckert points to the work of Campbell (1987) who demonstrated the relevance of imaginative value for commercial goods during the romantic movement.

[7] For Niklas Luhmann, any new information, when it is understood by some consciousness for the first time, takes the form of a surprise (Luhmann 1997).

The semantics of creative industry (Smith 1998), creative economy (Howkins 2001), and creative class (Florida 2004) deal with the property of surprise in a roundabout way: they attribute it to the intentional action of a particular type of actor who is capable of making goods that generate surprises. The "creative act" is an event in time during which the design of a music score, a cartoon episode, or a software patch is conceived by an individual or a team. The creative idea then needs a long production chain before it can surprise users. Recently, however, some authors have moved surprise to the opposite end of the chain. For these authors, surprise emerges within the experience of the user: unless the user attributes meaning to an event, no experience takes place. The delineation of a sector of "experience goods" adds a few branches to the creative industries sector: it suggests that the creativity of users in generating their own surprises turns many activities such as gambling or sport fishing into potential experience goods.[8]

The two approaches actually complement each other: both try to grasp a phenomenon that is not individual but happens between those who create and those who experience. Creators and producers offer performances and commodities[9] that they hope will appear novel to users. The creators who offer new experiences are themselves users of such experiences, turning the conventional value chain into a value spiral, where each successful surprise product leads to a successive generation of new surprise goods.[10]

Surprises that are fit for commercial products are carefully calibrated in their deviation from user expectations. The user must not be bored by evident repetitions or shocked by danger and provocation. Familiar surprises, combining thrill with comfort, are the most frequent and successful commercial variety.

Surprises establish strong links between individual emotion and social expression. When surprises are experienced in groups and collectives—as in games or artistic performances—these expressions become part or even the center of the performance. As the excitement of others is experienced on top of one's own experience, the total effect is enhanced. Durkheim (1995) called this effect "collective effervescence" and attributed a central cohesive function to such performances, particularly to religious rituals. The proposed conception extends Durkheim's contribution: effervescence is not limited to types of experiences molded by immutable tradition but is generated within experiences that can be designed and sold to a variety of audiences.[11] Since surprise

---

[8] The notion of experience goods was first used in economic theory to designate goods whose uncertainty of performance could be reduced by using or experiencing them. Pine and Gilmore (1999) were the first to use the term in its positive connotation. Recent cultural policy suggestions have been based on the distinction of an experience goods sector. See Power (2009) and Bille (2009). For a more detailed account of the transition in the meaning of the term, see Hutter (2011).

[9] The term "product" covers both varieties.

[10] See Hutter (2006) for an elaboration of the "value spiral."

[11] The success of "megachurches" suggests that even religious rituals are not immune to innovation introduced by faith entrepreneurs. See Stark (2008), and the concluding chapter of this volume.

experiences, like Durkheim's rituals, fade in individual memory and as a topic in social communication, they are replaced by new waves of products in daily, monthly, or yearly rhythms. Familiar surprises should flow constantly and yet not lose their characteristic irregularity—this is the innovation challenge in the creative/novel experience industries.

A broad arsenal of modes for generating surprises is available. At least five modes can be identified: (1) competitions with unpredictable outcomes, as in sports; (2) gambling events, where money or other assets can be bet against the odds of probability; (3) toys, games, and trips that generate mild variations; (4) oscillations in the specifications of goods that have specific functions, as in the length and color of skirts or in the size and shape of automobiles; and (5) the generation of amazement. This fifth mode will be the focus of the discussion, since it is the most versatile of the five.

Amazement is the richest mode because it can be built on any kind of expectation. Some particular practice of communication by word, image, sound, or bodily movement meets with specific, usually subconscious expectations. In amazement, such expectations are exceeded. A performance may be funny, skillful, or sublime, or all three at the same time, as in a Woody Allen movie. It may demonstrate courage, or virtuosity, or ingenuity—in all cases, the spectator or user goes through an experience of amazement. Amazement is a strong, albeit transitory, emotion. If the performance leading to the experience of amazement relates to a narrow bodily skill, as in a circus trick, the product has to keep changing. If the experience integrates a wide range of amazement features, as in an opera production, additional performances in a different setting and with a new audience can be enough to generate renewed amazement. Amazement may be accompanied by the shock of unexpected novelty or of provocation. These additional features increase amazement but are rarely appreciated without that deeper, more complex dimension.

Artworks, whether novels or rap songs or films, are particularly valued as sources of amazement. The artistic performance of an instrument amazes. So does the artistic liberty of employing pigments in a certain way, or the artistic skill of shaping language into verse. Attention to the effects of artworks can help to discover and understand features that are just as relevant for the success of less singular creative industries' goods.

Although many artworks have the potential for amazement, only a few out of the total number of works offered are successful in finding an audience. All others are ignored, dismissed, merely glanced at, or explicitly rejected. If amazement is a subjective mental experience, if feelings of elation and disappointment can be described but not transferred to others, then how have these works attained and, in even fewer cases, maintained and increased their value? Artworks will be used as an instructive case because the most finely calibrated social valuation practices have evolved around them.

Two Value Anchors: Praise Value and Price Value

PRAISE AND PRICE VALUATION ALONG THE VALUE CHAIN

How are stable values reached for specific artworks?[12] There seem to be two distinct mechanisms at work. One of them operates through judgments of praise: those who have come into contact with the product's performance talk about their experience and try to describe their feelings of elation or disappointment by comparing the work or the performance to other, older works that the person listening to the judgment might know or have heard about. The second mechanism operates through prices on art markets. As a growing number of persons want to share the experience they have heard praised, prices for the original or for copies go up and often stay at a stable level for long periods of time. The second mechanism is certainly the more transparent one, and it seems to dominate in most branches of the creative industries. But even the success of particular video games or pop songs depends on judgments of praise and the comparisons that such praise employs. While there may be polar cases when only price counts, the majority of cases will feature both mechanisms. Before examining the logical properties of these mechanisms in greater depth, we will take a closer look at four stages of the value chain.

Surprise is part of an event in which people create and perform something in order to amaze those who see it, hear it, or read it. Together, performance and audience response constitute the event. The performance emerges in two stages: a first stage in which a new work is conceived or created, and a second stage in which the novel work is produced and disseminated. Audience response also emerges in two stages: in a first stage, the members of the audience react to the performance, applaud during the event, and talk about their experience after the event. In a second stage, amateur surprise is distilled into the judgment of critics. These judgments are themselves available as novel goods in the shape of news media: they are experience goods in their own right. The critical judgments happen before the next round of performances and thus generate an ongoing sequence of communication events that alternate between performance action/reaction and audience reaction/new action.[13]

Judgments of praise are part of the communication between all four stages of this valuation chain. Artists find words of praise for their own work as compared to that of other artists, producers praise the works they have selected for performance, amateurs praise the amazing experiences they have gone through, and critics evaluate works according to more general

---

[12] For accounts of the historical value debates in the economic and the aesthetic field, see Hutter and Shusterman (2006) and the introduction in Hutter and Throsby (2008).

[13] The distinctions introduced are highly stylized. They refer to types of communication and do not reflect the much more complex personal patterns in reality. In fashion photography, for instance, photographers (creators) communicate as producers and advertisers, editors are producers and critics, and art directors also fulfill various roles. See Aspers (2001).

qualities of amazement. Prices are also used along the chain: artists pay for their training, producers buy rights to selected works, amateurs pay for access tickets and for ownership rights, and critics receive pay in return for their praise valuations.

The praise value generated by critics is of a particular nature. Artists are biased through their own creations, producers are assumed to speak in favor of their selection, and amateurs are swayed by their momentary emotions. All groups may be experts given their long history of experiences, but they are weak in expressing value in ways that are stable over long periods of time. The skill of the critics seems to lie in applying external criteria of valuation to a body of work, and to each single performance within an oeuvre, a style, or a career. In the genre of painting, for instance, the artistic valuations have been so stable that Old Master paintings are considered more secure assets than state-issued annuities. In the genre of film, critics' choices are frequently ignored by amateur audiences but tend to be accepted in the long run. The misjudgment of critics, perhaps most prominently in the case of Impressionist painting, shows that while short-term errors may be made, these are then corrected by the next generation of critics. Praise value, it seems, is more than just cheap talk that accompanies price valuation in markets. Praise value has an autonomy of its own that can, and frequently does, deviate from price value. What is it that makes rankings along scales of valuation so stable when the objects of the evaluations are internal experiences of amazement, highly dependent on individual cognition and social milieu?

THE NOTION OF VALUE ANCHORS

The quality ranking of events on any scale poses problems of comprehension. The ranking is inevitably relative because it is an ordinal sequence: regarding quality x, A is better than B, which is better than C, etc. Natural numbers that would add up to a sum expressible in absolute terms do not exist.[14] When positions are without a commonly shared point of reference, evaluations are difficult to compare between critics, and even between different judgments from the same critic. There is no external rule that determines which kind of work is more or less valuable, but comparisons need a common point of reference in order to make sense.

I call such a common point of reference a "value anchor."[15] The anchor successfully provides the fiction that, in a pool of relative judgments, there is a

---

[14] There were, however, quite serious attempts by writers like Roger de Piles or Jonathan Richardson to use natural numbers for determining the quality of the body of work by certain painters. See De Marchi (2008). A current quantitative approach uses data on reproductions to determine the "greatest artists" (Galenson 2001).

[15] The term "anchoring effects" has been used in the literature on market anomalies to express the bias that subjects in experiments display in their estimates toward a number they were originally given. In art auctions, an anchoring effect based on previous prices has been shown. See Beggs and Graddy (2009: 1027).

fixed point evident to all those who participate in the discussions surrounding a particular kind of private surprising experience.

To illustrate the nature and the effect of a value anchor, consider the case of the vanishing point as it is used in constructing the illusion of three-dimensional space in a picture plane: the vanishing point is a point like all the others in a painting, yet it is perceived with a second interpretation—it is assumed to be at an infinite distance. The double meaning of the point turns it from a sign into a sort of metasign. The point constructed to be the furthest from the picture plane is at the same time a statement about the spatial position of all other points on that painted surface.[16] The notion of infinity thus is able to serve as an absolute anchor from which to calculate all other spatial relations on the surface.

The use of infinity as a metasign follows formal logic. There are exactly three possibilities of constructing a metasign: ∞, 0, and $-\infty$.[17] None of the three is a natural number like 1, 2, 3, etc. They are positioned at the "end" of numbers, positive and negative, and "between" the two series, respectively. All three points are expressed as symbols, not as numbers. Two of them are vanishing points—points that are describable yet are positioned at an infinite distance. The third point, 0, signifies "nothing." All three symbols are successfully used in scientific and in commercial computation, although they have no counterpart in physical reality. Can they provide the absolute anchor needed for relative quality comparisons of singular works?[18]

I will argue that these anchor values are indeed used: "∞" is operationalized as the ideal of infinite praise; "$-\infty$" operationalizes negative praise or reproach. The symbol "0" signifies equality in value, expressed as price. All three value anchors find their application in the valuation of artworks and other surprise goods.

USING INFINITY TO ANCHOR QUALITY JUDGMENTS

The central claim of this chapter is that a particular anchor of absolute value stabilizes relative praise judgments. Praise experts might be artists in their own right, producers, collectors, or critics, whether this last group comprises scholars or independent writers. In speaking as experts, they all are, in Bourdieu's terms, priests rather than sorcerers, *auctoritates* rather than *autores* (1969: 105). It is not the competition between them that is under scrutiny but a feature that is common to all of them and makes them effective judges in the first place.

---

[16] See Rotman (1987) for a detailed argument on the use of zero, the vanishing point, and paper money as metasigns.

[17] A first attempt to interpret the three points is Hutter (2007a).

[18] This research question is very close to that of a study by Karpik on the "economics of singularities." Karpik turns to the examination of "judgment devices...as guideposts for individual and collective action" (2010: 57). Karpik interprets these judgment devices as a means to reduce the uncertainty introduced by the singular goods. He is not concerned with issues of scale stabilization.

The degree to which a performance exceeds the social and mental expectations of its own stylistic program is expressed in words which take as their reference an ideal point of infinite quality.[19] Like the vanishing point, an ideal of excellence is a metacommunication, a statement about statements. That is what makes it an anchor. The anchor of excellence serves a function analogous to the vanishing point that generates spatial illusion.[20] The quality in which a performance excels—the "originality" of movies directed by Quentin Tarantino, the "brilliance" of arias sung by Cecilia Bartoli—these qualities are a current standard against which other action films or aria performances are valued.[21] Like the vanishing point in a painting, the infinity illusion of the anchor need only work for a limited section of reality.

During most of the eighteenth century, the infinity anchor for the visual arts was situated in classical art. Ancient Greek marble sculpture marked the ideal of excellence (Haskell and Nicholas 1981). Since then, the periods of stable anchoring have shortened, and canons have been dismantled and reconstructed. In recent history, anchors of excellence have been attributed to the works of particular artists. Since 1900, the oeuvres of Claude Monet, Paul Cezanne, Pablo Picasso, Marcel Duchamp, Jackson Pollock, Andy Warhol, and Gerhard Richter have served that function.

To indicate infinite quality, the separate estimations of a work's features along various quality scales are related. The result is a set of judgments that address very fine points of deviation from expected performance and yet succeed in conveying an opinion on the degree of excellence of a particular performance or a body of work, thus ranking it in relation to other objects of artistic valuation. Critics' judgments typically relate the accomplishments of a single work to the context of an artist's complete oeuvre and to the context of the style to which the work is attributable. Even in art worlds that have no clear leading figure, praise value finds its anchor in a small number of works by an even smaller number of creators. Across genres and styles, there is a remarkable consensus with respect to those artists that are closest to infinite praise.[22]

A second logical possibility remains: $-\infty$ could serve as a vanishing point for negative judgments, for rejecting a work, or for protesting against its performance. Expressions of protest play a prominent role in political discourse when no characterization of the enemy seems radical enough (Hutter 2007a). In the case of surprise goods, disappointments are formulated in less drastic terms. There are expressions of reproach or even expressions of rejection when the experience violates established criteria of quality or decency. But while

---

[19] The frequent use of adjectives like "perfect," "ideal," and "pure" may serve as an indication for this claim.
[20] Attempts at isolating the essential qualities of artworks tend to include "excellence." An example is Kane (1997).
[21] Beckert (in this volume) recognizes the relevance of such standards when he suggests that the imaginary value of objects lies in their symbolic representation of "espoused ideals."
[22] See Galenson (2001), who uses bibliometric evidence to prove A-list status. Becker's "art worlds" are based on the consensual valuations of different qualities and genres (Becker 1982).

there are many ways to idealize beauty, there seem to be no corresponding ideals of ugliness.

USING ZERO TO ANCHOR PRICE VALUATIONS

The second type of value scale operates with "0" as its absolute point. Pricing uses the equivalence of two compared goods, or a difference of zero, as a value anchor. When two parties exchange goods, the action leads to the actual, observable loss of property, with the right to use the good just given away. The loss precedes the gain of access to a new experience. Something is given in exchange; it is traded.[23] All the words surrounding the transaction are peripheral; decisive is the value of the item given up. Historically, the search for items of equal value improved immensely when value became expressible in a common medium for such exchanges. That medium has taken shape as money, whether in the form of metal or paper or as book entries. Money volumes operate with their own anchor. They stabilize their value through a set of institutions that has grown over centuries. Since the late nineteenth century, the money anchor has been grounded in the fiction that the value of a volume of fiat-money in circulation is guaranteed by a "lender of last resort," a national or supranational reserve bank.[24] This construction has functioned effectively as a vanishing point for the trust of agents until recent years (Ferguson 2009).

The world of market exchange—used as a term for the sum of all the active, interconnected arenas in which sellers perform and buyers reward—has grown so differentiated and subtle that all events with potential scarcity get price offers, even if they are declared "priceless" or "not for sale" (Grampp 1989). Still, price valuation does not always take place. Music can be performed and applauded, stories can be written and quoted, and sketches can be drawn and commented on, thus establishing their praise value throughout an audience without the operation of markets. But when such performances are provided by for-profit firms, their price valuation is inevitable. Price valuation also becomes inescapable when some works reach a level of evident and visible scarcity at which they are inevitably compared with the exchange value of other products.[25]

There are, it is argued, two ways of anchoring the value of products: one is through the attribution of exchange equivalence, as in price; the other is

---

[23] Simmel (1978: 78) develops his theory of value on the basis of this mutual valuation: "By being exchanged, each object acquires a practical realization and measure of its value through the other object."

[24] The act of Parliament establishing the hitherto private Bank of England as the solitary issue bank of Great Britain did not take place until 1844, but the Bank had effectively assumed that role in the previous decades. See John Clapham (1944) and Hutter (2007b).

[25] In the market for visual artworks, gallerists have developed sophisticated ways of signaling quality through the use of specific "pricing scripts" (Velthuis 2005). In addition, however, gallerists engage heavily in praise judgments and in narratives linking their artists to other, already established artists.

through the comparison with a standard of infinite value, as in praise. For products that have internal, mental effects, such as works in the visual arts or in music, theater, and literature, the second anchor should have particular relevance. Expressions of praise value determine the willingness to pay for such goods, hence their economic value and the value added to total economic product. Over the course of time—measured in years or decades—a correspondence of praise value and price value develops. But the many discrepancies between quality judgments and market prices are an indication of the different social processes at work around the two valuation mechanisms (Hutter and Frey 2010).

The interpretation of the two metasigns is at this point merely a theoretical proposition. Logically, there exists the possibility of using both "0" and "∞" as reference points. If long-term stability of value rankings is a desirable goal, then the combination of the two symbolic references has obvious advantages. But can such communication practices actually be observed in the scenes around creative industries' products? Is "infinity" really a category of relevance in the countless relative comparisons made to express the qualities of novel experiences?

Evidence for "Infinity Operators" along the Value Chain

The attempt to identify the use of the "infinity anchor" in the communication around creative industries is guided by the following consideration: as surprise goods are created, performed, used, and critiqued, the different stages of the value chain are accompanied by a stream of quality judgments. Such judgments employ comparisons with other goods, but how and to what extent do they employ comparisons with ideals of various qualities? Presumably, the different stages have different means of expressing such ultimate references. In consequence, the operationalization of the "infinity anchor" in praise value will differ between the stages. A number of rhetoric practices along the value chain are identified below that point to the use of such infinity operators.

EXPERIENCE CREATORS AND PROFOUND EMOTIONS

Creators are clearly compromised in ranking their own works along scales of quality. Yet there is great interest in the judgment of artists, because their experience in making the work—writing a novel or composing a song—is different from that of the rest of the protagonists. As creators praise the works of others, their judgment is linked to the authority and reputation of their own work. That authority, in turn, is based on the pursuit of some kind of ethos, some internal ideal that guides all the creators' collective quality distinctions.

The ideal may be verbalized in reference to the profound emotions that guide creators' judgments. Such references should be expected not only among composers and painters but also among more applied creators, such as fashion designers, architects, and cartoonists. Because creators have an existential involvement in a particular type of creative process, it is credible that even small, surprising features of novel works will trigger in them an emotional response of profound depth. It is also credible for creators to express emotions of rejection and reproach in exaggerated terms. The exaggeration is part of the attempt to signal the particular position of the speaker toward the work in question.

An example of "zeal" as an infinity operator can be seen in the following quote by T. S. Eliot, who criticized Milton's poetry in a famous essay early in his career and defended his harsh reproach in a later statement: "Poets ... will exalt the virtues of those poets of the past who offer them example and stimulation, and cry down the merits of those poets who do not stand for qualities they are zealous to realize. This is not only inevitable, it is right."[26]

Furthermore, creators often express a strong desire to keep price value and praise value separate. They fear that praise value is compromised by the factors that influence prices in exchanges (Bourdieu 1993: 75–6; Velthuis 2005; Zelizer 1994). Independent artists might succeed in maintaining such a separation even if the prices paid for their works are the basis of their independence. Creators who are employed by commercial companies do not have that opportunity. The companies measure their success in terms of revenues, or profits after taxes, and the collective focus on price value strengthens the firms' ability to coordinate actions. On the other hand, the companies producing novel goods benefit if there is a discussion within the organization around the qualities of the works produced. One should observe, therefore, that companies find ways to work with varieties of praise values.[27]

EXPERIENCE PRODUCERS AND THEIR EXALTED PRAISE

After the first stage, in which a novel artwork or any other surprise good is created either by an individual or by a collaborative circle, there is a second stage, in which the event is prepared and actually performed. Such events are often recorded, and copies of these recordings are distributed to audiences that have access to reproducing media, such as cinemas, CDs, or televisions. Those who accomplish these tasks are called producers. Producers have enough experience to make quality judgments; in fact, they would fail commercially if their judgments were inaccurate. Producers have to make selections, since only a fraction of the works suggested by creators can be transformed into performances and recordings. The selective choice is a clear, transparent

---

[26] Quoted in Hutter and Shusterman (2006: 203).
[27] This type of heterodoxy even makes sense outside the creative sector, since firms generally rely on internal change to come up with innovations sooner than their competitors (Stark 2009).

indicator of value, but it is accompanied by massive, often expensive expressions of praise for the works selected, either through the producers themselves or through hired specialists.[28]

Producers in creative industries come in two varieties: executive producers shape the work, live or recorded, through their intervention, while "distributive" producers have to master the logistics of and the communication around the dissemination of copies. Producers also come in two sizes: large, globally active companies, with high economies of scope and scale in the production and distribution of recorded copies, and small local or regional firms. In every branch, not more than half a dozen "majors" and thousands of "independents" operate.[29] The observations below refer to both groups, even if their means and tools are vastly different.

Goods that are new are inevitably unknown, so the potential audience has to be informed. Announcing the advent of a new film, a television series, or a video game is a skill of its own. Advertising and promotion budgets take up 30–60% of total production expenditures in most creative industries (Hutter 2006: 101f.). A large part of these sums pays for the privilege of placing messages into a mass medium, be it print, broadcast, or the Web. Advertising messages typically operate with exaggerated claims to excellence. They select quotes from the most positive judgments of supposedly neutral critics. As well as using the authority of these quotations of exalted praise by critics, advertising messages attempt to be novel and surprising in their own way. The inventiveness of a message serves as an indicator for the inventiveness of the actual good that the message advertises.[30]

Another avenue of action operates through direct engagements with audiences, amateurs, as well as critics in order to influence their quality judgments. Direct engagements with amateurs take place through live performances such as concerts or readings, or film screenings attended by the director and the main actors. The events are usually priced low enough to generate excess demand, which can then be reported as a sign of attention. For some genres,

---

[28] Aspers (2001: 105f.) reports the prominent role of selection in the case of fashion magazine editors. He observes the crucial role that status plays when value is assigned to the work of certain magazines, artists, or advertising studios. Status hierarchies and contexts could be seen as a complementary strategy for value stabilization.

[29] A number of effects accumulate to generate this sharply asymmetric distribution. There are technical network effects, the effects of distributing a public good, and the effects of "preferential attachment": users prefer experiences that they can share with many others and communicate about. In consequence, some network nodes develop into central hubs while all the others remain peripheral (Barabási 2001). Further amplification of the asymmetry takes place through the mass media. Mass-media products are experience goods as well: the surprise lies in the observation of any kind of new information. Since unexpected changes in nature, apart from the weather forecast and occasional earthquakes, are fairly rare, most of the news refers to social events, preferably those whose protagonists are already linked to their audiences: in this way, a fraction of the marketable works is brought to even greater prominence.

[30] A third way to attract audiences to something unknown is by providing access to selected fragments of the new work. It is easy to create limited demo versions of works that have been programmed or recorded in digital media in order to grant users access to their potential performance.

regular direct contact with "hardcore fans" at festivals is part of the long-term production program.[31] Winning affection from amateurs for certain performers stabilizes these fans' responses to new performances and decreases the danger that they will switch to other arenas.

Another direct engagement with amateurs takes place through market research. Audience reactions to surprise goods are surprises in themselves. "Nobody knows" is still the iron law of the movie industry, as well as other creative industries' branches.[32] Word-of-mouth publicity is considered the most powerful medium for passing on recommendations to other users. Yet the producers have a keen interest in forecasting the reactions as accurately as possible. One way to deal with this predicament is to make products that are similar to versions that were successful in the past, whether this is done through content, performers involved, or some other dimension. But there is a limit to copying old successes, and the danger of producing a "flop" remains. Market research is intended to reduce the danger, but this research is hampered by the surprise feature. How can people be asked about their interest in something when they cannot be exposed to it on a test basis because the surprise would be leaked to the general audience? The contingency of amateur audience reaction is crucial for maintaining the process of creative destruction that selects new variations of goods and withdraws attention from last season's items.

While direct engagements with amateurs show little evidence of the use of infinity operators, engagements with critics do involve ideal quality judgments. The producers, be they museum directors, opera impresarios, or fashion designers, need the judgments of critics to validate their selections. These producers find ways of gaining critics' attention in the first place by providing them with the opportunities to publish their opinions in appropriate media like exhibition catalogues or fashion journals. The producers then select the most exalted quotes, the ones which relate most openly to pure qualities or ideals.[33]

To sketch in more detail the kind of empirical work needed to explore this claim, I have selected a short text on an artwork that was published in the catalogue for an auction at Christie's in 2005.[34] The work is one canvas from Andy Warhol's *Flowers* series. These works, when first exhibited in 1965, actually did overwhelm their first viewers with surprise. Bright fluorescent colors dazzled the eye, and the subject matter disappointed expectations of social critique. The text is a one-page entry praising the work that is up for sale. The writing first sets out the work's pedigree in terms of previous owners,

---

[31] See Keith Negus (1999) on audience relationships in country music.
[32] See Richard Caves (2000) and his identification of the essentials defining the creative industries.
[33] For a parallel development in the communication of qualities in scientific writing, see Franck (1999).
[34] See Invaluable.com (2005).

public exhibitions, and literary treatments, and then adds prose that contains the following selected phrases:

> The present work is one of only seven monumental-scale paintings from Andy Warhol's famous *Flowers* series... Warhol was at the height of his creative powers and international fame... the pictures belong to a long art historical tradition of still-life painting... Warhol's updated version is consciously banal, superficial, synthetic and enchantingly beautiful. Quintessentially sixties... Dealer Ivan Karp recalls, "... they were totally successful and *we sold them all!* ... That's it. That's one of those immortal images..." ... While the *Flowers* can be seen as the vacuous flip-side of... horror and violence, there are some critics who believe that they are still permeated by Warhol's deep obsession with death. "... No matter how much one wishes these flowers to remain beautiful they perish under one's gaze, as if haunted by death." (J. Coplans, "Andy Warhol: The Art", *Andy Warhol*, exh. cat., Pasadena Art Museum, 1970, 52)

Scarcity ("one of only seven"), the peak of creative powers, art historical tradition, enchanting beauty, and quintessence are invoked. A prominent art dealer is cited who connects the commercial success with the quality of immortality. The association with death is attributed to "some critics" and supported by a quote from a text written 40 years earlier by a critic for one of the first public exhibitions of the work. Such are the strategies for implementing infinity operators in producer-generated praise judgments.

EXPERIENCE AMATEURS AND THEIR SPONTANEOUS PRAISE

Those who perform a surprise good—creators and producers—may have had their own experience when the performance originated. But the good will not be successful unless novelty and amazement are experienced by a large and attentive audience. The statements providing the evidence above on the impact of such performances were attributed either to "amateurs" or to "critics." Both kinds of statements come from "users" of the experience.

Amateurs' statements refer to an internal reaction that needs no further legitimation for its valuation; they react, to use a phrase suggested by Dewey, with "ejaculations"[35] of applause. Their expressions and judgments are powered by their "love" for a genre. The internal sensations during their experiences provide them with the criteria to express their approval or disapproval during and after a given performance. Intensity and length of applause or whistling are prime indicators for the quality of a performance. In a few cases, the emotion boils to collective frenzy, with expressions that signal the extraordinariness of the experience through collectively altered behavior.[36]

A second way of expressing the love for specific experiences operates through ownership and thus through price value: the collector pays for

---

[35] The term is used in Dewey (1939: 6f).
[36] Here, the similarity to Durkheim's "effervescence" is particularly striking.

possession; the museum or concert visitor pays for access to the object or the performance that triggered amazement and enthusiasm. Collectors in particular can strongly influence the reputation of specific works. A similar effect takes place when unusually large numbers of copies are sold. But in none of these cases do infinity operators seem to play a significant role.

Amateur users also talk about their experiences. The power of word of mouth, which is particularly relevant in the movie industry,[37] was mentioned above as one of the strategic concerns of producers. But what kinds of rhetorical strategies are used by amateurs? First of all, the reports are subjective; they work because they are not abstracted to critical reflection. They use fashionable colloquial terms for surprise and amazement: "awesome," "out of this world," or "it blew me away." They may also refer to pure qualities like "peace," "energy," or "joy," but such abstractions are not dominant.

Overall, amateurs generate praise value that seems to have little use for infinity operators. Their messages establish a credible connection to personal experience. Amateurs also use price value because they give up disposable income for ownership and allocate their time budget to particularly favored surprise goods. "Crowd opinion" is proverbial in its propensity for change, its fickleness, and its instability. This observation fits well with amateurs' lack of use of the "infinite" qualities' value anchor.

EXPERIENCE CRITICS AND FUNDAMENTAL CRITERIA OF QUALITY

Critics, working either in an academic or a mass-media context, have command over mental or even material archives because they have attended many previous performances in the genre for which they claim expertise. They also store knowledge of what has been said or written by other critics and performers about similar events. On the basis of that mental and social knowledge, they establish their set of criteria for quality. They rank new events along scales that indicate the degree to which these criteria are fulfilled. Thus, the ranking of new events can be compared to the ranking of previous events. Inevitably, critics are involved in the institutions that characterize "art worlds" (Becker 1982; Danto 1981; Moulin 1995). These institutions link the critics into networks that are decisive for reaching consensus on judgments in such domains. But the process toward consensus is less germane to our issue than identifying the strategies that stabilize that consensus.

Critics' statements were already used in Section 3 to provide examples for the use of absolutes in establishing the quality rank of an experience good, particularly in the arts. The examples given, however, are yet to be supported by a more detailed investigation. Such an investigation could move along the lines suggested above. Standards of excellence are a first candidate for an

---

[37] See De Vany (2004).

infinity operator: are they strictly comparative, or are they thought of as ideals to which certain performers or works come very close? A proxy for such standards might be the work of certain artists who are declared to be masters. Another possibility would be various ultimate qualities like "purity," "immortality," "beauty," or "overwhelming power." These terms take on different appearances as they are recreated in the jargon of specific cultures of critical writing such as fine art scholarship, pop music reviews, or travel guides.

The award of prizes for excellent works is a rich source for the use of idealizing attributes. The attraction of prizes lies in their simplicity: there is one winner, maybe a few runners-up, and many losers. But every selection of a winner needs to be based on verbal expressions of judgment, even if these statements are not known to a larger public. Such selections are typically made by a jury of "independent" critics, and the critics defend their decision in oral and written statements. They use and presumably invent criteria and expressions of judgment for novel amazing experiences, which are charged with the profound value of infinity.

Such a thesis is not entirely in line with current opinion. Hutter and Shusterman (2006: 203) report that the logical form used for evaluative judgment is "inductive, deductive or something altogether different." Infinity operators are only likely to be found in deductive arguments where terms like "greatness" or "wholeness" are employed. If ideal points of reference play an important role for the stability of value rankings, then the emphasis on deductive valuation may be greater than believed.

Praise Value and Economic Growth

Surprise, the generation of novel experiences, has now been identified as the common characteristic of not only the products of artistic creation but all the goods produced in the rapidly growing sector of the creative industries. The subjective value of surprise can be high, and social valuations reflect that. This chapter has argued that there are two consistent valuation mechanisms in operation, one of them operating through the abstraction of prices processed in market institutions, the other one operating through the formulation of praise in valuation networks. Such praise value, it has been claimed, is sustainable if comparisons between subjective experiences, and thus expectations of future surprise goods, are anchored in references to ideal qualities. Evidence for such anchoring, however, remains fragmentary. A more thorough investigation into the valuation practices along the value chains of creative industries' goods is needed.

The stability of praise valuations has implications for growth opportunities in postindustrial economies: as long as use is linked to material resources, the creation of new exchangeable value is limited. Praise value, in contrast, is much more expandable—in principle, it extends to the infinity of ideal excellence. Such value is constructed, but if valuations can be stabilized, they are reliable enough to serve as a basis for future investment of creative and productive resources. The nonmaterial goods may not have the simple utility of food or housing, but stable praise values for novel experience goods can be an effective foundation for decisions on future factor input, investment, and consumption. The constant, infinite flow of surprise products and their valuations could indeed become a major driver of global economic growth.

■ REFERENCES

Aspers, P. (2001). *Markets in Fashion: A Phenomenological Approach.* London: Routledge.
Barabási, A.-L. (2001). *Linked: The New Science of Networks.* Cambridge: Perseus Publishing.
Becker, H. S. (1982). *Art Worlds.* Berkeley: University of California Press.
Beggs, A. and Graddy, K. (2009). Anchoring Effects: Evidence from Art Auctions. *American Economic Review* 99(3): 1027–39.
Bille, T. (2009). *The Nordic Approach to the Experience Economy.* Creative Encounters Working Papers. Copenhagen Business School.
Bourdieu, P. (1969). Intellectual Field and Creative Project. *Social Science Information* 8(89): 89–119.
—— (1993). *The Field of Cultural Production: Essays on Art and Literature.* New York, NY: Columbia University Press.
Campbell, C. (1987). *The Romantic Ethic and the Spirit of Modern Consumerism.* Oxford: Basil Blackwell.
Caves, R. E. (2000). *Creative Industries: Contracts between Art and Commerce.* Cambridge, MA: Harvard University Press.
Clapham, J. (1944). *Bank of England.* Cambridge: Cambridge University Press.
Danto, A. (1981). *The Transfiguration of the Commonplace: A Philosophy of Art.* Cambridge, MA: Harvard University Press.
Department for Culture, Media and Sport (DCMS) (1998). Creative Industries Mapping Document. London: Department for Culture, Media and Sport.
De Marchi, N. (2008). Confluences of Value: Three Historical Moments. In M. Hutter and D. Throsby (eds.), *Beyond Price: Value in Culture, Economics and the Arts.* New York, NY: Cambridge University Press, 200–19.
De Vany, A. (2004). *Hollywood Economics: How Extreme Uncertainty Shapes the Film Industry.* London: Routledge.
Dewey, J. (1939). *Theory of Valuation.* Chicago, IL: University of Chicago Press.
Durkheim, E. (1995). *The Elementary Forms of Religious Life.* New York, NY: Free Press.
Ferguson, N. (2009). *The Ascent of Money.* London: Penguin.
Florida, R. (2004). *The Rise of the Creative Class: And How It's Transforming Work, Leisure, Community and Everyday Life.* New York, NY: Basic Books.
Franck, G. (1999). Scientific Communication: A Vanity Fair? *Science* 286(5437): 53–5.

Galenson, D. (2001). *Painting Outside the Lines: Patterns of Creativity in Modern Art.* Cambridge, MA: Harvard University Press.

Grampp, W. (1989). *Pricing the Priceless: Art, Artists and Economics.* New York, NY: Basic Books.

Haskell, F. and Nicholas, P. (1981). *Taste and the Antique: The Lure of Classical Sculpture 1500–1900.* New Haven, CT: Yale University Press.

Howkins, J. (2001). *The Creative Economy: How People Make Money from Ideas.* London: Penguin Press.

Hutter, M. (2006). *Neue Medienökonomik.* Munich: Wilhelm Fink Verlag.

—— (2007a). Are Markets Like Protest Movements? A Theoretical Appraisal of Valuation Systems. *Soziale Systeme* 13(1/2): 32–45.

—— (2007b). Visual Credit: The Britannia Vignette on the Notes of the Bank of England. In F. Cox and H.-W. Schmidt-Hannisa (eds.), *Money and Culture.* Munich: Peter Lang, 15–36.

—— (forthcoming, 2011). Experience Goods. In R. Towse (ed.), *Handbook of Cultural Economics.* Cheltenham: Edward Elgar.

—— and Frey, B. (2010). On the Influence of Cultural Value on Economic Value. *Revue d' économie politique* 120(1): 35–46.

—— and Shusterman, R. (2006). Value and the Valuation of Art in Economic and Aesthetic Theory. In V. Ginsburgh and D. Throsby (eds.), *Handbook of the Economics of Art and Culture.* Amsterdam: North-Holland, 169–210.

—— and Throsby, D. (2008). *Beyond Price: Value in Culture, Economics, and the Arts.* Cambridge: Cambridge University Press.

Invaluable.com (2005). *Notes on Lot 38: Andy Warhol (1928–1987).* http://www.invaluable.com/catalog/viewLot.cfm?lotCode=8UIF2XOC&lotType=artist&aID=10873 (accessed May 14, 2010)

Kane, R. (1997). Four Dimensions of Value: From Experience to Worth Center. *The Journal of American Architecture and Design* 10: 9–15.

Karpik, L. (2010). *The Economics of Singularities.* Princeton, NJ: Princeton University Press.

Luhmann, N. (1997). *Die Gesellschaft der Gesellschaft.* Frankfurt: Suhrkamp.

Moulin, R. (1995). *De la valeur de l'art.* Paris: Flammarion.

Negus, K. (1999). *Music Genres and Corporate Cultures.* London: Routledge.

Pine, B. J. and Gilmore, J. H. (1999). *The Experience Economy: Work is Theatre and Every Business a Stage.* Boston, MA: Harvard Business School Press.

Potts, J. and Cunningham, S. (2008). Four Models of the Creative Industries. *International Journal of Cultural Policy* 14(3): 17.

Power, D. (2009). Culture, Creativity and Experience in Nordic and Scandinavian Cultural Policy. *International Journal of Cultural Policy* 15(4): 445–60.

Rotman, B. (1987). *Signifying Nothing: The Semiotics of Zero.* Stanford, CA: Stanford University Press.

Schlesinger, P. (2009). Creativity and the Experts: New Labour, Think Tanks, and the Policy Process. *International Journal of Press/Politics* 14(1): 3–20.

Schulze, G. (1992). *Die Erlebnisgesellschaft: Kultursoziologie der Gegenwart.* Frankfurt: Campus.

Simmel, G. (1978). *Philosophy of Money.* London: Routledge & Kegan Paul.

Smith, C. (1998). *Creative Britain.* London: Faber & Faber.

Söndermann, M., Backes, C., Arndt, O., and Brünink, D. (2009). *Kultur- und Kreativwirtschaft*. Berlin: Bundesministerium für Wirtschaft und Technologie.

Stark, D. (2008). *Searching Questions: Inquiry, Uncertainty, Innovation*. Working Paper. New York, NY: Columbia University.

——(2009). *The Sense of Dissonance: Accounts of Worth in Economic Life*. Princeton, NJ: Princeton University Press.

United Nations Conference on Trade and Development (UNCTAD). (2008). *Creative Economy Report 2008*. New York, NY: United Nations.

Velthuis, O. (2005). *Talking Prices: Symbolic Meanings of Prices on the Market for Contemporary Art*. Princeton, NJ: Princeton University Press.

Zelizer, V. (1994). *The Social Meaning of Money*. New York, NY: Basic Books.

Part III
Financial Markets

10 Forecasting as Valuation: The Role of Ratings and Predictions in the Subprime Mortgage Crisis in the United States

*Akos Rona-Tas and Stefanie Hiss**

Introduction

The subprime mortgage crisis that developed in the United States became the trigger for the deepest recession in US history since the Great Depression. It had a devastating impact on the entire global financial system. The crash of the US mortgage market was a massive breakdown of valuation and price setting, since mortgage debt had been grossly mispriced by credit rating intermediaries. First, consumer credit ratings from credit bureaus misrepresented the creditworthiness of borrowers. Then, corporate credit rating agencies miscalculated the probability of default of structured finance products.

We frame the forecasting activities of consumer and corporate rating agencies as price anchoring on credit markets. The credit bureau scores and rating agency ratings, which attempted to approximate the underlying "real" value of debt as closely as possible by forecasting its future performance, set an anchor for prices. Because scoring and rating were price anchoring mechanisms, and credit bureaus and rating agencies acted as market enablers, we interpret the market failure of the subprime mortgage market as a social process.

We start with the distinction between values and prices. The peculiarities of credit markets as markets for information explain why they need consumer and credit rating agencies to act as intermediaries and market enablers by anchoring prices. We apply this frame to the intermediaries' failure in the subprime crisis. Five mechanisms contributed to their failure: (1) willful ignorance of the social construction of measurement, (2) the omitted variable problem, (3) correlated defaults, (4) endogeneity of creditworthiness, and (5) conflicts of interest. We then speculate why the system worked when it did, and what seems necessary to prevent future market failures. Our analysis

---

* Research for this chapter was partially funded by the Volkswagen Foundation.

is based on interviews with lenders and rating agencies along with the study of publicly available documents, congressional hearings, transcripts of earning calls of large players in the mortgage market, and the secondary literature.

Forecasting as Price Anchoring

VALUES AND PRICES

Values and prices are two representations of worth in society. In many cases, values and prices diverge, and prices misrepresent the underlying values. Nonetheless, the two are interconnected and shape each other. Prices, formed on markets, on the one hand depend on the values on which the market is based. On the other hand, values, at least in part, are influenced by market prices, as illustrated by the problem of adverse selection and moral hazard on credit markets that we discuss below.

In order to come into being and survive, markets must solve the problem of valuation, a task different from and a precondition for price formation (Aspers 2009; Beckert 2009). What goods or services are considered worth trading? How are they measured? What counts? The answers to these questions determine the values a market is based on. They also define the borderline between the market and its surroundings. The market for emissions trading is a case in point: as long as carbon dioxide was not considered worth trading and/or could not be measured adequately, no market developed. To get the carbon market going, the valuation problems had to be solved. Carbon dioxide had to be valued on a large scale as a good worth bartering, capable of being measured and counted so that it could be transformed into a license to pollute (Engels 2006; MacKenzie 2009). These days licenses are traded and prices are formed within the relevant market borders, thus solving the problem of valuation was a precondition for market creation and price formation. The values chosen determine the shape of the market and influence the possible range of prices. These prices, in turn, affect the underlying values. When prices for carbon dioxide remain low, climate change as the threat embodied by carbon dioxide is considered less dangerous, irrespective of any potential market failure and resulting price misrepresentation.

Once in existence, markets produce prices. Without prices, there is no market, yet the existence of prices and a mechanism to establish them does not mean that prices represent values correctly. This raises questions about the relationship between value and price that is as old as the economy itself. Whether price is presented as a result of the cost of production, human labor, relative scarcity, or subjective preferences, most economic theories have agreed that behind the world of fickle prices there is a universe of more stable values. Prices and values are both a matter of social construction. Prices are tied to markets, while values may (pre)exist outside them. Housework and childcare, for example, are valued whether or not they are traded and priced on the market. The prices they realize on a market may diverge from the values attached to them. Thus, whether prices truly reflect the underlying values strongly depends—again—on the question of how values are counted and measured: not as a precondition for market creation, as above, but as an ongoing effort to converge prices and values.

In financial markets, value and price come very close to overlapping because the only thing that matters for actors in these markets is money in its most abstract form (Simmel 1978). Money gained and money lost depends solely on systems of prices. In a postmodern, self-referential way, there appear to be prices behind prices.[1] But even in financial markets, actors must be able to evaluate prices—whether they are too high, too low, or just right—and for that actors need to refer back to something more fundamental than price itself. Valuation can be based on a combination of narratives, organizational practices, and calculative devices (Beunza and Stark 2004; MacKenzie 2007; Smith 2007). If actors in financial markets could not think critically about prices, there would be no point in trading.

In perfect worlds with perfect markets, prices would equal the "real" value of goods or services. Hayek, one of the most fervent supporters of this view, saw price as the essence of all knowledge embodied in the market. The "marvel of the market" is that with the help of the forces of supply and demand, prices aggregate the dispersed knowledge about the commodity in a way unrivaled by central calculation or any other form of market coordination (Hayek 1945: 527). According to Hayek, this aggregation is a social mechanism and cannot be replaced by formal calculation.

Critics of Hayek point out that only in idealized markets where many preconditions are present can prices reflect underlying values (Jackson 2009; Stiglitz et al. 2009). Such preconditions include complete information, no barriers to entry, a sufficient number of market participants, and no externalities (Victor 2008). To make things worse, most markets are interrelated through prices, since prices in different markets refer to and constitute each other: when the price of mortgage credit is cheap, the total cost of housing becomes cheaper (even when home prices go up). The misrepresentation of values through prices in one market infects other markets—prices misrepresenting values can have contagious effects.

FORECASTING

There are at least two reasons why the "marvel of the market" fails in credit markets. The first is that actors must make choices under uncertainty (Beckert 2009; Knight 1985) that results from their inability to foresee the future.

---

[1] As meaning in Derridian deconstruction is infinitely deferred, so it seems that value is infinitely deferred in financial markets.

Valuation is almost always about the future. Even simple commodities bought for immediate consumption involve guesses about future pleasures or utilities they will bring, a prediction that may not be trivial (Gilbert 2006; Kahneman and Thaler 2006). In investment markets, future expectations are central, and in financial markets, with the exception of arbitrage, any purchase for resale or collecting dividends hinges on an estimate of future price or yield. In markets for commodity futures, insurance, and financial derivatives, prices are based solely on predictions. Measuring value as events yet to unfold in the future, rather than as costs or labor already expended in the past or even as subjective needs or objective scarcity revealed in the present, introduces an element of fundamental uncertainty that poses a formidable challenge to valuation and price formation.

Prediction markets, which build on Hayek's idea that price contains all the necessary information, claim to produce optimal forecasts. Predicting anything from election results to terrorist attacks, these markets aggregate information by allowing people to buy and sell future contracts that promise to pay a certain amount if a specific event happens (Cowgill et al. 2009; Surowiecki 2004; Wolfers and Zitzewitz 2004). The basic assumption of prediction markets is that because people must put money down, they will not commit to a prediction unless they feel certain that they are right, and the possibility of gaining money will give people the incentive to collect all available information. In theory, prediction markets would then run on the best possible information. Empirical studies of prediction markets showed them to often perform better than forecasts that were based on expert judgments or political polls, provided that the information necessary to make the relevant prediction was by and large available.

This brings us to the second reason why prices fail in markets based on forecasts. Information economics has pointed out what Hayek overlooked: disclosing or obtaining information is not always in the interest of all actors, and prices do not just reflect value but can influence it as well. Prediction markets can only succeed when these problems are absent: when there is no incentive to withhold information and the bet does not influence the outcome.[2]

In credit markets, withholding information can lead to a strategic advantage that may promote the self-interest of a player while distorting the flow of information and ultimately the price. Borrowers are interested in appearing more creditworthy than they are and in covering up adverse information that could result in higher interest rates, further fees, or outright rejection. Lenders

---

[2] Prediction markets must be anonymous; otherwise, bets that came from people who were assumed to have more knowledge would drive prices and give other players an incentive to bet strategically. Prediction markets must also have no effect on the outcome of their predictions. US Department of Defense discussions of setting up a prediction market in terrorism information floundered for this reason, when objections included the observation that a terrorist act with a low predicted likelihood could offer terrorists a way to deliver surprise (and even to make money, if they bet on their own action).

may also lack the incentive to obtain the best information. If banks can pass on the risk of bad debts to investors by securitizing and selling the loans, they may not collect and convey the best available data.

The effect of price on value is described by Akerlof (1970) in his famous fable of markets for "lemons" in the form of adverse selection and moral hazard. In credit markets, lenders who cannot tell good from bad borrowers must charge a price (interest rates) based on the average performance of the pool. Some borrowers will be better than average and will be overcharged by the average price. The price will repel these better borrowers, who will find loans too expensive, and attract bad customers, who intend to default and thus are willing to accept any price. If better borrowers leave, prices must go higher because the average quality of borrowers goes down. Borrowers who used to be around the average will then be overcharged, they too will leave, and prices will rise yet again. This continues until the only borrowers remaining will be those with no intention to repay the loan.

High prices will not just drive out good borrowers; they also make it harder for debtors to meet their obligations even when they intend to pay up. While adverse selection is a consequence of information asymmetry about the intention and economic situation of the borrower, moral hazard occurs because the quality of a loan at the time of pricing can change *after* the loan has been made and because the quality of a borrower can drop below what was originally forecast.[3]

RATING AND SCORING AS MARKET ENABLERS

Because the "marvel of the market" does not work in contemporary mortgage markets, prices are enabled by third-party institutions. While lenders and investors often do their own assessments, they rarely dispense with the services of specialized agencies that provide ratings of debtors. These ratings therefore anchor prices and allow mortgage providers to decide whether it is sensible to grant the loan and which interest rate to apply, just as the ratings inform investors whether it is a good idea to invest in securities backed by the revenue flow from those mortgages.

Two types of rating agencies perform price anchoring in the process of mortgage lending. Consumer rating agencies assess individual mortgage applicants, and corporate rating agencies subsequently assess securitized mortgage

---

[3] The standard treatment of information asymmetry assumes that (1) the borrower has the information advantage, (2) borrowers can walk away if they feel they are being overcharged, and (3) bad debtors face no penalties. These assumptions are often not realistic. Lenders may know less about the intentions and situation of borrowers than the borrowers themselves but know and understand better the details of the loan contract and have an interest in hiding or obscuring information. Individual customers rarely comprehend fully the terms of their contracts, which can run to many pages and include concepts such as compound interest and balloon payments that many people cannot fathom. It is also not true that borrowers can always decide not to borrow (or to go elsewhere for better terms). Finally, there are penalties for defaulting.

pools. To originate a mortgage, lenders must first assess the creditworthiness of the applicant. In the United States, for years the chief indicators of people's creditworthiness have been the credit scores calculated by the credit bureaus. These credit scores are intended to "objectively evaluate and 'score' credit applications and credit bureau data in order to assess likely future performance."[4] Credit scores anchor the price of the borrower's creditworthiness, while the terms of the loan the borrower gets are also influenced by a series of other incidental factors such as the federal funds rate, inflation, the lender's market power or market strategy, and, in the case of mortgage lending, trends in the housing market.[5] Once mortgages are granted, they are often collected and securitized, that is, bundled into pools, and securities are issued against the revenue stream of the mortgage payments made by the borrowers. These mortgage-backed securities are evaluated by corporate rating agencies.

The work that credit scoring and rating agencies do shows a few striking similarities with central planning, the target of Hayek's criticism. Just like planners, these agencies collect information in a bureaucratic fashion as local knowledge percolates up through standardized forms and reports, and then apply complex, scientific methods to analyze this information. Just as central planners do, these agencies present themselves as actors following only their own principles, unaffected by their social environments. While Hayek clearly overestimated the "marvel of the market," he rightly understood that the articulation of value, whether in the form of credit ratings or prices, is an irreducibly social process. In the remainder of the chapter, we will show how social processes by undermining or reinforcing the agencies' ability to forecast and thus produce ratings and scores, ultimately determined the degree to which these agencies enabled the market in securitized mortgages.

Short History of the Subprime Mortgage Crisis

By 2005, home ownership in the United States had reached an all-time high of 69%, with large increases among disadvantaged social groups such as Hispanics/Latinos and Blacks (US Census Bureau 2009).[6] The US mortgage debt in 2007 stood at $11 trillion, where 65% of these were securitized mortgages, making the US secondary mortgage market the largest fixed-income market in the world (Keys et al. 2008).[7] Subprime mortgages in 2007 were estimated to be worth around $1.5 trillion (Agarwal and Ho 2007). A subprime mortgage is

---

[4] http://www.myfico.com/crediteducation/glossary.aspx
[5] The lender needs forecasts for each of these factors in order to make a well-informed lending decision.
[6] The comparable numbers in some European countries: Germany 42%, France 55%, Great Britain 69%, Ireland 77%, Spain 85%.
[7] The size of corporate debt in the United States, by comparison, is $5.7 trillion.

one that does not meet the underwriting guidelines of Freddie Mac and Fannie Mae, the two federally chartered mortgage giants. These criteria include a good credit score, proper employment, and low loan-to-income ratio. Subprime mortgages are more expensive for borrowers: they carry higher interest rates, origination fees, penalties, mortgage insurance, and other costs. Subprime mortgages also represent a greater risk for lenders.[8]

The precursor to the subprime mortgage crisis was a long and steep increase in housing prices. Between 1997 and 2006, when they reached their peak, real home prices for the United States as a whole increased by 85% (Shiller 2008: 32). This rapid boom, coupled with low interest rates, resulted in aggressive lending on the expectation that future price increases would act as quasi collateral: even if the owners defaulted on their mortgages, lenders' losses would still be covered by the appreciation of the real estate. A wide subprime market developed for people whose credit indicators were below safe (or prime) levels. In 1995, $65 billion worth of subprime mortgages were originated; without adjustment for inflation, this figure had quintupled by 2003 and reached $625 billion by 2005, leveling off at $600 billion in 2006 (Ashcraft and Schuermann 2008; Chomsisengphet and Pennington-Cross 2006; US Senate 2007). The market quickly became concentrated. The top 25 players, led by lenders such as Countrywide Financial, HSBC, Washington Mutual, Citigroup, Wells Fargo, and Ameriquest Mortgage, issued over 90% of subprime mortgages (Ashcraft and Schuermann 2008). As the volume of subprime mortgages increased, the rate of securitization of these mortgages grew as well. In 1995, it was still under 30%; by 2003, it had reached almost 60% (Chomsisengphet and Pennington-Cross 2006) and by 2006 had climbed further to 75% (Demyanyk and Van Hemert 2008: 6).

The growth of the subprime lending market was made possible by federal actions aimed at deregulating the banking industry. The Depository Institutions Deregulation and Monetary Control Act of 1980 preempted state anti-usury laws that had set a ceiling on interest rates on mortgages, and the Alternative Mortgage Transaction Parity Act of 1982 permitted variable interest rates, balloon payments, and interest-only and minimum-payment loans. Four years later, the Tax Reform Act disallowed tax deductions for any consumer loan interest except mortgage interest, which made even expensive mortgage loans cheaper than consumer loans. This pushed demand for mortgages up as people started to finance their purchases through home equity loans. With property values rising throughout the last decade and interest rates staying relatively low, cash-out refinancing became very popular.

---

[8] In fact, the overall default rate for subprime mortgages rose to 13% by October 2007, double of what the rate was two years earlier. This figure was 19% for adjustable-rate subprime mortgages, triple the mid-2005 level (Truth in Lending 2008: 1674).

Ratings and Subprime Mortgages

Both consumer and corporate ratings bear responsibility for the subprime mortgage crisis. Lenders in the United States depend on the three large credit bureaus—Equifax, Experian, and TransUnion—to rate potential borrowers. Each credit bureau maintains files on about 210 million people and 1.5 billion credit accounts that cover over 90% of the adult population. For a fee, each bureau will provide the detailed credit history of the applicant and a credit score. All three bureaus use a scoring system that was originally devised by the Fair Isaac Corporation (FICO) and the score is known as the FICO credit score.

Consumer ratings are completely formalized. The FICO credit scores, which Freddie Mac and Fannie Mae have required to purchase a loan since 1995 (Straka 2000), are calculated by a statistical algorithm that summarizes credit history data in a single number that is designed to reflect the person's likelihood of nonpayment. The score runs from 300 to 850, with the median score around 720. The lender must decide on a cutoff to separate those whose applications are accepted. Those who are above the threshold then may receive different prices depending on their scores.

The securitization of mortgage debt demands a seal of approval from one of the credit rating agencies. Only a Nationally Recognized Statistical Rating Organization (NRSRO) can rate a debt instrument. This designation is conferred by the US Securities and Exchange Commission (SEC). There are currently ten NRSROs, but the three big ones—Moody's, Standard and Poor's, and Fitch—account for 99% of all outstanding ratings for asset-backed securities (ABSs). These three agencies form a triopoly, similar to the three credit bureaus in consumer ratings.

The three rating agencies have transformed enormously in recent decades and today they function as quasi-regulatory agencies because various regulations require a high rating issued by an NRSRO. Until the mid-1980s, the agencies were small local affairs, but since then they have grown into international giants. In 1986, Standard and Poor's had 40 analysts; by 2000, this number had increased by a factor of 50. Moody's went through a similar expansion and had 1,500 analysts by the beginning of the millennium (Partnoy 1999; Smith and Walter 2002). Fitch had been a small player until it merged with IBCA (International Bank Credit Analysts) in 1997. By the standards of the industry, the rating agencies have poor pay, high turnover, and overworked analysts (US SEC 2008*a*: 12). Corporate rating agencies, whose "opinions" are protected by the First Amendment of the US Constitution (Fight 2001), are emphatic that they do not make automated decisions as consumer credit bureaus do, but their move toward formalization is unmistakable as the scale of their operations increases.

Securitization begins when lenders collect a number of their residential mortgages into packages and put them in a trust fund. This trust fund serves as the collateral against which the securities are issued.[9] The securities are then sold all over the world to investors, but before they are offered for sale each package of loans is rated by a corporate rating agency. In order to rate each package, the agency needs data from the lender on each loan that includes the FICO credit score of the borrower as well as other information such as the loan amount, the geographic location of the property, the ratio of the loan amount to the value of the house, whether the real estate is being used as a primary residence, and whether it is a first or second lien. The pool of mortgages is structured into different levels (tranches) of risk from which to construct what are called residential mortgage-backed securities (RMBSs), a form of ABSs. The rating agency rates each tranche by running various models to test how many defaults can be expected under various assumptions. The rating results in a group of loans that *in toto* would be too risky to be rated as "investment grade" (a designation necessary by law for certain investors, such as pension funds, to buy them) but now has parts (tranches) that are designated as safe investments. In effect, the riskier tranches insure the safer ones. An even more complex form of investment instrument is known as collateralized debt obligations (CDOs). CDOs are structured like RMBSs, but CDOs can manage their obligations actively, that is, they sell them and buy others. While an RMBS has a static pool of debts of residential mortgages, CDOs can have different kinds of obligations (such as residential and commercial mortgages, car loans, and credit card debts) in their dynamic portfolios.[10] However, their transactions are limited by a set of complex rules that are designed to keep the rating of each tranche constant. These rules of debt management are also set by the rating agencies.

The rating of RMBSs and CDOs is more formalized than the rating of securities that are issued by actual companies. Both require the separation of the durable qualities of the debt from the short-term effects of the business cycle. This involves a series of judgment calls about the future of various markets. When RMBSs and CDOs are rated, there is a set of debt obligations to assess instead of a corporate organization. If a company encounters difficulties, good management can rescue it by bringing in more capital or by changing course. If a pool of debtors stops paying, it is unlikely that the issuer is going to do much, because now the debt and the risk belong to the investors. This allows for a more formal assessment because there are no "human factors" to contemplate—except, of course, for the thousands of mortgage holders. Moreover, corporate bonds all rise and fall with the fortunes

---

[9] We refer here to the lender as the one arranging the securitization, but often there was a different institution, called the arranger, that acted on behalf of the lender or originator. Later, the securities were often managed by yet another organization, called the manager, which collected payments from the debt holders and managed the payout.

[10] Certain types of CDOs are not backed by assets. These "synthetic" CDOs are based on credit default swaps. In essence, "synthetic" CDOs sell insurance against default of holdings in other financial instruments, such as CDOs that are backed by assets and are called "cash" CDOs.

of the company. RMBSs and CDOs, on the other hand, can be partitioned into better and worse parts, a quality tranching exploits.

In fact, before the crisis, RMBSs had been considered especially safe for two reasons. Experience showed that people in financial difficulty abandoned mortgage debt last and kept up their monthly payments well after they had defaulted on their car loans or credit cards. It was also believed that banks eager to take debts off their books to avoid setting aside legally mandated debt provisions were more likely to securitize good debt, as securitization opened up the bank's lending practices to public scrutiny.

Judgment comes into play in several ways when debt obligations are being rated, even though the rating of debt obligations is more formalized than the rating of securities issued by business enterprises. First, the analyst must assess the quality of the information provided by the issuer. Then, the analyst must adjust the model to the peculiarities of the given pool of obligations and figure out the proper ways of stress-testing them. Here, a lot depends on which economic forecasts the analyst chooses. In the end, the ratings are always decided by committee vote, and in some cases the results of the quantitative analysis are overridden (US SEC 2008*a*).

THE RATINGS' ROLE IN THE CRISIS

The crisis involved both consumer and corporate rating agencies in a two-step process. Residential mortgages were issued to consumers, who were typically rated by their FICO credit scores. The bundled debts that were sold to investors were rated by rating agencies.[11] A by-and-large automated system of underwriting was used in originating the mortgages, and a judgmental system—albeit heavily aided by formalized modeling—was deployed to securitize them.

Since the onset of the crisis, FICO and its score have come under strong criticism. One study by Fitch shows that the difference between the average FICO credit scores of defaulting and non-defaulting borrowers in 2006 was only ten points, a very small difference given the scale of the score (Fitch 2007).[12] It was revealed soon afterward that the power of the FICO credit score to predict delinquency or foreclosures had dropped considerably between 2001 and 2006 (Demyanyk and Van Hemert 2008; Rajan et al. 2008). Responding to criticisms, FICO toned down its claims of the score's predictive accuracy (Foster 2007) and in March 2008 rolled out an improved FICO credit score.

It was not just FICO that failed; corporate rating agencies are also being blamed. As the crisis evolved, the rating agencies had to revise their overly optimistic assessments. In the first ten months of 2007, the big three took a combined total of 9,496 so-called rating actions—corrections of earlier

---

[11] From a total of 394,635 ratings for asset-backed securities, Standard and Poor's accounts for 197,700, Moody's for 110,000, and Fitch for 72,278 (SEC 2008*b*: 35).

[12] Ten points is less than one-eighth of one standard deviation.

ratings—on US subprime RMBS tranches, compared with 836 in 2006 and 240 in 2005, an unprecedented admission of failure (Romey and Drut 2008: 9). The US Congress is currently investigating the role the three played in the subprime crisis. The SEC issued a detailed report faulting the rating agencies and proposing new regulations to shore up the ratings process, and the agencies pledged to take "remedial measures to address the issues" (US SEC 2008a: 39).

How Ratings Failed in the Subprime Mortgage Crisis

In this section, we will discuss five issues to evaluate consumer scoring and corporate rating: the social construction process of measurement, omitted variables, correlated defaults, endogeneity, and conflict of interest.

THE SOCIAL CONSTRUCTION OF DATA

The borrowers: Reactivity or gaming the system?

The accuracy of the ratings depends on the quality of the data used. No measurement is ever perfect. There is always a discrepancy between an indicator and the concept it intends to capture. The FICO credit score is computed exclusively on the basis of credit history, that is, information supplied by lenders. This score, called the behavior score, cannot be manipulated directly by the borrower misstating information, because the data circulates in a closed, standardized system from lenders to credit bureaus to lenders, completely bypassing borrowers. With no access to the system, consumers must change the lenders' reports to improve their scores.

Formalization facilitates transparency. Transparency ties the hands of the lenders, which was the very reason why formalization emerged as a solution to combat lending discrimination in the United States. Transparency, however, also makes it easier for the borrowers to manipulate the system, since both lenders and raters are obliged to disclose their operations, giving borrowers the opportunity to learn how to exploit the gap between indicator and concept by figuring out ways of increasing their score without improving their creditworthiness. FICO, mindful of this problem—and of protecting its proprietary interests—has done everything it could to keep its algorithm secret. Until a few years ago, people did not even have the right to know their FICO credit score unless they were rejected for having one that was too low. In 2000, California forced lenders to disclose scores regardless of the decision on the loan, and FICO soon changed tactics. These days anyone can purchase his or her own score. FICO now supplies a very general description of the various components of the score, but not its technical details. The average credit score began to rise when the veil of secrecy was lifted from the scores.

Improved scores are not necessarily a sign of their declining validity. FICO and the credit bureaus themselves have made efforts to help people improve their scores and address problems in their personal finances. How could we tell if the overall improvement in FICO credit scores was due to a real improvement in people's finances, rather than a result of gaming the system? If the improvements were real, we would see an increase in the overall average credit score, but no change in the average scores for nonperforming loans, just a decline in the general default rate. Between 2003 and 2006, however, the average score for bad borrowers grew and the average score for good borrowers stayed the same, shrinking the difference from 31 to 10 points (Fitch 2007).

Indeed, an entire industry emerged to advise people on how to improve their scores (Foust and Pressman 2008). There are countless websites offering credit score simulations where people can run what-if scenarios to find out how their FICO credit score would be affected by changing one or more things about their credit history. Most system gaming of this kind involves taking advantage of a hole in the system and does not entail anything illegal.[13] None of these strategies actually improves one's financial situation or decreases one's likelihood of default, yet they still raise one's score.

These tricks can yield enough extra points to push one above the cutoff point, making the difference between a yes and a no decision or better and worse terms. Gaming the system is a form of reactivity (Espeland and Sauder 2007) that belongs to the category of self-frustrating predictions, or those that occur when the consequence of making a prediction is that the forecast is less likely to hold (Buck 1963). Since credit scores are predictions about the future behavior of borrowers, in the long run, system gaming makes these scores less reliable predictors.

Reactivity posed a problem for corporate rating agencies as well in the run-up to the crisis. In rating RMBSs and CDOs, agencies embraced a transparency never entertained in consumer scoring. Rating agencies made the software their analysts used for evaluation available to their clients, who could run their proposed CDOs or RMBSs through the system and receive advice from the software on how to restructure these for the best possible rating (Benmelech and Dlugosz 2009).[14] The issuers were able to tweak the structure of their mortgage pools to their best advantage.

Corporate rating agencies embraced transparency to a greater degree than consumer credit rating agencies because their paying clients are the issuers

---

[13] Tricks do exist that clearly violate the law; these are deployed not by the clients but by the brokers and even the lenders themselves.

[14] For RMBSs and CDOs respectively Standard and Poor's uses *S&P Levels* and *Evaluator*, Fitch developed *ResiLogic* and *Vector*, and Moody's deploys *Moody's Mortgage Metrics* and *CDOROM* and *CDOEdge*.

who demanded it, and they could take their business elsewhere if they chose. The clients of the consumer rating agencies are the lenders, not the borrowers. Yet corporate rating agencies had the opportunity to use expert judgment to spot abuses; they could foil some attempts to game the system and adjust to others. That their expert judgment did not fulfill this role sufficiently was the result of the sudden increase in workload and the conflicts of interest, to which we will return later.

The lenders: Fiddling with data

While lenders supply scoring data in accordance with a standardized protocol, studies report that credit bureau records are often inaccurate (Avery et al. 2004; Cassady and Mierzwinski 2004; US GAO 2005). Lenders, the immediate sources of information, do have interests in distorting information about their clients. For instance, supplying good information to the credit bureaus will raise a client's score, making that client more desirable to other lenders and eligible for terms that would be more advantageous for the consumer and less profitable for the lender. Yet at the same time, banks can also build loyalty by not reporting skipped payments and small infractions to the credit bureau. The overall direction of the distortion is not obvious, and the result will be a credit score that is probably just noisier and not particularly biased. The annual free credit report that has been mandated by the Fair and Accurate Credit Transactions Act (FACTA) since 2004 is designed to correct some of the inaccuracies. Because lender provision of data is voluntary, the credit bureaus have little leverage over data quality and must trust that since lenders are both suppliers and consumers of the information, they have an interest in keeping data accurate.

Corporate rating agencies face a different situation. Investors—the de facto lenders—play no role in data gathering. The agencies get the information directly from the issuers (borrowers) and depend on the clients for the interpretation of the data, and must make various judgments in the process. Such judgments introduce new elements of discretion and new potential for bias and error. Corporate rating agencies do not rely solely on the consumer ratings when assessing RMBSs. They also consider additional information submitted by the lender that may include individual borrowers' incomes, employment, and assets, data that is supposed to be collected and verified by the loan originators (the original lenders). The quality of this information depends on the lender's interest in assessing customers thoroughly so as not to lose money (either as nonpayment when credit is granted or as lost business when credit is denied). Yet securitization relieves the original lender of responsibility for the consequences of bad decisions; they are passed on to those who bought the RMBS. As a result, the additional information that lenders provided on borrowers was often of poor quality or in many cases simply missing.

THE OMITTED VARIABLE PROBLEM

Another weakness of formalized models is that their algorithms depend on a prespecified set of variables and are therefore capable of only very limited learning. Scoring models give different weights to each factor. The models learn when the weights are periodically updated with the help of new data to reflect shifts in the relative importance of the factors. A factor that loses its relevance may end up with a weight close to zero, but factors omitted from the model at the outset will never appear. The model assumes that we know up front what the relevant variables are, and their list can change only by subtraction.

Omitted variables are a serious concern for the FICO credit score. Avery et al. (2000) show that omission of variables related to local economic conditions seriously biases and weakens scoring models. In the subprime meltdown, one important missing variable was income. Because the FICO credit score does not include it, income is usually checked separately by mortgage lenders. Income is added into the decision process through the use of a simple formula that sets the maximum loan payment as a percentage of the applicant's income. Another missing variable is "capacity" or "capital," as the FICO credit score does not include information about the borrower's assets.

When discussing their rating criteria, corporate rating agencies use general descriptions and explain by example rather than by stating a fixed list of factors and measurements. This allows the agencies to include new factors within their general outline and to deploy alternative measurements for established factors. When the agencies rate RMBSs, however, they must rely on the variables the lenders submit. While the agencies also use aggregate figures about the economy, the most important information is the data about the individual borrowers, and this must be collected in a standardized and coordinated fashion by the lenders, leaving the raters with very little flexibility to explore new variables when rating these types of financial products.

CORRELATED DEFAULTS

Default correlation describes when one's default depends not only on one's own characteristics (or history) but is affected by the defaults of others. Consumer and corporate rating agencies each take very different approaches to this problem. Consumer scoring algorithms assume that each borrower is statistically independent of all other borrowers.

In the consumer market, where the link between two loans is less direct, many of these correlations are close to zero most of the time since the fate of a car loan in Detroit is rarely influenced by a defaulting credit card holder in California if the two borrowers are strangers to each other. FICO credit scores are calculated based on overall credit records of people all over the country and count on this zero correlation.[15] Yet while the independence assumption may be valid in certain periods of economic stability and across a wide spectrum of loans, it is clearly invalid in turbulent times and in particular segments of the credit market. Hence, the resulting FICO credit scores are distorted (Calem and LaCour-Little 2001; Löffler 2003).

The independence assumption makes modeling aggregate probabilities easy. If two defaults are independent, then the probability of both happening is just the product of the probability of each happening. Parameters, the weights that link the borrowers' characteristics to the credit score, are calculated using this assumption. But if the defaults are not independent but correlated, calculations become much more complicated and require additional information that is usually unavailable.

Correlated defaults are of special concern on the subprime mortgage market (Cowan and Cowan 2004) because foreclosures affect housing values in the entire neighborhood. They depress real estate values and make the neighborhood de facto poorer, creating negative equity in some homes, which, in turn increases, the probability of further foreclosures and still-lower home prices. When borrowers default on their mortgages, it also dampens the demand for construction, and that can lead to further defaults as those working in and around the construction industry lose their jobs.

Correlated defaults can also emerge through imitation. Seeing others walk away from their loans makes it more acceptable to do so, resulting in a cascade of defaults. Once defaults reach a critical mass, in fact, the problem becomes redefined as a collective, political issue that requires government intervention. This further increases the temptation to abandon one's debt.

To make things even more complicated for modelers, each mechanism generates a different correlation, and the ultimate relationship may depend on the shifting relative importance of each. The complexity of the model grows quickly; the correlation is between cases (or classes of very similar cases), which means that with N customers, there are $N \times (N-1)/2$ correlations; in a small portfolio of a thousand people, one may have to work with almost half a million correlations.

In corporate lending, the relationships are more direct and the correlation among loans is of great concern. If a bank lends to two financially dependent companies, the default of one has a direct effect on the other's ability to pay its debts. There need not be any more general factor that underlies the two defaults. This is why when companies are rated there is always a thorough "market analysis," which tries to map how the success of the rated company depends on the success or failure of others by looking at the supply chain and the competitors.

---

[15] In many cases, default correlation can be thought of as a special case of the omitted variable problem. Real estate prices or local unemployment could be included as additional variables, but they will still not fully account for the volatility created by the domino effect.

The more formalized rating of RMBSs and CDOs has relied heavily on formal models of correlated defaults. In August 2004, Moody's and Standard and Poor's began to estimate correlated defaults using a method called the Gaussian copula, which provided a relatively simple formula. The calculations were based not on historical observations of how loans stood or fell together but on the relationship between the values of the insurance taken out on each (Li 2000). This model had its critics early on (Malevergne and Sornette 2003) and has been vilified since the collapse (Salmon 2009; Taleb 2007), but it was once used widely because it gave a simple solution to an intractably complex problem. One sign of trouble was the "correlation smile": the finding that the asset correlations implied by the market were not uniform across the tranches but higher in the most senior and most junior tranches and lower in the mezzanine (Feld 2007; Hager and Schoebel 2006). This suggested that the Gaussian copula, based on the normal bell-shaped Gaussian distribution, underestimated "fat tails," that is, the probability of observing very high or very low correlations, and therefore underestimated the likelihood of the kind of financial catastrophe that happened.

The correlation of defaults for the ABS—and the RMBS in particular—was due not just to economic, political, and social forces but also to the fact that it was originated by the same lender and serviced by the same servicer. If the mortgages are granted in a systematically incorrect way (e.g., the originator is too lenient) or if the servicer responsible for collecting the payments and prodding tardy payers is not doing its job well in some systematic pattern, default correlations will rise. Furthermore, there is a model risk as well, where a distortion in the estimation models used by the lenders to approve the loan can also contribute to the correlation of the defaults.

ENDOGENEITY OF CREDITWORTHINESS

Another important assumption of consumer credit scoring models is that a person's creditworthiness determines that person's credit score and not the other way around, or, in statistical parlance: an individual's riskiness as a borrower is not endogenous with respect to the same individual's score. To some extent, this is obviously untrue. Low scores result in worse loan conditions that in turn increase the riskiness of the borrower. Here, the score is at least partially the cause, and not just the consequence, of creditworthiness. This inversion is inevitable and there are at least three reasons why here the endogeneity problem is of significant concern.

First, poor performance on a particular loan and a subsequent drop in credit score can have an effect on the terms of the borrower's *other* existing loans. Most importantly, the interest rates on one's credit card debts may be hiked if one's credit score goes down, for example, as the result of missing a mortgage payment. Raising interest on an unrelated debt takes money out of the borrower's pocket and leaves the borrower with less money to meet those mortgage obligations, driving his or her credit score further down.

Second, in the United States, credit scores are used not just by lenders to evaluate creditworthiness but also by many others who can influence the borrower's ability to pay. Landlords routinely use credit scores to decide on tenants. People with low credit scores are more likely to be turned down or to be asked to pay a large deposit. Moreover, employers use credit scores in making hiring decisions. A low score can be a disqualifier. It is easy to see how a spell of unemployment can lead to missed payments, then to lower scores, and finally to lost job opportunities, which in turn result in more missed payments. Ninety-five percent of American car insurance premiums are based on credit scores, and people in financial difficulty will have to pay more to drive their cars, making it even harder to climb out of those difficulties.

Third, subprime lending targets vulnerable social groups. These tend to be lower-middle and working-class people, often minorities, who have little savings, few assets, limited skills, and restricted geographic mobility to follow the best job opportunities. They lead a precarious existence and are often just a paycheck away from financial ruin; this is why they are risky borrowers and have low credit scores. For them, a small change in credit score can have momentous consequences. Without the financial buffers of other groups, they can quickly find themselves in a vicious cycle in which financial difficulty begets low scores that then lead to even worse financial difficulty, a process where the score is as much the cause as the consequence of their economic ruin.

The expansive role of credit scoring in the United States brings brisk business to FICO and the credit bureaus because it opens up new markets for their scores. Banks also welcome having their bad clients punished by non-lenders. In normal times, this improves the predictive power of credit scores: it helps low scorers to default and high scorers to stay current. However, as it amplifies the effect of external shocks—such as unemployment, divorce, or health troubles (Sullivan et al. 2000)—the score's predictive power suffers because default rates will increase faster than scoring models would predict. The dramatic downturn in the mortgage market was another external shock that was exacerbated by the endogeneity problem. Consumer scoring was not the main cause but it contributed to the crisis by putting people in a debt trap.

Corporate ratings are also prone to the endogeneity problem. A drop in the rating of a company's debt can have serious consequences for the company's ability to pay its debts, and can result in similar vicious cycles, which is why the agencies claim that they are slow to change rates. This slowness, however, makes it very difficult to evaluate the agencies' prescience. Why do agencies downgrade securities only when the issuer's troubles are plain to see? Is it because the agencies did not spot the trouble in time, or do they react late because they want to mitigate the endogeneity problem and try to avoid making an already bad situation worse?

In the case of RMBSs, the rating has no direct effect on how many mortgage holders will stop making their payments. There is an indirect effect, however, because when RMBSs obtain high ratings easily, this encourages more securitization. The fact that the rating agencies were optimistic—indeed overly optimistic—about this investment vehicle ultimately abetted more aggressive lending, which in turn led to riskier mortgages and higher defaults. The ease with which an RMBS could pass muster reduced the incentives to lend carefully. The unrealistically high ratings thus begat more defaults in the next round of securitization. This mechanism acted not by changing the behavior of the homeowners but by altering the behavior of the lenders. While ratings influenced the quality of RMBSs, their direct effect on the price of RMBSs was amplified by regulatory requirements. As RMBSs were downgraded and their prices dropped, pension funds and other institutional investors mandated to hold only investment-grade assets were forced to sell their shares, accelerating the plunge.

CONFLICTS OF INTEREST

Unlike consumer credit scores, corporate ratings are "opinions," and raters therefore have discretion. One question US legislators are examining is whether this discretion was exercised in a self-serving manner. Since the early 1970s, rating agencies have been paid by issuers. Issuers want good valuations and naturally want to influence the ratings in a more favorable direction.

Currently under investigation is whether the rating agencies shortchanged investors and overrated RMBSs just because the agencies wanted the business. The SEC report found that the three agencies were vying for larger market share and pursued clients aggressively. That the issuers were highly concentrated aggravated this pursuit. Rating RMBSs was a very profitable business, and the agencies were reluctant to alienate their big customers. The agencies were also found to have violated internal rules that are intended to insulate analysts from fee negotiations with issuers, and the SEC complains that the rules designed to prohibit analysts from personally profiting from their ratings through personal securities holdings were not enforced in all instances (US SEC 2008a: 23–32).

A different kind of conflict of interest emerged from incompetence. With the ever-increasing complexity of these securitized debts, the rating agencies, unable to keep up with the "financial innovation" of the issuers, had to rely on the expertise of the issuers to rate the issuers' own newfangled products. The issuers (or arrangers) then would "work with" the rating agencies to test these RMBSs and CDOs.

While the corporate rating agencies are accused of conflicts of interest, FICO is charged at best with overselling its score and at worst with peddling a product of low quality. To put it sharply: corporate raters are accused of corruption and incompetence, FICO of incompetence only.

How Ratings Work When They Do

Two years after the collapse, it is hard to remember how robust and successful the rating agencies seemed to be. Everyone applauded the democratization of finance and the end of discrimination in lending that brought homeownership to minorities and to the less-than-affluent. Many marveled at the smartness and sophistication of structured finance and the wonders of the free market. In the conclusion, therefore, we will turn the original question upside down: Why did the rating agencies seem to work so well at establishing values and anchoring prices for many years? How could forecasting work? After all, prediction in the social world has always had an abysmal record.

The securitized mortgage credit market depended on not one but two highly rationalized systems of valuation and price anchoring: consumer and corporate ratings. The former is highly formalized, the latter is less so and keeps elements of individual judgment. In the case of RMBSs, however, the overall formalization was higher than for securities issued by corporations. The predictions of consumer rating agencies worked well for a while because what later turned out to be their defects were either contained or did not matter much at the time. Lenders operated a closed system of credit reporting. Consumers were not just unable to directly influence what information was registered with the credit bureaus, most did not even know they had been rated. Low default rates made the fact that FICO omitted important factors immaterial. Low default rates also reduced the significance of correlated defaults to a level that was negligible. The endogeneity of creditworthiness enforced the predictions through the mechanism of self-fulfilling prophecy. Conflicts of interest were never at issue as a cause of consumer rating bias. Over time, however, borrowers found out about the system and started to game it, undermining the predictive power of the FICO credit score. As lenders moved into new market segments, the omission of certain variables had consequences. As defaults grew, their correlations became stronger. As long as good clients got favorable loans and risky ones were mostly shut out, most borrowers could benefit from the positive effects of higher scores because they received loans on favorable terms. The punitive effect of the scores acted first and foremost as a deterrent. Once riskier customers were let in, the punitive effect of the score had detrimental effects on marginal borrowers, as they had to carry mortgages with exorbitant rates, which increased defaults.

Corporate ratings of securitized mortgages worked fine as long as the real estate market was on a steep upward trend. With smaller issuers, the rating agencies had more power to control data quality and avoid the omitted variables problem. The raters could demand the data they thought to be necessary. When securitization was in its infancy, lenders were more careful gathering information about customers because securitization opened their lending procedures up to external scrutiny. Moreover, because they securitized only a fraction of their mortgage portfolio, their general operating procedures were more cautious. With increased securitization, the balance between the need to win ever more customers and the obligation to continue lending prudently collapsed, and the originators of the mortgages became accessories to distorting the data, submitting files with missing information. This was easier for lenders to do as the issuer market became concentrated and the power shifted away from the agencies. Unlike the consumer raters, the corporate raters did try to model default correlations, but they used modeling techniques that underpredicted the likelihood of a catastrophe. Like the Black–Scholes model described by MacKenzie (2008), the rating agencies' Gaussian copula had both "cognitive simplicity" and public availability, after it was published by David X. Li in 2000 (Li 2000). It was an existing technique used in insurance to value annuities (Frees and Valdez 1996) and thus was in the public domain.

Unlike consumer rating, corporate rating has been self-conscious about the endogeneity problem. In good times, endogeneity gave the rating agencies a convenient excuse for late downgrades: they did not want to be active participants in the downfall of companies. Once the corporate rating agencies had to downgrade a large number of RMBSs, their action together with regulatory measures triggered panic selling; this drove the price (but not the value) of the RMBSs down. The collapse of the mortgage market, however, finally did have an indirect effect on default rates (value) by bringing the entire financial sector and ultimately the entire economy down.

Few people worried about conflicts of interest until the collapse. In economics, a large literature developed before the crisis that argued that rating agencies would never succumb to opportunism because of the prohibitive reputational cost they would have to pay (examples include Covitz and Harrison 2003; Crockett et al. 2004: 75; Walter 2004; but see Partnoy 1999). In the absence of direct data, economists had to argue from outcomes. It was hard to make the argument for odious mechanisms when the market seemed to be working well. Now direct evidence is available from the investigation conducted by the SEC (US SEC 2008*a*, 2008*b*) and the US congressional hearings.

Conclusion

The subprime mortgage crisis developed as a crisis of valuation and price anchoring. Price anchoring in credit markets is enacted as a series of forecasts about the future. In the US mortgage market, price anchoring is performed first and foremost by consumer and corporate rating agencies. Even though the agencies are private companies competing in a marketplace, they form stable triopolies. There have been several attempts to make the ratings business more competitive and to introduce new players, so far with little success.

There are good reasons why we find exactly three dominating agencies in both lines of business. Price formation must provide a focal point; otherwise, it cannot fulfill its coordination function. Having a multitude of rating agencies would provide too many anchors in a market where actors have no natural intuition about value. A plethora of raters also exposes the price anchoring process to rampant "rate shopping," allowing issuers to find the agency that rates them highest. Because issuers pay, a competition among rating agencies would likely compromise the rating process even more.

The rating industry is a monopoly in many countries, but this requires a deep trust in public institutions. A duopoly would not work, because two ratings can stand in irresolvable disagreement when setting a price in a particular case, but that conflict can be settled by a third rating. The triopoly is the optimal solution for when coordination is necessary but a monopoly is not trusted.

During the subprime mortgage crisis, both agency triopolies failed together. There was no credit bureau that raised the red flag about the FICO credit score and no corporate rating agency that blew the whistle on unrealistic assessments. Undoubtedly, there were powerful financial incentives for participating in the bubble, yet the common failure also suggests that none of the forecasters saw the trouble coming and that all shared a common if flawed understanding of the mortgage market. The crisis reveals the weak points of a system based on formalized prediction. Data is created in strategic social processes, models are never complete, the pattern of outcomes of interest is always complex, valuation and price anchoring are performative and influence what they evaluate, and the raters are subject to opportunism. Formalization and transparency that curbs discretion may guard against opportunism, but it also opens more opportunities for gaming the system and ultimately results in a loss of flexibility.

REFERENCES

Agarwal, S. and Ho, C. T. (2007). Comparing the Prime and Subprime Mortgage Markets. *Chicago Fed Letter* 241. Chicago, IL: The Federal Reserve of Chicago. http://www.chicagofed.org/webpages/publications/chicago_fed_letter/2007/august_24l.cfm. (accessed April 1, 2011).

Akerlof, G. A. (1970). The Market for "Lemons": Quality Uncertainty and the Market Mechanism. *Quarterly Journal of Economics* 84(3): 488–500.

Ashcraft, A. B. and Schuermann, T. (2008). *Understanding the Securitization of Subprime Mortgage Credit*. Federal Reserve Bank of New York Staff Report 318. http://www.newyorkfed.org/research/staff_reports/sr318. (accessed April 1, 2011)

Aspers, P. (2009). Knowledge and Valuation in Markets. *Theory and Society* 38: 111–31.

Avery, R. B. Calem, P. S., and Canner, G. B. (2004). Credit Report Accuracy and Access to Credit. *Federal Reserve Bulletin* 90: 297–322.

Avery, R. B., Bostic, R. W., Calem, P. S., and Canner, G. B. (2000). Credit Scoring: Statistical Issues and Evidence from Credit-Bureau Files. *Real Estate Economics* 28 (3): 523–47.

Beckert, J. (2009). The Social Order of Markets. *Theory and Society* 38: 245–69.

Benmelech, E and Dlugosz, J. (2009). *The Alchemy of CDO Credit Ratings*. Working Paper 14787. National Bureau of Economic Research. http://www.nber.org/papers/w14878 (accessed April 1, 2011).

Beunza, D. and Stark, D. (2004). Tools of the Trade: The Socio-Technology of Arbitrage in a Wall Street Trading Room. *Industrial and Corporate Change* 13(2): 369–400.

Buck, R. C. (1963). Reflexive Predictions. *Philosophy of Science* 30(4): 359–69.

Calem, P. S. and LaCour-Little, M. (2001). *Risk-Based Capital Requirements for Mortgage Loans*. Working Paper 2001-60. The Federal Reserve Board Financial and Economics Discussion Series. http://www.federalreserve.gov/pubs/feds/2001/200160/200160pap.pdf (accessed March 27, 2011)

Cassady, A. and Mierzwinski, E. (2004). *Mistakes Do Happen: A Look at Errors in Consumer Credit Reports*. National Association of State PIRGs.

Chomsisengphet, S. and Pennington-Cross, A. (2006). The Evolution of the Subprime Mortgage Market. *Federal Reserve Bank of St. Louis Review* 88(1): 31–56.

Covitz, D. M. and Harrison, P. (2003). Testing Conflicts of Interest at Bond Ratings Agencies with Market Anticipation: Evidence that Reputation Incentives Dominate. *Finance and Economics Discussion Series* 2003-68. Washington: Board of Governors of the Federal Reserve System.

Cowan, A. M. and Cowan, C. D. (2004). Default Correlation: An Empirical Investigation of a Subprime Lender. *Journal of Banking and Finance* 28: 753–71.

Cowgill, B., Wolfers, J., and Zitzewitz, E. (2009). *Using Prediction Markets to Track Information Flows: Evidence from Google*. Discussion paper. http://www.bocowgill.com/GooglePredictionMarketPaper.pdf (accessed April 1, 2011)

Crockett, A., Harris, T., Mishkin, F. S., and White, E. N. (2004). *Conflicts of Interest in the Financial Services Industry: What Should We Do About Them?* Geneva: International Center for Monetary and Banking Studies.

Demyanyk, Y. and Van Hemert, O. (2008). *Understanding the Subprime Mortgage Crisis*. SSRN Working Paper.

Engels, A. (2006). Market Creation and Transnational Rule-Making: The Case of CO_2 Emissions Trading. In M.-L. Djelic and K. Sahlin-Andersson (eds.), *Transnational Governance: Institutional Dynamics of Regulation*. Cambridge: Cambridge University Press, 329–48.

Espeland, W. N. and Sauder, M. (2007). Rankings and Reactivity: How Public Measures Recreate Social Worlds. *American Journal of Sociology* 113(1): 1–40.

Feld, M. (2007). *Implied Correlation Smile*. Master's thesis, Institute for Statistics and Econometrics, CASE Center for Applied Statistics and Economics, Humboldt – Universitaet zu Berlin.

Fight, A. (2001). *The Ratings Game*. Chichester: John Wiley's and Sons, Ltd.

Fitch (2007, April 27). *Subprime Collateral Trends and Early Payment Defaults*. US Residential Mortgage. Special Report.

Foster, C. (2007). *Scoring for Success in a Turbulent Mortgage Market*. View Points, November/December. Fair Isaac Company.

Foust, D. and Pressman, A. (2008, February 7). Credit Scores: Not-So-Magic Numbers. *Business Week*. http://www.businessweek.com/magazine/content/08_07/b4071038384407.htm (accessed April 1, 2011)

Frees, E. W. and Emiliano Valdez, J. C. (1996). Annuity Valuation with Dependent Mortality. *The Journal of Risk and Insurance* 63(2): 229–61.

Gilbert, D. (2006). *Stumbling on Happiness*. New York, NY: Knopf.

Hager, S. and Schoebel, R. (2006). *A Note on the Correlation Smile*. Working Paper. Eberhard-Karls-University of Tuebingen.

Hayek, F. A. (1945). The Use of Knowledge in Society. *The American Economic Review* 35(4): 519–30.

Jackson, T. (2009). *Prosperity without Growth: Economics for a Finite Planet*. London: Earthscan.

Kahneman, D. and Thaler, R. H. (2006). Anomalies Utility Maximization and Experienced Utility. *Journal of Economic Perspectives* 20(1): 221–34.

Keys, B. J., Mukherjee, T., Seru, A., and Vig, V. (2008). *Did Securitization Lead to Lax Screening? Evidence from Subprime Loans*. EFA 2008 Athens Meetings Paper.

Knight, F. H. (1921/1985). *Risk, Uncertainty, and Profit*. Chicago: University of Chicago Press.

Li, D. X. (2000). On Default Correlation: A Copula Function Approach. *The Journal of Fixed Income* 9(4): 43–54.

Löffler, G. (2003). The Effects of Estimation Error on Measures of Portfolio Credit Risk. *Journal of Banking and Finance* 27: 1427–53.

MacKenzie, D. (2007). Is Economics Performative? In D. MacKenzie, F. Muniesa, and L. Siu (eds.), *Do Economists Make Markets? On the Performativity of Economics*. Princeton, NJ: Princeton University Press.

——(2008). *An Engine, Not a Camera. How Financial Models Shape Markets*. Cambridge, MA: MIT Press.

——(2009). Making Things the Same: Gases, Emission Rights and the Politics of Carbon Markets. *Accounting, Organizations and Society* 34: 440–55.

Malevergne, Y. and Sornette, D. (2003). Testing the Gaussian Copula Hypothesis for Financial Assets Dependences. *Quantitative Finance* 3(4): 231–50.

Partnoy, F. (1999). The Siskel and Ebert of Financial Markets? Two Thumbs Down for the Credit Rating Agencies. *Washington University Law Quarterly* 77(3): 620–714.

Rajan, U., Seru, A., and Vig, V. (2008). *The Failure of Models That Predict Failure: Distance, Incentives and Defaults*. SSRN Working Paper.

Romey, C. and Drut, B. (2008). Analysis of Subprime RMBS Ratings in the USA. *Risk and Trend Mapping* 4. Autorité des marchés financiers. http://www.amf-france.org/documents/general/8136_1.pdf (accessed March 27, 2011)

Salmon, F. (2009). Recipe for Disaster: The Formula That Killed Wall Street. *Wired Magazine* 17(3): 74–9.

Shiller, R. J. (2008). *The Subprime Solution: How Today's Global Financial Crises Happened, and What to Do about It*. Princeton, NJ: Princeton University Press.

Simmel, G. (1907/1978). *The Philosophy of Money*. London: Routledge.

Smith, C. W. (2007). Markets as Definitional Practices. *Canadian Journal of Sociology* 32(1): 1–39.

Smith, R. C. and Walter, I. (2002). Rating Agencies: Is There an Agency Issue? In R. M. Levich, G. Majnoni, and C. Reinhart (eds.), *Ratings, Rating Agencies and the Global Financial System*. Boston: Kluwer, 289–318.

Stiglitz, J. E., Sen, A., and Fitoussi, J.-P. (2009). *Report by the Commission on the Measurement of Economic Performance and Social Progress*. http://www.stiglitz-sen-fitoussi.fr/documents/rapport_anglais.pdf (accessed March 27, 2011)

Straka, J. W. (2000). A Shift in the Mortgage Landscape: The 1990s Move to Automated Credit Evaluations. *Journal of Housing Research* 11(2): 207–32.

Sullivan, T. A., Warren, E., and Westbrook, J. L. (2000). *The Fragile Middle Class: Americans in Debt*. New Haven, CT: Yale University Press.

Surowiecki, J. (2004). *The Wisdom of Crowds: Why the Many Are Smarter Than the Few and How Collective Wisdom Shapes Business, Economies, Societies, and Nations*. New York, NY: Doubleday.

Taleb, N. N. (2007). *Black Swan: The Impact of the Highly Improbable*. New York, NY: Random House.

Truth in Lending: Proposed Rule. 73 Fed. Reg. 1672 (2008). 12 CFR pt. 226. http://www.federalreserve.gov/reportforms/formsreview/RegZ_20080109_ifr.pdf (accessed March 27, 2011)

US Census Bureau (2009). *Quarterly Homeownership Rates by Race and Ethnicity of Householder for the United States: 1994–2009*. http://www.census.gov/hhes/www/housing/hvs/charts/files/fig08.pdf (accessed March 27, 2011)

US Congress. Senate. Committee on Finance. (2007). *The Housing Decline: The Extent of the Problem and Potential Remedies*. 110th Cong., 1st session, December 13. Testimony of Michael Decker.

US Government Accountability Office. (2005). *Credit Reporting Literacy: Consumers Understood the Basics but Could Benefit from Targeted Educational Efforts*. GAO-05-223.

US Securities and Exchange Commission. (2008a). *Summary Report of Issues Identified in the Commission Staff's Examinations of Select Credit Rating Agencies*. By the Staff of the Office of Compliance Inspections and Examinations Division of Trading and Markets and Office of Economic Analysis. http://www.sec.gov/news/studies/2008/craexamination070808.pdf (accessed March 27, 2011)

—— (2008b). *Annual Report on Nationally Recognized Statistical Rating Organizations*. http://www.sec.gov/divisions/marketreg/ratingagency/nrsroannrep0608.pdf (accessed March 27, 2011).

Victor, P. A. (2008). *Managing without Growth: Slower by Design, not Disaster*. Cheltenham: Edward Elgar.

Walter, I. (2004). Conflicts of Interest and Market Discipline among Financial Service Firms. *European Management Journal* 22(4): 361–76.

Wolfers, J. and Zitzewitz, E. (2004). Prediction Markets. *Journal of Economic Perspectives* 18(2): 107–26.

11 Selling Value in Kenya's Nairobi Stock Exchange

Christopher Yenkey

Introduction

This chapter approaches the issue of value creation in emerging financial markets by exploring the state's use of advertising to stimulate share ownership among new, domestic investors in the frontier stock exchange in Kenya. Creating a stock exchange as a formal organization is a relatively easy task to accomplish. A stock exchange can operate with just a few key components, requiring only a supply of companies willing to sell shares publicly, some minimum number of investors willing to purchase the shares, and a location in which intermediaries can meet to exchange bids and offers. Over the centuries, this has taken place in such unlikely venues as a coffeehouse and under a buttonwood tree, as were the cases in the early years of the Amsterdam Stock Exchange in the seventeenth century and the New York Stock Exchange in the late eighteenth century, respectively. While it is fairly easy to create a stock exchange as a location in which shares can be traded, such an arrangement will be impaired from performing its intended functions—of mobilizing nascent capital, facilitating price discovery, and generating more liquid secondary markets—until a sufficiently large number of participants are assembled. The recruitment of a sufficient number of participants is one distinguishing feature that separates a stock *exchange* from a stock *market*. A stock exchange as a formal organization can exist even when it fails to accomplish its stated goals, and indeed many newly created stock exchanges exist formally but remain functionally irrelevant because of low levels of participation (Sing 1997; Yartey and Adjasi 2007).

The recruitment of investors into frontier stock exchanges is a concern in scores of developing countries that have established capital markets in recent decades. The number of stock exchanges worldwide has doubled since 1985, with more than 70 formal exchanges having been established in this time period dominated by the spread of neoliberalism (Mondo Visione 2007). The global push to establish capital markets in developing countries brings to the front a previously overlooked aspect of the sociological study of financial markets: how to legitimate investor capitalism to new populations in countries that often lack a number of institutional structures that support such market structures. Potential investors in the frontier stock exchanges of Lithuania,

Tanzania, or Slovenia, to name just a few, possess no previous experience with the practice and often lack knowledge of the firms whose shares are made available. In addition, this intangible financial technology is introduced into developing countries frequently characterized by numerous institutional weaknesses, including weak property rights regimes, volatile macroeconomic environments, and low incomes. This chapter addresses the question of how an actor living in such a vulnerable environment might come to value share ownership despite these negative stimuli.

Sociologists have long framed such questions in terms of the legitimacy of a product or a firm as it is adjudicated by potential consumers. A number of definitions of legitimacy relate to the degree to which an organization or practice conforms with both formal and informal social norms, including rules, regulations, and cultural beliefs and practices (for a detailed review, see Deephouse and Suchman 2008). Numerous empirical studies have explored this interplay between accepted norms in the developed economy of the United States, but the purpose of this chapter is to investigate how legitimacy is constructed outside the context of the developed, often Western, markets in which it is often studied. Potential adopters of shareholding as a new practice in a developing country are frequently constrained by a lack of alternative investment options, which in turn contributes negatively to an already restrictive class mobility structure. In such an environment, are potential investors expected to decline an opportunity for socioeconomic advancement because they lack familiarity with a newly offered financial product?

Unlike previous studies of how legitimacy is constructed in developed market settings, I argue that in the context of developing countries, legitimacy is more strongly related to the aspirations of the potential investor than it is about achieving parsimony with norms and practices already taken for granted. The new product offered need not be seen as consistent with past practices in order to achieve a high level of legitimacy and therefore adoption. Instead, the proposed product, in this case share ownership, achieves legitimacy by coming to represent an ideal that is in especially high demand in developing countries: upward socioeconomic mobility. This ideal is built around an expectation of future value: a potential investor does not need to understand what a share is but must come to believe that share ownership represents a rare opportunity to improve one's material well-being.

Sociologists have previously studied this aspirational basis for consumer demand. Campbell (1987) writes of the role played by the "imaginative hedonist" in the formation of modern consumer society, arguing that the spirit underlying modern consumerism is less related to the material value of goods. Instead, judgments of product desirability are partially driven by practices similar to daydreaming, where an actor imagines achieving a particular state and then consumes the goods that the actor believes will help achieve that state. Extending this argument, Beckert (2010) distinguishes physical value, which is based on the function an object performs, from imaginative and positional value. In more affluent consumer societies, where a higher proportion of consumer expenditures is spent on nonessential goods purchased with disposable income than on the provision of basic needs such as food and shelter, positional value is similar to patterns of consumption studied by Veblen and Simmel, where the products consumed by an actor help to situate that actor in a social space. Imaginative value, Beckert argues, is different in that the consumed object "performs as an arbitrator or bridge between the subject and a desired but intangible ideal" (2010: 9). The case study presented here makes use of these concepts, but in an empirical setting, where the physical or material value of a good is not so clearly detached from the "daydream" of a lifestyle less defined by material limitations. The connection I draw between aspirational emotions and economic action among Kenyan investors is similar to behaviors studied by other researchers. Studies of individual participation in state-sponsored lotteries, for example, show that lower income groups make up the majority of lottery ticket buyers, a reflection of hopes of improved material well-being (McConkey and Warren 1987; see Beckert and Lutter 2009 for a review). This mixing of aspirations with material gains is related to work by Keister (2000), who studies how American households seek wealth accumulation in adherence to notions of the "American dream," which amounts to an ideological commitment that each generation should leave its heirs materially better off. Here, parents engage in rationally calculated investment behaviors toward the goal of material gain, but the catalyst for these is a more ideational commitment to provide greater resources to their children than they received from their own parents.

But how does one choose a course of action intended to realize such aspirations? Suchman condenses numerous conceptions of legitimacy based on calculated self-interest into what he calls pragmatic legitimacy, which he defines as "the self-interested calculations of an organization's most immediate audiences" (1995: 578). Potential investors in developing countries have the same material motivations as do investors in developed countries—both groups purchase shares because they believe that doing so is in their financial best interest. This assumption, however, reveals nothing about *how* potential investors come to associate share ownership with material gain, particularly in light of the lack of prior experience of the new investors who are the focus of this analysis. Potential investors in Kenya frequently lack access to objective sources of information that might be used to judge the attractiveness of a given investment, such as records of past firm performance or access to financial advisory services. As a result, these actors are increasingly reliant on perceptions of firm performance rather than on objective calculations of it.

This chapter investigates one major source of these perceptions: the state's use of mass advertising campaigns intended to persuade inexperienced investors that share ownership represents an opportunity for upward social mobility. The larger issue at hand is the state's effort to construct a more functional market apparatus, a more macro-level issue in line with previous research on market construction (e.g., Aspers 2009; Callon 1998). However, the scope of this chapter is more limited. Following loosely in the footsteps of Bourdieu's study (2005) of the French suburban housing market, this chapter studies how an advertising campaign for an initial public offering (IPO) in Kenya elicits an aspirational response from potential investors. This chapter is less directly aimed at understanding Kenyan consumers and has an overt focus on how the state seeks to activate them.

ADVERTISING'S ROLE IN GENERATING FAMILIARITY AMID UNCERTAINTY

The concept of "invest in what you know" was popularized by investment adviser Peter Lynch (1990) in the late 1980s. Prior to that, this idea was formalized by economist Robert C. Merton (1987), who constructed an asset pricing theory recognizing that a large proportion of investors' trade is based on familiarity rather than on performance. A growing sociological literature investigates the role played by advertising in producing this effect. For example, Kihlstrom and Riordan (1984) argue that potential consumers understand that advertising is a costly use of resources, and therefore firms that engage in large advertising campaigns are seen by consumers as more profitable, more stable, and consequently a more desirable investment. Grullon et al. (2004) find that advertising intended to improve a firm's position within product markets has a spillover effect into capital markets, and Pollock and Rindova (2003) show that increased media coverage for listing firms drives up IPO share prices.

Previous studies such as these suggest that advertising not only has a positive impact on willingness to invest in a particular share, but this effect is felt more strongly among less experienced, less financially literate investors. Advertising performs a similar role in Kenya as it does in the United States, and this chapter investigates how such expectations are constructed among inexperienced investors in the frontier stock exchange in Kenya through the state's use of large-scale advertising campaigns. I will argue that the demand for share ownership is not the result of individual calculations of firm performance; instead, perceived value is constructed through advertising campaigns that make use of symbols of socioeconomic advancement, attainable through share ownership, to attract inexperienced investors. In this manner, potential investors need not become familiar with the share as an object itself. Instead, value is constructed by convincing the investor that the source of that object possesses scarce resources which satisfy the desired ideal.

Before exploring a specific advertising campaign used to recruit new Kenyan investors into the stock exchange, it is helpful to understand the opportunity structure in which such campaigns take place. The following section introduces the reader to the Kenyan investing public as well as to recent policies adopted by the Kenyan state to make share ownership financially possible for large segments of the population.

The Kenyan Context: Mass Retail Investing in a Volatile Environment

The Nairobi Stock Exchange (NSE) was formally established in 1954 as an overseas affiliate of the London Stock Exchange during the period of British colonial rule. British businessmen governed the market, excluding indigenous participation, until Kenyan independence in 1963. From independence in 1963 until 2005, the NSE operated as a closed group controlled by a small number of stockbrokers, who restricted access to share ownership at the expense of market growth. A lax regulatory environment allowed firms listed on the stock exchange, most often in cases of privatizations of state-owned firms, to sell shares to a small group of stockbrokers, pension funds, government officials, and other Kenyan elites. However, these barriers to entry for small-scale shareholders were directly addressed in the Privatization Act of 2005, passed by the Kenyan Parliament in that year. With the belief that the state stood to benefit from the economic growth potential of a more active capital market, the 2005 Act contained several provisions that forced the NSE and its intermediaries to accept a higher degree of retail shareholding.

Formally, the Act requires that any firm listing on the NSE make at least 25% of its shares available to no fewer than 1,000 shareholders. The Act also requires approval by the state regulatory agency, the Capital Markets Authority (CMA), of several key features of each initial public offer (IPO), including the initial share price to be charged, the minimum number of shares allowed in a single application, and the allocation of IPO shares across different types of investors such as retail, institutional, and employees of the listing firm. The CMA was given the authority to restrict the use of price discovery techniques, resulting in IPO procedures where all investors subscribe to their desired number of shares during a subscription period held over the course of several weeks prior to the shares being listed on the exchange. In the event of an oversubscription to the IPO, which occurs regularly, share allocations are made to each applicant according to a pro rata policy, whereby each investor receives a proportion of subscribed shares based on the total subscription level in the IPO. The end result of these provisions is that by withholding approval for listings, the state is able to set fixed prices for IPO shares and dictate what proportion of those shares will be reserved for small-scale retail investors. The state can also force listing companies to set low minimum buy-in levels, which has the effect of reducing the financial barrier to entry for lower income investors.[1] While the formal provision of the Act requires that 25% of shares be allocated to at least 1,000 investors, the interpretation and application of that provision goes far beyond what is formally required. With share prices

---

[1] The use of such politicized offer terms is common in emerging markets, where states adopt listing requirements that incentivize participation by retail investors. For a more in-depth review of the practice, see Jones et al. (1999).

fixed, minimum buy-ins held low, and allocation policies controlled by the regulator, the state effectively forces listing firms to allocate a high percentage of IPO shares to retail investors, who are now able to buy in small lots without the worry that their applications could be priced out by higher bids from institutional investors.

A former chief executive of the CMA discusses the functional goals of this policy:

The theory here was to be sure the shareholding was reasonably wide to give liquidity in the marketplace. This is a standard requirement for most emerging markets and stock exchanges. You see, most emerging markets stock exchanges—they have that level of pressure. The government came up with a policy... which was a privatization policy that stated clearly that the allocation of the shares in [the] IPO would be distributed on the basis of ensuring wider participation of the investors, and therefore individuals were given a higher priority than institutional investors.

At the time of passage of the Privatization Act of 2005, there were an estimated 140,000 total shareholders in the exchange, but by the end of 2008 that number had grown to almost 1.5 million in a country of approximately 8.5 million households. For the first time in Kenyan history, a critical mass of individuals have started to transition out of traditional, tangible assets such as real estate, land, and livestock as preferred savings vehicles and into intangible assets like stocks. This transition has occurred in an environment characterized by low incomes and low savings rates, a weak property rights regime, high information asymmetries, and unstable bureaucratic and macroeconomic environments. For example, per capita GDP in Kenya in 2006 was approximately $700, and fewer than one-third of households earn more than double the poverty wage. Given that access to disposable income and household savings is a prerequisite for purchasing shares or other savings or investment vehicles, the low average incomes in Kenya and the low percentage of the population living above double the poverty line would predict that few would purchase shares.

In addition to the low average income in Kenya, the protection of property rights that some scholars argue is necessary for capital market investment (La Porta et al. 1997) is also conspicuously lacking. Kenya ranked 84th on the World Bank's 2008 Investor Protection Index, which measures the strength of the regulatory framework surrounding legal enforcement of contracts and disclosure of material information to shareholders. The weakness in the rule of law in Kenya is also manifested in the extreme level of corruption in Kenya, exemplified by Kenya's global ranking of 150th in Transparency International's 2007 Corruption Perceptions Index.

Despite these background conditions, approximately 1.3 million new investors have purchased shares at the NSE since early 2006. This boom in the investing population in Kenya reflects the state's effort to ensure that a broad range of Kenyan society has the opportunity to participate in the stock exchange. Of the 1.47 million total accounts on the exchange, more than

86% are Kenyan citizens registered as retail investors, while just over 12% are registered as Kenyan companies. Reflecting some success in the state's effort to attract a shareholding base that more closely resembles Kenya's overall population, the median portfolio value among all investors is $68. Among retail investors, portfolio values at the 99th percentile are just under $9,000, while for company investors, portfolio values for the top 1% are closer to $40,000. The distribution of portfolio values across investors reflects the high levels of wealth stratification seen in the overall Kenyan population, as the author estimates that more than 60% of total market capitalization is concentrated in the accounts of fewer than 10% of investors.[2] Growth in participation in this market has been an almost entirely domestic affair, as approximately 1% of all accounts is held by non-Kenyans, and half of those are non-East Africans. Contrary to common assumptions about the large degree of foreign ownership across emerging markets, recent research has shown that foreign investment in African capital markets is practically nonexistent outside of South Africa (Moss et al. 2007).

Seven firms have undergone IPOs on the NSE since the passage of the Privatization Act in 2005, and new investors reacted with differing levels of demand to each of these offers. The author calculates that fewer than 30,000 of the approximately 1.3 million investors new to the NSE since early 2006 purchased their first shares outside of an IPO event, a fact that strongly suggests any explanation of the legitimation of shareholding in Kenya should focus on attributes of these IPOs. Table 11.1 shows descriptive statistics for each of the seven firms that have listed on the NSE since mass retail shareholding was enabled by the Privatization Act of 2005. In addition to showing the total number of new investors recruited into the stock exchange in each IPO, Table 11.1 shows the level of state ownership of each firm, the firm's size in terms of gross revenue (in thousands of Ksh) in the year just prior to listing, the advertising budget in Kenyan shillings (Ksh) designated for the IPO itself, each firm's financial performance as measured by the average change in yearly gross profit over the three years prior to listing, the cost of the minimum buy-in required of each investor in Ksh, and the change in price of shares of the previous IPO at the time of listing. Several regularities are worth noting. First, state-owned firms attract the lion's share of new investors, recruiting more than 943,000 new investors in IPOs of four firms either entirely or majority-owned by the state. This compares to a total recruitment of almost 215,000 new investors for all IPOs of firms that are either entirely private or have the state as a minority shareholder. IPOs of state-owned firms are also associated with lower minimum buy-ins and considerably larger budgets for general advertising as well as IPO-specific advertising. With the exception of the two

---

[2] Measures of total numbers of investors and the portfolio value of each account are made possible through access to the databases of the Central Depository and Settlement Corporation (CDSC), the legal entity that serves as the clearing and settlement authority for all transactions on the NSE. Descriptive data presented here is from a snapshot taken on June 9, 2009 of all shareholding accounts.

Table 11.1 Descriptive statistics of each initial public offer

Firm name (in order of listing)	No. of new accounts created during IPO	% state ownership	Gross revenue for year prior to IPO (000s Ksh)	Ad budget for IPO (Ksh)	Avg. 3-year % change in gross profit	Minimum buy-in (Ksh)	% change share price prev. IPO at time of listing
KenGen	203,755	100	11,021,000	101,000,000	−28.1	5,950	n/a
Scangroup	58,253	0	2,343,628	8,640,000	54.2	5,225	207.1
Eveready	135,192	35	2,244,635	8,000,000	−3.0	4,750	133.8
Access Kenya	21,325	0	577,881	3,210,000	9.5	50,000	−9.4
Kenya Reinsurance	58,587	100	3,034,743	57,700,000	−24.2	19,000	32.5
Safaricom	665,786	65	47,447,490	7,128,000	7.9	5,000	47.5
Cooperative Trust Bank	15,220	100	8,275,856	68,018,417	49.1	9,500	−36.8

Sources: Prospectuses for firms listed, NSE databases.

Table 11.2 Correlations between number of new NSE accounts opened and firm, offer and market-level attributes

% state ownership	0.58
Gross revenue one year before listing	0.86
Total budgeted advertising expense for the IPO	0.68
Average % change in gross profit rate over three years prior to listing	−0.51
Value of minimum subscription allowed	−0.66
% change in share price of previous IPO shares	0.50

Sources: Prospectuses for firms listed, NSE databases.

most recent listings, state-owned firms also show the weakest financial performance in the three years prior to listing.

Table 11.2 presents correlation coefficients between the number of new investors recruited by each firm in the first five IPOs following passage of the Privatization Act of 2005, and the attributes of each firm relative to its IPO and the market. The correlations presented in Table 11.2 suggest that the decision by an actor to first enter this market is less oriented toward past firm performance. Instead, actors appear to be drawn into the practice of shareholding by larger firms who employ large advertising campaigns and who offer shares at low minimum buy-ins. New investors are also increasingly drawn to IPOs that follow a previous IPO that experienced more positive gains in share price after listing. The traits of larger firm size, low minimum buy-in, and large advertising expenditure were the exclusive purview of the state-owned firms being privatized via the NSE during this time.

While it is not the purpose of this chapter to argue that any one attribute of a firm or its IPO is the most influential in attracting new investors, a quantitative analysis is restricted by the low number of IPO events. Instead, the strong correlation between advertising expenditures and recruitment of new investors, especially relative to other potential influences, suggests that much can be learned by better understanding how the state conducts its advertising campaigns in its quest to recruit new investors.

Advertising and Value Creation in the Kenyan Market: Aspirations and Expenditures

This section begins by discussing theories of how state ownership of a firm, independent of other characteristics, signals value to potential investors in Kenya. Next, I present a case study of an advertising campaign for a recent privatization carried out through an IPO on the NSE. Finally, I explore how the state allocates its advertising budget for three privatization IPOs across the country, showing that the state allocates resources toward recruiting a broad range of Kenya's population rather than targeting upper-income groups.

THE STATE AS A SIGNAL OF WEALTH AND CLASS MOBILITY

Political science has a well developed literature that demonstrates the role of the state in determining access to material resources and wealth-generating opportunities, and therefore ultimately determining social class in African countries. Sklar (1979) was among the first to make the argument that the state filled the void left by departing colonial governments in many African countries, including Kenya, when independence swept the continent in the early 1960s. The response of the Kenyan state to the end of colonial rule was similar to that in many other newly independent African countries, which was to nationalize most means of production and concentrate these resources in the hands of a governing elite that was predominantly headquartered in the capital city. As a result, a ruling elite emerged in the 1960s and 1970s that controlled the majority of the wealth in most African nations. Diamond (1987) continues this analysis by elaborating several pathways through which Africans can access state-owned resources and thereby gain access to a higher class position. Among these, and central to the theory presented here, is the role played by clientelism and state patronage. Here, individuals who achieve a position in the state such that they have access to resources are expected to transmit such resources back to their local community via kinship and ethnic networks. In this manner, a well-placed individual can support a large constituency by redistributing state resources to supporters. It is also true, therefore, that in order to gain access to scarce resources in an African state, it is necessary to have such a link to the government.

Given that the majority of citizens in Kenya have no such patron to serve on their behalf, and given that the citizens understand that a large proportion of resources in Kenya are controlled by the state, it is not surprising that a mindset develops that stimulates Kenyans to try to gain access to the state in some manner as a means of improving their material well-being. Bratton et al. (2004) find evidence through the Afrobarometer survey of public perceptions of market liberalization policies in sub-Saharan Africa that a high proportion of respondents believe that economic policies and recent economic reforms increase income inequality by favoring individuals with close ties to state organizations.

This suggests that Kenyans are predisposed to see state-owned firms as access points to resources needed to improve one's class position. Therefore, when an opportunity arises to partake in ownership of a state-owned enterprise, new investors in Kenya will be predisposed to take advantage of that opportunity without seeking additional information with which to calculate expected returns. In short, state ownership of the firm acts as a cognitive heuristic that signals value in the shares offered net of other characteristics of the firm that potential investors might consider. Even if potential investors are hesitant or unfamiliar with the act of purchasing shares, the possibility of sharing in the ownership, and therefore the wealth, of a state-owned firm signals an expected value that outweighs the reticence to engage in an unfamiliar practice.

The individual's view of the state as facilitating class mobility is complementary to the state's motivation for adopting the politicized offer terms discussed previously. While the individual seeks class mobility via access to state resources, the state seeks to mobilize pockets of nascent capital and increase liquidity in the emerging capital market by deepening market participation among the general public. Seen in this way, the state and the populace become codependent in their search for material resources.

THE STATE'S USE OF ADVERTISING: SYMBOLS, ASPIRATIONS, AND PERCEIVED VALUE

The remainder of this section examines how a particular privatization IPO advertising campaign is carried out in Kenya. Data presented here was collected through archival research of internal documents obtained from the Nairobi-based advertising agency that executed the campaign and semi-structured interviews conducted in the field with representatives of the advertising agency, executives of the listing firm, and Kenyan market regulators. The focus of this analysis is the IPO of the Kenya Reinsurance Corporation, the fifth IPO in the post-Privatization Act era. This IPO is particularly illustrative because it represents a concerted effort by the state to build a sense of value around a completely unknown company operating in an unfamiliar industry. Unlike the IPO of state-owned telecom giant Safaricom, a highly visible and popular firm in Kenya which generated the highest number of new investors into the market (see Table 11.1), Kenya Re started its IPO process as an almost total unknown to the general public. Additionally, Kenya Re exhibits the most strongly negative financial performance of any of the post-Privatization Act listing firms. The Kenya Re IPO benefited somewhat from the publicity given to four earlier IPOs, but as suggested by the correlations in Table 11.2, the Kenya Re IPO most likely was at a disadvantage given the poor share price performance of the two IPOs that preceded it and the company's higher than average initial share price. However, Kenya Re has by far the highest advertising expenditure, when measured as a percentage of firm gross revenue, of any of the seven firms that have listed since the Privatization Act. Finally, because all IPO advertising campaigns for state-owned firms listing on the NSE are handled by the same advertising agency, that uses a consistent strategy in all IPO compaigns an analysis of one campaign serves as a representative sample of all others.

The advertising agency begins by assessing what it calls the "consumer psychographic types" of potential investors within the Kenyan population. These are ideal types of potential investors that advertisers use to understand how categories of potential constituents might react to different advertising strategies. The three categories of potential investors are summarized in Table 11.3. The common theme running across these groups is an orientation toward familiar, stable, and lower risk brands or products. The consumer is best approached with a product seen to virtually guarantee positive returns and minimize risks, and that is strongly associated with previously understood and accepted practices. These attributes are directly in line with the definition of legitimacy discussed above, but with the exception that Kenya Re at the outset is an unknown firm and these qualities will have to be constructed through the advertising campaign.

To do so, the agency outlines a four-stage advertising campaign for each IPO, geared toward portraying the offer according to the attributes to which mainstreamers, aspirers, and succeeders are likely attracted. Table 11.4 provides a description of each of these four stages. The first stage, called the awareness phase, makes no mention of the IPO itself, seeking only to increase

Table 11.3 "Psychographic types" of consumers, as defined by advertising agency

Consumer type	Characteristics
Mainstreamer	Conformist, conventional, passive, habitual; favors big and well-known brands
Aspirer	Materialistic, affiliative, oriented to extrinsics such as image, appearance, persona; attractiveness is more important than quality of contents
Succeeder	Strong goal orientation, confidence, work ethic; supports status quo, stability; brand choice based on reward, prestige, "the very best"

Table 11.4 Four-stage advertising strategy used in Kenyan privatizations

Phase	Goal
Awareness	Build familiarity with the company name and the industry/type of business conducted; establish the function of the company: what it does; convey a high level of financial performance and large firm size
Pre-listing	Establish pride of ownership; present the IPO for the first time and communicate it as a way for the individual to share in the strength of the firm
Listing	Provide information on how and when to purchase shares: time frame of subscription period, application procedures, and locations where applications are accepted
Countdown	Create a sense of urgency; inform potential investors that there is only a limited time to subscribe to shares; activate the feelings of demand created in previous phases

consumer recognition of the firm's name and line of business as well as creating an image of profitability. The second stage, called the pre-listing phase because it takes place just before the subscription period opens, introduces the idea that for the first time outsiders can become owners of this profitable company but without providing details of how ownership is actually negotiated. In the listing phase, the third phase, the logistics of how, when, and where to purchase shares are introduced. The final phase, the countdown phase, ensures that potential investors understand that becoming an owner of the firm is a limited time offer. Advertisements in this phase seek to create a sense of urgency by making a prominent display of the number of days left until the opportunity expires.

As stated in internal advertising agency documents, this four-stage strategy "represents a process that investors go through of learning, feeling, and finally doing." Beginning with the recognition that potential investors are not familiar with these companies, the advertiser builds a familiarity for the company by associating the firm with a product or line of business that the public is already familiar with. Next, that product or line of business is shown to be part of a profitable enterprise. After these claims of profitability, the individual is introduced to the idea that it is possible to share in these resources by becoming an owner in the firm. Finally, the potential investor is instructed on how to act on this opportunity within a limited time frame. Each of these advertising phases is accomplished using strong symbolic references, images that represent ideals that are cognitively accessible to an unfamiliar public.

Through the use of focus groups before this campaign began, the advertising agency identified a pervasive image of strength and stability known to the Kenyan public: the baobab tree. The account manager for the advertising agency that conducted the campaign explains:

What we did first was to have an identifier for this IPO, and you can see that we have the Kenya Re logo, but then we came up with this tree [the baobab tree] because our focus group research asked people to tell us something that said "solid." We told [the focus group] the characteristics of Kenya Re: it won't go down, it would not do this and that, and this is the kind of tree people told us about. It is a specific species of tree. It is very solid. We use this tree and tell them that "Kenya Re secures your future."

The baobab tree has a particular significance in African culture. Often referred to as "the tree of life," it has long been a symbol of stability and comfort in difficult times, providing shelter and nourishment, with edible fruit and bark that are used for a number of traditional remedies and products. The baobab tree is a common landmark on the African savannas; its trunk stores large quantities of water and is often tapped during periods of drought. In the awareness phase advertisements for Kenya Re, an example of which is shown in Figure 11.1, this traditional symbol of comfort and stability serves as a backdrop to a more contemporary symbol of an upper-middle-class lifestyle: a large home. As explained by one advertising agency strategist:

When you're doing [IPO] advertising, you want to show something that's aspirational. You have to use a vision that people can understand. This is a home. There is an insurance company behind the home. And behind the insurance company is Kenya Re. And it's a nice home, huh?

Figure 11.1 Creating familiarity with the industry in awareness phase advertisements

The consumer is introduced to the firm and the reinsurance industry through these symbols, as the advertisements state that home insurance, a more familiar product, is itself backed by reinsurance, thus making the potential consumer aware that even insurance companies purchase insurance, and Kenya Re is the source for that reinsurance. In advertisements placed during the latter part of this first phase, claims are made of the strong performance of the company. In the background of these performance claims, examples of which are shown in Figure 11.2, the consumer gets a closer view of the tree as more details of the company are provided.

Performance claims create a direct link between the symbols of prosperity suggested in earlier advertisements and a concrete method by which share ownership can deliver on those aspirations. Claims of high profit rates, growing financial clout, high market share in a common commodity, and other claims are designed to provide a justification for the idea that this particular company can fulfill the aspirations established in the earlier ads. The advertising agency's account manager for the campaign clarifies the idea further:

Figure 11.2 Establishing firm performance in awareness phase advertisements

Figure 11.2 Continued

You remember we had our tree, which was our symbol for Kenya Re; it's growing bigger and bigger, and now you're moving out to the branches; we're zooming in and getting more specific and telling people that our investment standard is eight billion and we're growing bigger every year. You really have to play. The idea is to play around with the numbers and interpret the numbers to people and tell them what they mean.

This playing and interpreting, however, can prove to be a bit of a gray area. In one ad, Kenya Re's credit rating is claimed to be "an impressive international rating of B+." Objectively, a B+ corporate bond rating is indicative of highly speculative, non-investment-grade firms by all major ratings agencies. Even if Kenya Re's claim of B+ is meant to suggest a credit score among the highest of the B ratings, this falls somewhere between an upper- and lower-medium-grade risk category. However, a population of potential investors unfamiliar with formal credit rating schemes is more likely to associate "B+" with an above-average exam score than a below-average credit rating. In another Kenya Re ad, also shown in Figure 11.2, it is claimed that pretax profit reached Ksh 719 billion in 2006 and that it is increasing each year. An investigation of the audited financial statements provided in the IPO prospectus, however, suggests that this is an exaggerated interpretation of the company's financial strength. First, Kenya Re's pretax profit in 2006 is listed in the audited statement as only Ksh 647 million (just under US$1 million), but more significantly, the post-tax profit of the company sharply declined in 2006, falling by almost 50% from 2005. The 2006 post-tax profit for the company was at its lowest since 2002.

Such exaggerated performance claims, however, fit with the advertiser's understanding of the receptivity of the psychographic types of potential investors mentioned earlier. Mainstreamers in particular, who make up the largest group of expected investors, are believed to be highly susceptible to claims of low-risk, high-return investments. In the agency's internal documents, the mainstreamer is "eternally optimistic and will vehemently try to maintain a decent standard of living. If the share offer is perceived to be at zero risk, with higher returns and affordable, they would definitely consider subscribing despite market conditions." For these potential investors, the strategy is to demonstrate that the firm has achieved a significant size, which in the unstable environment of sub-Saharan Africa can be a powerful symbol of stability and resources. In fact, the agency recognizes that firm size is an important part of potential investors' perceptions of value. In an internal advertising strategy document for the KenGen IPO, the first IPO following the 2005 Privatization Act, the advertising agency states, "It is vital for the company to look, feel, and act big. Big companies have big bottom lines and therefore big returns for the investors."

Figure 11.3 shows an example from the countdown phase, meant to generate a sense of urgency among potential investors. Here, the central message is that this opportunity is available only for a limited time. This series of advertisements provides a literal countdown of the number of days remaining in the subscription period, with ads counting down the fifth, third, second, and final day to submit a share subscription.

The discussion so far has focused exclusively on the print campaigns, but in addition to the print campaigns, radio programs are used even more extensively to access potential investors in more remote areas. In fact, the number of interactions between consumers and the advertising campaign is designed to be more than ten times higher for exposure to a radio advertisement than a print advertisement. Newspapers are considered a luxury item for most Kenyans, as only a minority of Kenyans are able to afford the price of a daily newspaper. Just under 500,000 newspapers are printed each day in Kenya, and each costs approximately 75 cents, about 40% of a Kenyan's average daily income. Radio, on the other hand, is recognized as reaching a much wider audience more frequently. The content of the radio advertisements follows the same pattern as the print campaigns in both intent and substance: the company is introduced in a manner that associates it with the same symbols and aspirations as does the print campaign, the profitability of the firm is introduced next, and the concept of becoming an owner by way of the IPO, along with the logistics of how to do so, is introduced last.

The radio campaigns, however, afford the advertiser one more way in which to incorporate location-specific familiarity into the campaign. Radio

Figure 11.3 Countdown phase advertisement

campaigns rarely use pre-taped messages, as is the norm with ad campaigns for existing consumer goods. Instead, local radio personalities, including disk jockeys and talk show hosts, are paid to present these concepts in a less formal, conversational manner, using local languages and dialects and references to local landmarks or other well-known symbols. Because such "advertisements" cannot be presented in paper form, little space is allocated for a discussion of radio campaigns here. However, a representative from the advertising agency summarizes the power of radio campaigns in addressing a culturally heterogeneous Kenyan population, made up of more than 40 different tribes and speaking even more languages:

What happens is that it is very difficult to target different parts of the country, but on radio you can do that because there are 42 different radio stations. So, when you're targeting Nairobi, you only pick those that broadcast in Nairobi. If you're targeting upcountry, you look at the research that shows what stations are stronger in different areas. In the pre-offer period, we use a different strategy to push people to go subscribe for those shares. It's called a radio activation. We empower the presenters, we give them a lot of information [similar to what is contained in the print campaign], and these presenters push the message to those people. On each radio station [in each region], they push the message in their own languages, so it tends to be more believable.

ALLOCATING ADVERTISING BUDGETS: DEMONSTRATING THE STATE'S COMMITMENT TO MASS RETAIL SHAREHOLDING

Employing different radio stations to target different parts of the country brings up the final element of IPO advertising considered in this chapter: the allocation of the state-owned firm's advertising budget across the country. IPOs, being rational business ventures, might be expected to stray somewhat from the stated goal of a populist-oriented approach to recruiting large numbers of investors in which advertising campaigns would focus on areas of the country with higher population densities or higher concentrations of upper- and middle-income groups (Meyer and Rowan 1977). This section of the chapter tests whether the state's rhetoric of mass retail investing is consistent with its allocation of advertising budgets, by quantifying how the radio portion of the respective advertising budgets for three privatization IPOs is allocated across the geographic and socioeconomic distributions of the Kenyan population. Data for the first three privatizations following the passage of the Privatization Act of 2005 is presented here in order to better establish the pattern in advertising expenditures across privatization IPOs. In addition to the Kenya Re privatization that has been the focus so far, data is presented for the IPOs of KenGen, the state-owned electricity utility, and Eveready East Africa, a familiar consumer goods firm that specializes in disposable batteries. The Kenyan state owned just over one-third of this multinational corporation until its 2007 IPO, when the state divested the majority of its shares and private owners floated a much smaller portion. The privatization of telecom firm Safaricom is not considered here, because advertising data for that IPO is not distinguishable from spending on other forms of advertising and therefore does not provide a consistent comparison across firms.

IPO advertising expenditure data was obtained from a Nairobi-based market research firm. Each radio advertisement has been assigned a valuation equal to the retail price an advertiser would be expected to pay for a particular ad to run in a particular outlet. The actual rate paid by the advertiser is unknown, as purchasers of large quantities of advertising are often able to negotiate discounts with various media outlets. What is available is a measure of the total volume of advertising to which a geographic region is exposed, and this volume is expressed in terms of its expected price. The volume of IPO advertising in these privatization IPOs is calculated using the geographic footprints of the 42 radio stations that broadcast across 16 regions in Kenya and the amount of radio broadcast time allocated for each IPO on each station. While data is available on all forms of media expenditure for each IPO, a focus on the distribution of spending on radio advertising is warranted for a few reasons. First, radio is the only medium virtually guaranteed to be experienced by all Kenyans, as lower income citizens are significantly less likely to come into contact with either print or television advertisements. Second, the geographic footprints of Kenya's 42 radio stations are more precise than those for print or television media, allowing for reliable calculations of the amount of advertising broadcast in each geographic region. Furthermore, radio advertising is the dominant media type employed in IPO advertising campaigns, comprising more than 70% of the total advertising budgets across IPOs.

Figures 11.4 and 11.5 show scatterplots of advertising expenditures in the three privatization IPOs across the 12 most populated regions in Kenya, with Figure 11.4 showing expenditures relative to the total population of the region and Figure 11.5 showing expenditures relative to the proportion of that region estimated to be in the highest socioeconomic status group. Only the 12 most populated regions are considered here because several of Kenya's regions contain few if any investors and receive little or no advertising exposure. Even if the state's goal is to establish widespread share ownership, it is an unavoidable reality that some of the country's regions are sufficiently poor that share ownership is not viable. For that reason, the analysis here restricts the focus to only those regions with a reasonable chance that some minimum number of individuals from the general population might adopt the practice.

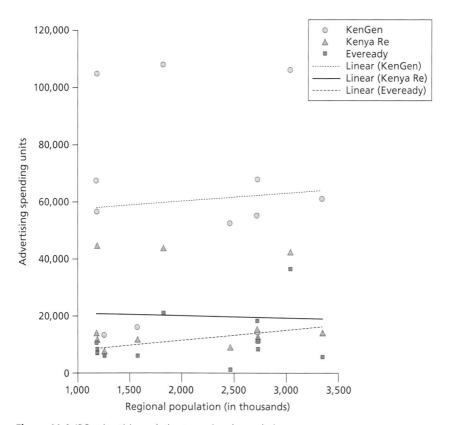

Figure 11.4 IPO advertising relative to regional population

Data for total population and socioeconomic status is taken from the 1999 Kenya Population and Housing Census. The proportion of the regional population considered to be of high socioeconomic status is measured as the percentage of residents of that region who report living in a permanent dwelling with an improved floor and roof, with access to an improved water source and a flush toilet. Given the difficulties of collecting valid income data in developing countries, measurements of socioeconomic status based on measures of standards of living rather than reported income are preferred.

Figure 11.4 shows the retail value of radio advertisements broadcast in the 12 most populated regions in Kenya in each IPO. Figure 11.5 plots the expenditure measure against the percentage of the region's population that meets the above definition of high socioeconomic status. Both scatterplots suggest that the Kenyan state is sincere in its commitment to recruit shareholders from the general population, because the state allocates consistent proportions of advertising resources for each IPO across regions regardless of population or concentration of wealth among the population. The trend lines for advertising in the KenGen IPO are only slightly positive, suggesting that advertising budget

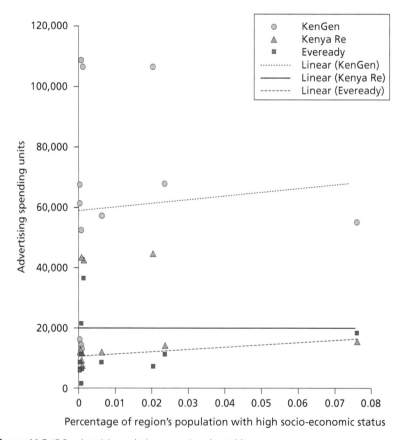

Figure 11.5 IPO advertising relative to regional wealth

allocations for this first IPO only slightly favor more heavily populated areas and more wealthy regions in Kenya. The trend line for Kenya Re IPO advertising spending is slightly negative for the total population and flat when graphed against the wealth of the region's inhabitants. Trend lines for the Eveready IPO are slightly positive, perhaps consistent with the firm's two-thirds majority private ownership prior to the IPO. Eveready is also the smallest firm of these three, one-third smaller in terms of gross revenue in the year prior to listing than Kenya Re and one-fourth the size of KenGen. When interviewed, Eveready executives reported that the firm had tried to minimize the total number of investors resulting from the IPO because of the high cost of servicing shareholders for a small firm.

The slight difference across the three IPOs, consistent in both scatterplots, may suggest that the state slightly favored more populated and more wealthy areas of the country in its first effort to recruit new investors during the KenGen IPO, but that by the time of the fifth IPO it had begun to target more of the country's lower income investors. However, this interpretation is called into question when one considers the range of advertising expenditures allocated to the least wealthy regions in Kenya. In all IPOs, the regions with the lowest concentrations of wealthy inhabitants experience both the lowest and the highest allocations of radio advertising budgets, equal to or greater than the expenditures in more wealthy regions. Additionally, in all three IPOs the region with both the highest concentration of wealthy residents and the largest population is the region including Nairobi, the capital city, which is the furthest point to the right in both graphs. Both graphs show that Nairobi receives less advertising resources than many other smaller and poorer regions and is also below the trend line for all 12 regions. The only exception to this trend is that Nairobi receives a slightly higher level of spending during the Eveready IPO than predicted by the trend line, a finding in line with a more private-sector approach to investor recruitment.

These patterns of allocating larger portions of IPO advertising budgets to smaller and poorer regions of the country are consistent with the state's overt goal of recruiting the general public into share ownership. They are also consistent with an explanation that residents of larger, wealthier, more urban areas might require less persuasion to take part in such an opportunity, since they might be expected to already be familiar with these large state-owned firms as well as the practice of shareholding. Or, if they are not familiar with these, they are perhaps more accustomed to other intangible assets and trade practices, such that these wealthier residents require less convincing to subscribe. The comments from one Kenya Re executive are in line with earlier work on the disproportional effects of advertising to retail as opposed to institutional investors:

Of course there was a lot of advertising, and we ran lots of publicity. Kenya Re owns lots of well-known properties [around Kenya]. This visibility helps. Especially with the retail investors it helped. I think with the institutional investors, fund managers, they know more and rely less on the advertisement. It helped mainly with the retail investors.

Concluding Discussion

This chapter began by identifying a tension that arises for many emerging stock exchanges in developing countries around the world: how to recruit a sufficient number of participants, such that the formal organizational structure established by policy makers is better able to realize its functional goals of mobilizing nascent domestic capital and improving liquidity in the secondary market. Numerous weaknesses in the formal and informal institutional environment in Kenya might be expected to make potential investors reticent to adopt the practice of shareholding, including weak property rights, volatile macroeconomic indicators, low incomes, a lack of previous experience with share ownership, and a historical preference for the use of tangible assets, such as land and livestock, as savings vehicles. The focus of the analysis presented here is state use of advertising campaigns that convey share ownership as a rare opportunity to access the state's material wealth by purchasing shares in a privatization IPO. Such a purchase signals an opportunity for socioeconomic advancement to a broader range of the Kenyan population than would normally have access to it. This process of democratizing shareholding in state-owned firms began with the regulatory reform in 2005 that enforced low initial share prices on the stock exchange, and the process continued with large-scale advertising campaigns for IPO events, which informed citizens of the approaching opportunity in order to mobilize their participation.

The analysis of the advertising campaign presented here differs in two important ways from earlier work by sociologists on the role played by advertising in affecting financial market outcomes (Grullon et al. 2004; Kihlstrom and Riordan 1984; Pollock and Rindova 2003). In earlier works, scholars investigated the effects of the presence of advertising on asset prices in financial markets. In the Kenyan context, however, prices are set by the state. Accordingly, the more appropriate measure of how advertising affects market construction is the extent to which new investors are persuaded to enter the market, rather than the prices they pay to do so. But it is also important to understand the content of the advertising itself, and this has been a key focus of this chapter. I have argued that Kenyans are predisposed to see the state as a rare source of material resources, both in the post-independence era of the 1960s and 1970s (Diamond 1987; Sklar 1979) and also in recent years, as neoliberal market reforms have swept Africa (Bratton et al. 2004). The aspirational nature of advertising campaigns therefore becomes a key feature affecting individual valuations of stock market participation, as potential investors come to associate share ownership with participation.

Approximately 90% of all investors in Kenya are lower-income, first-time market participants. This participation rate of lower-income actors in the Kenyan stock market bears a striking resemblance to participation in lotteries in developed countries, as studied by Beckert and Lutter (2009). These authors argue that individuals in vulnerable financial positions are increasingly willing to gamble on low-probability outcomes in the hope of improving their financial position. I argue that this willingness to accept risky, and in this case unfamiliar, behaviors and practices can inform our sociological conception of mechanisms that convey legitimacy on a practice, causing us to include in this conception signals that convey a high degree of aspirational valuation on products or practices previously unknown. In this way, the practice or the product itself need not be understood and accepted but rather can be considered valuable based on the image or ideal that it represents (Beckert 2010). In Kenya, the ideal is class mobility in an environment where mobility is extremely hard to come by, as opposed to an ideal based on consumption of luxury goods that convey a position in a social-status hierarchy, but the two examples are sufficiently similar theoretically. I would argue that investors are attracted to this ideal, rather than the practical reality it makes possible, by pointing to the extremely low levels of initial investment made by most investors. With these low initial investments, even very positive returns of 200% or more would not be sufficient to alter an investor's class position in Kenya. No amount of investing at the low levels enforced by the Kenyan state would provide access to the large homes or other symbols of material wealth featured in the advertising campaigns.

The argument presented here about how advertising campaigns legitimate share ownership to an unfamiliar population therefore has more in common with Preda's argument (2005) that promoting stockbrokers as a high-status group, or "men of honor," in the early centuries of investor capitalism in New York, London, and Paris helped institutionalize stock market participation. The trend in Kenya has been considerably more populist, with the state implementing policy reforms that allow the government to circumvent the negative influences of early Kenyan stockbrokers on mass participation and reach out directly to a public hungry for access to formal financial structures that were seen as exclusionary in the past but are now open to participation by the general public.

The larger question of whether or not a functional market has been created in Kenya remains to be seen. Certainly, a much larger amount of domestic capital has been mobilized in Kenya with the advent of mass retail investing, especially considering that the majority of stock exchange participation comes in the form of IPO share subscriptions. In this way, it is perhaps more useful to think of the Kenyan stock exchange, at least in terms of the masses of lower income investors recruited in recent years, as the sale of a product (shares) to a consumer base that resulted from a successful advertising campaign. But stock exchanges are not thought of as product markets; they are considered to be arenas for exchange in which an asset is initially purchased not for consumption or possession but rather as a store of value expected to be remobilized at some point in the future, something that requires selling the share and therefore providing liquidity to the market. However, other work by the author who investigates trading behavior by new investors after they enter the stock exchange suggests that the vast majority of the more than one million inexperienced investors recruited into the stock exchange have yet to transact their shares (Yenkey 2010). The material gains to be made by purchasing shares, the core ideal expressed in the advertisements, can only be realized by recognizing and acting on an appropriate time to sell those shares. The study presented here thus differs from previous work that investigates the construction of market actors as more active exchange agents (e.g., MacKenzie 2009). Elsewhere, I suggest that initial share ownership is an ideal much more easily communicated than share trading, a more complex set of actions that require a greater degree of market experience to negotiate (Yenkey 2010). Future research will need to focus on better understanding the type of market that arises from the constructive efforts described here.

■ REFERENCES

Aspers, P. (2009). *How are Markets Made?* MPIfG Discussion Paper 09/2. Cologne: Max Planck Institute for the Study of Societies.
Beckert, J. (2010). *The Transcending Power of Goods: Imaginative Value in the Economy*. MPIfG Discussion Paper 10/4. Cologne: Max Planck Institute for the Study of Societies.
——and Lutter, M. (2009). The Inequality of Fair Play: Lottery Gambling and Social Stratification in Germany. *European Sociological Review* 25(4): 475–88.
Bourdieu, P. (2005). *The Social Structures of the Economy*. Cambridge: Polity Books.
Bratton, M., Mattes, R., and Gyimah-Boadi, E. (2004). *Public Opinion, Democracy and Market Reform in Africa*. Cambridge: Cambridge University Press.
Callon, M. (1998). *The Laws of the Markets*. London: Blackwell Publishers.
Campbell, C. (1987). *The Romantic Ethic and the Spirit of Modern Consumerism*. Oxford: Oxford University Press.
Deephouse, D. L. and Suchman, M. C. (2008). Legitimacy in Organizational Institutionalism. In R. Greenwood, C. Oliver, K. Sahlin, and R. Suddaby (eds.), *The SAGE Handbook of Organizational Institutionalism*. Thousand Oaks, CA: Sage, 49–77.
Diamond, L. (1987). Class Formation in the Swollen African State. *The Journal of Modern African Studies* 25(4): 567–96.
Grullon, G., Kanatas, G., and Weston, J. P. (2004). Advertising, Breadth of Ownership, and Liquidity. *The Review of Financial Studies* 17(2): 439–61.
Jones, S. L., Megginson, W. L., Nash, R. C., and Netter, J. M. (1999). Share Issues Privatizations as Financial Means to Political and Economic Ends. *Journal of Financial Economics* 53: 217–53.
Keister, L. (2000). *Wealth in America*. Cambridge: Cambridge University Press.
Kihlstrom, R. E. and Riordan, M. (1984). Advertising as a Signal. *The Journal of Political Economy* 92(3): 427–50.
La Porta, R., Lopez-de-Silanes, F., Shleifer, A., and Vishny, R. W. (1997). Legal Determinants of External Finance. *Journal of Finance* 52(3): 1131–50.
Lynch, P. (1990). *One Up on Wall Street*. New York: Penguin Books.
MacKenzie, D. (2009). *Material Markets: How Economic Agents Are Constructed*. Oxford: Oxford University Press.

McConkey, C. W. and Warren, W. E. (1987). Psychographic and Demographic Profiles of State Lottery Ticket Purchasers. *The Journal of Consumer Affairs* 21: 314–27.

Merton, R. C. (1987). A Simple Model of Capital Market Equilibrium with Incomplete Information. *The Journal of Finance* 42(3): 483–510.

Meyer, J. and Rowan, B. (1977). Institutionalized Organizations: Formal Structure as Myth and Ceremony. *American Journal of Sociology* 83(2): 340–63.

Mondo Visione. (2007). *The Handbook of World Stock, Derivative and Commodity Exchanges*. London: International Financial Publications.

Moss, T., Ramachandran, V., and Standley, S. (2007). *Why Doesn't Africa Get More Equity Investment? Frontier Stock Markets, Firm Size and Asset Allocations of Global Emerging Market Funds*. Center for Global Development Working Paper 112. Washington, DC: Center for Global Development.

Pollock, T. G. and Rindova, V. P. (2003). Media Legitimation Effects in the Market for Initial Public Offerings. *The Academy of Management Journal* 46(5): 631–42.

Preda, A. (2005). Legitimacy and Status Groups in Financial Markets. *The British Journal of Sociology* 56(3): 451–71.

Sing, A. (1997). Financial Liberalization, Stockmarkets, and Economic Development. *The Economic Journal* 107(442): 771–82.

Sklar, R. L. (1979). The Nature of Class Domination in Africa. *The Journal of Modern African Studies* 17(4): 531–52.

Suchman, M. C. (1995). Managing Legitimacy: Strategies and Institutional Approaches. *Academy of Management Review* 20(3): 571–610.

Yartey, C. A. and Adjasi, C. K. (2007). *Stock Market Development in Sub-Saharan Africa: Critical Issues and Challenges*. IMF Working Paper WP/07/209. Washington, DC: International Monetary Fund.

Yenkey, Christopher. (2010). The Social Structure of Speculation: Investor Attributes and Short-Term Share Trading in Kenya's Emerging Stock Market. Unpublished manuscript. Ithaca, NY: Cornell University.

12 Coping with Contingencies in Equity Option Markets: The "Rationality" of Pricing

Charles W. Smith

Introductory Overview

This chapter is largely engaged in an empirically grounded account of equity option pricing practices. The central objective of this account is to show how such pricing is determined by particular coping mechanism used to manage distinct types of contingencies associated with these markets. These contingencies are tied not only to the complex and abstract character of these particular financial instruments, but also to the highly technological and global nature of equity option markets. As such, the chapter seeks to expand our understanding of the ways in which ambiguities, uncertainties, and contingencies are actually addressed in ongoing market practices. More concretely, as the chapter will attempt to document, actual pricing in these highly contingent pregnant markets tends to reflect a range of adaptive strategic actions rather than theoretically grounded attempts to calculate inherent value.[1]

The decision to focus upon equity option markets is due not only to the highly contingent nature of these markets but also to the fact that they tend to be more accessible cognitively and methodologically than most derivative markets, grounded as they are upon equities; they are also the derivative markets that the author has most intensely studied. The descriptive materials garnered from these markets' trading practices and presented here, however, are not intended as documentary verification of the theses presented, but rather as particular illustrations intended to elucidate the broader theoretical arguments

---

[1] This focus upon actual pricing practices is linked to the decision not to embed this discussion in any serious manner with existing theoretical texts that might be seen as associated with this discussion. On the one hand, both the markets and the concrete practices being discussed have not been subject to the specific types of concerns presented in this chapter; on the other hand, the general theoretical themes that are introduced in the discussion tend to have such lengthy and diverse histories that any reasonable set of citations is not likely to be helpful in either clarifying the texts or properly placing this discussion within its broader theoretical context. The particular citations made represent cases where the author feels that the reader might obtain further clarification to specific points made in the text or closely related to other discussions bearing on similar issues, though often from quite different perspectives.

being forwarded, which relate to the ways in which contingencies in general are handled. Given that these markets remain comparatively esoteric, some introductory comments would seem to be appropriate.

Equity Option Markets and Their Management

Despite the fact that equity option markets have recently been subject to a great deal of discussion and analysis, bearing on a wide range of subjects including the 2008 financial meltdown, they remain highly opaque and obscure to all but a relative few. This is not surprising given that options are not only inherently complex and quite esoteric financial instruments but are also utilized in a variety of complex and esoteric ways within financial markets. Fortunately, most of these complexities need not be addressed here given this chapter's much more limited objective, which is exploring how equity options are actually, not theoretically, priced within equity option markets. Broader questions dealing with underlying theoretical/mathematical issues, the legitimacy or overall impact of these options on the economy and society at large, as well as technical discussions bearing on their proper usages are not subjects of this chapter. Insofar as this chapter does have a broader concern, it is, as noted above, with exploring the ways in which the equity option pricing practices speak to certain broader issues bearing on the "rationality" of pricing practice and hence the social construction of meanings and values in general.[2]

Given that the exponential growth in option markets since the 1980s has been due in large measure to the general acceptance of the Black–Scholes–Merton option-pricing model, this stated objective might sound minimally incongruous. Most financial options and their various markets only exist in a very real sense by means of these pricing models. Without these pricing models, it is highly unlikely that these markets would exist in their present vibrant form. What is commonly overlooked, however, is that while practically all equity options are "theoretically" priced in accordance with Black–Scholes–Merton and related pricing models, in actuality they are continually priced and repriced in the marketplace, that is, through market transactions.[3] Admittedly,

---

[2] To ward off any possible misunderstandings, it should be emphasized that given this focus, this chapter deals with price-setting practices in auction markets, not production markets.

[3] The literature bearing on how options are priced, most of which does not speak to the issues under discussion in this chapter, falls into a number of different categories. The largest of these is probably the vast "how to trade options" literature written for the investor/speculator sellers and public. Most of this literature seeks to explain and show how options and various option strategies can be applied profitably in the marketplace. As such, this literature generally builds on the mathematical economic literature generated by mathematical and behavioral economists expanding upon and modifying earlier treatises on this subject. See for example McMillan (2002, 2004) and Natenberg (1994). The economic literature ranges from numerous quite technical mathematical economic treatises and articles to more political

"theoretical" prices play a role in determining transaction prices, but only, as I will attempt to show, in a quite secondary and general manner. To understand this difference, it is necessary to understand how equity options are actually traded in contrast to the way they are theoretically defined.

Equity options are "rights" to buy (calls) or sell (puts) particular stocks or other equity financial instruments at a particular price (the strike price) within a particular time period (expiration date).[4] Whereas the buyer of such options acquires the right to buy or sell the stock in question, the party that sells such rights assumes the "obligation" to deliver or accept the stock in question if the buyer elects to exercise his/her right in accordance with its specified conditions. The Black-Scholes-Merton and other pricing models are theoretical/mathematical models for determining what any particular option is theoretically worth in terms of various factors including its strike price, the present price of the underlying financial instrument, the length of time until its expiration date, present interest rates, and, perhaps most importantly, the volatility of the underlying financial instrument.

Such options are commonly presented as means for limiting losses due to unexpected major price moves of the underlying equity, or as means of generating additional income without incurring any major risk. Theoretically, this can be done in a variety of ways. An owner of stocks, by buying a put—usually at a modest price—below the present price of the stock, can guarantee his or her ability to sell the stock at the put strike price within the time period specified. On the other hand, this same person could elect to sell calls above the present price of the stock and earn additional income without major risk because he or she already owned the stock that would have to be delivered if it did exceed the strike price of the call before the option expired. In both cases, the closer the strike price of the option to the present price of the underlying stock, the greater the cost of the option and the more likely that it would be exercised. Both of these cases are commonly referred to as "covered" transactions, though the proper name for the put transaction is a "protected" transaction.[5]

One can also buy and sell options without owning the commensurate stock. This is referred to as buying or selling "naked." There is little financial danger in buying calls or puts naked except for the money spent in buying them; the

economic volumes, all of it quite unconnected to the themes and issues of this chapter. The economic sociological literature by and large does not address equity options; that which does, however, relates to some of the themes raised in this chapter though it tends not to be similarly empirically grounded (see particularly Mackenzie 2006; Mackenzie and Millo 2003). For related economic sociology literature empirically grounded in markets, see Stark (2009), Beunza and Stark (2003), Knorr Cetina (2003, 2007), Knorr Cetina and Bruegger (2000, 2002), Smith (2007a, 2007b), and Zaloom (2006).

[4] All financial options function in basically this manner, differing only in the types of financial instruments to which they are linked.

[5] The difference in terminology is because the term "covered" is properly used to designate a situation where one possesses the underlying stock necessary to cover an obligation to buy or sell, whereas in the put situation there is no obligation to sell the stock at the strike price. One rather has purchased the "protective" right to do so if the stock declines.

profit possibilities are, in contrast, quite high, though less likely, if the underlying stock has a significant move in the right direction before the option expires. A call costing $1, with a strike price of $105 for a stock presently trading at $100, for example, would increase ten times in value if the stock went to $115. The situation would be the same if one elected to buy a put similarly below the present market price and the stock went down in a similar manner. Not surprisingly, as noted earlier, the probabilities of losing one's initial investment in such situations tend to be higher than making a substantial profit. One would lose one's entire "investment" not only if the stock went in the opposite direction but also if it stayed pretty much the same or moved only slightly in the desired direction.

One can also sell puts and calls naked. In these situations, one automatically receives the present premiums that constitute the option price sold.[6] Doing so can be very dangerous, however, since the seller becomes liable beyond the strike price of the options sold if there is any movement of the underlying equity before the option's expiration date. If, for example, one elected to sell either the call or the put in the cases above and the stock then went against the seller by 25 points—up in the call case or down in the put case—the seller would lose $20 for every $1 taken out. A substantial amount of collateral is therefore required in order to make such "naked" sales. An important added factor if this occurs is that the amount of collateral required increases if the underlying stock moves against the seller.

While a substantial number of option contracts are bought and sold individually as in the various examples just noted, such transactions make up only a percentage of options traded.[7] A high percentage of option contracts—nearly all informed estimates being in excess of 50%—are bought and sold as part of a variety of "linked" option strategies, in which different option contracts are traded in combination with other contracts. For all practical purposes, the various contracts that constitute such strategies tend to be "naked," though by the very nature of these strategies different contracts offset/hedge the risks entailed in other contracts. A number of the more common such strategies have names including "spreads," "straddles," and "butterflies," each of which can take a number of different forms, including what are often referred to as "legged" transactions that entail different expiration dates. If these do not serve to indicate how complex such strategies can become, it should be noted that there are other even more exotic strategies that often combine these strategies in a variety of ways. (Complex option strategies can also be used in setting up various arbitrage strategies, which function quite differently than

---

[6] Since in the examples given, the strike prices are not in-the-money, the price of the options is pure premium. The phrases "in-the-money" and "out-of-the-money" refer to whether the strike price has or does not have any inherent value at the moment based on the price of the underlying financial instrument.

[7] Unfortunately, there is no hard data on what this percentage is since it is not possible to document the various "links" among all transactions. Knowledgeable estimates range from 30 to 80%; the most knowledgeable fall between 50 and 60%.

the strategies being discussed here. This difference will be described in greater detail later.)

What further complicates matters is that the various option contracts that make up these multi-part strategies can not only have different expiration dates but can also be initiated at different times. New strategies are added and old strategies are closed down or allowed to expire. As a consequence of this, traders do not manage particular strategies per se but rather ongoing "positions" made up of a variety of interlinked contracts "opened" (begun) at different times with different expiration dates. The equity option market is itself in large measure constituted by the ongoing management of such "positions," which include not only monitoring various combinations of linked transactions but also continuing the buying and selling of contracts. Given that these new transactions, like most transactions entailed by the various option strategies, are often entered into by means of "limit" orders, even the acts of buying and selling need to be monitored while being executed.[8] These demands are such that it becomes practically impossible in these situations to properly price specific options and as a consequence this is seldom done. Since the individual price of any given option within this ongoing process is unimportant in contrast to the net cost or price difference of the encompassing strategy, this does not cause a problem. Even the net cost of a particular strategy is likely to be secondary to an even more encompassing overall market position. As such, even the net cost—within reason—of a particular strategy may not be as significant as the need/desire to put it into place to protect a larger overall market position.

To further complicate matters, one's overall market position is subject to other factors such as one's margin position, buying power, tax situation, and other things, all of which are influenced by changes in price of the underlying equities of the options. Faced with all of these constantly changing and linked factors, it is not only difficult to price individual option contracts at any given moment but also unreasonable. The relationship between pricing and initiating the various linked transactions that constitute managing a complex auction position is the reverse of that common to most auction markets; transactions govern individual pricing rather than vice versa. As such, these transactions also speak to another deeper issue, namely the difference between knowing and doing and the privileging of one over the other.

To see meanings as emerging from practices rather than guiding these practices requires rethinking the normal ways we see meanings and practices as related.[9] It also requires us to rethink what we normally understand to be the function of meanings, particularly prices. In the process of wrestling with

---

[8] Unlike a market order, which accepts whatever the market bid or ask is at the moment, a limit order sets a limit, usually somewhere in between the bid and ask offer, on what price it will accept.

[9] The sociological literature bearing on the relationship between "meanings" and "practices" encompasses numerous works in the sociology of knowledge, social constructivism, pragmatism, ethnomethodology, and critical realism, to name just a few perspectives that address some of the issues raised in this chapter, too numerous to be noted in a chapter such as this, let alone discussed. As a consequence, the citations made in what follows are at best highly selective and limited to a few that

these issues, I was drawn back to a response I received from a highly respected, very knowledgeable stock market trader many years earlier to one of my opening questions: "How do market professionals make sense out of the market?" With a mischievous smile, he responded, "Every professional on Wall Street can give you a great explanation of why the market did what it did yesterday, but none of them can tell you what it is going to do tomorrow." In essence, he was saying that one's ability to cope with the market was not dependent upon one's ability to "make sense *of* the market." It depended upon one's ability to "act sensibly *in* the market." This distinction between "making sense of something" and "acting sensibly in particular situations" has its own lengthy history, grounded as it is in the very old philosophical conundrum of the deep disconnections between meaningful accounts of particular realities, how these realities are experienced, and how these realities can be managed.

Acting Sensibly versus Making Sense

The inherent tensions between explanatory accounts and experienced reality can be traced back to the pre-Socratic philosophers, particularly Parmenides, Zeno, and Heraclitus. This tension is linked to a number of classical philosophic disputes bearing on the relative importance of universals versus particulars, reasoning versus sensations, stability versus change, and ideations versus materialism, to mention just a few, all of which overlap each other in various ways. In the context of option markets and auction markets in general, these factors tend to manifest themselves primarily around the consequences and significances of uncertainties and contingencies, a matter succinctly caught in Kierkegaard's often quoted line that echoes what the trader told me: "Life can only be understood backwards, but it must be lived forwards." Or perhaps even more pointedly, given the underlying intention of the trader quoted, by the nastier saying, "Those who can, do; those who can't, teach"; or, to stay with the trader, "advise and make recommendations."

Markets are, of course, not the only situation in which we confront contingencies and uncertainties.[10] We confront them pretty much everywhere. In doing so, we rely on a variety of means for coping with them. "Making sense," which commonly takes the form of finding, creating, and imposing some sort

---

have shaped this discussion in one way or another. Three particular works and their authors, however, clearly deserve to be minimally noted here: Mead (1934), Garfinkel (1967), and Bhaskar (1979).

[10] In using the words "uncertainties" and "contingencies," I am here underscoring the extent to which my market trader understood equity markets as being subject to "uncertainty" rather than statistically predictable "risk" (Knight 1921). In this respect, he clearly reflected the dominant view of financial market traders in contrast to that of the majority of mathematical economists associated with option valuations. It is also the view that governs the "acting sensibly" modality that is central to this chapter.

of ordering narrative account on events initially experienced as chaotic, is probably the most common way of doing this. Another fairly general method is to engage in one or another familiar "routine or performance." While "making sense" entails imposing some sort of cognitive order, "routines and performances" entail imposing some sort of behavioral order; habits commonly fulfill this task. "Acting sensibly," in contrast, is a less widely utilized method and does not seek to impose an overall order; it is rather a method for handling the disorder. Though used with different frequency, all three methods work in different situations where different objectives are desired. The "where, when, and by whom," however, varies considerably. Such is clearly the case when we examine financial markets.

Successful registered representatives such as brokers, financial advisers, and financial commentators not only make their living by being able to "make sense" of the market to their respective constituencies but are also expected to do so (Smith 1981, 1999). Most individual lay investors, in contrast, do best by adopting a limited number of traditional investment routines and performances, investing a set amount of money in a set distribution of types of investments at regular intervals and then regularly recalibrating. They tend to do better not trying to "master" the market but rather by sticking to well-worn paths (Smith 1981, 1999). It is only a relatively few active traders who successfully utilize "acting sensibly" as a central coping method. And even these few tend to utilize this method primarily in the most fluid, contingency-prone markets, such as the equity option market. Given that it is with this market that we are primarily concerned, it is on this method that we intend to focus. So what goes into acting sensibly that it enables a practitioner to cope with contingencies?[11]

COPING WITH CONTINGENCIES BY ACTING SENSIBLY

The major difference between "acting sensibly" and the other two major strategies for coping with contingencies, "making sense" and "routines and performances," is that acting sensibly accepts contingencies as ontologically real. The "disorder" and unpredictable outcomes are not seen to be due merely to ignorance of one sort or another. Such disorder is seen rather to be rooted in ontologically grounded conflict of one form or another; the coming into contact with each other—becoming contingent—of different systems for example. The problem is not simply an instance of not "understanding" what is happening that can be covered up/denied by imposing a post hoc account on it or ignoring it through "staying the course." Real contingencies, in the form of disjointed events, require us to actually confront and manage

---

[11] While the "acting sensibly" modality plays a secondary role in most financial markets, as it does in most relatively stable situations, it is and has been favored by some, who are generally referred to simply as "traders" (Smith 1981, 1999). They are, in a very real sense, the poets of the market and like most poets, to quote James Dickey, they are those who "stand outside in the rain hoping to be struck by lightning."

them. Most of us do not do this very well. Fortunately, we are not normally confronted with these situations and when we are, we can generally distance ourselves from them.

There are some people, however, who for one reason or another—generally because of the nature of their jobs—confront such situations regularly. For these people, learning how to act sensibly is a matter of survival. Market traders are a prime example, as are certain types of surgeons, litigators, and kayakers, to name a few other examples that I have spent some time studying; they tend to function in one way or another on the edge (Smith 2005). Relatively little in the way of a general overview of what goes into such behavior has been presented for reasons that hopefully will become clearer. In essence, however, this absence is due to the fact that there are few if any obvious tangible commonalities in the ways that "acting sensibly" is utilized in different situations. Having been wrestling with this problem for some time, however, I would like to suggest a few.[12]

THE FIVE BASIC ELEMENTS IN ACTING SENSIBLY

Let me start by simply listing and giving a brief summary of each of what I would suggest are the five basic elements that go into acting sensibly. After doing that and before going into much detail regarding each, I will attempt to describe in more detail some of the conditions and elements that apply in equity option markets. This should better enable us to see how these various strategic steps are applied in these particular markets.

1. Identifying and Prioritizing Objectives

The key point here is to recognize that in acting sensibly there is no single objective. The constantly changing conditions that generally apply require one to hold simultaneously a number of different objectives, which need to be continually reprioritized.

2. Monitoring Manifest and Potential Markers

In acting sensibly, the major difficulty is not simply that there are numerous markers that must be monitored but that these markers come and go. The crucial task here is not to become fixated on any given set of markers at any given time, since new markers of importance are apt to appear suddenly while others are likely to disappear.

3. Identifying and Juggling Rules of Thumb

The need to identify and juggle a range of "rules of thumb" underscores the fact that in acting sensibly one needs continually to make modest adjustments,

---

[12] The various steps of acting sensibly that I want to suggest grow out of qualitative ethnographic research projects of different "acting sensibly" activities over the past decade or so, particularly financial option markets and to lesser degrees online/search engine markets, high-risk surgeons and litigators, and kayaking.

with the emphasis on "modest." Grand strategies seldom, if ever, work. It is necessary to match appropriate practical minimalist actions to particular situations.

4. Adjusting and Correcting One's Course

The need to adjust and correct one's course is linked to identifying and juggling rules of thumb. The emphasis here, however, is upon recognizing the ways and extent to which previous actions or lack of actions need to be addressed to successfully attain one's present objective(s).

5. Maintaining an Escape Route

The principle of "Maintaining an Escape Route" completes the circle back to "Identifying and Prioritizing Objectives," since a viable escape route is always an alternative objective. The underlying assumption here is that when all else is said and done, survival remains the objective of last resort. What might constitute a viable escape route at one moment, however, may not constitute a viable escape route later. As such, monitoring and maintaining a viable escape route commonly also entails identifying and locating new escape routes as conditions change, much as is the case in identifying and monitoring markers. Most importantly, however, electing to utilize an escape route represents a clean break from "Adjusting and Correcting One's Course." It requires that one abandon ship.

It is time to see how these elements play out in equity option markets, particularly how they affect pricing. Before doing this, however, it is necessary to return briefly to the different dynamics of the arbitrage strategies noted earlier and the dynamics of what has been labeled "managing one's position," which is our present focus. This difference is of particular importance since it highlights the crucial differences between pricing built on making-sense foundations and pricing built on acting-sensibly foundations.

While both of these strategies entail complex and generally serial purchases and sales of mixtures of call and put contracts, they differ in the types of signposts and markers that guide these transactions. Arbitrage strategies are generally tied to discrepancies in market prices and theoretical prices generated by pricing models (Natenberg 1994). These discrepancies are such that they are only observable when portrayed in electronic graph and chart form. In this respect, these strategies are like managing position strategies, in that they are also sensitive primarily to differences between and among prices rather than individual prices per se. These differences, however, as just noted, are linked to theoretical values/prices, which are generated by governing narratives and accounts that claim to provide a theoretical basis for making sense of these prices. These strategies, in short, are inherently "chartist" strategies.

Chartist strategies are clearly not new to financial markets. If anything, they have tended to be the dominant strategies proposed by the "how to become rich in the market" books and services offered to the public. There is a twist to these particular chartist strategies within option markets. First, unlike the chartist strategies in other financial markets that are normally dismissed and snubbed by market professionals, these arbitrage strategies are pretty much limited to floor traders and market makers in option markets for the simple reason that the discrepancies tend to be small and short term, making it practically impossible for others to profit from them. There is another deeper problem that is difficult to resolve that speaks to these strategies, namely whether the success of some market makers employing these strategies is due to the discrepancies between the actual and theoretical values of particular contracts or merely the gap in the bid and ask prices of the contracts to which market makers have access. Given my skepticism as to the utility of any form of making-sense coping mechanisms in the highly contingent character of option markets, I am inclined to favor the latter position, though such strategies cannot be ignored. It is the managing of one's position strategies, however, that I would suggest is the best evidence of the dominant successful coping strategies prevalent within equity option markets. It is to these strategies and the five components of acting sensibly as they apply to these strategies, therefore, that we return.

Identifying and prioritizing objectives in managing option positions

Ask most people why anyone would invest in any equity instrument, be it an equity option contract, an equity index fund, an individual stock, or pretty much any other type of equity financial instrument, and you are likely to be told that the reason is "to make money." If only it were that simple. Making money may well be an objective of most people invested in equity markets of one sort or another, but is rarely the primary reason that they became invested initially, nor is it usually why they are invested at any given moment. They are invested in financial markets because they had and have money and they needed and need a place to put it. There are of course banks, bonds, mattresses, and other places where they could put their money, and they often do, but equity markets are the places where most people are inclined to put at least some of their surplus funds.

Naturally, there are other reasons to put funds into these markets, such as excitement at being part of the market, sharing experiences with other investors, self-image, etc. (Smith 1981, 1999). First and foremost, however, one needs to have some funds. Even then, and ignoring the other reasons that might have played a role in directing funds into equity markets rather than under the mattress or toward government bonds, the stated objective of "making" money grossly oversimplifies what normally becomes a much more complex and changing objective, which tends to mirror the overall feel and flow of the market. In bullish/up markets, objectives are often simply to make money; in less bullish conditions, however, one is likely to be satisfied with making a little money and in a bearish market not to lose any money or perhaps too much money. In a crash, one might be quite happy simply not to be wiped out.

Just as important as the fact that objectives will change is the fact that such changes are likely to circle back on each other as the overall market and one's own position change. As such, the task is seldom to pick one objective but to continually evaluate and rank a multitude of objectives. In doing this, it is not so much what one would like to choose, but what choices are possible and reasonable. The decision, especially when dealing with option contracts, is not simply, "Do I want to become more aggressive or more defensive," but "How can and how should I do this?" It is not, as when dealing with stocks, the simple question of whether to buy or sell, though even then one must decide what to buy and what to sell and how much of each. When dealing with options, the choices are much more numerous and varied, as indicated earlier.

For example, one might want to "protect" a particular strategy by building underneath it another strategy. Let us assume, for instance, that one has earlier set up a SPY 10-by-20, 5-point put spread starting 5 points below a market price at that moment of 105 that had 11 weeks to run before expiring, for a net credit of $350.[13] Next, let us assume that with two days left before expiration of these contracts, the SPY has dropped 8 points, which is 2 points above our trader's bull's-eye—the price where he or she would make the most money possible from this particular spread ($5,350—the $350 taken out to begin with, plus the $5,000 on the 5-point spread). If the SPY closed at this price, the trader's profit would be $3,350—the $350, plus $3,000 on the 3-point spread. At that particular moment, however, his strategy is likely to be worth considerably less, perhaps as little as $600. The reason for this is that the premium of his in-the-money 100 put would have shrunk to very little, while the premium of his out-of-the-money 95 put would still be fairly high. While our trader would no doubt want to maintain his position in the hope of getting the full benefits of his present position, he knows that he is quite vulnerable to a significant loss if the SPY continues to decline. He might decide to convert this spread into a quasi butterfly strategy by building another 10-by-20, 5-point put spread underneath his present position.

---

[13] SPY is the symbol for the main S&P index fund. A 10-by-20, 5-point put spread, five points below the market at 105, would be a strategy in which ten 100 put contracts were purchased that allowed the buyer to sell 1,000 SPY shares at $100, and twenty 95 put contracts were sold that obliged the seller to purchase 2,000 SPY shares at $95. Assuming a 2.75 price to buy at 100 and a 1.55 price to sell at 95, this would generate a net credit of $350. If the SPY goes down less than five points before the options expire in 11 weeks, the trader will get to keep this $350. If the SPY goes down between 5 and 15 points, the trader will make between $350 and $5,350, with 15 points down as his bull's-eye of $5,350. Once the SPY goes down over 15 points, however, the trader will begin to give back this $5,350 at the rate of $1,000 for every point the SPY goes down. At 30 points down, he would have lost $9,650.

To do this would probably not cost him much, and it would protect him: he then would not lose any money until the SPY dropped another 6 points. He would still have his bull's-eye at 15 points below where he started, but would now not start losing money until the SPY dropped 26 points, rather than 20. One major problem, however, would be that at 26 points down, he would be losing $2,000 per point rather than $1,000. With one week to go, coupled with the significant drop that has already occurred in this scenario, our trader might want to build this additional put spread. Unfortunately, he might find that he has not got the resources to do so, even though the actual cost of the additional 10-by-20 spread would be minimal, because there is insufficient margin power to cover this new spread that results in part from the additional margin liability generated by the first spread. His choices might be limited to closing the spread he has and forfeiting the opportunity for a significant gain, or risking a major loss by doing nothing. He could also elect to buy back some or all of the puts he was short of and sell other puts at a lower price but with a later expiration date (what is called going "down and away"), for little if any additional costs, but then he would have to maintain this position for a longer length of time. He might also elect to sell some "out-of-the-money calls," namely calls with strike prices above the present price of the underlying stock, in an attempt to offset possible losses that a further decline might entail. Depending upon the size of this particular strategy, he could also elect to do a little bit of each of these additional strategies. In making this decision, our trader will also be influenced by whatever other positions he or she is holding at the moment. The bottom line is that in such situations, our trader is apt to be much more focused on staying afloat and managing the various positions than in attempting to impose some sort of ordering account on the situation. This requires being highly focused on one's condition and environment, which brings us to our second component of acting sensibly.

Identifying and monitoring markers in managing option positions

The key difficulty with monitoring markers when acting sensibly is, as noted earlier, that a given marker, no matter how important it might become, is not always there. When one is acting sensibly, markers have a tendency to come and go. In equity option markets, traders are normally permanently aware of things like the established highs and lows of both the market and the individual stocks that they are following, as well as recent trading ranges. The markers that come and go, however, tend to be the most important element: changes in volatility, narrowing and widening of differences between bid and ask prices for a given instrument, changes in differences between theoretical and actual prices, differences in premiums between puts and calls, differences in trading volume levels, changes in various sentiment indicators, and overall "noise" level.

In asserting that these markers both come and go, I do not mean to imply that they actually disappear but rather that their presence is not noted given their low profile under most conditions. Much the same can be said for the ways in which the flow of news, or more accurately the way the market responds to such news, is treated.[14] Even the most significant market markers over time are likely at any given moment to remain sufficiently dormant as not to be noticed. A further complication is that some key markers take the form of the expected not happening: these markers make their mark by continuing to remain dormant when one would expect them to materialize. The "dog that didn't bark" evidence made famous by Sherlock Holmes is an example of this. The absence of any increase in the trading volume or volatility of a stock or even market sector after experiencing an unexpected earnings jump or decline would be a market example.

Equally, if not more significant than the comparatively quiescent nature of many markers is the fact that in acting sensibly it is crucial that one not over-fixate on such a marker in the expectation that it will become more salient. Succumbing to such temptations can serve to make one miss the emergence of some other marker. The line "I may not know what I am looking for—or even better, what will catch my attention—but I'll recognize it when I see it," aptly describes the proper orientation when it comes to monitoring markers, and successful traders try hard not to allow themselves or others to disrupt this studied and disciplined form of inattentive attention. In their case, the line might be expanded to include "... and don't try to tell me what it is."

When a marker appears, it still needs to be interpreted within the existing context. The very emergence of most markers, given that most tend to be dormant most of the time, normally indicates a change of some sort; in themselves, however, they seldom indicate the nature of the change. For a marker to be useful, it not only needs to be recognized, it needs to be properly interpreted. Ideally, it should indicate something about a probable or possible near-term market change of some sort. Unfortunately, grasping what type of change is often difficult. This is true even for private, personal markers, such as one's own intense emotional response, which are important markers for acting sensibly in all circumstances with which I am familiar. A sudden adrenaline rush or an increase in one's irritability nearly always means something significant is happening, but it does not really indicate precisely what this is in any particular situation. If all does become "clear," and one has a sense of the type of action that should be taken, there is still the question of exactly what, if anything, to do, which brings us to our third component.

---

[14] News by itself, such as analysts' reports and recommendations, does not in and of itself constitute a "market marker" as the term is being used here. Traders cannot avoid giving such items attention, especially when media hype is involved. It is primarily the response or lack of response of the market that could act as a significant market marker for the trader, rather than the news itself.

Juggling rules of thumb in managing option positions

As with "objectives" and "markers," when it comes to "rules of thumb" there is always more than one rule that deserves attention, and these are often contradictory to each other in one or more respects, which explains the need to juggle. As in managing "objectives" and "markers," this juggling normally also requires resources of varying sorts; proper timing is also generally important. As implied above, the decision to apply this rule or that rule occurs within a specific context and in response to particular markers being monitored, which requires continuous monitoring; it is also necessary to give special attention to whatever feedback signals arise in response to what one has done or is doing. This often requires one to reverse or minimally change gears, if not direction. Throughout all of this, it is usually also important to keep one's interventions as simple as possible: do not overreact, do not oversteer, do not drop the reins, and do not panic or celebrate.

When it comes to specific market-oriented rules, different players have different proclivities. A representative list of some of the more popular rules, however, would include the following: when buying or selling, particularly in combination, limit oneself to small spreads between bid and ask prices; when uncertain about taking any action, consider doing half of what was contemplated; when in serious doubt, get out; never fall in love with any position; try to sell naked puts in down markets and calls in up markets; be patient; be disciplined; establish reasonable "stops," both up and down, where you need to take some action; be prepared to go "down and away" with your puts and, with care, "up and away" with your calls; be prepared to take a short loss. There are many more, and each can take various forms. The central point here, however, is not so much in the details of what each rule requires but rather that each rule is quite limited in what it requires. There are no grand strategies built into these rules individually or collectively. There is, however, a governing rule of sorts, which brings us to the fourth component of acting sensibly.

Adjusting and correcting course in managing option positions

The need to correct course in order to avoid veering into dangerous territory occurs in many situations and sounds like a fairly easy thing to do, at least when compared to generating a completely new course. Unfortunately, this is not always or even usually the case, since we are commonly disinclined to make small adjustments. We generally prefer either continuing in the same direction—what is sometimes called "holding one's course"—hoping that somehow we will return to less dangerous territory; turning around; or stopping where we are. Another quite common response is to convince ourselves that we never intended to follow "that" course in the first place. This response commonly entails attempting to locate ourselves in a quite different place than we actually are, often in terms of a representational model of some sort. It is similar to trying to find a location on a map that seems to correspond to where one thinks, or would like, one to be, in contrast to seriously exploring one's present location and adjusting one's course from there. It is this latter type of adjustment of correction that goes into acting sensibly, not the former.

In the market, this means examining and evaluating the positions one actually holds, not the market in general or positions one might have held if one had previously done something different. It requires one to determine what to hold, sell, and buy, generally in combination with one another; it also requires examining and evaluating one's available resources. It means focusing on what is actually happening, not what could happen, not what might happen, and not what one would like to happen. It is not an easy thing to do. It usually means accepting some losses that one had not initially expected, with little positive in return. It is primarily a process of limiting more costly later losses of one sort or another. With "corrective" actions, less is nearly always better than more. It is important to avoid jumping out of a frying pan only to land in the fire.

Most of the actual actions taken belong to the choices described in the "Juggling Rules of Thumb" section in response to the "markers" of one sort or another noted in the "Identifying and Monitoring Markers" section: reducing one's position; building upon an existing spread or other type of strategy; buying back part of a strategy and selling an "equivalent" part "up and away" or "down and away," depending on the situation; "taking in" equity or buying equity to offset a position; etc. There is also a very real sense in which any adjustment or change in course also entails reprioritizing one's objectives. In the more dire situations, the objective that is apt to be most prioritized is simple survival. In order to insure survival, however, more is often required than correcting course. There are times when it becomes necessary to close down or exit a position, which brings us to the fifth component in acting sensibly.

Maintaining an escape route in managing option positions

In acting sensibly, maintaining and monitoring an escape route functions as the "prime directive." Survival is what acting sensibly is all about. As such it is not surprising to realize that escape has in many ways already been built into the first four components. While generally not an explicit "objective," for example, it is always an implicit, fallback objective when objectives are being identified and monitored. Similarly, in monitoring markers, there is often what might be called a catastrophe warning tag. The tag signals major potential danger that may demand an escape route. Markers with this tag take priority over all other markers. Much the same situation holds true when it comes to juggling rules of thumb, in which rules that demand at least a change of some sort, if not an outright escape move, nearly always take priority when activated. Finally, escape also functions as the ultimate course correction insofar as it entails abandoning the present course entirely.

There is a somewhat ironic twist to all of this, however, in that as latently omnipresent as such escape routes might be, they can become lost among other objectives, markers, rules, and corrections. Escape exits and routes seldom come in bright red lights as do the exit signs in theaters, or with blinking lights as do the exit paths in commercial aircraft. There is similarly no map that designates "escape routes," for the simple reason that in situations such as option markets, where acting sensibly tends to be the coping process of preference, viable escape routes and exits tend to change continually. As a consequence, attempts to preselect an escape route are likely to be counterproductive.

In a highly ordered system where making sense is generally the coping strategy of preference, emergency exit signs can generally be usefully posted, but not in the twisting, rushing currents of situations like those that are characteristic of equity option markets. As a consequence, "maintaining an escape route" in these situations is more a matter of attention and intention than locating a place. What distinguishes such escape routes from "course corrections" is that escape routes are not intended to lead one to a safer course but rather, as indicated above, to remove one from the scene. This is an important distinction that an observer can easily miss. For the actor in question, however, it is a very decisive move. A few examples might help to clarify this difference.

Near the end of the "Adjusting and Correcting Course" section above, a number of commonly used corrective actions were noted. Where all of these actions differ from "exit" actions is that they serve to maintain the basic underlying position. An exit action, in contrast, closes down or minimally "locks down" the underlying position. Buying—rather than selling—puts below or calls above to cover an existing "short" position would be an example of such an exit. Such action nearly always entails putting additional sums into a position to limit further losses. This can also be done sometimes by buying the underlying equity/stock. For litigators, this distinction takes the form of deciding to end an interrogation that has taken an unexpected and dangerous turn as quickly as possible, rather than redirecting it back in the direction preferred. For surgeons, an exit of this type often takes the form of electing to close the patient up when confronted by an unresectable growth rather than attempting to make minor "repairs."

What all of these situations have in common is that in all cases, the actions taken are a direct response to a perceived danger whose cost cannot be absorbed. It is not the danger per se that is the issue; in most situations where acting sensibly is the preferred strategy, there is nearly always risk of significant loss of some sort involved. In these cases, the danger is seen to be too damaging to be borne. When acting sensibly, risk of sustainable loss is one thing; terminal loss, be it of life, money, or anything else, is another thing. This difference speaks directly to a deeper difference mentioned earlier, namely the difference between treating discontinuities and contingencies as ontological and thus inherent in reality, rather than as merely epistemological or cognitive limitations or failures in our understanding of this reality. Acting sensibly assumes the former view. Loss is real, not merely a theoretical probability. The monetary value of most options represents only a small fraction of the value of the underlying financial instruments to which the options are tied. As such, a significant but not enormous or mind-boggling increase or decrease in the price of such underlying instruments in a period of a few weeks—let us specify a 30% move—might easily generate losses that would completely wipe out a relatively conservative option position if not managed judiciously. These are terminal losses, as the 2008 financial collapse has shown. As this financial collapse reveals, clearly not everyone involved with options was acting sensibly. The great majority of those who got most hurt were those who thought that they could manage options by making sense of them. Those who survived by and large fell into two groups: those who pretty much avoided options and derivatives and remained loyal to a number of making-sense strategies, and those who traded options and derivatives throughout but did so by holding true to their individual acting-sensibly approach, grounded in their recognition of the inherently contingent nature of the market.

Pricing as a Product of Acting Sensibly, Not Theoretical Valuation

So what might we deduce from these markets about pricing? Financial markets, as noted in the beginning of this chapter, offer exceptionally rich strategic research sites, to use Robert K. Merton's phrase (1987), for examining and reflecting upon "pricing." What makes them even more special is that financial markets commonly evolve and change over time, including the emergence of qualitatively new markets such as the equity option market in the 1970s, providing us data bearing on ways in which these pricing practices change (MacKenzie and Millo 2003; Smith 2007*b*). In the 1970s, stock market pricing and evaluations were subject primarily to the governing narratives and framings that dominated at that time: Fundamentalists, Insiders, Chartists, and Traders (Smith 1981). The proponents of each orientation had their own ways of making sense and imposing meanings on the market and determining what different stocks were, or should be, worth. Their "making sense" frames also told them what to do and what not to do if they wanted to be financially successful in the market. Though each approach had its own views and rules, each was fundamentally stable and covered pretty much all contingencies that might arise. Over the next few decades, these governing narratives were subject to some modifications, but their basic "making-sense" orientations remained (Smith 1999). These orientations continue to dominate presently.

While all auction markets are subject to such governing narratives to some degree, these narratives tend to be subject to greater variations and modifications when the items being auctioned are less homogeneous than are financial instruments. If the stock market is about "defining value," the great majority of nonfinancial auctions are about "the construction of value" (Smith 1989: 174–82). The degree to which these narratives are subject to modification tends to be correlated to both the homogeneity of what is being auctioned and the regularity of the auction itself; the more homogeneous the items and the more frequent the auction, the more fixed the governing narrative. What are generally referred to as commodity auctions, which include financial auctions, as a consequence tend to be subject to the most stable and dominant narratives; collectible auctions with their more varied items commonly exhibit more varied and flexible narratives. What are commonly referred to as one-of-a-kind or sale auctions, given the highly idiosyncratic items auctioned and the highly irregular intervals between the times most of these items come to market, in turn, are subject to the most extemporaneous narratives. In collectible and one-of-a-kind auctions, the auction itself became a vehicle for collectively creating the governing narrative for that particular auction and consequential pricing of items (Smith 1989: 165–74).

It is the argument of this chapter that the fluidity, volatility, and contingency of option markets have served to limit, if not eradicate, the relevance of these governing narratives in determining prices further. Rather than directing and guiding transactions, prices in option markets tend to be the products of transactions. The transaction prices of most equity and fixed-income instruments tend to be determined and to reflect a variety of other financial monetary values such as earnings, dividends, cash flow, past prices, interest rates, inflation, etc. As such, these "external" transaction prices are a key element, probably the key element, in making sense of the market, giving it a rational order that can then be used to guide future actions. In contrast, as described in the account of managing an option position, individual prices are not in themselves that important. What is important is one's overall exposure to various degrees of loss under a wide range of possible situations. What is your exposure if the market goes up, down, or sideways, in the short term, long term, etc.? What is important are the likely comparative net outcomes for your market position, that is, your particular market holdings, under these different situations, not the particular price of any specific option contract.

In managing a position, consequently, prices do not govern actions so much as emerge as the footprints left by traders managing their various positions. Even then, prices are not vehicles for quantifying particular qualities or parameters. They tend rather to be means for tying together or "glossing" a range of different factors into a single agreed-upon measure capable of enabling participants at that given moment to freely exchange a particular set of financial rights or obligations. In serving as the means for enabling a free exchange of some item, such consensual prices are not functioning in an unusual manner. This is how consensual prices function in all markets. To agree upon a price for a particular item does not necessarily or even usually mean that there is agreement as to the inherent value of that item in terms of any particular aspect of the item. All it means is that there is an agreement on a monetary exchange value. This fact is often unnoticed in relatively stable markets, where pricing tends to be subject to dominant "making-sense" narratives that implicitly imply that the shared price reflects a shared view of the item's inherent value. In option markets, in contrast, where narratives play little or no part and contract prices are commonly generated in "acting sensibly" management of a range of different market positions, the extent to which a consensual price reflects little more than a momentary consensus about that specific contract's price is more transparent.

In privileging practices over accounts, option markets speak not only to Zeno's Paradoxes and the Kierkegaard and Trader quotes presented earlier but also to a number of other fundamental theoretical concerns bearing on the relationship of explanatory accounts and what might be called "material reality." I can do little more in this chapter than identify some of the most important, which I do primarily to indicate some of the broader issues to which recent developments within financial markets, particularly the growth of option and derivative markets of varying sorts, speak, especially when these markets are examined from a broad sociologically informed perspective. In doing so, I need to begin with an important disclaimer.

In claiming that "acting sensibly," as embodied in equity auction markets, is an understudied and underappreciated form of coping with contingencies, I in no way mean to minimize the importance of either "making sense" or "routines and performances." Without the Black–Scholes–Merton and other "making-sense" option-pricing models and the range of established financial market practices, the present vibrant equity option markets would not and could not exist. The underlying theme of this chapter is not that acting sensibly should replace making sense and routines and performances in coping with contingencies[15] but rather that it needs to be added to the other two if we are to have any success in coping with the full range of contingencies that we are apt to confront. The factors that make this so have been recognized for centuries, namely, the unavoidable limitations of any account, no matter how sophisticated or elegant, to successfully encompass all of the possible outcomes of any relatively complex system over any significant length of time. This point has probably been proven most clearly by Gödel's incompleteness theorems. Equity option markets might be considered special only insofar as they have a particular ability to evidence this fact repeatedly and dramatically.

---

[15] This chapter itself is clearly part of the "making-sense" genre, even if its subject matter might be "acting sensibly," though in my own defense it is a "making-sense" account that offers no predictive powers.

Concluding Thoughts

Why even the most sophisticated accounts fail to fully explain the simplest of events is another question. Of the various formulations that have been forwarded to explain this situation, those that accept an "open system" vision of reality have tended to be among the most perceptive, particularly those associated with the Critical Realism discussions of the last few decades (Bhaskar 1979; Manicas 2006). While not ignoring the various forces at work generating equilibriums and stability, the creation of every system or structure can only be expected to exert new disruptive pressures on other systems and structures insofar as all are interconnected through being open to the others. It is specifically when relatively stable, but inherently open systems, previously quite distant from each other, come into more intimate contact and consequently begin to exert greater pressures on each other that these systems become subject to "contingencies." The underlying "causal" forces at work within the previously separate systems begin to impact on the other systems, generating quite different and novel consequences. As a result, what might have been taken as given and permanent within each previous separated system is likely to be subject to unexpected change of some sort or other.

While more academically dominant efforts of generating and imposing predictive, ordering accounts of events often function to resist if not reject such contingencies, they are commonly recognized by those forced to confront them in their day-to-day activities. No place is this more the case than in financial markets in general and option and derivative markets in particular, where the limitations of all grand narratives are understood, if not always publicly acknowledged. This denial is not surprising. If sociology has revealed anything, it is the extent to which "knowledge" in practically all forms is not only social in origin and form but exists to hold social groups together by providing them with a shared, ordered account of their "world." From Durkheim's "collective conscience" (1933) to Giddens's "ontological insecurity" (1984), knowledge's prime role has been to provide us with "meaningful accounts" capable of supporting the inherently social human condition. It has been and continues to be the primary impetus of traditional folkways, religious accounts, and modern science. And "rationality," in admittedly various forms, is the guise to which all would-be accounts seeking to be accepted as "knowledge" aspire.

Here again, there have been many from Heraclitus to Nietzsche who have taken more critical stances or have at least expressed concern. How else to explain Weber's notion of the "iron cage" quality of the ever more "rational" social structures that he at other times appeared to celebrate (DiMaggio and Powell 1983)? Whatever our reservations and concerns might be, however, our need, habit, even passion to see our world as ordered tends to dominate even to the extent of leading us to deny our reoccurring experiences of our world as inherently contingent (Garfinkel 1967). This is a condition that pervades pretty much everywhere, nowhere more so than in academic disciplines, as indicated above. Academic disciplines have an innate tendency to generate ordered accounts. Academics, like priests, get paid for providing answers, the simpler and more all-encompassing the better. The social sciences, including sociology—whatever its claim as reformer and challenger to the status quo—are fully susceptible to this tendency. Having said that, it is also true that academic disciplines—particularly sociology, with its heritage of approaching knowledge critically—can be a valuable antidote for this tendency, especially when grounded in proper research settings such as financial markets, which provide a rich, varied, and ongoing source of data applicable to numerous issues including that with which this story began, "defining value." Few situations provide us with such fertile research sites for exploring the different and often new, even surprising, ways we seek to cope with different forms of contingencies.

If the account of option markets presented above has merit, for example, there is an ironic twist in what our financial markets might be telling us. In looking back over the past few centuries, the general consensus has been that there has been a continual, if sometimes erratic, growth of rationality and sense-making in the manner in which we experience our world and lives. Nowhere has this growth of rationality been more hailed than in the transformations of our economic lives and markets (Weber 1947, 1958). Options and option markets have been one of the latest actors to take the stage in this unfolding drama, starring as the instruments able to master risk and uncertainty by means of their highly sophisticated, mathematically grounded rationality. In these financial markets, however, these instruments seem to have given rise to a very different type of rationality, the rationality of acting sensibly: a rationality that approaches all governing accounts with deep skepticism; a rationality that assumes contingencies to be the norm. Whether right or wrong, this is clearly a message that deserves our attention both as it applies to financial markets and beyond.

Conversely, few disciplines are as well situated to shed new light on these markets and probe their depths as economic sociology. Unlike prevalent economic thinking that privileges theoretical models and other "making-sense" tools, sociology has a long history of debunking governing accounts and narratives. This is not to deny the emphasis that sociology over the years has placed on normative structures, but the discipline also has other roots, including deep pragmatic roots (Mead 1934) that approach meanings of all sorts with greater appreciation for their instrumental and emotive character. In order to mine the abundant data of evolving and emerging financial markets, however, it is necessary to utilize the full bag of theoretical and methodological tools that social science has to offer. This includes the need to collect ethnographic data as well as the quantitative materials generated by various public and private organizations. It requires generating descriptive accounts in addition to analytical modeling. It also will require messing up our hands, minds, and sensibilities. A contingent world by definition is not a cognitive or even a physically or ethically neat, ordered place. Markets tend to be fast moving, often dangerous currents, with plenty of rocks and even a few falls, but they can also be stimulating, instructive, and exhilarating.

REFERENCES

Beunza, D. and Stark, D. (2003). Tools of the Trade: The Socio-Technology of Arbitrage in a Wall Street Trading Room. *Industrial and Corporate Change* 13(2): 369–400.

Bhaskar, R. (1979). *The Possibility of Naturalism*. Brighton: Harvester Press.

DiMaggio, P. and Powell, W. W. (1983). The Iron Cage Revisited: Institutional Isomorphism and Collective Rationality in Organizational Fields. *American Sociological Review* 48(2): 147–60.

Durkheim, E. (1933). *The Division of Labor in Society*. New York, NY: Free Press.

Garfinkel, H. (1967). *Studies in Ethnomethodology*. Englewood Cliffs, NJ: Prentice-Hall.

Giddens, A. (1984). *The Constitution of Society*. Berkeley, CA: University of California Press.

Knight, F. H. (1921). *Risk, Uncertainty, and Profit*. Boston, MA: Hart, Schaffner & Marx; Houghton Mifflin Company.

Knorr Cetina, K. (2003). From Pipes to Scopes: The Flow Architecture of Financial Markets. *Distinktion* 4(2): 7–23.

—— (2007). Markets as Definitional Practices: A Comment on Charles W. Smith. *The Canadian Journal of Sociology* 32(4): 487–90.

—— and Bruegger, U. (2000). The Market as an Object of Attachment: Exploring Postsocial Relations in Financial Markets. *Canadian Journal of Sociology* 25(2): 141–68.

—— —— (2002). Global Microstructures: The Virtual Societies of Financial Markets. *American Journal of Sociology* 107(4): 905–50.

MacKenzie, D. (2006). *An Engine, Not a Camera: How Financial Models Shape Markets*. Cambridge, MA: MIT Press.

—— and Millo, Y. (2003). Constructing a Market, Performing Theory: The Historical Sociology of a Financial Derivatives Exchange. *American Journal of Sociology* 109 (1): 107–45.

Manicas, P. T. (2006). *A Realist Philosophy of Social Science: Explanation and Understanding*. Cambridge: Cambridge University Press.

McMillan, L. (2002). *Options as Strategic Investments*, 4th ed. Paramus, NJ: Prentice-Hall.

—— (2004). *McMillan on Options*. Hoboken, NJ: John Wiley & Sons.

Mead, G. H. (1934). *Mind, Self and Society*. Chicago, IL: University of Chicago Press.

Merton, R. K. (1987). Three Fragments From a Sociologist's Notebooks: Establishing the Phenomenon, Specified Ignorance, and Strategic Research Materials. *Annual Review of Sociology* 13: 1–28.

Natenberg, S. (1994). *Option Volatility and Pricing: Advanced Trading Strategies and Techniques*. New York, NY: McGraw-Hill.

Smith, C. W. (1981). *The Mind of the Market: A Study of Stock Market Philosophies, Their Uses and Implications*. Totowa, NJ: Rowman and Littlefield.

—— (1989). *Auctions: The Social Construction of Values*. New York, NY: Free Press.

——(1999). *Success and Survival on Wall Street: Understanding the Mind of the Market*. Lanham, MD: Rowman and Littlefield.

——(2005). Financial Edgework: Trading in Market Currents. In S. Lyng (ed.), *Edgework: The Sociology of Risk-Taking*. London: Routledge, 187–200.

——(2007a). Continuities in Markets as Definitional Practices: A Response to Aspers, Knorr Cetina, and Prus. *Canadian Journal of Sociology* 32(4): 505–11.

——(2007b). Markets as Definitional Practices. *Canadian Journal of Sociology* 32(1): 1–39.

Stark, D. (2009). *The Sense of Dissonance: Accounts of Worth in Economic Life*. Princeton, NJ: Princeton University Press.

Weber, M. (1947). *The Theory of Social and Economic Organization*. New York, NY: Free Press of Glencoe.

——(1920/1958). *The Protestant Ethic and the Spirit of Capitalism*. New York, NY: Charles Scribner and Sons.

Zaloom, C. (2006). *Out of the Pits: Traders and Technology from Chicago to London*. Chicago, IL: University of Chicago Press.

Part IV
Organizations

13 Valuing Products as Cultural Symbols: A Conceptual Framework and Empirical Illustration

Davide Ravasi, Violina Rindova, and Ileana Stigliani

Introduction

Before World War II, Piaggio was a large diversified producer of civil and military vehicles, ranging from small ships to trains and airplanes. After the war, in order to meet the growing need for affordable means of transportation, the company launched a scooter called the Vespa, which in subsequent years enjoyed enormous market success in Italy and abroad and defined a dominant design in its product category. The popularity of the Vespa line rested on a mix of clever design, appealing form, and the gradual incorporation of the scooter into a web of cultural practices that marked the changing lifestyles and emergence of new identities in postwar Europe (Hebdige 1988). In the 1980s and early 1990s, the decreasing popularity of Vespa scooters was associated with a general decline in the fortunes of the company. In the late 1990s, however, the relaunch of new Vespa models in honor of Piaggio's 50th anniversary played a central role in the turnaround of the company. The growing media and market interest in the years that followed suggested that over time Vespa had acquired a cultural significance that made the product far more than a simple scooter. This significance eventually earned the Vespa a considerable price premium over competing products.

The case of Vespa illustrates how under certain circumstances, products can come to be valued by consumers not only for what they do but also—and sometimes mostly—for what they mean (Ravasi and Rindova 2008). Research from several strands of the social sciences and humanities provides evidence that consumers' assessments of product value are rooted in intersubjective, sociocultural meanings, which are based on the systematic embeddedness of products in social relationships (e.g., Bourdieu 1984; Holt 1998; McCracken 1988; Sahlins 1976). As a result of this embeddedness, products become tangible, material expressions (symbols) of social categories. Consumption is therefore driven by motives that relate not only to what different products are useful for but also to how their owners fit into the system of social relations

(DiMaggio 1987; Douglas and Isherwood 1979). The value consumers assign to products is only in part "functional"—the extent to which these products can be used to satisfy practical needs. Part of the value consumers extract from products is "symbolic"—the extent to which these products can be used by consumers to position themselves within their social space. Management research to date, however, has given limited attention to the relationships between the cultural meanings attached to objects, the consumer value they deliver, and how these aspects influence demand. Some of this lack of attention may be due to the commonly accepted view of consumer demand as based on idiosyncratic consumer preferences outside producers' control (see Frenzen et al. 1994 and Beckert 2009 for critiques of this view).

One way to explain the limited attention in management research to the symbolic value of products is the management field's historical disinterest in consumption practices and processes (see Priem 2007 for an insightful critique of this bias in strategy research). In management studies, research seems to implicitly assume a demarcation between utilitarian goods (home appliances, fast-moving consumer goods, home electronics, etc.), mainly valued by consumers because of the practical benefits they deliver, and non-utilitarian or "cultural" products (media, arts, entertainment, etc.). Hirsch loosely defines the latter as "'nonmaterial' goods directed at a public of consumers, for whom they generally serve an aesthetic or expressive, rather than clearly utilitarian, function" (1972: 641–2). These non-utilitarian goods are assumed to be valued both because of the experience they deliver (Lampel et al. 2000) and because their consumption enables individuals to symbolically position themselves within a system of social relationships (Aspers 2009; Bourdieu 1984; DiMaggio 1987).

Research in the sociology and the anthropology of consumption, however, provides ample evidence that consumers use a broad range of "utilitarian" products as cultural resources to construct, maintain, or enhance personal and social identities (see Belk 1988; Davis 1992) and status (see Holt 1998), and that this form of "symbolic consumption," which initially affected mainly personal adornment and clothing, has been gradually extended to products as diverse as consumer electronics, beverages, and means of transportation (Holt 2004; McCracken 1988). While these diverse streams of research have provided rich accounts of symbolic consumption in terms of consumers' motivations and practices, they have given relatively limited attention to the questions of how producers influence the symbolic content of their products.

Past research in the sociology and anthropology of consumption has generally indicated how product design, advertising, and other market communication activities can endow products with cultural meanings through the use of verbal, visual, and material cues (e.g., Holt 2004; Wernick 1991), but previous scholarship has not investigated in depth the organizational conditions within which these processes occur and which may have an impact on their effectiveness. In this chapter, we first draw on work in the anthropology and sociology of culture (Bourdieu 1984, 1985; DiMaggio 1987, 1994; Douglas and Isherwood 1979; Sahlins 1976) to discuss how products acquire sociocultural meanings and become vehicles for communication, and how core competences and resources—namely cultural capital and symbolic capital—enable producers to endow products with desirable cultural meaning—that is, symbolic value. We then report on an empirical study investigating how heritage artifacts preserved in corporate museums and archives facilitate dynamics of accumulation and deployment of cultural and symbolic capital.

The Sociocultural Meanings of Products

Research in cultural anthropology (Douglas and Isherwood 1979; McCracken 1988; Sahlins 1976) and sociology (Bourdieu 1984; Simmel 1997) has provided converging observations that patterns of consumption convey and generate sociocultural meanings about owners' status and identities. Research in this tradition observes how products acquire intersubjective, sociocultural meanings because of their systematic inclusion in social practices and relationships (Sahlins 1976).

Because the social meanings of goods are determined within the system of social relationships and institutions that underlie and constitute the cultural world, they tend to be relatively stable and to be taken for granted by actors who are embedded in this system of relationships (Douglas and Isherwood 1979). Consumer research shows, however, that individuals not only "appropriate" the meanings embedded in the products they purchase and use, they also frequently act as co-producers of these meanings. Consumers actively work "to transform symbolic meanings encoded in advertisements, brands, retail settings, or material goods to manifest their particular personal and social circumstances and further their identity and lifestyle goals" (Arnould and Thompson 2005: 871).

Consumer behaviorists use the term "symbolic consumption" (Hirschman and Holbrook 1980) to refer to the purchase and use of products as identity- and status-markers, and "symbolic value" (Belk 1988; Mick 1986; Solomon 1983) to refer to the value of products as symbols of status and identity. Symbolic consumption choices are driven by individual understandings of the intersubjective, (sub)cultural meanings that are associated with an object and—by transfer—with its owner/user (DiMaggio 1987; McCracken 1986). The potential to become symbols and to offer symbolic value is not limited to the small subset of products commonly recognized as "status symbols." Rather, consumers are co-opting an increasing array of products in their efforts to fulfill their "identity projects" (Ahuvia 2005; Mick and Buhl 1992)—understood as consumers' efforts to express or claim actual or aspirational positions in the system of social relationships in terms of status, identity, or both. Whereas early research primarily emphasized the symbolic value of objects that are more identity-relevant because of their proximity to a person's body (Belk 1988), more recent studies have documented symbolic consumption in a broad array of product categories, including beverages (Holt 2004), motorcycles (Schouten and McAlexander 1995), cars (Luedicke 2006), computers (Belk and Tumbat 2005; Eisenman 2007), and cellular phones (Pantzar 2003). More generally, cultural sociologists (Bauman 2001; Ewen and Ewen 1982) and anthropologists of consumption (Holt 1998; McCracken 1988) share the idea that symbolic consumption is a central characteristic of advanced capitalist societies.

Symbolic Production through Design and Advertising

The idea that symbolic value has both subjective and intersubjective components, of which the latter is linked to social and cultural categories, suggests that consumers and producers can seek to strategically position themselves within a social system through the products they consume and produce (Aspers 2009). In turn, the cultural meaning of products is shaped by the engagement of producers and consumers in the creation, manipulation, and dissemination of signs and symbols, and the inclusion of products in social practices (Hirschman 1986; Ravasi and Rindova 2008). Institutional intermediaries, such as acknowledged experts (Wijnberg and Gemser 2000) and the media (Lounsbury and Rao 2004), influence the process by drawing attention to specific practices of production and consumption, and by promoting and legitimating the cultural categories that guide their collective interpretation (Lounsbury and Rao 2004).

Past research into the influence of producers on the cultural world has mostly focused on advertising and branding (Ewen 1976; Goffman 1979; Holt 2004; Wernick 1991). From a cultural point of view, advertising and other market communications activities disseminate representations about how a product can fit within existing social relationships in a society or subcultural segments of it. In the process, such communications transfer the sociocultural meanings arising from this association to the product (Holt 2004; Wernick 1991). Through this process, advertising supplies consumers with "bundled meanings" that suggest possible ways of interpreting the product through allusions to occasions of use and/or types of users (Scott 1994).

Recent research in management indicates that visual and material cues embodied in product form may be just as powerful in eliciting culturally embedded understandings about an object (Hargadon and Douglas 2001; Rindova and Petkova 2007). As cultural sociologist Paul du Gay observes: "design produces meaning through encoding artifacts with symbolic significance; it gives functional artifacts a symbolic form" (du Gay et al. 1997: 62).

Designers use specific elements of form to produce this meaning, such as shape, color, material, and texture to evoke the associations with desirable sociocultural meanings derived from various sociocultural domains, including other industries, consumer subcultures and countercultures (Ravasi and Rindova 2008), fashion, architecture, and the arts (Molotch 2003; Verganti 2006).

From a cultural perspective, advertising and design rely on similar processes by drawing from existing cultural conventions, symbols, and images to constitute a product as a symbol (Scott 1994; Wernick 1991). Both advertising and product design accomplish a process of representation, through which meaning is constructed and attached to products through the use of signs and language (du Gay et al. 1997). In this respect, both advertising and product design attempt to imbue a set of technologies with particular cultural meaning. However, whereas design encodes meaning directly in the object, advertising attaches additional meanings to the artifact already created by product design. Wernick summarizes these differences as follows: "Advertising transfers meanings on to a product from outside, through repeated imagistic association. Through design, on the other hand, that same signification is stamped onto it materially" (1991: 15).

The symbolic potential of products, however, may or may not be recognized and/or appreciated by consumers. As cultural theorists observe, producers provide "a series of possibilities that have to be realized in and through consumption" (du Gay et al. 1997: 59). Although designers and advertisers attempt to encode meaning in objects, consumers decode them by selectively noticing and interpreting only some of the many cues that make up a product's form or characterize its communication. The constitution of a product as a symbol ultimately depends on the meaning its design invites, and the expressive options it stimulates consumers to envision.

In summary, although ultimately the creation of symbolic value depends on how consumers evaluate products in light of their identity projects, producers can influence this process strategically by using cultural referencing in their product form design. Product design and advertising then become signification processes aimed at the production and constitution of material symbols. The use of product form design and advertising to engage in signification expands the symbolizing potential of products and creates new expressive options for consumers. When consumers recognize these options as relevant to their identity projects, they engage in symbolic consumption of these products, thereby realizing their symbolic value. When producers develop new products that have high cultural resonance and become cultural means for expressing consumers' identities, producers of goods also become producers of culture, whose choices influence the system of meanings associated with goods that circulate in a given society.

Organizational Resources for Symbolic Value Creation

To strategically imbue products with culturally relevant signs, producers need to develop specialized resources that enable them to gain deep understandings of the symbolic aspects of consumption, including how consumers use the products that circulate in a given society to express identity and status, and what position a firm's products hold within this broader symbolic system. In this section, we discuss two such specialized resources, which we term cultural capital and symbolic capital.

ORGANIZATIONAL CULTURAL CAPITAL

The concept of organizational cultural capital builds on Bourdieu's observations about how and why individuals engage in cultural consumption. According to Bourdieu, when analyzed at the individual level cultural capital involves possession of cognitive, affective, and even bodily means for "appropriating" meanings associated with art and other objects with complex aesthetic properties (Holt 1998). We use the concept of "cultural capital" at the organizational level to refer to the set of cultural resources, and the capabilities to manipulate them, that are deployed in value-creation strategies (Dalpiaz et al. 2010). These resources include concepts and understandings about the sociocultural world, and material artifacts of cultural significance, from which further knowledge can be extracted. Some of these resources are internalized by the firm in practices, texts, language, and material possessions; others rest with members engaged in the production of signs and symbols (designers, advertisers, etc.).

Designers and advertisers have been described as acting as "cultural intermediaries," as their cultural capital allows them to locate themselves at the interface between production and consumption and to imbue commodities with symbolic meanings (Bourdieu 1984; du Gay et al. 1997). Ethnographic studies of advertising agencies show that advertisers rely on both "formal practices of research" and their "informal dispositions and cultural identifications" to "extract" situated cultural knowledge from the consumer culture within which they are immersed (Kelly et al. 2005). This research has shown that advertisers draw largely on their personal experiences of the cultural world, and how they use their cultural references as raw material to construct meaningful advertising messages. Similarly, it has been suggested that certain design consultants act as "brokers of languages" (Verganti 2006), as they combine superior skills in understanding and anticipating the emergence of new product meanings with knowledge of the formal languages with which these meanings are expressed, as well as deep involvement in different industries, fields, and institutions where new trends in formal languages are experimented with, shaped, debated, and acknowledged.

The cultural knowledge that designers and marketers possess does not allow them to map every product to a specific set of meanings, but rather to envision possible bundles of meanings coming to surround an object on the basis of its formal properties or the way in which it is communicated, and to make judgments with regard to the cultural status of objects (Aspers 2009). Therefore, cultural capital enables designers, advertisers, and/or the organizational decision-makers who have to sign off on their creations to make more sophisticated judgments about what to change and what to preserve in a given form or the way in which it is communicated, to capture essential meanings while offering the possibility for new meaning-making.

Like other types of organizational knowledge, organizational cultural capital is partly held by individuals and partly embodied in collective practices, processes, structures, and tools (Nahapiet and Ghoshal 1998; Walsh and Ungson 1991). Occasional employment of cultural intermediaries may not be sufficient to give an organization the capacity to systematically engage in symbolic value creation. At an individual level, cultural capital is largely tacit and difficult to evaluate—even certified academic attainments, such as a degree in industrial design, may only attest to a minimum threshold. A certain amount of resident cultural capital is likely to be required in order to properly evaluate and coordinate the work of external intermediaries (Cohen and Levinthal 1990). Little is known, however, about the structures and processes that allow organizations to accumulate, preserve, and deploy cultural capital.

ORGANIZATIONAL SYMBOLIC CAPITAL

Some of the potential meanings that can be evoked by product design and advertising are associated with the producer itself. The association between a product and a producer is often alluded to by more or less explicit verbal and visual signs, such as a name, a logo (the three-pointed star of Mercedes, e.g., or the "bitten apple" commonly found on Apple computers and mp3 players), or other physical features (the Burberry checkered tartan or the red label in Prada shoes). These signs—which are generally understood as elements of brands—were initially used by producers in order to reassure consumers about the origin of their goods and the respect of certain quality standards regarding the functional properties of their products (Keller 1997: 27–8). In more recent times, however, the names of companies such as Apple, Harley-Davidson, Nike, and Armani—to name but a few of them—seem to have become more general identity markers, as the sets of meanings that surround these names tap into a broader user and use-related imagery than the mere functional properties of their products might justify. Their names and logos have become what marketers refer to as "lifestyle brands," in order to emphasize how these signs no longer stand for quality and functionality, but rather have become the means through which consumers transfer onto themselves meanings that are producer-specific and then use these to express personal or social identities (McCracken 1988). For example, the Harley-Davidson logo is apparently one of the most popular tattoos in the United States, and accounts exist of Apple or Nike enthusiasts who have had the logos of these companies branded on their skin. We refer to such producer-specific signs, and the meanings ascribed to them that create cultural expressions of identity and distinction, as "symbolic capital." Symbolic capital refers to the extent to which members of a social group collectively ascribe appealing social meanings to a producer and recognize an association with that producer—mainly through the purchase, use, and/or display of its products—as a relevant expression of personal and social identity.

As we pointed out earlier, the attachment of meaning to an object ultimately occurs because of consumers' adoption and incorporation of the object itself into their consumption practices. The acknowledgment of a product as relevant for the fulfillment of individual identity projects is likely to manifest in a number of consumption patterns, which contribute to building or reinforcing an intersubjective social meaning of the object as repeatedly co-occurring with certain types of people, occasions, events, etc., and not with others. The more that a product is readily identified in common perception and/or public discourse as having been developed by a particular producer—by virtue of design, communication, media coverage, or simply word-of-mouth—the more the meanings ascribed to the product contribute to the accumulation of the producer's symbolic capital (see also Aspers 2009). The set of meanings associated with the product in turn serves to construct or reinforce the social position of its producer as a "producer of meaning." In this way, whenever a new product is released on the market by a producer of high symbolic capital, part of the meanings that are generally associated with the producer and its name are transferred to the object, which becomes the material conduit by which consumers may appropriate these meanings and ultimately transfer them onto themselves (McCracken 1988).

It is important to keep in mind, however, that producer choices may both create and erode symbolic capital. For instance, design choices that are inconsistent with the meanings that are generally ascribed to a producer, such as a "boring" gray Apple computer, a baroque, flowery Armani dress, or an Alessi kitchen tool in cheap plastic, are likely to raise doubts about the validity of current interpretations, and possibly lead to a revision of the set of meanings associated with the producer—hence leading to a modification of that producer's symbolic capital. Sustaining symbolic capital over time consequently requires producers to systematically design and communicate products in ways that are consistent with the meanings that consumers ascribe to them.

An Empirical Application: Historical Artifacts as Embodied Cultural Capital

The concepts of cultural and symbolic capital—and their influence on symbolic value creation—emerged as central explanatory variables in an exploratory study undertaken to investigate the growing phenomenon of *corporate museums*. A corporate museum is an exhibit-based facility, owned and operated by an organization, which collects and displays artifacts (products, visuals, photographs, prototypes, and other material from the corporate archives) illustrating the history and/or operations of the organization to employees, guests, customers, or other visitors (Danilov 1992; Nissley and Casey 2002). This definition excludes pure archives, art, and antique collections maintained by firms, and other types of corporate collections that are not focused on the organization, its history, and its production. Corporate museums are found in a variety of industries, including automobiles, motorcycles, furniture, fashion, food, beverages, and banking.

Our study was aimed at understanding why organizations engage in the organized collection and display of a variety of historical artifacts, and how these collections affect organizational practices. Our emerging interpretations point at the important role that these collections play in the process of symbolic value creation. Specifically, we observe that these historical artifacts serve as "repositories of cultural knowledge," enabling designers and brand managers to reconstruct an understanding of the sociocultural meanings surrounding the organization and its products and of the material forms through which these meanings have been expressed. The cultural knowledge embodied in these historical artifacts, then, supports the development of design and advertising that are coherent with cultural meanings and expectations in society, and as such facilitates the deployment of previously accumulated symbolic capital into new product releases.

The case reported here is part of a larger study of four organizations: Alessi, Alfa Romeo, Ducati, and Piaggio. Our study relied on data from both secondary and primary sources. Our core source of data was 42 interviews with 38 informants: museum curators, key employees in each organization, and, when possible, external actors interacting with the museum. Data analysis followed common procedures for grounded theory building, starting with open coding to uncover common themes and initial set of categories to break up the data for further comparative analysis (Glaser and Strauss 1967). Throughout the process, triangulation among different sources and comparison across cases helped us prune, refine, and strengthen our emerging categories until we arrived at a framework that could be considered robust across informants and across cases. The interpretation reported here is consistent with our observations about how corporate museums were established, structured, and used at all four organizations.

SYMBOLIC VALUE AND SYMBOLIC CAPITAL AT PIAGGIO

Piaggio is currently one of the four largest producers of two-wheeled vehicles in the world. Historically, the fortunes of the organization in the second part of the last century were tied to its Vespa scooter—sold in millions of units all over the world and considered the "archetype" of the product category. The Piaggio Museum, founded in 1994 and opened to the public in 2000, contains unique pieces such as the Vespa Dalí, decorated personally by the Spanish artist, or the Vespa 125 that Gregory Peck and Audrey Hepburn rode in the movie *Roman Holiday*. At the time of our study, the collection included a rich archive comprising more than 150,000 documents and attracted around 25,000 visitors a year.

In Italy, the Piaggio name is strongly associated with its iconic products—the Vespa scooter and the Ape minivan. The Vespa was designed in 1946 by Corradino D'Ascanio. D'Ascanio was an airplane engineer (until World War II the production of airplanes was a core business for Piaggio), and the design of the original Vespa incorporated several features from aircraft design, such as the air-cooled engine, the stressed skin framework, and the stub axles. The new product, combining formal harmony, comfort, and convenience, met with immediate success in Italy and abroad and established a standard for the design of scooters to come. By the mid-1960s, in many European languages the word "Vespa" was considered a synonym for "scooter." Furthermore, over time the Vespa name acquired a broader cultural significance—as a symbol of youth, independence, emancipation, and coolness—that went far beyond its technical and functional properties as a scooter (see Hebdige 1988). As one of our informants put it, "Vespa is now an integral part of the culture, [and] not only [the] Italian culture."

Early on, we argued that objects acquire symbolic value as they are used by consumers to construct individual and social identities. Multiple observations suggest that this has been and to a large extent still is the case for Vespa. Over the last 60 years, since its first release in 1946, enthusiastic consumers—who went to the point of identifying themselves as "vespisti"—have formed hundreds of fan clubs around the world, using historical vehicles at cultural events such as gatherings, historical reenactments, and other forms of interactions, such as the spontaneous "silver swarms," mass assemblies of thousands of Vespa riders in large cities in the late 1940s and early 1950s.

The existence of a collector market for historical scooters offers additional evidence of the significance these organizations have acquired for some individuals and communities. These grassroots activities have been reinforced by the inclusion of the Vespa scooter in more than 80 national and international movies—including *Roman Holiday* and Fellini's *La Dolce Vita*—and other expressions of popular culture such as art and literature. As sociologist Omar Calabrese observed:

The Vespa is also one of the elements that forms a stable part of the landscape of our everyday lives... We find it in the scenario of tens of films... It was snapped by Renato Guttuso and decorated by Salvador Dalí. It was photographed alongside the Pope, the Shah of Iran... Gary Cooper, Gregory Peck, Ursula Andress and Audrey Hepburn rode it... Most importantly, however, the Vespas [sic] has been immortalized in millions of family photos, an object that accompanies personal memories and trips... (Calabrese 2002: 22–3)

Indeed, some of our informants observed how the fact that Vespa had become a cultural symbol required Piaggio to carefully handle the symbolic capital accumulated over the years. The Vespa's design, advertising, and other activities had to be sure not to violate culturally ingrained interpretations and meanings that surrounded the product. As the communications manager remarked:

Just think of how many people fell in love on a Vespa. Think of the movies where Vespa appears. All of this is transferred to the product and is part of the soul of the product. Then again, all of this constrains the product. That is, the product can't change much either, because it has some responsibility to its public.

While the rich collective imagery and cultural significance of Vespa gave Piaggio's scooter additional symbolic value, it also meant that the company had to take great care with any communications or design that might interfere with Vespa's cultural significance. The Vespa name and image constituted symbolic capital that Piaggio had taken advantage of for decades, but had also been wary of undermining: Piaggio essentially stopped redesigning the Vespa after 1979, and the company minimized its advertising campaigns from the late 1970s to the mid-2000s.

HISTORICAL ARTIFACTS AS CULTURAL CAPITAL

Although our informants frequently expressed feelings of wonder, awe, and admiration when referring to objects included in the museums, these objects were not considered mere pieces of artwork to behold and contemplate. Several informants stressed that the museum had been created first and foremost to preserve, and in some cases to recover, organizational knowledge and therefore to constitute what many of them referred to as the "historical memory of the organization." Although much factual information about the history of an organization, such as accounting statements, commercial files, and personnel records, was preserved in various internal archives, our informants believed that the museums enabled organizations to preserve and organize a different type of knowledge.

Objects stored in the Piaggio museum were considered by the company's designers and engineers as fundamental to developing an understanding of the distinctive combination of formal features—the "style" (Hebdige 1979)—that had historically characterized Piaggio's products. According to the chief designer at Piaggio, prolonged exposure to the old vehicles contained in the museum was essential to building a deep understanding of the distinctive identifying features of the products:

Designers must have such a product culture that they manage to identify the signs, the elements of style that define and characterize a brand... When I arrived at Piaggio, I already had a strong cultural background on the product, which I expanded at the museum. The museum had a very important role in this respect. When I was working at the Lancia design centre in Turin, I would hang out in the Lancia Museum.

In the mid-1990s, as a core initiative that was part of a broader turnaround process, Piaggio top management decided to celebrate the 50th anniversary of Vespa with a new release and a relaunch of the product and the brand. Informants from the marketing department and the technical office discussed the importance of the material collected in the museum—material which at that point was not yet on display—for the success of this initiative. Indeed, the team entrusted with the task of designing a new Vespa for the 50th anniversary of the product turned to the museum before even sketching a line. As the team leader remarked:

I came to see how prototypes were made, what the philosophy of D'Ascanio was... and I tried to understand how much care was taken in the course of the last 60 years to derive one model from the previous one... Between 1946 and 1977, the Vespa was modified every year, with great patience... At this stage, you humbly go to the museum and try to capture the differences in the models from the different years. That's why I tried to analyze motorcycles in detail, to understand the underlying philosophy and to try to readapt it to the GT and GTS.

Eventually, the team came to define a number of features, such as the shape of the front plate, the rear "hips," the stub axle, and the steel frame, as distinguishing the Vespa—in all of its various releases—from other motorcycles.

Products, however, were not the only type of artifacts the museums collected and displayed. Piaggio, just like the other organizations included in our study, had been involved in cultural events, such as exhibitions and races; its products were included in movies or other representations of the general culture and the company had received ample coverage by the media. These events had left visible traces in photographs, books, catalogues, and other artifacts documenting the inclusion of the organization's products in the cultural life of national and local communities. According to one of our informants, these artifacts collectively helped marketers and communicators make sense of the cultural practices and images with which the organization and its products had been associated in the past, and which formed the collective imagery that still surrounded the Vespa. For example, according to the Vespa brand manager:

Although everybody talks of the museum as a collection of Vespas displayed in the halls, at the museum there are thousands of advertising campaigns, logos, interpretations of the Vespa phenomenon. Vespa invented the first Dadaist campaign in the world of communication... The museum allows you to visually associate products and concepts.

The rich collection, consisting of thousands of photographs and images, documents how the Vespa became a part of the Italian and international cultural landscape. At one point, the Piaggio Museum sponsored a special exhibition involving prominent Italian journalists and sociologists in order to articulate and emphasize the links between the pioneering advertising communication of the company and the evolution of national culture and lifestyles (Calabrese and Fanfani 2002). According to our informants, these artifacts reflected the important sociocultural role that the organization played in the evolution of the industry or society. At the Piaggio Museum, displays of old press articles, photographs and excerpts from movies, and other forms of cultural expression traced explicit connections between the rising popularity of the Vespa motorcycle and the changing lifestyle and transportation habits in Italy, the emancipation of the less fortunate classes, and the constitution of "the young" as a social category. This perspective was made explicit by Piaggio's technical innovation manager:

Historically, Vespa was born to satisfy the Italian population's need for mobility right after the Second World War. Then it went through a peculiar evolution over time, so that by now Vespas are not objects anymore, they are history.

This rich collection was used as the basis to develop a deep understanding of both the sociocultural meanings associated with the Vespa (brand knowledge) and the distinctive material manifestations of these meanings (design knowledge). We argue that the combination of these two forms of knowledge constitutes a form of organizational cultural capital, since at Piaggio it allowed employees to reconstruct an understanding of (1) what induced people to categorize a scooter as a "Vespa"; (2) what users and occasions of use it was associated with in the collective imagery; and (3) the variety of meanings that had been layered onto the product over the years. Our informants argued that it was essential to preserve this embodied knowledge so as to support activities that would take the symbolic capital the organization still possessed and deploy it in new commercial endeavors, in order to relaunch the product after years of crisis.

DEPLOYING SYMBOLIC CAPITAL THROUGH DESIGN AND ADVERTISING

Designers, engineers, and marketers at Piaggio believed that because some of their products were deeply embedded in the national culture and carried strong identity-relevant meanings for some audiences, this generated expectations about the "appropriate" way to design and communicate new products. They viewed the knowledge embodied in the museum collections as essential to understanding, for instance, the elements of design and the marketing messages that would likely fit the beliefs and expectations of these groups. This fit was considered important for preserving and exploiting the peculiar meanings associated with the Piaggio name and its products—that is, its symbolic capital.

Many of these expectations were perceived to be focused on product form and characteristics, but they went beyond technical and economic considerations. As the technical innovation manager at Piaggio explained to us:

[When we developed the Vespa GT] we had to reconcile numerous historical, iconographical, design, technical and market constraints... We had to think of a form that was "Vespistic," because even if the technological content changes, the recognition of Vespa is tied to its iconography. The problem with objects that have become icons in the collective imagery is that they are now sort of the property of each and every one of us. We all have an idea of how a Vespa is done... In the museum there's the real one. It could be seen through my eyes or yours. But all models are here.

The same informant proudly remembered how the respect for these elements of style made even new unbranded prototypes immediately recognizable:

[The] GTS was a classic Vespa, but at the same time completely new, if compared to the still widely popular PX... Before the official presentation, I went for a ride around Rome. I stopped at a traffic light, and a guy on a Yamaha stopped beside me and asked, "What Vespa is that?" There was no logo on the scooter; it was recognizable because of its line and shape.

Issues of fit with institutionalized cultural meanings and expectations affect not only design or technical decisions but also advertising and marketing decisions as well. At Piaggio, for example, informants discussed the importance of the museum in inspiring and supporting the development of campaigns that resonated with ingrained cultural understandings about the organization. As the brand manager of Vespa explained:

The museum gives you a chance to immerse yourself in the Vespa world. When somebody comes to work for me, I send them for at least a couple of days to the museum.

One of our informants remarked how the rich collection of objects and images collected in the museum had been important in inspiring the communication that recaptured the heritage of the product and the brand and tapped into Piaggio's symbolic capital to enhance the appeal of the product:

Now that I work at the press office, I realize how much I take advantage of the museum. Now that we have the 60th anniversary of Vespa, I have magazines from all over the world asking me for photographs, stories, anecdotes, and for me the archive is a precious resource... The rebirth of Vespa could not have happened without a recovery of the historical memory of Piaggio... Everything we use now—photographs, movie posters, the *Dolce Vita*, John Wayne on a Vespa, etc.—comes from the historical archive.

When Piaggio marketers reviewed the museum collection carefully in the late 1990s, they were able to identify specific, consistent meanings in the discourse about Vespa—mobility, freedom, emancipation, youth, joy, environment. Thanks to innovative use of wordplay and graphics, Vespa's earlier communications had now also become part of the collective meanings associated with the scooter. The themes and style of this older advertising inspired the communication campaigns of the late 1990s and early 2000s that accompanied the renewed popularity and growing sales of the product.

As the case of Piaggio illustrates, museum collections enable organizations to preserve cultural knowledge embodied in historical artifacts (products, photographs, drawings, etc.). These artifacts allow for detailed observations and immersion into artifacts that have generated the sociocultural meanings associated with an organization and its products, as well as the study of the distinctive forms that have characterized these products. They serve therefore as material repositories of cultural knowledge and constitute organizational cultural capital. Organizational cultural capital, in turn, enables organizational members to make choices—in design, advertising, etc.—that external constituents would perceive as reflecting the cultural meanings associated with the organization and its products. As a result, they serve to preserve and enhance the symbolic capital of the organization, and to imbue new products with symbolic value.

Discussion

Our study improves our understanding of how organizations become "producers of culture." Specifically, we discuss how collections of historical artifacts in corporate museums can be used to accumulate cultural capital and to preserve and enhance symbolic capital. Consistently with research in sociology, we recognize that products acquire meanings beyond their immediate instrumental uses. Our study extends these ideas by observing how some organizations or their products may acquire significance for the construction, expression, and/or preservation of the identity of individuals and communities, and how through such significance, the organizations or products acquire value "beyond technical or economic considerations" (Selznick 1957)—that is, they acquire symbolic value. Our study further suggests that the acquisition of symbolic value represents both an opportunity and a constraint for organizations. As an opportunity, organizational symbolic capital allows organizations to charge premium prices and to enjoy loyal customers, to the extent that these meanings and associations are perceived as socially desirable, because consumers will be willing to pay a premium in order to appropriate the cultural meanings associated to a producer's name and products. Furthermore, consumers will express enthusiastic support for the organization, which contributes to the circulation of additional meanings about the organization and to the desirability and value of its symbolic capital.

Symbolic capital, however, is not only a resource but also a potential source of constraints. As we explained in the first part of the chapter, the (symbolic) value of a product is determined by relatively autonomous processes of consumption and institutional intermediation that are only partly controllable by producers. To the extent that the value of its products is in part culturally determined and culturally embedded, then, a producer needs to take into account institutionalized expectations about the appropriate way to design, manufacture, communicate, and commercialize these products. Conformity to these expectations is essential for the perceived "authenticity" of the product.

Violation of institutionalized expectations about the essential properties of a product may call into question the association between the actual product and the culturally embedded notion of it (or of its producer), and hence the capacity of this product to carry the set of meanings associated with this idealized notion. In other words, products that are considered inauthentic risk being stripped of their cultural significance and losing their expressive capacity as vehicles to signify individual and social identities. In fact, our informants repeatedly expressed their concern that violating the expectations of some key constituents might gradually erode the particular symbolic capital their organizations enjoyed. Conversely, developing products and communication that resonated with culturally ingrained expectations was perceived as fundamental for periodically reestablishing, in visual and tangible ways, a symbolic connection between the present and past events and products of the organization, since these had become charged with historical and cultural significance for the constituents themselves.

As exemplified by the case of Piaggio, the extent to which the organizations we studied were endowed with symbolic capital affected the amount of pressure on their members to act in ways that resonated with constituents' expectations. Preservation of symbolic capital, however, required them to first construct a valid interpretation of these culturally ingrained expectations. In order to ensure that new products were designed, produced, and communicated in ways that would be perceived as authentic, organization members had to build an understanding of the essential properties that defined the idealized notion of their products, and of the web of meanings that constituents associated with them. In this respect, the historical objects preserved in the museums provided the embodied cultural capital necessary to make choices that would be rooted in the accumulated cultural meanings of the organization and its products. To appreciate the importance of this organizational practice, it is important to note that product designs and communication are often seen as emerging from an individual designer's or marketer's vision, or in the imitation of current trends in the industry (Rindova et al. forthcoming). Museum collections play an important role because they store the same artifacts that over time formed the collective experience of a community and produced a collective interpretation by consumers of the organization and of its products. Access and exposure to these artifacts through the museum collections helped organizational members to reconstruct a sense of the organization as it might be perceived by its stakeholder audiences. As a result, the knowledge gleaned from the historical artifacts collected in museums enabled organizations to take actions that were perceived as both coherent with the organization's distinctive character and style, and as fitting with established cultural interpretations.

Conclusion

Research in strategy and organization studies is paying increasing attention to how producers draw on cultural and symbolic resources to support innovation and competition (Dalpiaz et al. 2010). Investigation of the organizational resources and structures through which producers can engage in symbolic value creation, however, is still in its infancy. While evidence from several fields in the social sciences points to the increasing relevance of cultural dynamics in consumption and value creation, strategy and organizational researchers (with some notable exceptions) have not engaged actively with these issues (see Lawrence and Phillips 2002; Ravasi and Rindova 2008; Rindova et al. 2011).

The dynamics of value creation described in this chapter differ from the conventional wisdom in strategy and innovation research, where the pursuit of value creation is associated with technological innovations that enable functional changes that appeal to existing or new customers (e.g., Bower and Christensen 1995). Our approach proposes a complementary perspective by drawing attention to the role of organizations as producers of cultural objects that are valued by consumers, because these objects provide consumers with additional possibilities to express identity and status through consumption choices. Building on research in cultural sociology and the anthropology of consumption, we discuss how concepts such as symbolic value, cultural capital, and symbolic capital, when applied to the organizational level of analysis, can increase our understanding of how producers of consumer goods can produce cultural symbols valued by customers. We used the case of Piaggio, which is part of a comparative study of the uses of corporate museums, to illustrate the distinctive organizational practices that emerge when organizations attend to the accumulation of cultural and symbolic resources. We hope that these insights will stimulate future organizational research on the practices, processes, and consequences for organizations engaging in symbolic value creation.

REFERENCES

Ahuvia, A. C. (2005). Beyond the Extended Self: Loved Objects and Consumers' Identity Narratives. *Journal of Consumer Research* 32(1): 171–84.

Arnould, E. J. and Thompson, C. J. (2005). Consumer Culture Theory (CCT): Twenty Years of Research. *Journal of Consumer Research* 31(4): 868–82.

Aspers, P. (2009). Knowledge and Valuation in Markets. *Theory and Society* 39(2): 111–31.
Bauman, Z. (2001). Consuming Life. *Journal of Consumer Culture* 1: 9–29.
Beckert, J. (2009). The Social Order of Markets. *Theory and Society* 38: 245–69.
Belk, R. W. (1988). Possession and the Extended Self. *Journal of Consumer Research* 15: 139–68.
—— and Tumbat, G. (2005). The Cult of Macintosh. *Consumption, Markets and Culture* 8(3): 205–18.
Bourdieu, P. (1984). *Distinction: A Social Critique of Judgment and Taste*. Cambridge, MA: Harvard University Press.
—— (1985). The Market for Symbolic Goods. *Poetics* 14: 13–44.
Bower, J. L. and Christensen, C. M. (1995). Disruptive Technologies: Catching the Wave. *Harvard Business Review* 73(1): 43–53.
Calabrese, O. (2002). Birth and History of an Object of Desire. In O. Calabrese and T. Fanfani (eds.), *Chi Vespa è... già domani*. Bologna: Editrice Compositori, 19–23.
—— and Fanfani, T. (2002). *Chi Vespa è... già domani*. Bologna: Editrice Compositori.
Cohen, W. and Levinthal, D. (1990). Absorptive Capacity: A New Perspective on Learning and Innovation. *Administrative Science Quarterly* 35: 128–52.
Dalpiaz, E., Rindova, V., and Ravasi, D. (2010). Where Strategy Meets Culture: The Neglected Role of Cultural and Symbolic Resources in Strategy Research. In J.A.C Baum and J. Lampel (eds.), *Advances in Strategy Management, Volume 27: The Globalization of Strategy Research*. Bingley: Emerald, 175–208.
Danilov, V. (1992). *A Planning Guide for Corporate Museums, Galleries, and Visitor Centers*. Westport, CT: Greenwood Press.
Davis, F. (1992). *Fashion, Culture, and Identity*. Chicago, IL: University of Chicago Press.
DiMaggio, P. (1987). Classification in Art. *American Sociological Review* 52: 440–55.
—— (1994). Culture and Economy. In N. Smelser and R. Swedberg (eds.), *The Handbook of Economic Sociology*. Princeton, NJ: Princeton University Press.
Douglas, M. and Isherwood, B. (1979). *The World of Goods: Towards an Anthropology of Consumption*. New York, NY: Basic Books.
du Gay, P., Hall, S., Janes, L., Mackay, H., and Negus, K. (1997). *Doing Cultural Studies: The Story of the Sony Walkman*. London: Sage.
Eisenman, M. (2007). Cultivating Taste: Constructing the Importance of Product Aesthetics in Technological Industries. In G. T. Solomon (ed.), *Proceedings of the Sixty-Sixth Annual Meeting of the Academy of Management* (CD), ISSN 1543-8643.
Ewen, S. (1976). *Captains of Consciousness: Advertising and the Social Roots of the Consumer Culture*. New York, NY: McGraw-Hill.
—— and Ewen, E. (1982). *Channels of Desire: Mass Images and the Shaping of American Consciousness*. New York, NY: McGraw-Hill.
Frenzen, J., Hirsch, P. M., and Zerrillo, P. C. (1994). Consumption, Preferences and Changing Lifestyles. In N. J. Smelser and R. Swedberg (eds.), *The Handbook of Economic Sociology*. Princeton, NJ: Princeton University Press.
Glaser, B. G. and Strauss, A. L. (1967). *The Discovery of Grounded Theory*. New York, NY: Aldine.
Goffman, E. (1979). *Gender Advertisements: Studies in the Anthropology of Visual Communication*. New York, NY: Harper and Row.

Hargadon, A. B. and Douglas, Y. (2001). When Innovations Meet Institutions: Edison and the Design of the Electric Light. *Administrative Science Quarterly* 46: 476–501.

Hebdige, D. (1979). *Subculture: The Meaning of Style*. London: Methuen.

——(1988). *Hiding in the Light. On Images and Things*. London: Routledge.

Hirsch, P. M. (1972). Processing Fads and Fashion: An Organization-Set Analysis of Cultural Industry Systems. *American Journal of Sociology* 77: 639–59.

Hirschman, E. C. (1986). The Creation of Product Symbolism. *Advances in Consumer Research* 13: 327–31.

——and Holbrook, M. B. (1980). *Symbolic Consumer Behavior*. Ann Arbor, MI: Association for Consumer Research.

Holt, D. B. (1998). Does Cultural Capital Structure American Consumption? *Journal of Consumer Research* 25: 1–25.

——(2004). *How Brands Become Icons*. Cambridge, MA: Harvard Business School Press.

Keller, K. L. (1997). *Strategic Brand Management. Building, Measuring, and Managing Brand Equity*. Upper Saddle River, NJ: Prentice-Hall.

Kelly, A., Lawlor, K., and O'Donohe, S. (2005). Encoding Advertisements: The Creative Perspective. *Journal of Marketing Management* 21: 505–28.

Lampel, J., Lant, T., and Shamsie, J. (2000). Balancing Act: Learning from Organizing Practices in Cultural Industries. *Organization Science* 11(3): 263–9.

Lawrence, T. and Phillips, N. (2002). Understanding Cultural Industries. *Journal of Management Inquiry* 11(4): 430–41.

Lounsbury, M. and Rao, H. (2004). Sources of Durability and Change in Market Classifications: A Study of the Reconstitution of Product Categories in the American Mutual Fund Industry, 1944–1985. *Social Forces* 82(3): 969–99.

Luedicke, M. K. (2006). Brand Community Under Fire: The Role of Social Environments for the HUMMER Brand Community. *Advances in Consumer Research* 33: 486–93.

McCracken, G. (1986). Culture and Consumption: A Theoretical Account of the Structure and Movement of the Cultural Meaning of Consumer Goods. *Journal of Consumer Research* 13: 71–84.

——(1988). *Culture and Consumption: New Approaches to the Symbolic of Consumer Goods and Activities*. Bloomington, IN: Indiana University Press.

Mick, D. G. (1986). Consumer Research and Semiotics: Exploring the Morphology of Signs, Symbols, and Significance. *Journal of Consumer Research* 13: 196–213.

——and Buhl, C. (1992). A Meaning-based Model Advertising Experience. *Journal of Consumer Research* 19: 317–38.

Molotch, H. L. (2003). *Where Stuff Comes From: How Toasters, Toilets, Cars, Computers, and Many Other Things Come to Be as They Are*. New York, NY: Routledge.

Nahapiet, J. and Ghoshal, S. (1998). Social Capital, Intellectual Capital, and the Organizational Advantage. *Academy of Management Review* 23(2): 242–66.

Nissley, N. and Casey, A. (2002). The Politics of the Exhibition: Viewing Corporate Museums through the Paradigmatic Lens of Organizational Memory. *British Journal of Management* 13: S35–S45.

Pantzar, M. (2003). Tools or Toys: Inventing the Need for Domestic Appliances in Postwar and Postmodern Finland. *Journal of Advertising* 32(1): 83–93.

Priem, R. L. (2007). A Consumer Perspective on Value Creation. *Academy of Management Review* 32(1): 219–35.

Ravasi, D. and Rindova, V. (2008). Symbolic Value Creation. In D. Barry and H. Hansen (eds.), *New Approaches in Management and Organization*. London: Sage, 270–84.

Rindova, V. P., Dalpiaz, E., and Ravasi, D. (2011). A Cultural Quest: A Study of Organizational Use of Cultural Resources in Strategy Formation. *Organization Science* 22(2): 413–31.

——and Petkova, A. (2007). When is a New Thing a Good Thing? Technological Change, Product Form Design, and Perceptions of Value for Product Innovations. *Organization Science* 18(2): 217–32.

Sahlins, M. (1976). *Culture and Practical Reason*. Chicago, IL: University of Chicago Press.

Schouten, J. W. and McAlexander, J. H. (1995). Subcultures of Consumption: An Ethnography of the New Bikers. *Journal of Consumer Research* 22: 43–61.

Scott, L. M. (1994). Images in Advertising: The Need for a Theory of Visual Rhetoric. *Journal of Consumer Research* 21: 252–73.

Selznick, P. (1957). *Leadership in Administration: A Sociological Interpretation*. Evanston, IL: Row, Peterson.

Simmel, G. (1905/1997). *Simmel on Culture: Selected Writings*. London: Sage.

Solomon, M. R. (1983). The Role of Products as Social Stimuli: A Symbolic Interactionism Perspective. *Journal of Consumer Research* 10: 319–29.

Verganti, R. (2006). Innovating Through Design. *Harvard Business Review* 84(12): 114–22.

Walsh, J. P. and Ungson, G. R. (1991). Organizational Memory. *Academy of Management Review* 16(1): 57–91.

Wernick, A. (1991). *Promotional Culture. Advertising, Ideology and Symbolic Expression*. London: Sage.

Wijnberg, N. M. and Gemser, G. (2000). Adding Value to Innovation: Impressionism and the Transformation of the Selection System in Visual Arts. *Organization Science* 11(3): 323–9.

Postscript

14 What's Valuable?

*David Stark**

John Dewey is an appropriate starting point for discussing a volume on *The Worth of Goods: Valuation and Pricing in the Economy*—not least because Dewey's *Theory of Valuation*, published in 1939, was a major contribution to the study of the core problems addressed in the chapters collected here. Like Dewey, all of the authors in this volume argue that valuation cannot be reduced to pricing. While insisting on this distinction as the *sine qua non* of a sociological approach to valuation, they also sound a note of caution about being too quick to accept some other received distinctions. Like Dewey, several challenge the opposition between calculation and judgment, and many point to the ways in which value and values are frequently entangled.

Perhaps more than anyone who has written on this topic, Dewey was aware not only of how everyday language constrains our thinking but also of how it can reveal insights about the concepts we deploy. In his *Theory of Valuation*, Dewey explores the double meanings in ordinary speech and points to words such as "praise" and "appraise" that parse in different directions from a common root. After noting the twins "estimate" and "esteem," Dewey observes that it is suggestive "that praise, prize, and price are all derived from the same Latin word; that appreciate and appraise were once used interchangeably; and that 'dear' is still used as equivalent both to 'precious' and to 'costly' in monetary price" (Dewey 1939: 5–6).

Dewey's triplicate of price, prize, and praise—to which I add a fourth, perform—will serve as an organizing device for this concluding chapter. The point is not to make sharp conceptual distinctions among these categories but to use them as a springboard to address the themes raised by the authors in this volume.

Price

As I write this in the summer of 2010, oil continues to spew into the Gulf of Mexico from the BP Deepwater Horizon drilling site. Federal government

---

* This chapter was written while I was a Visiting Professor in the Program on the Cultural Sources of Newness at the Social Science Research Center Berlin (WZB). I am grateful to its director Michael Hutter and to the WZB for their support.

estimates indicate a flow rate of 35,000–60,000 barrels of oil per day, but this figure is disputed, with BP officials claiming a lower rate and some scientists pointing to evidence that it is higher. But whatever the final tally, it is clear that the BP oil spill is an environmental and economic catastrophe, damaging the fragile ecology of the marshlands, killing sea- and wildlife, robbing fishermen and others of their livelihoods, and posing the possibility of yet-unforeseen threats to numerous species in the now-polluted waters of the Gulf.

The BP oil disaster offers a unique challenge and opportunity to economic sociology because it is an acute case of price determination. What is the price that BP should pay for the destruction of lives, livelihoods, and the natural environment? And just as important, how should this price be determined?

Marion Fourcade's chapter, "Price and Prejudice: On Economics and the Enchantment (or Disenchantment) of Nature," is an exemplary demonstration that economic sociology can contribute much to this national debate. Fourcade's case is that of the Exxon Valdez supertanker that ran aground in March 1989, despoiling Alaska's Prince William Sound with a spill of 30,000 tons (nearly 11 million gallons) of crude oil. Her study focuses on the $1.025 billion out-of-court settlement to compensate for environmental damage to the area. The crux of the analysis highlights how various federal and state agencies hired environmental economists who recommended a method (new at the time) of passive use damage evaluation—"passive use" because it focuses on resources that people are unlikely to use directly. The key technique in this method was a "contingent valuation survey" administered in four locations across the United States.

Survey respondents were given visual and oral information about the spill and its effects, as well as informed about a Coast Guard program to prevent future spills. Basically (and not at all unlike being asked how much you would pay for a basket of groceries), they were asked how much their household would be willing to pay for the program to be implemented. The result was $31 per median household. The economists aggregated these individual "preferences," multiplying by the number of US households, to derive the figure denoting America's total willingness to pay (a measure of utility loss) for the environment of Prince William Sound. That figure, in turn, was the basis for the government's legal case and therefore the key determinant of the price that Exxon paid in the ultimate settlement.

Fourcade dissects the "epistemic culture" of the economists' contingent valuation, specifically its assumptions about aggregating individual preferences that are disconnected from the preferences of other individuals and therefore of any real social context. And she criticizes the confined character of the survey instrument, specifically its framing of asking citizens how much they would be willing to part *with their own money* rather than asking them how much the violator should pay from corporate coffers.

I have a strong affinity to Fourcade's work because it resonates so much with arguments I made in the opening and closing pages of my book, *The Sense of Dissonance*. The challenge for economic sociologists is to develop concepts and analytic strategies that address the problem that *value* is almost always bound up with *values*. In fact, all the really interesting questions about economic value are always, inextricably, tied to questions about moral economy and hence my book's subtitle: *Accounts of Worth*(Stark 2009). In studying the limitations of the ways in which Exxon was called to account, Fourcade addresses this problem head-on.

Yet the conclusions that Fourcade draws from her study invite some critical reflection. Although she does not use the exact words, essentially Fourcade points to the price that we pay (as a society) whenever we make a monetary valuation of a non-market, public societal good. The very act of putting a "price" on something tips the scales in favor of the economists' expertise and their market or quasi-market framings. The title could be restated: not simply "price *and* prejudice" but price *yields* prejudice. I wonder if this need be the case.

Does "price" somehow inevitably come down to "market price"? Are all monetary valuations necessarily market pricings? There are some good reasons to think not. Economic historians and economic anthropologists provide numerous examples. State socialism might provide others. (Some would argue, however, and not without reason, that monetary valuations under central planning were not really prices, in fact, and that monetary valuations were some other kind of numerical assignment but not really money.) These are interesting questions—for economic sociologists and for the critical study of accounting. They quickly take us into questions about calculation. If we posit that there are non-market orders of worth, do these have distinctive rationalities that are nonetheless recognizable as "calculation"?[1]

Ordinary language never resolves theoretical questions. But it can sometimes suggest a moment of insight. In this case, the telling phrase in common parlance is when we say that someone has "paid a price." The revealing aspect of *paying a price* is that context typically indicates that the price that was paid was *not calculated on market terms*. It is, nonetheless and quite emphatically, a price. Indeed, a non-market price. We hear the phrase in many domains: Someone who acquired wealth by such disloyalty to friends that the price was dishonor; a former colleague who accepted a senior administrative university post at the price of her academic standing; a painter or writer who achieved celebrity status at the price of no longer being taken seriously as a creative artist; a politician who... and so on.

Thus, in everyday language, "price" can be an expression that points quite directly to the very heart of the problem, where differing orders of worth are somehow *compared* without ever being made strictly *commensurable*. Such a price is not a market price but it is a price that is identifiable. It can and often

---

[1] As Wendy Espeland (Espeland and Stevens 1998) shows in her work, the challenges grow even greater when the commensurabilities are being constructed in societies in which the dominant logic is a market logic.

does have a magnitude ("a big price," "a small price"). The timely question, in the BP case, is how can it be made quantifiable?

Assume for the moment that citizen surveys might play a useful role in assessing damages. This, in any case, was the approach taken by the economists following the Exxon Valdez oil spill.[2] My imagined "survey" is not a policy recommendation but instead a thought experiment intended to stimulate thinking about alternative ways to "measure" public incommensurables. Unlike contingent valuation, such a survey would not ask respondents what they would be willing to pay and then use that figure as the basis for assigning BP's damages. Instead, participants would be asked to think about something that the public *is already paying for* (and that therefore already has a price) and these "comparisons" would then be used as the basis for assessing the damages that BP should pay.

The purpose of this survey, respondents would be told, is to help determine the price that BP (and allied companies such as Halliburton that share liability) should pay for causing the disaster and for the consequent damage. What is it worth to restore the Gulf Coast and to enact protective measures to ensure that nothing like this ever happens again? Respondents would not be asked to give any figures other than simple counts that make a comparison to something that already exists. How many space shuttle flights would BP's damages be worth? Two? Ten? Twenty? More? Here, too, the respondent would not be given any figures about these expenditures. The basic idea of the exercise is a kind of implicit barter: Point to something that people already have an idea about as serving some public purpose, and then ask how many of these some other thing is worth. How many fifth-generation fighter bombers? Twenty, fifty, a hundred? How many next-generation aircraft carriers?

Ten space shuttle flights would be $15 billion. That is given by the average cost per flight ($1.5 billion) based on the cost of the entire space shuttle program. But maybe the question should be how many space shuttle *programs* (the above program was estimated at $170 billion in 2008 dollars). The program cost of the Lockheed Martin F-22 Raptor fighter plane has been estimated at $65 billion, and a 2009 report estimates that the new Gerald Ford-class aircraft carriers will cost $14 billion including research and development.[3] Even just a couple of such programs start to add up to serious money.

Note that this thought exercise does not ask citizens to "put a price" on nature or the environment—a difficult operation, as Fourcade shows.[4] Instead, the problem is framed as determining the "price to be paid" in a case of

---

[2] In mid-June 2010, Reuters reported that "Credit Suisse [was] putting BP's share of the tab to as much as $12 billion, *taking Exxon Mobil's Valdez spill in* 1989 *as [a] benchmark* and including $4 billion of fines" (Maharg-Bravo 2010; emphasis mine).

[3] Figures respectively http://en.wikipedia.org/wiki/Space_Shuttle; http://en.wikipedia.org/wiki/F-22_Raptor; http://en.wikipedia.org/wiki/Gerald_R._Ford_class_aircraft_carrier (both accessed June 20, 2010).

[4] In addition to her chapter in this volume, see also another chapter involving a comparison of the Exxon Valdez case to an oil spill in France (Fourcade 2010).

retributive justice. Some might argue that the price to be paid should not be limited to monetary penalties. A tough prison sentence for the CEO of a highly profitable company might yet be the most effective retributive justice if the aim is not only to restore the environment but also to change the behavior of the senior executives of other highly profitable corporations.[5]

The obvious alternative to citizen surveys or retributive justice via the criminal courts is assessment of damages by expert appraisal. It is to this aspect of the sociology of worth—appraising and prizing—that we turn.

Prize

In so doing, we turn again to John Dewey, who makes the following observation in his *Theory of Valuation*:

[W]hen attention is confined to the usage of the verb 'to value', we find that common speech exhibits a double usage. For a glance at the dictionary will show that in ordinary speech the words 'valuing' and 'valuation' are verbally employed to designate both *prizing*, in the sense of holding precious, dear (and various other nearly equivalent activities, like honoring, regarding highly) and *appraising* in the sense of *putting* a value upon, *assigning* value to. This is an activity of rating, an act that involves comparison, as is explicit, for example, in appraisals in money terms of goods and services. (Dewey 1939: 5)

Here, Dewey points out that valuation can also occur through prizing and appraising in addition to market pricing. Several of the chapters in this volume suggest that parallel to and interacting with economies of prices, we find economies of prizes and appraisals. Peter Gourevitch, for example, shows how consumers who value fair trade products depend upon NGOs to certify the validity of product claims. Akos Rona-Tas and Stefanie Hiss similarly demonstrate how pricing in financial markets depends on the appraisals of ratings agencies. Marie-France Garcia-Parpet shows the disruptive and persistent effects that wine critics have when expert ratings reshape consumer tastes and the very practices of viticulture. And Ashley Mears points to the career structures of fashion models who must balance higher prices in commercial (catalogue) modeling against work in editorial shoots that, while lower paid, are nonetheless highly prized.

Taken together, these chapters indicate that, in addition to market *competition*, valuation in modern economies increasingly occurs through organized

---

[5] In mid-June 2010, President Obama negotiated a $20 billion compensation fund which BP will pay into an escrow account. Statements by Obama, the White House, and subsequent editorial commentary specifically referred to the firm's profitability (some specifically mentioning recent estimates of BP's $20 billion in annual profits), suggesting that the price to be paid could be linked to profits.

(or semi-organized) *competitions*. I briefly discuss how tests and contests interplay with ratings and rankings, point to some promising new research on the sociology of competitions, and then suggest what might be valuable in top-ten lists, taking these as a marker of an even more widespread phenomenon of consumer ratings and rankings.

Rankings, an ordinal list, can result from tests or from contests. We start with contests, and take first the forms of these in which competitors play against each other. The score in such a contest indicates which player (team) performed better (earned more runs or goals, ran faster, jumped higher) against another or others on a given day. The score of a soccer match is the result of a direct, head-to-head competition. And the aggregation of these scores (e.g., in win–loss records) results in rankings—whether of a soccer league or of all the professional tennis players or of all the Grand Master chess players in the world. Note that in such contests, there are referees and timekeepers but not judges. Technology contests (the fastest computer, the lightest airplane, robotic cars on ever-more challenging terrain) operate according to similar principles.[6]

But there is another kind of scoring in contests where judges are involved. Contestants do compete with each other in a given event at a given time. But the scores, from which rankings are derived, indicate the degree of conformity to some set of relatively standardized criteria for evaluating performance. Think of Olympic sports such as gymnastics, with their indices of "technical" and (contested) "artistic" scoring. In a sense, these are contests organized around more or less simultaneous tests. In principle, judges are not supposed to be ranking the performers directly but instead should be rating them according to how well they pass the set of tested performance criteria. Thus, in contests organized around tests, rankings result from ratings. These can be the averaged scores of several judges (as in various Olympic sports), the aggregations of scores across multiple judges (as in cumulative grade point averages), or an aggregation or index of the scores of a single judge across several evaluation criteria (as in rankings by critics in technology fields such as software).

Contests in grant and fellowship competitions frequently mix ranked scores with head-to-head agonistic competition. This is the case, for example, in grants competitions at the National Science Foundation (Lamont 2010). In such a mixed system, judges, juries, or "scientific review panels" use scoring procedures ("rate this candidate") to produce a "short list" of finalist competitors, frequently available at the outset of their face-to-face meeting. Jurors typically contend that this is merely a "provisional" or "rough" ranking. The

---

[6] The most famous such technology inducement prize was in 1714, when the British Parliament offered a prize of £20,000 (more than $3 million in current US dollars) for a method of determining longitude at sea to within one-half a degree. This technology competition launched a boom in navigational research, and the prize was eventually awarded in 1773 (to the dismay of the eminent astronomers who entered the competition) to a clockmaker. On competitions versus grants, see Hanson (1998), Che and Gale (2003), Newell and Wilson (2005), and Leonhardt (2007).

subsequent head-to-head competition directly comparing finalist proposals frequently overturns the initial scored "rankings." It is telling that panelists often refer to this moment of agonistic competition as "agonizing" work.

The mixed character of grants and fellowship competitions also points to an important feature of certain types of competitions: the selection criteria guiding the judges are not given at the outset but emerge during the jury's deliberations. Such is frequently the case in architectural competitions, as Kristian Kreiner (2007, 2009) demonstrates in a series of exemplary studies. At first glance, the evaluative principles governing the jurors' decision seem to be fixed at the outset: they are established in the "program," the brief specifying the problems that the architectural design must solve. But the various features of the client's desiderata are frequently contradictory: not all can be optimized or even harmoniously satisfied. Indeed, as Kreiner shows, the greater the elaboration of multiple performance criteria, the more likely the winning entry will ignore the program, with aesthetic principles trumping other evaluative principles in the jury's decision. More importantly, Kreiner examines in detail the processes and practices whereby jurors (and hence clients) use the entries to learn more about the actual problems that can be solved and the operative principles for assessing a successful performance (Jacobsen et al. 2010). What seems to be a case of analytic problem solving turns out to be a situation of interpretation (Lester and Piore 2004). Architectural competitions are an example of Dewey's pragmatist approach, through which we discover our principles for evaluation in the action of valuation. They are a social technology for exploration in the search when we do not know what we are looking for but can recognize it when we find it (Stark 2009).

As we have seen, contests can be deliberately designed to yield rankings from ratings (experts' scores on various types of "tests"). But it can also happen that ratings can have an unintended consequence, yielding a ranking. For example, despite their protests that their ratings of colleges were never intended as a ranking, the scores of the National Academy of Sciences could easily be converted into a ranking and were quickly followed by a plethora of privately produced "College Rankings" (*US News and World Report*, Princeton Review, and others) with lists of the top 100 universities, the 25 top-ranked liberal arts colleges, and the ten best business schools. What began as an assessment then became a contest as schools began to modify their admissions policies and (in some cases) their procedures for evaluating faculty teaching performance in efforts to move up in the rankings (Espeland and Sauder 2007).

In an era of globalization, rankings do not stop at the national level: university presidents and vice chancellors now proudly proclaim that the goal of their tenure in office will be to move their institution into the ranks of the top 50 universities in the world. Ministries of science and education produce "research assessment exercises," whether they do so in the name of finding more efficient means to allocate scarce tax dollars or (more unstated) to prod institutions of higher education to better compete for higher-tuition-paying foreign students. As Lucien Karpik shows in his chapter on pricing a scientific paper in France, the consequences are not always beneficial for science.

In the field of finance, bond ratings, like cumulative grade point averages, yield a ranking: AAA, AA+ AA, AA−, A+, A, A−, BBB+, BBB, B, and so on. In the case of the bonds for Residential Mortgage Backed Securities (RMBSs), as Rona-Tas and Hiss elaborate, these ratings are themselves derived from consumer credit ratings such as the FICO credit score. Recent research by Carruthers (2010) and MacKenzie (2010) suggests that these corporate bond ratings played a major contributing role in the recent financial crisis.

Ratings and rankings are taken *ad absurdum* in the proliferation of top-ten lists. As a Google search will quickly reveal, there are top-ten lists of everything, including the top ten stupidest top-ten lists. Entire sites are devoted to the genre: TopTenz.net, for example, has thousands of lists organized according to 15 categories, with drop-down menus revealing dozens of subcategories. Although it has a long pedigree—think of Moses' list of the top ten prohibitions—in its current form, the genre probably began in the 1950s, when the standard jukebox held 40 singles. Out of this emerged Top 40 radio programming, with the notion of a Top 40 list later refined in the 1970s to the cloying voice of Casey Kasem's weekly countdown, which defined what would be played on popular music radio—with lucrative results for the major record labels. David Letterman's nightly top-ten lists echo Kasem's countdown, even as his deadpan reading mocks the very project of the genre.

Top-ten lists are frivolous; yet their very ubiquity invites a moment of reflection. Taking them (not too) seriously requires an understanding of the humorous component of the genre. Parody is most effective when it gets under our skin to jab at a social practice in which we are complicit. Who has not resorted to a favorite critic's list of the top ten best movies of the past year when one could not decide on a film to rent? Or taken into account a wine's ratings when choosing a bottle to take to a dinner party? Or consulted an online guide of users' ratings when choosing a hotel, restaurant, vacation package, software program, or new electronic gadget? Which is the dean or department chair who has never perused the rankings of graduate programs?

And so we laugh because we laugh at our partial dependence on lists of ratings and rankings to navigate the uncertainties of finding what is valuable in the overly abundant world of consumer choices.

We laugh also because when the humorous genre works best, it does so by exposing a mixture of assessment criteria so ad hoc and absurd as to defy all rhyme or reason in the selection principle, whereby any element on the list can be "ranked" as higher or lower than any other. Such ironic lists thus evoke an unsettling sense that many of the rankings and ratings that we (along with our deans, our creditors, and our regulatory agencies) use are organized on an ordinal scale but were cobbled together from disparate and incommensurable principles of evaluation.

Many, perhaps most top-ten lists, however, are not ironic. What is immediately striking is how many are deadly earnest. Once again, Dewey is insightful. In the passage quoted at the outset of this section, Dewey goes on to distinguish appraisal and prizing:

> The double meaning is significant because there is implicit in it one of the basic issues regarding valuation. For in *prizing*, emphasis falls upon something having definite *personal* reference, which, like all activities of distinctively personal reference, has an aspectual quality called emotional.

Prizing, Dewey notes, has an emotional quality with a definite personal reference. This is exactly what one sees in the emphatically nonironic and nonexpert top-ten lists that are awash on social networking sites. "If expert critics and juries can award prizes, so can I," they seem to exclaim. "Here's my list, the objects I prize, and the reasons for this decidedly personal attachment."

Dewey then goes on to contrast the effectual moment of prizing with the intellectual moment characteristic of appraisal:

> Valuation as *appraisal*, however, is primarily concerned with a relational property of objects so that an intellectual aspect is uppermost of the same general sort that is found in "*estimate*" as distinguished from the personal-emotional word "*esteem*." That the same verb is employed in both senses suggests the problem upon which schools are divided in the present time. Which of the two references is basic in its implications? Are the two activities separate or are they complementary?

The move is typical of Dewey. Just when we think we have grasped the analytic separation of the emotional and the intellectual—as with the too-quick parsing of means and ends—he invites us to wonder, "Are they separate or are they complementary?"

Dewey's query is a fruitful insight for the sociological investigation of what is valuable. Online ratings and rankings by consumers now provide new sources of data on prizing and appraising—new means to register value judgments in the economy.[7] Personal top-ten lists are but the tip of the iceberg of a vast digital repository, much of it time-stamped data. Whereas economists have long had time-sensitive data on price movements, we now (or will soon) have alternative databases on the movements of prizing and appraising that register consumer attachments. These "valuemeters" will need new measures and metrics (Latour and Lepinay 2009: 16). They can be quantified, but these metrics of personal value judgments need not be expressed in terms of money. In fact, we will need to avoid the quick temptation to assess how prizing and appraising translate to pricing. That is the work for corporate (and start-up) research departments. The task for economic sociology will be to develop new metrics of what is valuable (the prizings and appraisings that give us access to

---

[7] User ratings are likely to be disruptive of conventional reviews by established critics. For an account of such disruption in the tourist industry, see Scott and Orlikowski (2010).

value judgment). These metrics are valuable precisely because they are metrics that are alternatives to prices.

Surprise! Praise

From price and prize, we turn to the third of Dewey's triplicate—praise. Here, we examine the capacity of a good not simply to be appraised but to evoke a sense of amazement, to inspire, to be an object that connects or conveys the user to a world of imagination. Several of the chapters in the volume address this theme.

Following George Shackle's definition that "a good promises performance," Jens Beckert distinguishes three dimensions of the performance of goods. A good's *physical* performance refers to what it does in the physical world. Beckert notes that one's valuation of the good depends not only on properties of the object but also on one's knowledge of how to use it. *Positional* performance refers to the mode of valuation according to which a good locates its owner in a differentiated social world. Although he does not exploit the phrase, Beckert is here pointing to the ways in which our "belongings" signal our identities (of class, lifestyle, or group membership)—in short, where we belong in social space. Positional value crucially depends on whether third parties recognize the same meanings and signals that the owner intends such goods to perform.

Whereas physical performance refers to the ability to achieve some transformation in the physical world and positional performance rests on the ability to perform a transformation in the social world of public symbolic meanings, the *imaginative* performance of goods refers to a transformation of consciousness in the realm of one's own imagination (see also Hennion 2004). Interpreting Durkheim's *The Elementary Forms of the Religious Life* as a treatise on valuation and drawing on Durkheim's notion of the totem, Beckert argues that imaginative goods can perform like relics, allowing the owner to be in touch with intangible values or aesthetic ideals. They are a "bridge to the transcendental." In this capacity to "transcend the here and now" (think, for example, of a bottle of wine that affords a material connection to the time of Halley's Comet or to the year of one's birth), imaginative goods are transportation systems. "Did you enjoy the opera?" a friend asks. "I was moved."

Beckert is attuned to the fact that a given object might have all three forms of value: a designer handbag (of a type shown to have been carried by a celebrity) can be used as an accessory, signal lifestyle membership, and—in its capacity as a secondhand relic—create for its owner an association with the charismatic personage. Citing Campbell, Beckert refers to imaginative goods as "aids to the construction of daydreams." Marketers are acutely aware of the symbolic properties in even the most profane of items. If you have seen an ad for Home Depot, you have seen how a can of paint can be marketed as a marital aid: an opportunity for the couple to converse while choosing the color. The guy paints the bedroom; fade out at happy embrace.

Beckert goes on to note that whereas religious relics maintain distance, the purchase of the object of imaginative value brings it into the profane world. Actual use of the object sets in motion a dynamic of disenchantment, with disillusionment creating an unending demand for new products, the arousal of new hopes, and yet new disappointments in the search for "imaginative salvation." Mick Jagger, too, observed this cycle of disappointment—of objects "tryin' to fire my imagination. But I can't get no satisfaction."

If Jens Beckert examines performance values, Michael Hutter analyzes the value of performances. Like Dewey, Hutter finds valuation tuned in multiple registers—cognitive and affective, intellectual and emotional. His contribution to this volume focuses on the emotion of *surprise*. Hutter refers to goods that are desired for their ability to generate surprises as "experience goods." Such goods can not only be theatrical or musical performances, books, fashion, movies, and television series but also electronic gadgets such as video games—anything that evokes a "Wow," indicating the users' experience of amazement, whether profound or fleeting. A mobile phone might seem to be a piece of hardware—until one hears a colleague talking excitedly about its performance: "It's just amazing!" The business models of Apple's iPhone and Google's Android are keyed to their performances as experience goods, with an endless stream of new "apps" generating opportunities for fresh surprises.

For Hutter, surprise is a function of expectations and uncertainties. Experience goods turn on uncertainty in a doubled sense. First, because they are singular, the user cannot be certain about the quality of the experience beforehand. But the concertgoer or the purchaser of a new DVD does have expectations, and these can either be exceeded or disappointed. We experience surprise when expectations are overwhelmed. Second, experience goods generate (they turn on) new uncertainties during the experience itself: a minor chord disrupting resolution to the dominant key, a sudden revelation of the heroine's motivations, a rally that ties the score in the ninth inning, a new level in a video game. For Hutter, surprise goods do not reduce uncertainty; they generate "a kind of uncertainty that is desired by the users because of the strong and positive emotions" it evokes.

Because the management of expectations and uncertainties is so important for the "praise value" of experience goods, commercial products are carefully calibrated not to deviate too much from user expectations. They should be neither too boring nor too startling. "Familiar surprises, combining thrill with comfort," Hutter concludes, "are the most frequent and successful commercial variety."

Contemporary megachurches in the United States offer a fruitful case to explore Beckert's concept of "imaginative performance" and Hutter's concept of "experience goods." At first glance, a religious setting might seem too far removed from Hutter's examples of circuses, rock concerts, and video games.

Similarly, the church would seem too obviously "transcendental" to apply concepts that Beckert develops for the profane worlds of handbags and wine bottles. But the case invites you to defer these objections until closer inspection.

Evangelical, nondenominational "megachurches" (defined as congregations with more than 2,000 members) are the fastest growing segment of religious affiliation in the United States. I began studying several megachurches in Oklahoma City in 2006. The date was not arbitrary, for it was the centennial anniversary of the publication of Max Weber's "'Churches' and 'Sects' in North America," for which Weber (atypically) conducted field research in Missouri, North Carolina, and Oklahoma.[8] The setting thus seemed appropriate for witnessing new developments in the Protestant ethic and the spirit of capitalism.

VictoryChurch.tv and LifeChurch.tv are two such Oklahoma City megachurches. Indeed, these are their posted names, inscribed on large signs (complete with logos resembling the Nike swoosh or dot-com start-ups) reaching high above gargantuan parking lots. Each church began in the mid-1990s with a handful of members. VictoryChurch, for example, first worshipped in the cafeteria of a public high school. Within a decade, weekly attendance had grown to over 6,000 (at VictoryChurch) and over 13,000 on five "campuses" (LifeChurch). Both megachurches achieved such growth through an innovative recombination of the cultures of church and commerce.

The architecture of these churches is the first signal of such recombination. There are no steeples; in fact, from the street one sees no crosses or other religious symbols. After outgrowing the high school cafeteria, VictoryChurch leased space in a declining shopping center, one of the familiar "strip malls" that line the thoroughfares of most American cities. From these still-modest operations (the suburban equivalent of an urban "storefront" mission church), it quickly expanded to acquire the entire retail property (80,000 square feet, 9,000 square meters). From the parking lot, one sees the signage of its various facilities: a bookstore (at which one can purchase CDs, DVDs, and other materials produced by the church's audiovisual department), a coffee shop (serving Starbucks-branded coffee), an arts and crafts studio, and the church's own religiously themed toy store whose logo evokes that of Toys "R" Us. Unlike some of the other even larger Oklahoma City megachurch campuses, VictoryChurch does not have a gym or fitness center.

With its membership continuing to grow and having exhausted all of the available space in the shopping center, VictoryChurch faced a moment of decision. It needed to build a new sanctuary (although that term is avoided in favor of "auditorium"). It had the land and abundant resources to erect any

---

[8] To my knowledge, this is the only instance in which Weber (fully accustomed to work in the archives) conducted ethnographic field research. His accounts in "'Churches' and 'Sects' in North America: An Ecclesiastical and Sociopolitical Sketch" are among his most vibrant writing. See, for example, his description of a baptism along the banks of a river (Weber 1906/1985).

kind of building for worship. Yet it eschewed the more conventional "church" architecture, opting instead for a minimalist structure that in almost every respect—from its vast scale to the undisguised ventilation units running along the ceiling—resembles a Wal-Mart retail center.

LifeChurch is a similar story of adopting the Wal-Mart "box" architecture. Like VictoryChurch, it has a reception area modeled after that of a megaplex cinema. At LifeChurch, upcoming sermons ("Invasion" is one example) are announced in glass-framed posters with a format identical to those greeting customers standing in line at a cinema box office. Both megachurches have food courts and a smaller version of their retail store (cash registers at the ready) immediately adjacent to the auditorium. Do not hesitate to take your mega-size Coca-Cola drink into the service. And if you would like the youngsters to grab a bag of cookies or potato chips to munch on during the service, these are available in large bins, free for the taking. Need to find your way around the facilities? Here is the pastel color-coded map, just as in any other mall.

I mentioned "service." But this is not the term of art adopted in these megachurches. Whether on Sunday morning or Friday or Saturday evening, the preferred term is "experience." These megachurches are fully equipped to deliver that experience. Entering into the auditorium, we see that whereas the basic architectural construction was inexpensive, no penny has been spared on audiovisual equipment. Here is the multichannel (iDR-48 MixRack and iLive-T112 Control Surface) console for digital mixing of sound and video that would be the envy of any corporate media studio. At VictoryChurch, the mixing console is square in the middle of the auditorium; at LifeChurch, it is housed in the "Control Room" staffed by technicians and a producer who selects the media objects.[9] There is much to display. Both churches have no less than five video cameras (two fixed and three handheld mobile units deployed throughout the auditorium). VictoryChurch has a very large screen, but LifeChurch dwarfs this with three screens, each as large as you would find at a drive-in movie theater, displaying a sometimes dizzying array of split-screen moving images.[10]

Dimmed lights, spotlights, stroboscopic effects, and loud Christian rock music—prayers in PowerPoint. Sermons at LifeChurch are repeatedly punctuated by two-minute video "messages" that bear an uncanny resemblance to commercial interruptions, informing the worshippers about past or upcoming

---

[9] The backstage control room at Victory also functions as a production studio. If you find an experience especially meaningful, you can notify an usher. Wait a few minutes after the end of the service and for $7.50 you will receive a DVD of that particular service.

[10] In private conversation, the staff at LifeChurch refer to Senior Pastor Craig Groeschel as "the communicator." "Craig really understands the camera," one young staffer explained. "For an ordinary public speaker, when they get to that emotional high point, they'll step forward and look into the eyes of the audience. Not Craig. He turns and looks right into camera three because he knows it's a dedicated close-up. It's like, if it's not on the screen, it's not happening. Even people in the front rows: they'll look up to the screen. We know. We've done the studies."

series of sermons available on DVD. But "experiences" vary. Those on weekend nights, catering to a younger set, tend to be louder. Typically, at least one of the Sunday morning experiences (offered in various time slots) tends to be a bit less enervating.

The pastors of these megachurches are the heirs of the televangelists, who appeared first on the radio and later on television. One of the true pioneers was the evangelist Oral Roberts ("put your hands on the radio"), operating from nearby Tulsa. This next generation of preachers is adopting new technologies. LifeChurch and VictoryChurch simulcast their services; each has a fully elaborated website with deep categories, streaming video, and online payment systems ("click here to donate"); each proudly announces its "social networking" capabilities and presence on Facebook and Twitter. The website of LifeChurch has a bar along the top announcing the "Next Online Experience In," followed by a set of digital countdown boxes: "01 HR, 42 MIN, 15 SEC," and so on. Several years ago, LifeChurch launched a venue in Second Life, where visitors can choose to have their avatar raise one hand in the "praise" posture, elevate above the digital floor, or even sport a halo.

But these megachurches are not just adept at using technologies. More significantly, they are media savvy in the sense of being familiar with a wide variety of media genres and capable of repurposing them. What the various "experiences" have in common is that they "quote" an established media genre. Some of these repurposings are so obvious as to need little interpretation: the youth minister, like the member of a "boy band" with shirt untucked and a headset microphone, involving the crowd at a rock concert. But even the relatively more subdued Sunday experiences harken back to some genre in the world of profane media. One "series" of sermons screened at the Sunday experiences, for example, has senior pastor Craig Groeschel going out with a film crew, "invading" the homes of LifeChurch members: Reality TV. That there is no altar or pulpit gives the megachurches flexibility in arranging the podium platform. Thus, one also encounters Pastor Craig in a different genre, sitting behind a kind of desk. To his right is a couch where he is joined first by a Christian celebrity, then by a regular church member, then by another celebrity, each of whom Pastor Craig interviews, eliciting a mixture of light banter and emotional testimonials. Without doubt, a late-night talk show.

Beckert's model of imaginative performance applies, but *in reverse*. Whereas Beckert directs our attention to how a profane object can transport users, bringing them into touch with some idealized state, here the megachurch preachers can be seen to be working in the opposite direction, repeatedly bringing us back into touch with the most mundane elements of entertainment culture, thoroughly suffusing the sacred with the profane. I do not write about theology, and I hesitate to speak of liturgy (whether megachurches are liturgical—even unconventionally—remains an open question in religious studies). But in their dramaturgical forms, these practices are decidedly "down to earth."

They are also in accord with megachurch recruitment strategies. Life and Victory aim to attract "seekers"—those who might not know exactly what they are looking for and who sense that they are not finding it in their experiences in the established denominational forms. "Love God but hate church?" their websites say, "You can find a place with us." In their competition with the mainline denominations, megachurches thus attempt to lower emotional transaction costs for these seekers. From the architecture to the food court to the structure of the experiences, the message is clear: "If you are comfortable walking into a shopping mall with your cutoff jeans and 7-Eleven Slurpee drink, you can feel comfortable doing the same in your experience with us." Are these businesses disguised as churches? Perhaps. But in place of that denunciation, it is more telling to regard them as churches disguised as businesses.

In contrast to the earlier nondenominational "tent revivals," megachurches do not practice "the call," inviting walk-ons to "come to the front and accept the Lord" in a sudden and dramatic "conversion experience." Instead, they recall Michael Hutter's observations that familiar surprises of the "successful commercial variety" entail a careful calibration of expectations and uncertainties. Such management of expectations can be seen in this passage, featured prominently on the website of LifeChurch:

> **Not sure what to expect?** We want your experience at LifeChurch.tv to be a great one, so we let you set the pace. Want to hang back and observe for a while? No problem. Want to meet a few people and learn more about us? There are lots of friendly faces ready to help. Either way, you'll be greeted by a warm environment, great music, and teaching that will make you think. [Emphasis in the original.]

We have come a long way from Max Weber. Whereas the work ethic of Weber's protestant was motivated by the fact that salvation (atonement, satisfaction of the debt of sin) in the hereafter could not be a known certainty on this earth, here the religious entrepreneurs[11] of commodified spirituality offer a different message. The experience goods of these megachurches seem to come with a promise: "Satisfaction Guaranteed."

Perform

Whereas in the preceding section we addressed the valuation of performances, in this concluding section, we examine valuation as performance. Charles Smith addresses skilled performances of valuation in his chapter, "Coping with Contingencies in Equity Option Markets." Smith distinguishes among

---

[11] The website of LifeChurch lists five members of the "Directional Leadership Team." The second job title listed (after "Senior Pastor") is "Innovation Leader."

three strategies for confronting uncertainties. The first, *making sense*, entails imposing some kind of narrative account on events initially experienced as chaotic. *Routines and performances*, the second strategy, imposes some sort of behavioral order. The third, *acting sensibly*, is the least common but the most interesting, and does not seek to impose an overall order: it is a method for handling the contingent and the disorderly. In his rich study of option traders, Smith analyzes the practices of juggling multiple rules of thumb in managing option positions.

Daniel Beunza and I take a similar analytic approach when moving from how models make markets to understanding how traders actually use models (Beunza and Stark forthcoming). We offer an ethnographic account of merger arbitrage as a reflexively skilled performance, with reflexivity socially distributed inside and outside the trading room. Merger arbitrage traders use a graphical representation (the "spread plot") of the positions of their rivals to check the probability estimates that they have independently derived from their own models and proprietary databases. If the spread changes in a direction different from their own estimates, the discrepancy prompts traders to re-search their databases ("Are we missing something?" asks the senior trader at the merger arbitrage desk) in an effort to uncover cognitive blind spots created by their categories.[12]

As in Smith's strategy of acting sensibly, these traders are not imposing an order but are actively managing contingencies. Beunza and I, however, depart from Smith in two ways. First, whereas Smith's analysis of trading views the strategies independently of organizational contexts, our analysis brings this aspect to the foreground. Our analysis, moreover, is not simply attentive to the organizational *setting* (the particular trading room of a particular investment bank). Instead, we demonstrate that "reflexive modeling" requires a distinctive form of *social organization*. It is this pointing to moments of reflexivity in the process of managing uncertainty that marks our second departure from Smith. Such a reflexivity is not a narrative order and is emphatically not an intellectualist exercise of transcending subjective experience. Neither is it "objective," but it is nonetheless objectified in the instrumentation, market devices, and material practices of merger arbitrage in the era of quantitative finance.

What is value? In answering this question, several of the chapters in this volume reiterate the distinction between "subjective" and "objective" approaches to the theory of value. In a recent chapter, Fabian Muniesa (2011) follows Dewey in arguing that a pragmatist approach displaces this subjective/objective dichotomy by replacing the notion of value with the action of valuation. Muniesa shows that Dewey's *Theory of Valuation*, published in 1939, was but the last in an ongoing philosophical debate launched in 1913 and extending through the 1920s and 1930s. Dewey enters the debate at the

---

[12] "Models, Reflexivity, and Systemic Risk: A Critique of Behavioral Finance" is a chapter with a twist. When the system lacks requisite diversity (or dissonance), the unintended outcome of the attempt to deal with the fallibility of financial models is systemic risk.

zenith of the "realist–idealist" controversy. On the realist side, value is a property of a good, independent of assessments; on the idealist side, it is a property of consciousness. On one side, value is "provoked"; on the other, it is "appraised."

Dewey enters this debate with a deliberate "flanking movement."

[T]he conclusion is not that value is subjective, but that it is practical. The situation in which judgment of value is required is not mental, much less fanciful. It is existential, but it exists as something whose good or value resides (first) in something to be attained in action and (secondly) whose value both as an ideal and as existence depends upon judgment on what to do. Value is "objective," but it is such in an active or practical situation, not apart from it. To deny the possibility of such a view, is to reduce the objectivity of every tool and machine to the physical ingredients that compose it, and to treat a distinctive "plow" character as merely subjective. (Dewey 1915, cited in Muniesa 2011: 4)

Muniesa suggests that a contemporary pragmatist approach to valuation will make "the distance between value and its measure (and also between value as appraised and value as provoked) collapse in an analytically constructive manner." The result, he concludes, is "an understanding of valuation as some sort of performance."

With Muniesa's shift from value (a noun, a property) to valuation (a process, a practical action), we see that the terms in our Deweyan list of price, prize, and praise were verb forms all along—*to price, to prize, to praise.* To these, we must now add a fourth, *to perform.*

The verb "perform" figures prominently in the literature on performativity, a concept preoccupying economic sociology these days. That attention is well deserved because the notion that the use of a model can improve its predictive fit is a powerful idea. But the impact of the insight is diminished in statements such as "economists perform the economy" or "models perform markets." The verb is there, but we lose the full meaning of the message if our attention quickly turns back from the action to the subject (economists, models, etc.).

Performativity occurs when the use of a model improves its predictive fit. My definition is far from "saying something makes it so," or "believing something makes it happen," or even from regarding performativity as an updating of Robert Merton's notion of "self-fulfilling prophecy" (Merton 1948). Prophecies, beliefs, statements, theories, and models perform nothing in themselves. It is only in their instantiation in material practices, in technologies, in devices, and through the *use* of these that models can improve their predictive fit. Original formulations of the concept (MacKenzie and Millo 2003) stress the *how*; but less careful applications seem to fall back on the *who* or the *what*.

In emphasizing that it is the use of the model, we do not return to some prior humanism: "We should never forget that, after all, it's *people* who perform." Once again, the subject becomes the prominent figure, here the noble human subject. Such statements pose as restoring to real people their true dignity as autonomous human agents. But it is a cheap humanism, because it strips human beings of what makes them human—their coevolution as a species with the cultural and material tools through which they reshape their worlds.

The object of study for sociology is not human beings but *being human*. That simple rephrasing immediately highlights the sociotechnologies that are apart from our brains and bodies but are a part of our humanity. For the economic sociology of valuation, there is no calculation apart from calculating devices, no judgments apart from judgment devices (Callon and Muniesa 2005; Callon et al. 2007; Karpik 2010). Yes, we calculate, we judge, we perform. We, assemblages of humans and nonhumans, perform.

In the activities of valuation, how do we perform, where, and when? One possible starting point to answer these questions is that we frequently do so in organizations—be they businesses, state agencies, universities, nonprofits, or civic associations. This aspect of valuation is relatively unexplored in this volume. With the exception of the chapter by Ravasi, Rindova, and Stigliani on the use of industrial museums in companies such as Vespa and Alfa Romeo, none of the contributions examine valuation in a particular organizational context.

Dewey's answer, in the passage quoted above, is that valuation involves an "active or practical situation." Following Dewey's insight, organizations offer a fruitful vantage point to study situations. In doing so, we move from methodological individualism (e.g., as in rational choice models of human behavior) and from methodological institutionalism (prevalent in much of economic sociology) to methodological situationalism. Situations occur in practical settings. They can be a fleeting event or they can have longer duration. But we know what is meant when someone says, "We have a situation here." It suggests that something is problematic. Indeed, it is almost redundant to say that a situation is perplexing or troubling. Situations are methodologically privileged because they are moments when the open-ended character of the world is revealed.

Situations must be investigated in situ. This is the analytic strategy I adopted in *The Sense of Dissonance: Accounts of Worth in Economic Life*. My argument draws on ethnographic observations in three very different organizations: a machine-tool factory in socialist Hungary, a new-media start-up in Manhattan's Silicon Alley, and the trading room of a major international investment bank on Wall Street. In each organization we find actors confronting the question "What's valuable?" Moreover, in each, there are discrepant answers to the question because there are multiple performance principles at play. Rather than reaching agreement and coordinating their actions on the basis of shared understandings, these organizations thrive by actively maintaining competing principles of evaluation. Through the organization of dissonance, perplexing situations about worth are not the cause of paralysis but are opportunities for innovation.

If diversity of principles of valuation is itself valuable for organizations, then it might also follow that diverse approaches to the study of valuation will be of value for economic sociology. The chapters in this volume are an important contribution to that open-ended inquiry.

REFERENCES

Beunza, D. and Stark, D. (2010). *Models, Reflexivity, and Systemic Risks: A Critique of Behavioral Finance*. Working Paper. New York, NY: Columbia University Department of Sociology.
Callon, M. and Muniesa, F. (2005). Economic Markets as Calculative Collective Devices. *Organization Studies* 26(8): 1229–50.
——, Millo, Y., and Muniesa, F. (eds.) (2007). *Market Devices*. Malden, MA: Blackwell.
Carruthers, B. (2010). Knowledge and Liquidity: Institutional and Cognitive Foundations of the Subprime Crisis. In M. Lounsbury (ed.), *Markets on Trial: The Economic Sociology of the U.S. Financial Crisis, Part A (Research in the Sociology of Organizations, Volume 30)*. Bingley: Emerald Group 157–82.
Che, Y.-K. and Gale, I. (2003). Optimal Design of Research Contests. *American Economic Review* 98(3): 646–71.
Dewey, J. (1915). The Logic of Judgments of Practice, Part 1. *The Journal of Philosophy, Psychology, and Scientific Methods* 12(9): 505–23.
——(1939). *Theory of Valuation*. Chicago, IL: University of Chicago Press.
Espeland, W. N. and Sauder, M. (2007). Rankings and Reactivity: How Public Measures Recreate Social Worlds. *American Journal of Sociology* 113(1): 1–40.
——Stevens, M. (1998). Commensuration as a Social Process. *Annual Review of Sociology* 24: 312–43.
Fourcade, M. (2010). *Cents and Sensibility: Economic Valuation and the Nature of "Nature."* Unpublished manuscript. Berkeley, CA: University of California, Berkeley.
Hanson, R. (1998). *Patterns of Patronage: Why Grants Won over Prizes in Science*. Working Paper. Berkeley, CA: University of California, Berkeley.
Hennion, A. (2004). The Pragmatics of Taste. In M. Jacobs and N. Hanrahan (eds.), *The Blackwell Companion to the Sociology of Culture*. Oxford: Blackwell, 2004.
Jacobsen, P. H., Jensen, D. T., and Kreiner, K. (2010). Asymmetric Information and Collective Ignorance: Dilemmas in Dialogue-based Architectural Competitions. Presented at the Constructions Matter Conference of the Center for Management Studies of the Building Process at the Copenhagen Business School, May.
Karpik, L. (2010). *Valuing the Unique: The Economics of Singularities*. Princeton and Oxford: Princeton University Press.
Kreiner, K. (2007). Strategizing in Unknowable Worlds: Preparing for Success in Architectural Competitions. Presented at the EURAM Annual Conference, May.
——(2009). Architectural Competitions: Empirical Observations and Strategic Implications for Architectural Firms. *Nordic Journal of Architectural Research* 21(2–3): 37–51.
Lamont, M. (2010). *How Professors Think: Inside the Curious World of Academic Judgment*. Cambridge, MA: Harvard University Press.
Latour, B. and Lepinay, V. A. (2009). *The Science of Passionate Interests: An Introduction to Gabriel Tarde's Economic Anthropology*. Chicago, IL: Prickly Paradigm Press.

Leonhardt, D. (2007, January 31). You Want Innovation? Offer a Prize. *New York Times*, http://www.nytimes.com/2007/01/31/business/31leonhardt.html (accessed September 16, 2010).

Lester, R. K. and Piore, M. J. (2004). *Innovation: The Missing Dimension.* Cambridge, MA: Harvard University Press.

MacKenzie, D. (2010). The Credit Crisis as a Problem in the Sociology of Knowledge. Presented at the SASE Annual Meeting, June.

—— and Millo, Y. (2003). Negotiating a Market, Performing Theory: The Historical Sociology of a Financial Derivatives Exchange. *American Journal of Sociology* 109: 107–45.

Maharg-Bravo, F. (2010, June 10). BP Uncertainty is an Opportunity for the Brave. *Reuters Breakingviews.* http://blogs.reuters.com/columns/2010/06/10/bp-uncertainty-is-an-opportunity-for-the-brave/ (accessed September 6, 2010).

Merton, R. K. (1948). The Self-Fulfilling Prophecy. *The Antioch Review* 8(2): 193–210.

Muniesa, F. (forthcoming, 2011). A Flank Movement in the Understanding of Valuation. In L. Adkins, R. Burrows, and C. Lury (eds.), special issue of *The Sociological Review*.

Newell, R. G. and Wilson, N. E. (2005). *Technology Prizes for Climate Change Mitigation.* Discussion Paper. Washington, DC: Resources for the Future.

Scott, S. V. and Orlikowski, W. J. (2010). Reconfiguring Relations of Accountability: The Consequences of Social Media for the Travel Sector. Presented at the Academy of Management Annual Meeting, August.

Stark, D. (2009). *The Sense of Dissonance: Accounts of Worth in Economic Life.* Princeton, NJ: Princeton University Press.

Weber, M. (1906/1985). "Churches" and "Sects" in North America: An Ecclesiastical Socio-Political Sketch. *Sociological Theory* 3(1): 7–13.

INDEX

Accountability 96–7
accounts of worth 46
acting sensibly 26, 278–81, 334
　elements of 279–81
　pricing as product of 288–90
Adam, Georgina 191
advertising 213
　budget allocation 264–7
　creative industries 212–15
　familiarity from uncertainty 250
　image in 258
　phases of 258
　　awareness 259–61
　　countdown 262–3
　　performance 260–2
　radio campaigns 262–3
　state use of 256–63
　symbolic capital 309–11
　symbolic products 300–1
aesthetic economy 157
Akerlof, George 90, 109
amazement 205
Appadurai, Arjun 190
appellations 22–3
Appellations d'Origine Contrôlée 22
appraisal 327
Aristotle 3, 8–9
art
　praise value 207
　pricing scripts 210
　as source of amazement 205
art auctions 178–200
　charity 187–90
　emerging cultural economies 190–2
　Hirst sale 192–4
　lack of 182–4
　nineteenth-century France 184–7
　posthumous sales 186
　pricing mechanisms 179–82
Arthur Anderson company 3
Aspers, Patrik 164
aspirations 249
asset-backed securities 230
auction theory 44
auctions 180–1
　art *see* art auctions
　charity 187–90
Audouze, François 140

Bartoli, Cecilia 209
Becker, Gary 10
Beckert, Jens 13, 183, 328–9
Belloc, Bernard 69
Beringer, Jacob 143
Beunza, Daniel 334
Bevan, Roger 183
Blache, Paul Vidal de la 136
Black–Scholes formula 44, 242
Black–Scholes–Merton option pricing
　model 273–4, 290
Bloch, Ernst, *The Principle of Hope* 123
bond ratings 326
boundaries 159
Bourdieu, Pierre 12, 110, 136, 184
branding 22, 25
bundled meaning 300
Butel, Paul 140
buzz 170

Caillebotte, Gustave 185
Calabrese, Omar 306
calculative tools 19
Callon, Michel 19, 25
Campbell, Colin 121
capital
　cultural 302–3
　symbolic 303–4
CERCLA 54
Chamberlin, Edward 15
charity art auctions 187–90
chartist strategies 280–1
Chauvin, Pierre-Marie 145
Chiffoleau, Yuna 142
China, art auctions 190–1
cicerones 20
circuits of commerce 156, 158–9
citation model 65–6
class mobility 255–6
clientelism 255–6
Coase, Ronald 48, 90
coercion 78
cognitive simplicity 242
collateralized debt obligations 19, 231–2
collective conscience 291
collective effervescence 204
Collins, Randall 189
committee model 67

commodification 46
compensation 51–5
competition 69–70, 323–4
    quality 71–2
    types of 72
confluences 20
consumer surplus 28
consumerism 15–16, 248
consumption
    ethical 86–105
    sociology of 110
    symbolic 298, 299
contingencies 272–94
    acting sensibly 26, 278–81, 334
    making sense 277–8, 334
contingent valuation 53, 55, 57
coordination 5
corporate museums 304–5
corporate ratings 239
corporate social responsibility 88–9
correlated defaults 236–8
cost-benefit analysis 54
course corrections 280, 285–6
creative act 204
creative disturbance 24
creative industries 202–20
    advertising 212–15
    construction of 203–4
    experience amateurs 215–16
    experience critics 216–17
    information and surprise 203–5
    live performances 213–14
    market research 214
    prizes 217
    producers 212–15
    value anchors 207–11
credit bureaus 230
credit markets 226–7
credit ratings 227–8
    borrowers 233–5
    conflicts of interest 240
    correlated defaults 236–8
    failure of 233–40
    lenders 235
    omitted variables 236
    operation of 241–2
    rate shopping 243
    reactivity 234
    role in subprime mortgage crisis 230–3
creditworthiness 238–40
critics 216–17
cultural capital 302–3
    historical artifacts 307–9
cultural intermediaries 302–3
cultural symbols 297–316
culture, epistemic 50, 319

D'Ascanio, Corradino 306
Dazed and Confused 155, 164–5, 174
Deepwater Horizon oil spill 319–20
definitional mechanisms 45
Degas, Edgar 186
Delsaut, Yvette 136
demand 28, 123
design 300–1
    and symbolic capital 309–11
desirability 14
Devore, Allison 96
Dewey, John 26, 319, 323
    Theory of Valuation 319, 323, 334
diaz de la Peña, Narcisse-Virgille 185
differentiation 120–1
digitized metrics 65–6
direct bargaining 179
disillusionment 121, 122
distributive producers 213
du Gay, Paul 300
Duchamp, Marcel 194, 209
Durand-Ruel, Paul 186–7
Duret, Théodore 185
Durkheim, Emile 7, 107, 124, 125, 204, 291
    Elementary Forms of the Religious Life 107, 112, 328
    Professional Ethics and Civic Morals 107

economic growth and praise value 217–18
economic orientation 72
economic valuation 41–3
economic value 8–11, 43–7
    dimensions of 11–13
    legal production of 47–50
economics
    roles of 47
    of singularities 64
Eliot, T. S. 212
Emin, Tracey 188
emotions 211–12
emulation 73–4
Enron 3
Entwistle, Joanne 164
environmental disasters
    Deepwater Horizon oil spill 319–20
    Exxon Valdez oil spill 50–7
epistemic culture 50, 320
Equifax 230
equity options 272–94
    covered transactions 274
    legged transactions 275
    linked 275
    management 273–7
        course corrections 285–6
        escape routes 286–8
        markers 283–4

prioritization 281-3
    rules of thumb 285
  naked buying/selling 274-5
  see also shareholding
escape routes 280, 286-8
Espeland, Wendy 321
ethical consumption 86-105
  corporate social responsibility 88-9
  Fairtrade 7, 86-7
  monitoring 88
  NGOs 89-90
    costly activity in other fields 100-1
    funding 95-7
    governance structures 91-5
    monitoring of 89-90
    professionalism of 99-100
    target audiences 90-1
    transparency 97-9
evaluation 9, 14-23
  judgment devices 19-23
  standard and status markets 17-19
excellence 209
executive producers 213
expectations 329
Experian 230
experience amateurs 215-16
experience creators 211-12
experience critics 216-17
experience goods 204, 329
experience producers 212-15
expert models 88
expertise 88
Exxon Valdez oil spill 50-7, 320-3
  meta-analytics 55-7
  passive use damage valuation 51-5

Fair and Accurate Credit Transactions Act (FACTA) 235
Fair Labor Association 92, 93
Fairtrade 7, 86-7
Fannie Mae 230
fashion modeling 155-77
  aesthetics of 156-9
  bookers 156, 169, 170
  buzz 170
  clients 171
  commercial work 161, 164
  competition in 157-8
  Devan 162-3
  earnings 164
  editorial work 161
  look 156, 162-3
  market structure 161-9
  modeling agencies 161-2
  payments 163-5
  pecking order 172

  perks 165-6
  prestige 167-9
  pricing 169-74
  risks 166-7
  value in 155-6
fellowships 324-5
FICO credit score 230, 232-4, 241
financial markets 225
  equity options 272-94
  shareholding 247-71
Fitch 230
fixed prices 180
Fligstein, Neil 134, 136
forecasting 223-46
  as price anchoring 224-8
formal devices 72
Fourcade, Marion 6, 17, 194, 320-1
France
  art auctions 184-7
  Evaluation Agency for Research and Higher Education 79
  research reform 64-70
  wines 131-42
Freddie Mac 230
functional value 13, 108-9
future value 26

Gallo Brothers 144
Garcia-Parpet, Marie-France 20, 45, 323
Garnier, Gilbert 136
Gassac, Daumas 150
Gaugin, Paul 185-6
Gaussian copula 238, 242
GDP 252
Geismar, Heidi 189
Ginestet, Bernard 140
goods 106-28
  functional value 108-9
  imaginative performance 110
  performance of 108-11
  physical performance 108-9
  positional performance 109-10, 111
  positional value 107, 113
  symbolic value 117
  totemistic qualities 112-15, 121-2
  transcendental power 115-18
Gourevitch, Peter 21, 321
governmentalism, crisis of 77-9
grants 322-3
greenwashing 92, 93
Groeschel, Craig 332
Guibert, Aimé 132-4, 146

haggling 179, 181
Heraclitus 277, 291

Herrman, Gretchen 181
heterarchy 24
hierarchies 5
Hirst, Damien 179, 183, 185, 188
　art sale 192–4
Hiss, Stefanie 17, 22, 321
historical artifacts 307–9
holding course 280, 285–6
Hutter, Michael 12, 184, 329

identity objects 299
imaginative hedonism 248
imaginative performance 110
　megachurches 330–3
imaginative value 13, 106–28, 249
　dynamics of 120–4
impact factors 63, 66
India, art auctions 190–1
individualistic value 12
infinity 208–10
infinity operators 203, 211–17
initial public offerings 250, 251, 253–4
　advertising
　　budget allocation 263–7
　　state use of 256–63
investment-value 11–12
investments 248
　advertising 256–63
　familiarity 250
　reasons for 249
investors, psychographic types 257, 262
Islamic Relief 100

Jagger, Mick 329
Jefferson, Thomas 141
Jensen, Michael 187
Jevons, Stanley 42
Jevons, William 9
Johnson, Hugh 146
judgment devices 19–23, 71
　types of 72

Karpik, Lucien 19, 131, 208
Kelly, Simon 185
Kenya
　advertising
　　budget allocation 264–7
　　state use of 256–63
　Capital Markets Authority 251
　corruption in 252
　GDP 252
　Nairobi Stock Exchange 247–71
　Privatization Act 251, 253
　protection of property rights 252
　state as signal of wealth/class mobility 255–6

Kenya Reinsurance Corporation 256–67
KIVA 98–9
Klein, Yves 194
Koons, Jeff 188, 194
Kreiner, Kristian 325
Krug, Charles 143

Laferté, Gilles 134
Lancaster, Ryon 15
Laporte, Catherine 142
Laroche, Michel 149
law of one price 58
legal system, economics of 47–50
lenders 235
Li, David X. 242
lifestyle brands 303
limit orders 276
liquidity premium 11
live performances 213–14
logic of excellence 75–7
logic of glory 75–7
logos 303
look 156, 162–3
　edgy 162, 163
Luhmann, Niklas 203
Lynch, Peter 250

McAfee, Preston 180
McDonalds 101
MacKenzie, Donald 19
McMillan, John 180
making sense 277–8, 334
manifest markers 279
marginal utility theory 9–10, 42
markers 283–4
　manifest 279
　potential 279
markets 4–5
　as definitional mechanisms 45
　financial *see* financial markets
　status 18–19, 158
　winner-take-all 157
market exchange 210
market orders 276
market price 27
market research 214
Marshall, Alfred 15
Marx, Karl 9, 41, 42
　commodity fetishism 115
Mears, Ashley 18, 323
megachurches 330–3
Menger, Carl 9
Merton, Robert 250, 288, 335
meta-analytics 55–7
metric
　digitized 65–6

manual 67
Millo, Yuval 19
Mintz, Sidney 134
Mitterand, François 141–2
Mondavi, Robert 144
Monet, Claude 185, 209
monetary compensation 47–50, 57–9
monetary valuation 58–9
money 8
  as commodity 42
  cultural ambivalence towards 57–9
  and power 42
  social implications of use of 41–2
money judgments 46
Moody's 230, 238
moral values 6, 7
Morice, Charles 186
Morisot, Berthe 185
multidimensionality 70
multistakeholder concept 92, 94
Muniesa, Fabian 334–5

Nairobi Stock Exchange 247–71
  formation of 251
  initial public offerings 250, 251, 253–4
  new investors 254
  portfolio values 253
  shareholders 252
Nationally Recognized Statistical Rating Organizations 230
negotiation 29, 181
neoclassical economics 10, 28
neocompetition 73–7
  emulation and rivalry 73–4
  glory and excellence 75–7
  types of rankings 74–5
networks 5
  personal 20
new knowledge 203–4
NGOs 89–90, 101–3
  costly activity in other fields 100–1
  funding 95–7
  governance structures 91–5
  monitoring of 89–90
  professionalism of 99–100
  target audiences 90–1
  transparency 97–9
Nike 92
non-governmental organizations *see* NGOs
non-utilitarian products 298

objectives 279
omitted variables 236
ontological insecurity 291
orders of worth 25
organizational cultural capital 302–3

organizational symbolic capital 303–4
out-of-the-money calls 283

Parker, Robert 145
Parmenides 277
Parsons' pact 46
passive use damage valuation 51–5
peer review 66, 67–8, 81–2
peer-run journals 67–8
peer-run organizations 67–8
performance 260–2, 328, 333–7
  imaginative 110
  live 213–14
  physical 108–9, 326
  positional 109–10, 111
performance indicators 66, 75
perks 165–6
Petit, Georges 187
Piaggio 297, 305–7
  design and advertising 309–11
Piaggio museum 307–9
Picasso, Pablo 209
Pissarro, Camille 185
Podolny, Joel 18
Polanyi, Karl 44
Pollack, Barbara 191
Pollock, Jackson 209
Poor's 230, 238
positional performance 109–10, 111
positional value 107, 113
Post-it notes 109
posted prices 180, 181
  rigidity of 183
potential markers 279
practices 118–20
praise 326–31
praise value 202, 206–7, 329
  and economic growth 217–18
prediction markets 226
prestige 167–9
price 27–30, 224–5, 319–23
  as artifact 44
  fixed 180
  market 27
price anchoring 224–8
  forecasting 225–7
  values and prices 224–5
price setting 27
price value 203, 206–7
pricing 3–4
  fashion 169–74
  as product of acting sensible 288–90
  rationality of 272–94
  research lines 30–2
pricing mechanisms 179–82
  conditions determining use of 182

pricing scripts 174
pricing technologies 44, 45
Prince William sound, oil spill 50–7, 320–3
prioritization 279, 281–3
prizes 217, 322–8
producers, role of 15
product awareness 259–61
product classification 16
product differentiation 15
product performance 260–2
product surplus 28
productivity indicators 66, 74
Purchasing Power Partnership Model 101

qualification 17
quality competition 71–2
quality criteria 216–17
quality judgements *see* value anchors
quasi price 74

radio advertising 262–3
Rainforest Action Network 98
rankings 20, 324
　bond ratings 326
　global 325–6
　top-ten lists 326
ratings *see* credit ratings
rationality of pricing 272–94
Ravasi, Davide 24
Red auction 188
reflexive modeling 334
regimes of value 6
Reich, Robert 92
relational value 12
religious symbols 112–15, 121–2
Renoir, Pierre-Auguste 185
research reform 64–70
residential mortgage-backed securities 231–2, 240
Resources for the Future 54
Ricardo, David 8
Richter, Gerhard 209
Rindova, Violina 24
ritualistic practices 118–20
rival ethical brands 94
rivalry 73–4
　rankings 74–5
Robbins, Lionel 9
Roberts, Oral 332
Rodet, Antonin 149
Rona-Tas, Akos 17, 22, 321
Rousseau, Theodore 185
routines 334
rules of thumb 279–80, 285

Schulze, Gerhard 203

scientific evaluation 63–85
　A-list journals 66
　competition 69–70
　　democratic tyranny 77–82
　　loss of social status 80–1
　　return to peer review 81–2
　　strategic state 77–9
　impact factors 63, 66
　measurement tools 65–7
　　citation model/digitized metrics 65–6
　　committee model/manual metric 67
　neocompetition 73–7
　　emulation and rivalry 73–4
　　glory and excellence 75–7
　　types of rankings 74–5
　peer review 66, 67–8, 81–2
　performance indicators 66, 75
　productivity indicators 66, 74
　research reform 64–70
scientific singularities 70–2
　definitions 70–1
　judgment devices 19–23, 71–2
　quality competition 71–2
scoring 227–8
securitization 230–1
self-fulfilling prophecy 335
semiotic socialization 165
setting 334
Shackle, George 108, 328
shareholding 247–71
　advertising
　　budget allocation 264–7
　　state use of 256–63
　growth of 247–8
　see also equity options
Simmel, Georg 9, 25, 110
　logic of differentiation 120
　Philosophy of Money 121
singular goods 19
Sisley, Alfred 185
Skalli, Robert 147–8
Smith, Adam 8
Smith, Charles 26, 181, 333–4
social dimension 116
social entrepreneurship 95–6
social organization 334
Social Responsibility Investment Funds 97
social status, loss of 80–1
social values 41–3
sociocultural meaning 299–300
space dimension 116
spread plots 334
standard markets 17
Stark, David 23–4, 25, 26, 46
status markets 18–19, 158
status symbols 299

Stigler, George 10
Stigliani, Ileana 24
subprime mortgage crisis 223–46
   Alternative Mortgage Transaction Parity
      Act (1982) 229
   correlated defaults 236–8
   credit ratings
      failure of 233–40
      role of 230–3
   Depository Institutions Deregulation and
      Monetary Control Act (1980) 229
   history of 228–9
   Tax Reform Act 229
substantial devices 72
Sullivan, Michael 191
supply 123–4
surprise 329
surprise economy *see* creative industries
surprise generation 205
surprise goods 203–5
symbolic capital 303–4
   constraints 311–12
   design and advertising 309–11
   Piaggio 305–7
symbolic consumption 298, 299
symbolic orientation 72
symbolic qualities 110
symbolic value 13, 297–316
   design and advertising 300–1
   organizational cultural capital 302–3
   organizational symbolic capital 303–4
   Piaggio 305–7
   sociocultural meaning 299–300
   violation of expectations 312

Tarantino, Quentin 209
Theory of Value (Debreu) 42
time dimension 115–16
top-ten lists 326
totemistic qualities 112–15, 121–2
tradability 45
transcendental power 115–18
transparency 97–9, 233–4
Transparency International, Corruption
      Perceptions Index 252
TransUnion 230
trickle-down effect 25
Trompette, Pascal 20

uncertainties 5, 277–8, 329
Underwriters Laboratory 91
Union Carbide 94
United Nations
   Conference on Trade and Development
      (UNCTAD) 203
   Global Compact 94, 95

use-value 11–12
user ratings 327
utilitarian products 298
utilitarian value 108–9
utility 42
   loss of 55
Uzzi, Brian 15

valorization 9
valuation 3–4, 327
   contingent 53, 55, 57
   economic 41–3
   passive use 51–5
   research lines 30–2
value 5–8, 224–5
   dimensions of 5–6
   economic *see* economic value
   functional 13, 108–9
   future 26
   imaginative 13, 106–28, 249
   moral 6, 7
   organizational basis of 23–4
   positional 107
   and price 27–30
   regimes of 6
   relational 12
   subjective 42–3
   symbolic 13, 297–316
   through friction 24–7
   typology of 111
value anchors 207–8
   infinity 208–10
   zero 210–11
Veblen effect 10
Veblen, Thorstein 13, 110
Velthuis, Olav 28
Vespa scooter 297, 305–9
   design and advertising 309–11

Wal-Mart 100–1
Walras, Léon 9, 28
Warde, Alan 120
Warhol, Andy 209, 214–15
wealth 255–6
Web of Science 65
Weber, Max 125, 136, 333
Wente, Karl 143
Wetmore, Charles 143
White, Harrison 15, 29
Williams, Raymond 163
willingness to accept 58
willingness to pay 58
wines 131–54
   aging of 138
   AOC status 133, 134–5, 147, 150
   consumption patterns 143–7

wines (*Continued*)
  cooperatives 149
  critics 145–6
  elitism in 136–9
  French 131–42
  INAO 135
  industrialization of 134
  as investment 138–9
  Languedoc-Roussillon 147–8, 150
  New World wines 142–3, 149
  table wines 135
  terroir 134–6
  vin de pays 135–6, 148, 149–50
  Vin de Pays d'Oc 136–42, 148, 149
  vintages, value of 140–1
winner-take-all markets 157
Worker Rights Consortium 92, 93
World Bank, Investor Protection Index 252
Worth, Charles Frederick 118

Yenkey, Christopher 14
Yue Minjun 190

Zbaracki, Mark 29
Zelizer, Viviana 7, 59, 115, 156, 178
Zeng Fanzhi 190
Zeno 277, 290
Zhang Xiaogang 190